A FIELD GUIDE TO

WESTERN
TREES

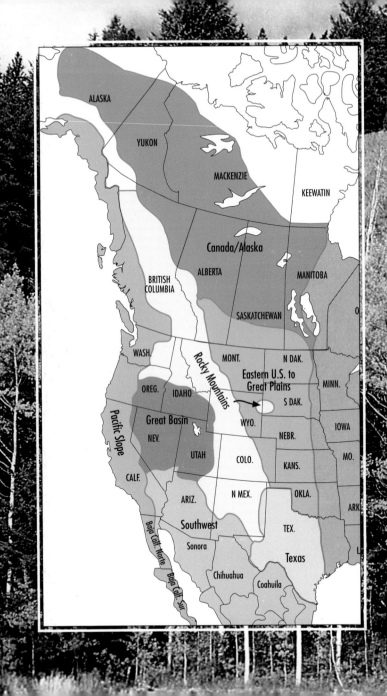

THE PETERSON FIELD GUIDE SERIES®

A FIELD GUIDE TO

WESTERN TREES

WESTERN UNITED STATES AND CANADA

GEORGE A. PETRIDES

Illustrated by
OLIVIA PETRIDES

FIRST EDITION, *Expanded*

SPONSORED BY THE NATIONAL AUDUBON SOCIETY,
THE NATIONAL WILDLIFE FEDERATION, AND
THE ROGER TORY PETERSON INSTITUTE

HOUGHTON MIFFLIN COMPANY
BOSTON   NEW YORK

For information about permission to reproduce selections from this
book, write to Permissions, Houghton Mifflin Company,
215 Park Avenue South New York, NY 10003

PETERSON FIELD GUIDES and PETERSON FIELD GUIDE SERIES
are registered trademarks of Houghton Mifflin Company.

Visit our Web site: www.houghtonmifflinbooks.com.

LIBRARY OF CONGRESS CATALOGING-IN-PUBLICATION DATA

Petrides, George A.
A field guide to western trees : western United States and
Canada / George A. Petrides ; illustrated by Olivia Petrides.
p. cm. — (The Peterson field guide series ; 44)
"Sponsored by the National Audubon Society, the National Wildlife
Federation, and the Roger Tory Peterson Institute."
Includes bibliographical references (p.   ) and index.
ISBN 0-395-90454-4
ISBN 978-0-395-90454-1
1. Trees — West (U.S.) — Identification.   2. Trees — Canada, Western —
Identification.   3. Trees — West (U.S.) — Pictorial works.   4. Trees —
Canada, Western — Pictorial works.   I. Title. II. Series.
QK133.P48 1998
582.16'0978 — dc2   98-13524   CIP

Book design by Anne Chalmers
Typeface: Linotype-Hell Fairfield; Futura Condensed (Adobe)

PRINTED IN THE UNITED STATES OF AMERICA

DOC 10 9 8 7

To my wife, Miriam,
and to our children,
George Henry, Olivia, and Lisa
and their fine families
— G. P.

To my father, George, for the many years of communicating
his enthusiasm, knowledge, and love of nature.
To my mother, Miriam, whose garden artistry
has continually delighted and instructed me.
— O. P.

EDITOR'S NOTE

This new Field Guide includes all the native and naturalized trees of western North America, from the arctic tree line in Alaska and Canada to northern Mexico. Nearly 400 native trees and others escaped from cultivation are illustrated in full color, along with new comparison charts, range maps, keys to plants in leafless condition, and text distinctions between similar species.

This is the 44th book in the Peterson Field Guide Series. The first, *A Field Guide to the Birds*, was published in 1934, and the principle on which it was founded—a schematic treatment pointing out the visual or field differences between species—proved a sound one. Checklist or phylogenetic order was often subordinated to an artificial but more practical arrangement of the figures on the plates, so as to make things easier for the tyro. For example, the chimney swift was placed with the swallows, and ducklike birds such as the coot were placed near the ducks. It was inevitable that Field Guides to botanical subjects should follow. In fact, as far back as 1941 I had planned to do a book on trees and had actually started when I learned that Dr. George Petrides was deep in a very similar project.

Dr. Petrides, a veteran field naturalist with a record of teaching and research, first in the National Park Service and the U.S. Fish and Wildlife Service and then at Michigan State University, had long felt the need for an approach to plant recognition that his students in ecology and game management would understand. It is well enough to be tutored in basic plant taxonomy, but more often than not the student, even after considerable training, is still confused when confronted by many problems of identification.

Upon examining his work I concluded that his version adhered to the basic principles of the Field Guide system even more than mine, so I switched my time budget to wildflowers, offering him bits of supplementary material—tree silhouettes, drawings of fruits and flowers, etc.—that would have gone into my own book on trees. He had based his approach mostly on leaf, twig, and bud characters. The resulting *Field Guide to Trees and Shrubs,* first published in 1958, covered the trees, shrubs, and woody vines that grow wild in the northeastern and north-central United States and in southeastern and south-central Canada. It was in a sense a pictorial key, using obvious similarities and differences of form and structure by which the beginner could quickly run down his tree, shrub, or vine. True, some botanists may have raised their eyebrows because the plants were not in the traditional order of their relationships, but there were many formal botanies so arranged; it would have been pointless to produce another. This innovative Field Guide was an effective shortcut. Actually, the student could also learn the relationships (even if indirectly) because a key in the appendixes made things quite clear. The leaf and twig plates were the ingenious and painstaking labor of Dr. Petrides, while the other figures (silhouettes, drawings on the legend pages, etc.) were mine. A much revised second edition of that Field Guide was published in 1972, and it was joined in 1988 by Dr. Petrides's *Field Guide to Eastern Trees,* beautifully illustrated by Janet Wehr.

The *Field Guide to Western Trees* is illustrated with artful paintings by the author's daughter, Olivia Petrides. Ms. Petrides holds degrees from Kalamazoo College and the School of the Art Institute of Chicago. She teaches drawing and painting at the School of the Art Institute of Chicago. Her paintings emphasize details that may not be present or clearly visible in a photograph.

In the *Field Guide to Western Trees,* we have the welcome third member of a trilogy. Don't leave it at home; take it along on your woodland rambles or on your drives in the countryside. We have learned much in recent years about the contributions of trees to the health of the global environment; this handy book will inform you about the green mantle that clothes our "small blue planet," the only home we've got.

ROGER TORY PETERSON

PREFACE

In working toward a simplified and useful guide to tree identification in western North America, I adopted five objectives: (1) To provide field marks that will identify a tree at any season, not just when it is in leaf or in flower. (2) To include all trees native to the area plus those foreign species that regularly survive and reproduce there, thus ensuring that any tree encountered in the wild will be found in the book. (3) To divide the western species and distinctive varieties into small groups that look alike, so that similarities and differences can readily be compared whether or not the plants are related. (4) To avoid technical terms like *coriaceous, cordate,* and *dentate* when it is just as accurate to translate these terms directly into *leathery, heart-shaped,* and *toothed.* (5) To include, where space permitted, a sampling of trees introduced into western parks and landscape plantings from the eastern United States and abroad.

It is hoped that my daughter's fine illustrations, as well as the identification charts, text descriptions, distribution maps, and general remarks given in this volume will enable the easy interpretation of tree floras in whatever part of the West one may be traveling or working.

In geographic area, this handbook covers the lower 48 states from the Great Plains westward as well as all of western Canada and Alaska. It is a companion volume to the *Field Guide to Eastern Trees* and includes all northern areas west of Hudson's Bay and all other lands from the eastern portions of Manitoba, North Dakota, South Dakota, Nebraska, Kansas, Oklahoma, and Texas to the Pacific Ocean. It goes north to the arctic tree line and south to the Mexican boundary. Since the distribution of many trees of the American Southwest extend also into northern Mexico, their ranges there are also mentioned.

The species considered are mainly those that dendrologist

Elbert L. Little, Jr., tallies for the area in his *Checklist of United States Trees*. I have retained the definition of a tree used in Little's *Checklist*. According to the Forest Service authorities, a tree is a woody plant attaining a height of 13 feet (4 m) or more and having a single trunk at least three inches (nearly 8 cm) in diameter at breast height (4½ ft.; 150 cm). Every tree known to grow to tree size is included.

Within the region described before, all native and naturalized trees are considered except for the hawthorns (*Crataegus*), whose many species and hybrids are not always identifiable even by specialists. The guide discusses examples, however, from this group.

Botanical varieties and forms below the rank of species are not considered unless they differ markedly from the typical species. The discussion encompasses 419 species in 136 genera, including one of many hawthorns. Several shrub species also are mentioned where these are sufficiently similar to a tree under discussion as to cause confusion.

The reasons for learning about trees vary from the purely recreational to the strictly serious. Like nearly all other creatures, we depend totally on green plants, which convert inorganic chemicals into organic foods and also help to maintain essential atmospheric gases in a healthful balance. There is growing concern that people are destroying the environment on which they depend for their prosperity and survival. Many human ills are related to the destruction of plants.

In any area the presence or absence of certain plant species or their tendencies to increase or decrease may reflect erosion, overexploitation, pollution or the lack thereof in that particular spot. In addition to serving as indicators of environmental quality, trees and shrubs play important aesthetic and monetary roles because of their beauty. Anyone who doubts that ecology and economics are interlinked has only to consult a forester, a soils scientist, a watershed biologist, a wildlife ecologist, a fisheries limnologist, or a hydrologist. Simpler yet, though, ask any urban dweller or real estate broker about the positive effect of green space on morale and property values.

A number of people assisted generously in the preparation of this book. Dr. Gustaaf A. de Zoeten, Professor and Chairman of the Department of Botany, Dr. John Beaman, Professor of Botany and Curator of the Beal-Darlington Herbarium at Michigan State University, and Dr. Alan Prather as Dr. Beaman's successor, offered office space, provided technical advice on plant nomenclature, and gave me access to the remarkably complete and thoroughly cataloged collections in their care. Martha Case, Elaine Chittenden, and Kimberley Medley, graduate assistants at the herbarium, gave generously of their time in cataloging specimens. Barbara Trierweiler, secretary and librarian, and Romayne Volk, preparator, also gave highly capable assistance. Niles Kevern, Professor and Chair of the Department of Fisheries and Wildlife, Michigan State University, provided additional office facilities.

In offering substantial guidance toward understanding the tree floras of their regions, Robert Lonard, Professor, Department of Biology, Pan American University, Edinburg, Texas; A Michael Powell, Professor, Department of Biology, Sul Ross University, Alpine, Texas; W. Robert Powell, Professor, Department of Agronomy and Range Science, and John M. Tucker, Professor, Department of Botany, both of the University of California, Davis, California; Geoffrey A. Levin, Curator, Department of Botany, Natural History Museum, San Diego, California; Melinda Denton, Professor, Department of Botany and Curator of the Herbarium, University of Washington, Seattle; John Sawyer, Professor, Department of Botany, Humboldt State University, Arcata, California; Charles T. Mason, Jr., Professor and Curator of the Herbarium, University of Arizona, Tucson, Arizona; Leslie Landrum, Professor and Curator of the Herbarium, Department of Botany, Arizona State University, Tempe, Arizona; Lytle Blankenship, Professor Emeritus, Texas A & M University, College Station, Texas; Joe Ideker, Biologist, and his assistants Perry Grissom and Martin Bray, Santa Ana National Wildlife Refuge, Alamo, Texas; and Laurence A. Ryel, retired Michigan Department of Natural Resources wildlife biologist now living in Logan, Utah, were all most helpful. Dr. W. Robert Powell provided valuable details from his studies of the localized Washoe Pine. Dr. Landrum generously made available his preliminary notes on Arizona oaks, a portion of a planned new reference on Arizona flora. Dr. Tucker kindly sent the negative for Fig. 5, which first appeared in one of his fine papers on hybridization in southwestern oaks. Maria de los Angeles Calderoni of the Department of Biology at Pan American University, Edinburg, Texas, as well as Drs. A.M. Powell and Geoffrey A. Levin all were gracious in advising in the pronunciation of Spanish names. The late James W. Hanover of the Department of Forestry, Michigan State University, provided advice on Engelmann/Blue Spruce identifications. Judge James B. Strong of Olympia, Washington, provided helpful information on trees in his state.

I am proud of my daughter, Olivia, Adjunct Associate Professor at the School of the Art Institute of Chicago, who produced the fine illustrations in the book. She also contibuted useful suggestions in the field toward perfecting the identification charts and text. At the Field Museum of Natural History in Chicago, Tim

Plowman, late Chairman, and John Engel, current Chairman of the Botany Department, generously arranged for her to work in the John G. Searle Herbarium. Honora Murphy, Collections Manager at the herbarium, provided work space, sympathetic advice and cooperation. Nancy Pliml Alaks, herbarium assistant, and Jon Polishook, research assistant, were especially kind in offering their time and support. Kevin Swagel, herbarium assistant, also was most helpful.

Peter Wehr of the Michigan State University Museum made the excellent computer map renditions, which have been redone and colorized for this new design by Larry Rosche. Betti Weiss and the late Susan Hazard deserve much credit for their expertise in converting rough handwritten copy into a finished word-processed manuscript. Lisa White, Manuscript Editing Supervisor at Houghton Mifflin Company, accomplished patient and superb work in the final editing. Susan Kunhardt, her predecessor, once gave similar assistance. Anne Chalmers, designer, also gave careful and detailed attention to ensure that the comparison charts were clear and attractive. Harry Foster, principal editor of the Peterson Field Guide series, gave editorial support and helpful advice throughout the project. Dr. W. C. Muenscher, Professor of Botany at Cornell University, whose fine course in woody plants stimulated my interest in this subject during the late 1930s, also is remembered.

George A. Petrides

CONTENTS

A FIELD GUIDE TO
WESTERN
TREES

How to Use This Book

PLEASE READ THIS SECTION: In using field guides, people tend naturally to head straight for the illustrations, either ignoring the introduction and text or simply skimming them. Anyone who seriously wants to identify trees, however, should not overlook this part of the book. The following pages explain the difference between opposite and alternate leaves and between compound and simple leaves. Here, too, are definitions of several terms that reappear in later sections. Even the word *twig* has an essential specific meaning that may be new to you!

GENERAL ORGANIZATION

The text is divided into six principal sections, beginning with the most easily recognized types:

  I. Trees with needlelike or scalelike leaves
 II. Trees with opposite compound leaves
III. Trees with opposite simple leaves
 IV. Trees with alternate compound leaves
  V. Trees with alternate simple leaves
 VI. Trees with parallel-veined or padlike leaves (palms, yuccas, cacti)

The six basic leaf types and arrangements are illustrated at the end of this chapter.

Within each principal section, trees are placed in small groups beginning with the most recognizable characteristics (thorns, lobed leaves, toothed leaves, etc.) and ending with species having the fewest obvious distinguishing features. It is a good idea to work from front to back within the book as a whole and within each section.

The comparison charts and other keys, which are explained below under IDENTIFYING UNKNOWN PLANTS, will further help you identify species. Appendix A provides a comprehensive winter key to all non-evergreen species. A summary of family and other relationships of western trees appears as Appendix B. Meanings of some terms are summarized in the Glossary. A rule on the back cover permits conversion of inches to millimeters. References include works cited and other publications of interest.

LEAF TYPES AND PATTERNS

When they are in leaf, all woody plants fall into one of the six major categories described above. Some readers may already be familiar with these categories or need only a few minutes' review. Novices, however, should be especially careful to note the differences between simple and compound leaves. One must be especially careful not to misidentify the opposite leaf*lets* of some compound leaves as opposite *simple leaves.*

Plants whose leaves are obviously not needlelike or scalelike are *broad-leaved plants.* Among such plants, a *simple leaf* has only a single blade and is joined by its stalk to a twig or branchlet that is woody. A *compound leaf* has several distinct leaflets attached to a midrib that is not especially woody. It is the stalk of that midrib that is attached to the woody twig. When the leafstalk of either a simple leaf or a complete compound leaf falls or is plucked, a distinct *leaf scar* (Fig. 1) is left behind on the twig or branchlet. That leaf scar usually has a *bud* present above or within it. Tiny *bundle scars* (broken nutrient tubes) also are present as tiny dots within the leaf scar. In contrast to the definite leaf scar and bud on a woody twig, only an indefinite mark and no bud are evident on the midrib when a leaflet is plucked.

Distinguishing between simple leaves and the leaflets of a compound leaf soon becomes second nature to the developing naturalist. At least for a while, however, the novice should always pluck a "leaf" to see whether a leaf scar of definite shape, along with its associated bud and bundle scars, is left behind. This will tend to ensure that a leaflet is not misidentified as a leaf.

In a relatively few species (Pls. 19, 20, 25), the major leaflets of the compound leaf are themselves divided into minor (sub)leaflets. Such leaves are *twice-compound* and may involve 4 to 800 or more minor leaflets.

Both compound and simple leaves may vary in shape, size, texture, and other characteristics. Despite all variation, however, the two main leaf types of simple and compound are fundamental.

Opposite leaves may be either compound or simple. They occur in opposing pairs along the twigs. Whorled leaves, where three or more leaves arise together around the twig, occur only infre-

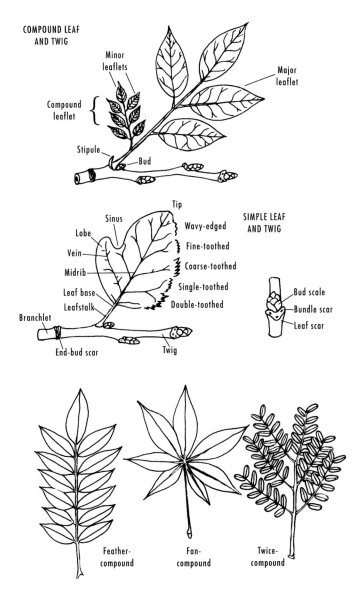

COMPOUND LEAF AND TWIG

Minor leaflets

Major leaflet

Compound leaflet

Stipule

Bud

SIMPLE LEAF AND TWIG

Tip

Sinus

Lobe

Vein

Midrib

Leaf base

Leafstalk

Branchlet

End-bud scar

Twig

Wavy-edged

Fine-toothed

Coarse-toothed

Single-toothed

Double-toothed

Bud scale

Bundle scar

Leaf scar

Feather-compound

Fan-compound

Twice-compound

Fig. 1. Leaf and twig terminology

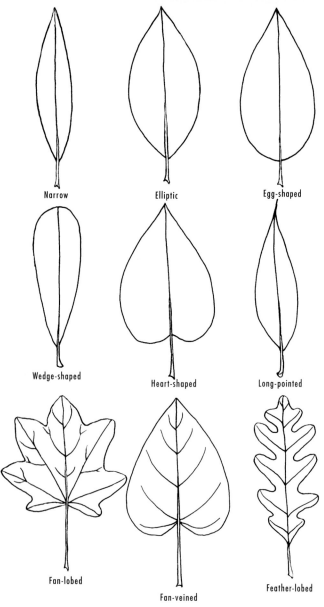

Narrow

Elliptic

Egg-shaped

Wedge-shaped

Heart-shaped

Long-pointed

Fan-lobed

Fan-veined

Feather-lobed

Fig. 2. Leaf shapes

quently. The few plants with whorled leaves are included in the opposite-leaved category.

Alternate leaves are arranged singly at intervals along the twigs. Just as one must be careful not to confuse opposite leaflets with opposite simple leaves so, in the other direction, some alternate-leaved plants bear *spur branches* on which leaves are densely clustered (see Fig. 3). These can be mistaken for opposite or whorled leaves if one is not careful to select strong-growing specimen twigs for study (see **Identifying Unknown Plants**, p. 8).

Broad-leaved plants are often called *hardwoods* by foresters, in contrast with the needle-bearing *softwoods*.

Twig and Bud Types

Twig and bud characteristics are important during winter and other times when trees are leafless. Probably because evergreen trees often predominate there, the characteristics of leafless western trees seem to have been somewhat neglected. Efforts have been made in this book, however, to assemble identification points for trees in leafless as well as in leafy condition.

A *twig* is not just any small division of a branch but the end portion — the part that constitutes the newest growth. The *branchlet* is the previous year's growth and is separated from the twig by a series of encircling *end-bud scars* (Fig. 1). The term branchlet also is applied to any small branch that is not a twig. When they are leafless, *non-evergreen* broad-leaved plants fall into two main groups: (1) those of Sections II and III with leaf scars arranged on the twigs in opposing pairs, or rarely in whorls of three or four, and (2) those of Sections IV and V, with leaf scars arranged singly on the twigs in a more or less scattered pattern (see Fig. 3). It is not always possible to identify with certainty the leaf scars of compound and simple leaves, though those of compound leaves are often larger and have more than three bundle scars.

Subdivisions made within the opposite- and alternate-leaved groups reflect the type of buds, the kind of pith, the number of bundle scars, the presence of milky sap, and other characters. Bud descriptions apply to mature winter buds. The term *chambered pith* is used here to include all types of segmented and transversely divided pith (the spongy core of a twig), including pith that is diaphragmed and partitioned. The main characteristics of twigs and buds are illustrated in Fig. 3.

End buds are designated as true or false (see Fig. 3), but the distinction is not always obvious. Some books mention end buds as present or absent rather than as true or false. In this volume, true end buds and clear sap may be considered to be present

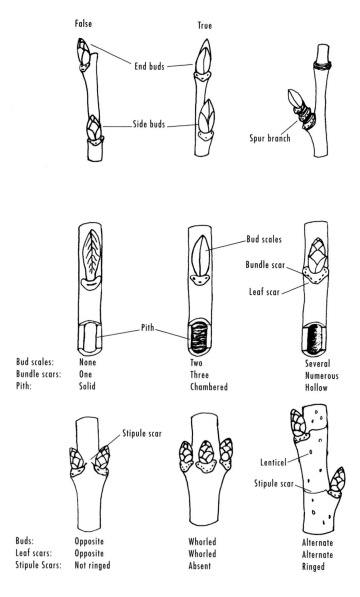

False   True

End buds

Side buds

Spur branch

Bud scales

Bundle scar

Leaf scar

Pith

Bud scales:	None	Two	Several
Bundle scars:	One	Three	Numerous
Pith:	Solid	Chambered	Hollow

Stipule scar

Lenticel

Stipule scar

Buds:	Opposite	Whorled	Alternate
Leaf scars:	Opposite	Whorled	Alternate
Stipule Scars:	Not ringed	Absent	Ringed

Fig. 3. Twig and Bud Terminology

unless otherwise stated. Central end buds are lacking in several species with opposite buds, as shown on Pl. 14.

PLATES

Each plate displays small groups of plants that most resemble each other in leaf and twig characteristics whether or not they are related to each other. Wherever possible, however, related species have been depicted on plates as close together as possible, given the main objective of grouping plants similar in appearance.

Not all specimens precisely match the illustrations, but the pictures do offer the designated critical points of identification. Stipules (see Fig. 1) have been illustrated only when they are of diagnostic value, since they often drop early.

On any one plate, the leaves of the several species have been drawn to the same scale in order to indicate their relative size. There may be differences in scale for plants shown on different plates. Leaf and plant sizes are given in the text. The illustrations of twigs, buds, and other small parts have often been enlarged to make their details more readily evident.

COMPARISON CHARTS

Opposite each plate is a comparison chart. These compact charts can be scanned readily, with similarities and differences among species quickly becoming evident. The charts offer an improved approach to "keying out" a plant in that they summarize and compare in one place the several differences between similar species. Even in a given season, trees can rarely be distinguished by a single field mark. Key features are not always present or may not be readily apparent on the specimen at hand (leaves, flowers, or fruits may be absent, for instance). The plates and appropriate comparison charts alone should suffice to identify an unknown tree.

The comparison charts indicate whether a species does (+) or does not (–) possess a particular characteristic or whether it possesses that characteristic in an intermediate or variable (±) form. In some cases, various space-saving combinations of these symbols are used to represent measurement data. In such instances, they are coded in a footnote. In general, the charts list first the features most important for identification. One should therefore read the plus-or-minus columns from left to right. Additional descriptive notes indicate further distinctive characteristics.

Because most species have limited distributions, it is helpful to recognize those that can be expected in the region being visited. The first column of each chart, therefore, attempts briefly to indicate the major geographic range of each species within the western United States and Canada. A footnote for each chart will identify the code letters involved. In general, they will agree with the regions mapped on the frontispiece and will proceed from north and west toward south and east.

Major areas coded are P = Pacific states and British Columbia, including southeast Alaska; C = Canada/Alaska (except for the northern Pacific slope, see P); B = Great Basin, involving most of Nevada plus nearby portions of adjoining states; S = southwestern states from southeast California to west Texas; R = Rocky Mountains; T = Texas; E = eastern trees that range westward on the Great Plains or are widely planted in the West; w = widespread distribution over several regions; I = species introduced from foreign areas and now growing wild in the West. Occasionally a special code letter (O = Oklahoma) will indicate a subregional distribution. Except for w (see above), lowercase (small) letters are used to indicate portions of an area (i.e., California) to which an entire plate (or major segment) is devoted.

Species occurring along the Mexican border can be expected to occur also in the adjoining state(s) of Mexico. B.C. in the text and charts always means British Columbia; Baja California is always spelled out. The distribution areas given in the charts and mapped on the frontispiece represent merely a general guide to assist in identification; reference also should be made to the more detailed maps in the text. General comments on the distribution of western trees also are given on p. 16.

Species not illustrated but similar to those on the plate have their names in parentheses on the chart. Key recognition points for these trees are given on the comparison chart and in the text.

IDENTIFYING UNKNOWN PLANTS

Collecting plants for identification and study is a practice that has long been sanctioned by science. Collections should be made, however, in moderation and under suitable conditions. Collecting wild plants must be balanced against the need to preserve natural values. In some areas, including national and state parks and monuments, it is illegal to collect plants without a permit.

From the standpoint of making an accurate identification, it is better to make identifications in the field than to collect specimens to be named at home or in camp. When collected specimens are examined later, you may find that important characteristics such as milky sap, spicy odors, bark pattern, and growth habits had not been noted. Fallen leaves and fruits that might have provided useful clues also may have been overlooked.

If, nevertheless, you find it desirable to collect a specimen for later study, keep in mind that a good specimen is essential for correct identification. Avoid dwarfed, twisted, and gnarled branches. From a vigorous specimen, clip 6 inches to a foot of the branch tip so that both leaf and twig characteristics are present.

With the unknown tree or specimen at hand and turning to the proper section of the book, you can scan the several plates and select the species that most resembles the unknown plant. When leaves are absent, use the leafless key at the end of the book as well as the illustrations and text descriptions.

In summer, the first step in identifying an unknown plant is to place it in one of the six main groups, according to leaf type and arrangement (see Fig. 4):

1. Leaves needlelike or scalelike	**Section I, p. 119**
1. Leaves broad. 2	
1. Palms, cacti, yuccas.	**Section VI, p. 376**
2. Leaves opposite or whorled. 3	
2. Leaves alternate. 4	
3. Leaves compound.	**Section II, p. 187**
3. Leaves simple.	**Section III, p. 205**
4. Leaves compound.	**Section IV, p. 219**
4. Leaves simple.	**Section V, p. 258**

You should turn next to the proper section, scan the plates, and select the species most like the unknown one. It is important then to review the facing *comparison charts* and to follow up by checking the *distribution maps* and reading the *text descriptions* of the several probable species. Verify that the specimen and its geographic range agree with the illustrations and text or else make another attempt to run it down. The text discussion of similar species may also help you to interpret identification marks.

Since the plates themselves are a pictorial key, you may prefer to disregard the sectional leaf keys and the comparison charts and rely upon spotting the proper illustration. It is often possible to proceed in this way if the species falls in Sections I through IV or in Section VI. Relatively few plants have needlelike, compound, opposite, or palm-frond leaves. Approximately half of all western trees have alternate simple leaves, however, and thus fall into Section V. Unless a Section V specimen has other quite distinctive characteristics, therefore, it may be best to follow the keys, tables, maps, and so on.

When a tree is without foliage, you must either find leaf remains on or under the specimen (and run some risk of picking up part of another tree) or rely on twig and other leafless characteristics. If you find dried leaves, you can attempt to proceed as you normally would with fresh foliage. Otherwise you should look for good twig specimens. Be sure to check for spur branches. Both the comparison charts and the leafless botanical key (Appendix A) should be used.

The most trying time for the identification of non-evergreen trees is usually early spring, when buds have burst but leaves are small and new twigs soft. For a few weeks then, some plants may be difficult to identify.

SPECIES DESCRIPTIONS

PLANT NAMES: Both common and scientific names are given for each species. Although for many species common names are well established, the same name or a similar one is sometimes also applied to a different, even unrelated, species. Ironwood, for instance, is used around the world as the common name for many species in numerous genera. In this book, species names that include the name of another unrelated group, for example Douglas-fir and Redcedar, are either hyphenated or joined together to indicate that they are not true members of the group.

The scientific names used in this book are mostly those established by the specialists who are compiling the *Flora of North America North of Mexico* (Morin 1993, 1997). This series, now in development, is becoming the basic reference for plant names and classification in the region. For species not yet reached by that flora, two sources are utilized. For trees that occur in California, the names of Hickman (1993) and his collaborators are adopted. For other species, the names listed are mainly those of Little (1979). Full citations of these references are given on page 408. Several oak species listed in Morin (1997) but found in only one locality or very limited area are not included here. Unless markedly distinctive in the field (i.e., Shore Pine, Shasta Red Fir, Lombardy Poplar), varieties or other subdivisions of species are not emphasized.

In an effort to assist in standardization, the common name approved by the U.S. Forest Service and given by Little's *Checklist* has generally been chosen for use in this book. In a few instances, if a name used in an earlier edition of this Field Guide seemed to offer advantages (by being more descriptive, by better indicating plant relationships, or by involving only one or two words), it was either retained or given in parentheses as a second choice. For some species in southern (tropical) Texas, the common names suggested by Little evidently are not in common use there. In a few such cases I have supplied the names employed by local botanists and confirmed by Correll and Johnston in their

Manual of the Vascular Plants of Texas. Pronunciation guides given here to names of Mexican origin have been provided by experts.

Scientific names have three essential parts: the name of the *genus* (plural, *genera*), the name of the *species* (plural, *species*), and the name or names, commonly abbreviated, of the botanist(s) who assigned the scientific names and who stand(s) as the authority(ies) behind it. In the case of *Acer negundo* L., for example, the initial stands for Carolus Linnaeus (also known as Carl von Linné), who is regarded as the father of systematic botany.

Varieties are recognizably distinct subpopulations of a species. In most instances, the distinction is minor. Only a few varieties in our area (i.e., Arizona Pine and Fernleaf Lyontree) are sufficiently different from the typical species to require separate identification. The parental forms of several other varieties (Texas Buckeye, Lombardy Poplar, and California Hazelnut) do not occur in the West, thus only the variety is described. In plant varieties, the varietal name and the name of the authority (or authorities) responsible for it follow the scientific name of the species. as in *Pinus ponderosa* var. *arizonica* (Engelm.) Shaw.

A main purpose of scientific nomenclature is standardization, so that botanists anywhere in the world may discuss a plant with the assurance that they are indeed dealing with the same species. Scientific nomenclature is an international cataloging system that also indicates plant relationships within certain limits. Unfortunately, scientific names may change as authorities decide that a species is more closely related to members of a genus different from that to which it was first assigned, that plants once considered to belong to two species should instead be regarded as two varieties of a single species, that a species originally thought to be new has already been named, and so forth.

The average naturalist should not be too concerned about the many peculiar ways in which scientific names are written. The rules of botanical nomenclature are much too involved to be fully reviewed here. The reader will probably find scientific names of value principally as they make it possible to locate the same species accurately in other reference books. If they are used in this way, care must be taken that the name of the author who assigned the name as well as the Latin portions of the scientific name are in agreement. (The same name has sometimes been applied inadvertently to different species by different authors.)

In the United States and Canada nowadays, scientific names tend to be anglicized when spoken, and most pronunciations are acceptable. One should not hesitate to use them. Anyone who can say arbutus, eucalyptus, rhododendron, or yucca is already using scientific names. In speech, the authors' names are usually omitted.

RECOGNITION: This guide limits plant descriptions largely to their general distribution and identification characteristics. A statement of the general distributional range of the species is followed by characteristics of foliage and twigs. Where individual differences may cause confusion in identification, their extent has been indicated in the text. I have attempted to describe degrees of hairiness where it was possible to do so, but the exact extent of hairiness in leaves and twigs is sometimes difficult to indicate in words. Nearly all leaves will show some fine hairs if they are examined closely under a hand lens. Plants described in the text or on the plates as being hairy are usually markedly so. On "hairless" plants, hairiness is not conspicuous.

Measurements are given for leaf lengths, plant heights, and trunk diameters, and sometimes for leaf widths, bud lengths, and other characteristics. Minimum and maximum leaf lengths are generalizations for normal leaves and *include the length of the leafstalk* unless otherwise stated. Sprouts of some species bear abnormally large leaves. The common minimum height and diameter for mature trees often are followed by the common maximum for each measurement and, in parentheses, the exceptional maximum. Diameters are for tree trunks at breast height (about $4\frac{1}{4}$ feet above the ground)—the forester's d.b.h. These figures are given as only general guides. The several maximum measurements are not usually all evident on a single specimen. All measurements are given in feet, inches, and fractions rather than in metric system units, since English units are more widely familiar in our area. The rule printed on the back cover permits leaf and bud measurements readily to be converted to metric units. Measurements given without other designation indicate length.

Flower and fruit data have been supplied only to the extent that, as general identification characteristics, they usefully supplement vegetative characteristics. Further details are provided mainly for those species not easily recognized by leaf and twig characteristics alone.

Flowers, of course, develop into fruits. The shape of a tree's fruit clusters, not always mentioned, therefore will be of the same type as the clusters described for the flowers. The extreme dates given for flowering and fruiting may need to be modified by a month or so, depending on locality. Where fruiting dates are lacking, dates for the flowers will indicate at least the earliest possible time when fruits might appear. Fruit colors apply to ripe fruits only. Descriptions of bark refer to the mature bark of large stems unless otherwise indicated. The habitat named indicates the vegetation or soil type in which the species is usually found.

General statements regarding the distinctiveness of certain species' characteristics apply to the area covered by the book.

SIMILAR SPECIES: Critical differences are discussed for species that most closely resemble one another, both when they are in foliage and when they are leafless.

DISTRIBUTION: Maps showing the limits of distribution in the areas north of Mexico have been published for most tree species in several volumes of Little's *Atlas of United States Trees*. These maps have been followed in preparing the book. Where the range is described verbally, distributional limits are reported from northwest to northeast and southwest to southeast. The distribution of a few species based mainly in Mexico is given from that country northward. Several tree groups (cypresses, junipers, ashes, poplars, yuccas) are mapped collectively in numerical style. This was done so that readers in a particular state or region could see at a glance which species are likely to be encountered there. The map for *Quercus dumosa* was taken from Elias's *Complete Trees of North America*.

REMARKS: General observations are given for plants that serve as sources of lumber, fuel, medicine, food, drink, poison, fiber, ornament, tannin, and Christmas trees, or are of special value in soil and wildlife management. References to wildlife are usually limited to game birds and to mammals of chipmunk size or larger. The origins of both scientific and common names are given where known. Good places to visit in order to see certain species also are sometimes mentioned.

BOTANICAL KEYS

When a dozen or so species are involved, the comparison charts offer advantages in scanning for similarities and differences. In cases where either a very few or a large number of trees must be classified, however, the charts are not handy. In such instances, as at the beginning of each section in the text and in Appendix A, traditional botanical keys are employed. The keys to plant identification may seem formidable at first but should be treated rather like a book's table of contents. Their function is merely to divide the subject matter, in this case plant species, into subsections, further sub-subsections, and eventually species or groups of species.

Using a key is simply a matter of following a trail that forks repeatedly but typically offers only two paths at any single fork.

The seeker continues to make choices between options, making certain at each point that the choice made fits the plant being identified, until an end point is reached. In cases of doubt, it may be necessary to follow each of the two routes offered and then to choose between the resulting determinations.

Everyone would like to discover a rare specimen. Before you conclude that you have found a species outside its usual range or have unearthed something entirely new to science, however, recheck carefully to verify that you do not have a case of mistaken identity. If it still seems likely that the plant is something unusual, you might collect a specimen (with flowers or fruits, if possible, and always with notes indicating the exact location, date of collection, and your own name and address). Carefully press it, dry it, and forward it to the department of botany at your state or provincial university or agricultural college with a request for confirmation of identification.

EQUIPMENT

Fortunately, tree identification requires little paraphernalia. Only two items are essential: a field guide or manual and a hand lens. *A good hand lens is as essential to the botanical naturalist as binoculars are to the birder.* The hand lens is especially helpful in ascertaining twig characteristics but is also essential for assessing leaf hairiness, leafstalk glands, etc. Furthermore, the lens discloses hidden beauty in small blossoms and other plant parts. Lenses for general use should magnify 6x or 10x. Holding the lens close to your eye makes it almost a part of you. Those manufactured by well-known optical companies are generally worth the slightly higher price usually asked for them. Hand lenses are economical and are practically indestructible. Secondhand ones can often be procured cheaply, especially in university towns. Though seldom necessary under ordinary circumstances, binoculars are handy when the foliage or fruits of tall trees are out of reach. They are useful also in botanical gardens and arboretums to check overhead leaves and to read distant name tags. Pruning shears can be helpful, too, especially in collecting thorny or fibrous specimens.

As previously noted, it is *strongly suggested that identification be made in the field,* where additional specimens and supplementary data are available. When you need to collect specimens, however, a large plastic bag will preserve them until they can be pressed. A roll of newspapers held by a strap, or even a large magazine, may also do well as a field carrier if specimens are being carried for early identification. Serious collectors, however, will want to acquire a plant press. These are available from any biological supply house.

In a press, plants are placed within newspaper pages which are inserted between blotters and placed between sheets of corrugated cardboard. The entire series is packaged between wooden frames and securely tied by straps. Specimens will dry quickly in dry weather if the press can be mounted outside a moving car. A stream of heated air blown through the press will also hasten drying. Otherwise, it is necessary to replace dry newspapers and blotters every few days to permit thorough drying and to prevent molds from invading the collections.

PLANT SUCCESSION

Every plant species, through evolutionary processes, has become something of a specialist. Each one lives in a certain type of *habitat* and thrives under a particular set of climatic, soil, and moisture conditions. On a newly available site, seeds or other reproductive parts of a number of species usually manage to be present, and some of these will sprout successfully. As a result a *plant community* composed of several species becomes established. As time goes on, plants and plant communities tend to alter the site so that it becomes less and less suitable for them (we are not the only species that fouls its nest!). Increasing soil fertility due to root decay and leaf fall, for example, may invite competition from species originally unable to become established on the site. Alternatively, increasing shade may prevent seedlings from surviving even though they are adjacent to, or are even surrounded by, their parents.

These factors and others bring about *succession* whereby plant communities and the soils they occupy pass through a series of stages until a stable community of plants and mature soil structure finally develops. This end product—a mature and relatively permanent community—is the *climax* plant association.

Primary plant succession occurs when community development begins and develops from a bare surface or in open water. Primary succession may begin on such areas as cliff faces, rock slides, gravel slopes, road cuts, sand dunes, lava flows, peat deposits, or on shallow lake bottoms, in bogs, or on river bars and deltas. In such places *pioneer* communities become established and are eventually succeeded by other plant communities, each of which tends to be more intermediate in its moisture requirements than its predecessor. That is, within the limits set by climate, succeeding communities beginning in a wet environment live on progressively drier sites, while those in a dry environment live on moister sites, with the climax community occurring on neither wet nor dry sites but on intermediate moist ones.

Secondary plant succession occurs when a plant community is entirely or partly killed or removed, exposing a soil that has already advanced to some degree toward maturity. Such plant destruction might be accomplished by fire, trampling, drainage, wind damage, lumbering, cultivation, or other means. The secondary plant community series that follows a change in the original vegetation generally differs from the primary successional series.

Species in developmental stages of plant succession may be geographically more widespread than those of the climax stage. Some species may occupy somewhat different habitats and successional stages in different portions of their ranges, whereas others are restricted to only a portion of a single climax area.

Knowledge of local successional stages is essential in studies of land use, soil conservation, forestry, wildlife management, and outdoor recreation. The amateur botanist will find it an interesting and valuable project to prepare a succession chart for his or her locality; see Oosting's *Study of Plant Communities*.

DISTRIBUTION OF WESTERN TREES

The temperature and precipitation limits that affect the survival of each tree species also govern the development of soils upon which they depend. Topography can cause climates, soils, and vegetation to vary widely between locations at different altitudes. The number of tree species to be found in a particular locality tends to be limited. In the West, different environments with different tree floras may be only a few miles apart.

Plants that grow at low elevations in the far north may occur on high slopes much farther south. A person ascending a mountain road from a southern lowland location may pass through several vegetative zones and finally reach timberline and alpine tundra with northern characteristics.

In Alaska and western Canada, the farthest-north belt of spruce-fir (boreal) forests extends south of the treeless arctic tundra and eastward across the continent to Newfoundland and Maine. Following the cold climates at increasingly higher altitudes, a zone of similar coniferous trees extends southward along the Rocky Mountains, Cascades, the Sierra Nevada and Coast Ranges deep into Mexico. Differing in the species of trees involved is the complex of Pacific Forest conifers that extends south along the Pacific slope from Kodiak Island, Alaska, to San Francisco Bay and beyond. Southward along the Pacific Coast a zone of shrubby chaparral or coastal scrub vegetation also contains a number of tree species.

Away from the coast, the Great Basin area lies between the Sierra Nevada and Rockies. It extends north to the grasslands of eastern Oregon, eastern Washington, and southern Idaho and south to the arid portions of southern California, southern Nevada, and northwest Arizona. Adjacent and to the south, the Mohave, Sonoran, and Chihuahuan deserts occupy much of southern California, Arizona, southwestern New Mexico, and southwestern Texas. With the numerous mountain areas within their borders, a varied tree flora is supported in these areas. East of the Rocky Mountains and south of the Canadian forests, the Great Plains range eastward to meet the deciduous forest of the eastern United States.

ILLUSTRATED PLAN
OF THE SIX MAIN SECTIONS

Figure 4

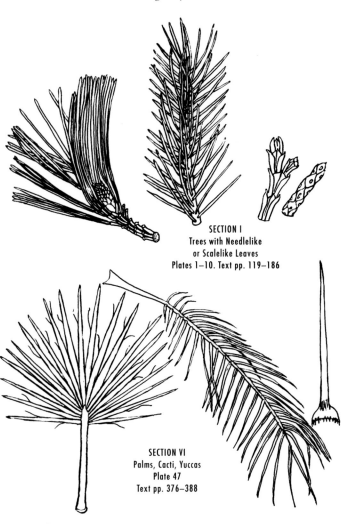

SECTION I
Trees with Needlelike
or Scalelike Leaves
Plates 1–10. Text pp. 119–186

SECTION VI
Palms, Cacti, Yuccas
Plate 47
Text pp. 376–388

LEAVES OPPOSITE OR IN WHORLS

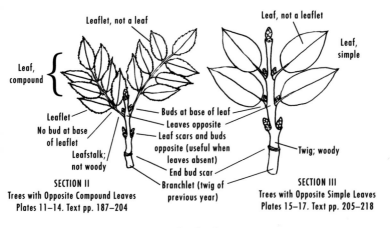

Leaflet, not a leaf

Leaf, compound

Leaflet

No bud at base of leaflet

Leafstalk; not woody

Buds at base of leaf

Leaves opposite

Leaf scars and buds opposite (useful when leaves absent)

End bud scar

Branchlet (twig of previous year)

SECTION II
Trees with Opposite Compound Leaves
Plates 11–14. Text pp. 187–204

Leaf, not a leaflet

Leaf, simple

Twig; woody

SECTION III
Trees with Opposite Simple Leaves
Plates 15–17. Text pp. 205–218

LEAVES (*not leaflets*) ALTERNATE

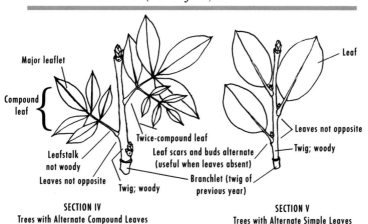

Major leaflet

Compound leaf

Leafstalk not woody

Leaves not opposite

Twice-compound leaf

Leaf scars and buds alternate (useful when leaves absent)

Branchlet (twig of previous year)

Twig; woody

Leaf

Leaves not opposite

Twig; woody

SECTION IV
Trees with Alternate Compound Leaves
Plates 18–25. Text pp. 219–257

SECTION V
Trees with Alternate Simple Leaves
Plates 26–46. Text pp. 258–375

PLATES

PLATE 1

CONE-BEARING EVERGREEN TREES WITH CLUSTERED NEEDLES: LARCHES, 1- AND 2-NEEDLE PINES, AUSTRALIAN-PINE

Larches: Needles 12–14 on warty spur branches, single on long twigs, drop in autumn. True Cedars: Foreign park trees resembling larches but evergreen, see p. 124. Pines I: Needles in bundles, evergreen, 1- and 2-needle pines[1] on this plate; 3–5-needle pines on Pls. 2–4.

SPECIES AND REMARKS	Major distribution[2]	Max. needle length (in.)	Needles shade of green[3]	Max. cone length (in.)	Size of cone prickles[4]	Many old cones on tree	Text page
TAMARACK *Larix laricina* (American Larch) Cone bracts hidden.	C	1	Y	¾	0	−	121
(EUROPEAN LARCH *Larix decidua***)** Twigs droop, bracts pointed.	I	1½	Y	1½	0	−	122
WESTERN LARCH *Larix occidentalis* Twigs ± hairy, bracts pointed.	PR	1¾	Y	1½	0	−	122
SUBALPINE LARCH *Larix lyalli* Twigs woolly, bracts toothed.	PR	1½	B	2	0	−	123
(TRUE CEDARS *Cedrus species***)** Evergreen, cones and scales broad.	I	1–2	B	2–5	0	−	124
SINGLELEAF PINYON *Pinus monophylla* Needle 1 (–2), thick, spine-tipped.	B	2¼	G	3	0	−	126
TWO-NEEDLE PINYON *Pinus edulis* Cone scales thick, blunt; southern.	R	2	D	2	0	−	127
LODGEPOLE/SHORE PINE *Pinus contorta* Cones not heavy, scales thin.	RP	3	YD	2	−	+	127
(AUSTRIAN PINE *Pinus nigra***)** Mature bark plates gray-yellow.	P	3–6	D	2–4	±	−	128
(JACK PINE *Pinus banksiana***)** Needles short, cones curved.	C	1½	Y	2½	−	+	129
BISHOP PINE *Pinus muricata* Cones stout, scales thick; coastal.	P	6	D	3½	+	+	129
(PONDEROSA PINE *Pinus ponderosa***)** Some 2-needle clusters; Pl. 3.	w	10	Y	6	±	−	135
AUSTRALIAN-PINE *Casuarina equisetifolia* Needles jointed, droop; not a true pine.	I	12	Y	1	0	±	129

[1] All with cones egg-shaped and short-stalked; leaf sheaths short except in Bishop Pine, Austrian Pine, and Lodgepole/Shore Pine.
[2] B = Great Basin; C = Canada/Alaska; I = foreign introduction, mostly plantings; R = Rocky Mts.; P = Pacific states and B.C.; w = widespread.
[3] B = blue-, D = dark-, G = gray-, Y = yellow-green.
[4] o = none; − = small, slender; ± = medium; + = large.
[5] Bracts are located between cone scales.

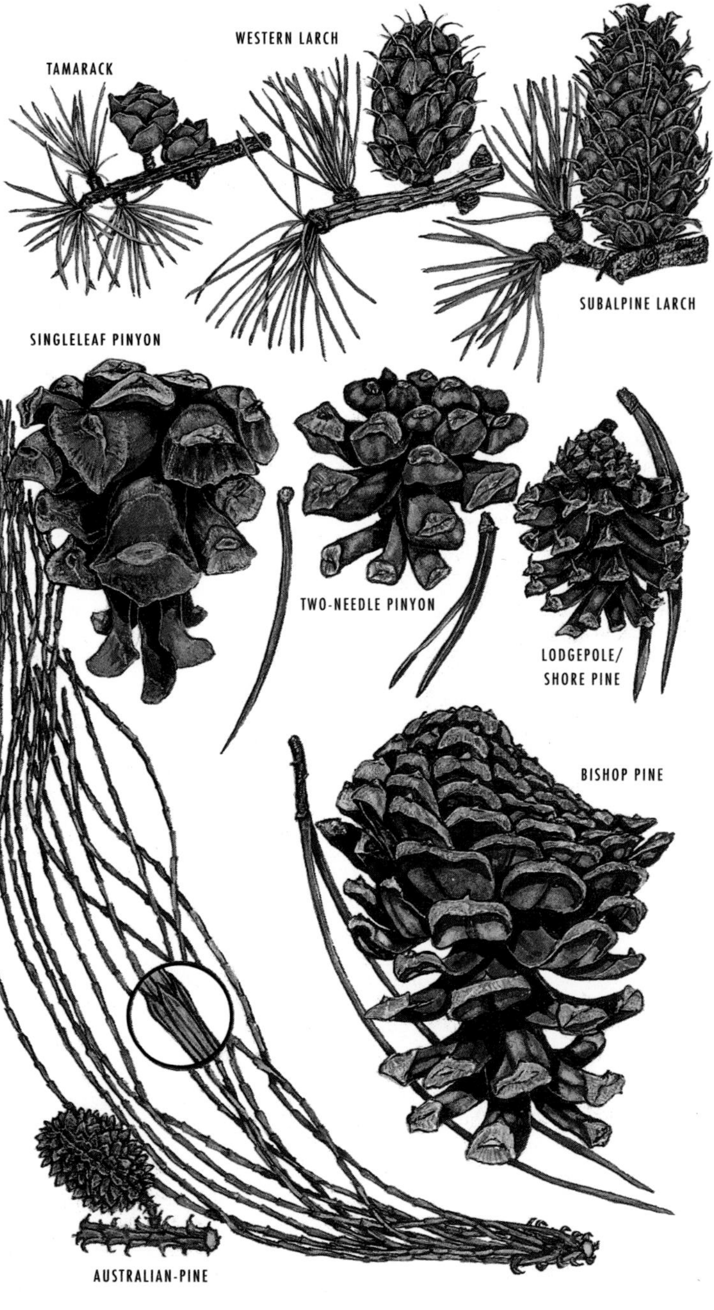

PLATE 1

TAMARACK

WESTERN LARCH

SUBALPINE LARCH

SINGLELEAF PINYON

TWO-NEEDLE PINYON

LODGEPOLE/
SHORE PINE

BISHOP PINE

AUSTRALIAN-PINE

PLATE 2

PINES II: 3-NEEDLE PINES OF CALIFORNIA AND ITS BORDERS

Six 3-needle (yellow or hard) pines occur mainly in Calif.[1] with three species barely extending into sw. Ore. and/or w. Nev. Needle bases bound by durable sheaths ⅛–½ in. long. Cones mostly stout, thorny, short-stalked. Mainly mountain slopes. Ponderosa Pine (Pl. 3) is also a widespread 3-needle species in Calif.

SPECIES AND REMARKS	California distribution[2]	Max. needle length (in.)	Cone length[3]	Cone thorn size[4]	Cone thorns curved	Many old cones on tree[5]	Text page
KNOBCONE PINE *Pinus attenuata* Cone curved, one side knobby.	w	6	M	M	+	+	130
MONTEREY PINE *P. radiata*[1] Cone off-center; scales thick.	cc	6	S	S	–	+	131
WASHOE PINE *P. washoensis* Local ne. Calif., w. Nev.	ne	6	VS	M	–	–	131
(PONDEROSA PINE *P. ponderosa*).[6] Cone dull; bark flaky, yellow.	w	10	S	M	+	–	135
JEFFREY PINE *P. jeffreyi*[7] Cone shiny; bark tight, rosy.	w	10	L	M	±	–	132
COULTER PINE *P. coulteri*[1, 8] Trunk single; cone massive, buff.	sc	12	VL	L	+	+	133
GRAY PINE *P. sabiniana*[1, 8] Trunk forked; cone heavy, dark.	w	14	L	L	±	+	134

[1] Three species occur naturally only in Calif. (2 also in nearby Mexico).
[2] cc = central coast, ne = northeastern mountains, sc = southern and central coastal mountains, w = widespread in California mountains.
[3] Cones: VS = very short, 2–4 in.; S = short, 3–6 in.; M = medium, 3–7 in.; L = long, 6–10 in.; VL = very long, 10–14 in.
[4] L = very large, M = medium, S = small or lacking.
[5] Also cone bases off-center and scale tips very thick.
[6] Some needles in twos, see Pls. 1 and 3; "bark" refers to mature trunk.
[7] Trunk with nice pineapple odor when nose pressed into bark furrows.
[8] Coulter Pine twigs ½–1 in. thick; Gray Pine twigs ⅛–½ in. thick.

PLATE 2

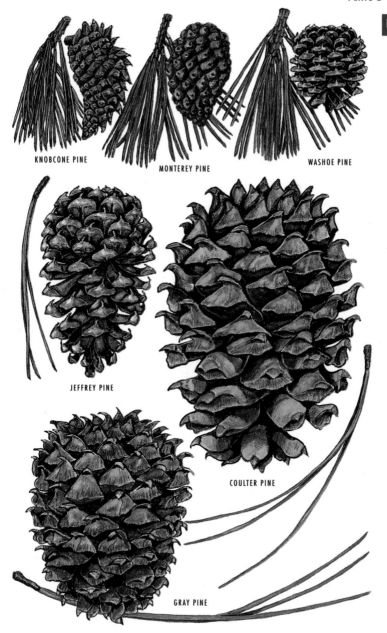

KNOBCONE PINE

MONTEREY PINE

WASHOE PINE

JEFFREY PINE

COULTER PINE

GRAY PINE

PLATE 3

PINES III: PONDEROSA PINE
PLUS 3-NEEDLE PINES OF THE MEXICAN BORDER

Ponderosa Pine is common throughout the western U.S. and s. British Columbia. Three other pines with needles in clusters of 3 are distributed from Ariz. to cen. Texas. Needle sheaths are soon shed in Mexican Pinyon and Chihuahua Pine. Cones mostly egg-shaped; stalks minimal in two species.

SPECIES AND REMARKS

	Major distribution[1]	Needle length (in.)	Needle shade of green[2]	Cone length (in.)	Cone prickle size[3]	Cone prickle curved	Many old cones on tree	Color of mature bark[4]	Text page
PONDEROSA PINE *Pinus ponderosa*[5] Twigs ¼–½ in. thick, sheaths ½–1 in.	w	4–10	Y	3–6	±	+	–	Y	135
MEXICAN PINYON *P. cembrioides* Needles stout; cone stalks short.	ST	1–2½	B	1–2	o	o	–	D	136
CHIHUAHUA[6] PINE *P. leiophylla* Needles slender, cone stalks ½ in.	S	2½–4	B	1½–3	–	–	+	D	136
APACHE PINE *P. engelmannii* Twigs ½–1 in. thick, sheaths 1–1½ in.	S	8–15	D	4–6	±	±	–	Y	137

[1] S = se. Ariz./sw. N.M.; ST = se. Ariz./sw. N.M./cen. and w. Texas; w = widespread.
[2] B = blue-, D = dark-, Y = yellow-green.
[3] o = none, – = small, ± = medium.
[4] D = dark, Y = yellow.
[5] See also Pls. 1 and 2.
[6] chee-WAH-wah.

PLATE 3

PONDEROSA PINE

MEXICAN PINYON

CHIHUAHUA PINE

APACHE PINE

PLATE 4

PINES IV: 5-NEEDLE PINES WITH NEEDLES 2½–13 IN. LONG

Five-needle (white or soft) pines have slender leaves bound at the base by deciduous sheaths whose remnants are ¹⁄₃₂–¹⁄₁₆ in. long. Cones mostly elongated and slim, dropping early, their scales thin and with small slender prickles or none, usually present beneath the tree. Arizona and Torrey pines have wider cones and long leaf sheaths. Seeds winged.

SPECIES AND REMARKS	Major distribution[1]	Needle length (in.)	Needle shade of green	Cone length (in.)	Cones long-stalked	Cone scales with prickles	Seeds longer than wing	Text page
SOUTHWESTERN WHITE PINE *Pinus strobiformis* Cones ± heavy,[2] scales turned back.	S	2½–3	B	5–9	–	–	+	138
SUGAR PINE *P. lambertiana*[3] Trunk bark scaly, ridged.	P	2½–4	B	11–20	+	–	–	138
WESTERN WHITE PINE *P. monticola*[3] Mature trunk bark often in small, square plates.	PR	2½–4	B	5–10	+	–	–	139
TORREY PINE *P. torreyana*[4] Twigs ¼–⅓ in. thick; local Del Mar, Calif. & S. Rosa Is. Cones may persist.	P	8–13	D	4–6	+	±	+	140
ARIZONA PINE *P. ponderosa var. arizonica*[4] Twigs 1¼–1 in. thick; parent species Pl. 3.	S	4–10	Y	2–3½	–	+	–	141

[1] P = Pacific states; PR = Pacific states, n. Rockies, and nearby Canada; S = Southwest.
[2] For a white pine species.
[3] Mature cone scale widths: Sugar Pine 1–1¼ in., Western White Pine ¼–1 in.
[4] Needles in 5s though member of the yellow pine group.

PLATE 4

SOUTHWESTERN
WHITE PINE

SUGAR
PINE

WESTERN
WHITE
PINE

TORREY
PINE

ARIZONA PINE

PLATE 5

PINES V: 5- (OR 4-)NEEDLE PINES
WITH NEEDLES 1–2½ IN. LONG

Like the typical white pines of Pl. 4 but with foxtail,[1] nut,[2] and stone[3] pine characteristics. Needles mostly 5 per bundle and bound by basal sheaths of minimal (⅟₃₂–⅟₁₆ in.) length. Cones fall early, stalks short or absent, cone scale prickles slender or lacking. Mostly alpine species. Needles sometimes to 3 in. long.

SPECIES AND REMARKS	Major distribution[4]	Needle length (in.)	Needle shade of green[5]	Cone length	Cones ± cylindrical	Cone scales thick	Text page
INTERMOUNTAIN BRISTLECONE PINE *Pinus longaeva*[1,8] Cone bristles ⅟₁₆–¼ in.	BR	1–1½	D	3–3½	+	–	142
FOXTAIL PINE *P. balfouriana*[1,6] Prickles tiny or none; 2 areas only.	P	1–1½	D	3–5	+	–	143
PARRY PINYON *P. quadrifolia*[2] 4 needles; sw. Calif. mountains.	P	1–1½	Y	1½–2½	–	+	143
WHITEBARK PINE *P. albicaulis*[3] Cones dark; scales pointed, closed.	PR	1½–2½	Y	1–3	–	+	144
LIMBER PINE *P. flexilis*[3,7] Cones buff, scales rounded, open.	RB	1½–2½	Y	3–6	+	±	145

[1] Bristlecone and Foxtail pines retain the needles along the last 10 years or so of branchlet growth, giving a foxtail appearance to each branch tip.

[2] Parry Pinyon, along with Singleleaf and Two-leaf pinyons (Pl. 1) and Mexican Pinyon (Pl. 2), produce tasty nuts.

[3] Resembling the Swiss Stone (Arolla) Pine (*Pinus cembra* L.) of cen. Europe; twigs very flexible in both Whitebark and Limber pines.

[4] B = Great Basin, P = Pacific states, R = Rocky Mts.

[5] D = dark-, Y = yellow-green.

[6] Native in Klamath Mts., n. Calif., and again in s. Sierras.

[7] Also e.-cen. and s. Calif.

[8] See text for related species in the Rockies, where scattered white resin dots on the needles assist in identification.

PLATE 5

BRISTLECONE PINE

FOXTAIL PINE

PARRY PINYON

WHITEBARK PINE

LIMBER PINE

PLATE 6

CONIFERS WITH SINGLE NEEDLES ON WOODY PEGS: SPRUCES

Cone-bearing evergreen trees whose dead branchlets and twigs are much roughened by tiny woody pegs. Mature cones woody, brown, hanging near twig ends. Needles short, mostly stiff and sharp, typically 4-sided but flattened in two species. Bark mostly thin and scaly. Hemlocks (Pl. 8) have weak needle-pegs.

SPECIES AND REMARKS	Major distribution[1]	Needles flattened[2]	Needle length (in.)	Needle shade of green[3]	Twigs hairy[4]	Cone length (in.)	Cone scale tips ragged	Text page
SITKA SPRUCE *Picea sitchensis* Branchlets/twigs droop; coastal.	P	+	¾–1	D	−	2–4	+	146
WEEPING SPRUCE *P. breweriana*[5] Branchlets/twigs weep strongly.	P	+	¾–1	Y	+	2–4	−	147
ENGELMANN SPRUCE[7] *P. engelmannii*[6] Bark brown, thin, scaly; needles flexible.	R	−	¾–1	BD	±	1½–2½	+	148
BLUE SPRUCE *P. pungens*[7] Bark dark, thick; needles stiff.	R	−	¾–1¼	BD	−	2½–4	+	149
WHITE SPRUCE *P. glauca* Tundras, drier soils; scales flexible.	C	−	⅜–¾	YB	−	1½–2	−	149
BLACK SPRUCE *P. mariana* Tundras, bogs; many old cones present; scales rigid.	C	−	¼–⁷/₁₆	BD	+	¾–1¼	+	150

[1] C = Canada and Alaska, P = Pacific states and B.C., R = Rocky Mts.
[2] With 2 rather than 4 white stripes; 4-sided needles easily twirled between the fingers.
[3] B = blue-, D = dark-, Y = yellow-green.
[4] Use lens after removing needles.
[5] Native Siskiyou Mts., Ore./Calif.
[6] Also Cascade Mts. south to n. Calif.
[7] Central cone scales diamond-shaped in Engelmann Spruce, rounded in Blue Spruce.

PLATE 6

WEEPING SPRUCE

SITKA SPRUCE

ENGELMANN SPRUCE

BLUE SPRUCE

WHITE SPRUCE

BLACK SPRUCE

PLATE 7

CONIFERS WITH NEEDLES SINGLE AND FLAT (OR 4-SIDED): FIRS

Narrow-crowned trees whose plucked needles leave smooth circular scars on the twigs. Needles short, mostly flat, blunt, grooved above, white-banded beneath. (White bands most evident on fresh new twig-end needles.) Buds mostly blunt. Cones erect, fleshy, often purplish, fall early. Young trunks mostly gray, smooth, with resin blisters. See Douglas-firs, Pl. 8.

SPECIES AND REMARKS	Major distribution[1]	Main vertical range[2]	Low needles in flat sprays[3]	Needles whitened above[4]	Shape of needle tips[5]	Needle length[6]	Buds resin-covered, shiny	Cone length (in.)	Text page
GRAND FIR *Abies grandis*[8] Needles of 2 lengths.	PR	L	+	−	N	M	+	2–4	152
WHITE FIR *A. concolor*[7] Needles long, U-curved.	PR	M	±	+	RP	L	+	3–5	153
SILVER FIR *A. amabilis*[8] Twigs hidden from above.	P	M	−	−	N	S	+	3½–6	154
NOBLE FIR *A. procera*[8,9] Needles thin, 2 stripes each side.	P	M	−	+	R	S	−	4–7	155
RED FIR *A. magnifica*[10] Needles 4-sided; Sierras and s. Cascades.	P	H	−	+	R	M	+	6–8	155
SUBALPINE FIR *A. lasiocarpa*[7] Top stripe single, crown narrow.	PR	H	−	+	RN	M	+	2¼–4	156
BRISTLECONE FIR *A. bracteata*[11] Needles spiny, buds pointed.	P	M	±	−	S	L	−	2½–4	157
(BALSAM FIR *A. balsamea*) Needles short; east of Rockies.	C	L	+	−	R	S	+	1–3	158

[1] = Canada; P = Pacific states, B.C., and north; R = Rocky Mts.
[2] L = low, 0–5000 ft.; M = middle, 1500–7000 ft.; H = higher elevations.
[3] − = needle bases J-curved so that needles are mostly upright and bunched on twig and branchlet tops.
[4] As well as beneath; use lens.
[5] Use lens on low needles: N = notched, P = pointed, R = rounded, S = sharp.
[6] S = short, ⅜–1 in.; M = medium, ¾–1½ in.; L = long, 1½–2½ in.
[7] For closely related species, see text.
[8] Pacific Northwest region.
[9] Cone bracts long-pointed, hiding cone scales; mainly Cascades, Wash./Ore.
[10] Needles easily twirled between the fingers.
[11] Cone bracts visible, ½–1¾ in. long; native Monterey, Calif., area.

PLATE 7

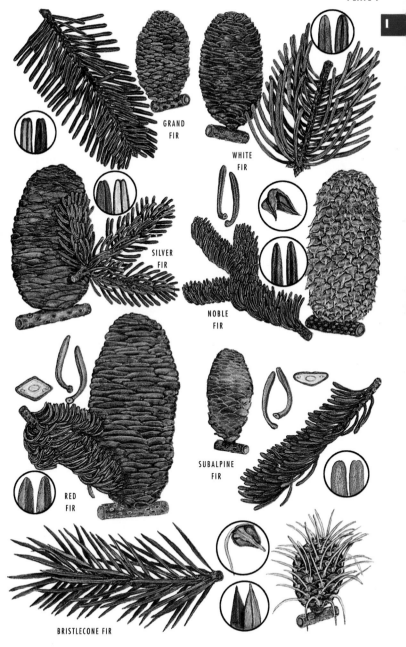

GRAND
FIR

WHITE
FIR

SILVER
FIR

NOBLE
FIR

RED
FIR

SUBALPINE
FIR

BRISTLECONE FIR

PLATE 8

OTHER CONIFERS WITH SINGLE FLAT NEEDLES

Trees evergreen, except Baldcypress. Foliage in flat sprays, except Mountain Hemlock. Douglas-fir needles leave circular scars on twigs like true firs of Pl. 7. Hemlock twigs have weak woody needle-pegs;[1] top shoot droops. Cones brown but fruits red, berrylike in Pacific Yew and green, olivelike in California Torreya.

SPECIES AND REMARKS	Major distribution[2]	Needles on thin stalks[3]	Needles white-banded beneath[3]	Needle bases extend on twig[3]	Needle length (in.)	Cones/fruit length[4]	Cone scales with thick tips[5]	Text page
COMMON DOUGLAS-FIR *Pseudotsuga menziesii* 3-point cone bracts, twigs droop.	PR	+	+	−	¾–1½	L	−	159
(BIGCONE DOUGLAS-FIR *Pseudotsuga macrocarpa***)** Twigs droop, cones/bracts larger; sw. Calif.	P	+	+	−	¾–1½	VL	−	160
WESTERN HEMLOCK *Tsuga heterophylla* Needles of several lengths.	PR	+	+	−	¼–¾	S	−	160
MOUNTAIN HEMLOCK *Tsuga mertensiana* Needles not in flat sprays.	PR	+	+	−	¼–¾	L	−	162
CALIFORNIA TORREYA *Torreya californica*[6,7] Needles stiff, spiny, scented.	P	+	+	+	1–3	M	O	163
PACIFIC YEW *Taxus brevifolia*[6] Needles soft, odorless.	PR	+	−	+	½–1	VS	O	164
REDWOOD *Sequoia sempervirens*[7,8] Coastal fog belt, cen. Calif./ sw. Ore.	P	−	+	+	½–1¼	S	+	165
BALDCYPRESS *Taxodium distichum* Deciduous; west to cen., s. Texas.	E	−	−	+	¼–⅞	S	+	166

[1] See spruces, Pl. 6.
[2] E = se. U.S., P = Pacific states and B.C., R = Rocky Mts., T = Texas.
[3] Use lens. White bands may be lost on dried or weathered needles.
[4] VS = very short, ⅜–½ in.; S = short, ¾–1 in.; M = medium, 1–1½ in.; L = long, 1½–3 in.; VL = very long, 4–7 in.
[5] O = fruits fleshy, not dry cones.
[6] Mendocino Co., coastal n. Calif., may be the only area where the ranges of these two species overlap.
[7] Stump sprouts common.
[8] High needles awl-shaped.

PLATE 8

WESTERN HEMLOCK

COMMON
DOUGLAS-FIR

MOUNTAIN
HEMLOCK

CALIFORNIA
TORREYA

PACIFIC YEW

upper

REDWOOD

lower

BALDCYPRESS

PLATE 9

CONIFERS WITH SMALL SCALELIKE LEAVES: "CEDARS" AND CYPRESSES

Leaves mostly under ¼ in., pairs alternate at right angles (use lens). Cones woody, brown, scales mostly 6–8. Cypress twigs often 4-angled. Trunks mostly furrowed and shreddy. For true cedars, see p. 124.

SPECIES AND REMARKS	Major distribution[1]	Foliage in flat sprays	Leaves with a gland dot[3]	Cone length (in.)	Text page
INCENSE-CEDAR *Calocedrus decurrens* Leaf-scales vase-shaped.[2]	P	+	−	¾–1	168
WESTERN REDCEDAR *Thuja plicata*[2,3,4] Scales "butterfly"-marked, sprays droop.	PR	+	±	½–¾	169
ALASKA-CEDAR *Chamaecyparis nootkatensis* Scales not marked, point out; sprays droop.[2]	P	+	−	⅜–½	170
PORT ORFORD-CEDAR *Chamaecyparis lawsoniana* Scales X-marked, twigs slender.[2,3]	on	+	+	¼–⅜	171
ARIZONA CYPRESS *Cupressus arizonica* Twigs thin, wide-angled.	S	−	+	¾–1¼	173
Cypresses Native to Restricted Areas in California/sw. Oregon[5]					
(TECATE[6] CYPRESS *Cupressus guadalupensis*) Trunk red-brown, smooth, peeling.	sc	−	+	¾–1¼	174
(MODOC CYPRESS *C. bakeri*) Cone scales warty.	on	−	+	⅜–¾	174
(MACNAB CYPRESS *C. macnabiana*) Cone scales with prominent "horns."	n	+	+	½–1	174
(GOWEN CYPRESS *C. goveniana*)	cn	−	−	½–¾	174
(SARGENT CYPRESS *C. sargentii*)	cn	−	+	¾–1	175
(MONTEREY CYPRESS *C. macrocarpa*[2])	cn	−	−	1–1½	175

[1] P = Pacific states and B.C., R = Rocky Mts.; S = Southwest; T = Texas. In Calif./Ore.: cn = cen./n. coasts; on = sw. Ore./nw. Calif.; n = n. Calif.; sc = sw. Calif.
[2] Cone scales: Incense-cedar, 6; Western Redcedar, 8–12; Alaska-cedar, 4–6; Port Orford-cedar and most cypresses, 6–8; Monterey Cypress, 8–14.
[3] Use lens to check for glands and white markings on undersides of fresh leaf-scales.
[4] Native coastal s. Alaska to n. Calif., also n. Rockies.
[5] May be planted elsewhere.
[6] teh-KAH-tay.

PLATE 9

INCENSE-CEDAR

WESTERN REDCEDAR

PORT
ORFORD-
CEDAR

ALASKA-CEDAR

ARIZONA CYPRESS

PLATE 10

TREES WITH SCALELIKE AND/OR AWL-SHAPED LEAVES: JUNIPERS, GIANT SEQUOIA, TAMARISK

Junipers: Leaf scales to ⅛ in.; twigs mostly ¼₆ in. wide; fruits fleshy, round, mostly white-powdered; trunks mainly reddish, shreddy. Common Juniper on p. 183. Giant Sequoia: Needles sharp, to ¼ in. long; cones woody, brown; mature trees huge. Tamarisks: Leaves tiny, scaly, deciduous; true flowers present, not a conifer. See Redshank, p. 186.

SPECIES AND REMARKS	Major distribution[1]	Color of mature fruits[2]	Fruits over 3/8 in. diameter	Leaf scales with gland dot[3]	Leaf scales long-pointed[3]	Leaves: shade of green[4]	Trunk single	Seeds per fruit	Text page
ROCKY MOUNTAIN JUNIPER *Juniperus scopulorum* Twigs thin (¹⁄₃₂ in.), droop.	W	B	—	+	+	D	+	2	177
WESTERN JUNIPER *J. occidentalis* Sierras and Cascades.	P	B	—	+	—	G	+	2–3	178
ONESEED JUNIPER *J. monosperma* Southern Rockies.	S	B	—	—	+	G	—	1	179
UTAH JUNIPER *J. osteosperma* Mature fruits red.	B	BR	±	—	+	Y	±	1–2	180
(CALIFORNIA JUNIPER *J. californica*) Mostly west of Sierras.	P	R	+	+	—	Y	—	2	181
(ALLIGATOR JUNIPER *J. deppeana*) Trunk bark thick, small squares.	S	R	+	+	+	B	+	4	181
(PINCHOT JUNIPER *J. pinchotii*) Bark furrowed, West Texas.	T	R	—	+	±	Y	—	1–2	182
(ASHE JUNIPER *J. ashei*) Bark shreddy, cen. Texas.	T	B	±	±	±	D	—	1–2	182
(WEEPING JUNIPER *J. flaccida*) Twigs pendent.	T	R	+	+	+	Y	±	4–12	183
(EASTERN REDCEDAR *J. virginiana*) West to plains states.	E	B	—	±	+	Y	+	1–2	183
GIANT SEQUOIA *Sequoiadendron giganteum* Leaf bases extend along twig.	P	R	+	—	O	B	+	many	184
FIVE-STAMEN TAMARISK *Tamarix chinensis* Flowers pink, twigs thin; imported.	w	R	—	—	+	Y	+	many	185

[1] B = Great Basin, E = eastern U.S., P = Pacific states, S = sw. states, T = Texas and nearby, w = widespread.
[2] B = blue to blue-black, juicy; R = red-brown, dry.
[3] Use lens; o = all leaves awl-shaped, sharp.
[4] B = bluish-, D = dark-, G = gray-, Y = yellow-green.

PLATE 10

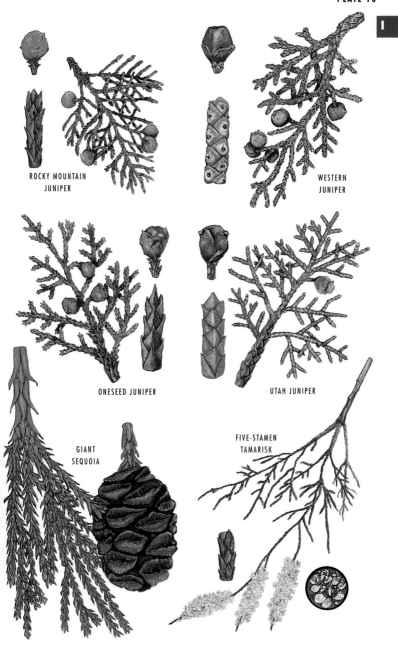

ROCKY MOUNTAIN
JUNIPER

WESTERN
JUNIPER

ONESEED JUNIPER

UTAH JUNIPER

GIANT
SEQUOIA

FIVE-STAMEN
TAMARISK

PLATE 11

TREES WITH OPPOSITE LEAVES FAN-COMPOUND OR TRIFOLIATE

Buckeyes have 5–9 leaflets arranged like the spokes of a wheel, end buds large, flower clusters showy, upright. Sierra Bladdernut and Barreta have only 3 leaflets per leaf. Several ashes and maples plus an elderberry and Fernleaf Lyontree also sometimes have trifoliate leaves.

SPECIES AND REMARKS	Major distribution[1]	Leaflets per leaf	Leaflets stalked	Buds sticky	Flower color[2]	Fruit type[3]	Text page
CALIFORNIA BUCKEYE *Aesculus californica* The only wild buckeye in Calif.	P	5–7	+	+	P	N	188
TEXAS BUCKEYE *Aesculus glabra*[4] Leaflets 4–6 in. long; cen. Texas.	T	7–11	–	–	Y	N	189
RED BUCKEYE *Aesculus pavia* Leaflets 1½–4 in. long; to cen. Texas.	E	5	±	–	RY	N	190
HORSECHESTNUT *Aesculus hippocastanum*[4] Leaflets 4–10 in. long; planted widely.	I	7–9	–	+	W	N	190
SIERRA BLADDERNUT *Staphylea bolanderi* Tiny leaflet tips; n./cen. Sierra.	P	3	+	–	W	I	190
BARRETA *Helietta parvifolia* Leaflets blunt, no teeth; s. Texas.	T	3	–	–	G	D	191
(ASHES *Fraxinus* spp., Pls. 12, 13) Fruits single-winged.	w	3–7	±	–	V	D	192
(MAPLES *Acer negundo*, Pl. 14; *A. glabrum*, Pl. 15) Fruits 2-winged.	w	3–5	+	–	G	D	205
(MEXICAN ELDERBERRY *Sambucus mexicana*) See Pl. 14.	PS	3–5	+	–	W	B	202
(FERNLEAF LYONTREE *Lyonothamnus floribundus*)[5] Leaves scalloped; s. Calif. islands.	P	2–7	–	–	W	D	198

[1] E = eastern U.S.; I = introduced from abroad; P = Pacific area; S = Southwest; T=Texas; w = widespread.

[2] G = greenish white, P = pinkish white, R = red, W = white, Y = yellow, V = variable.

[3] B = blue, fleshy; D = dry, see text; I = inflated, balloonlike, 1–2 in. long; N = large nut in thick husk.

[4] Nut husk prickly; Horsechestnut is a European tree.

[5] var. *asplenifolius*, Pl. 14.

PLATE 11

CALIFORNIA BUCKEYE

TEXAS BUCKEYE

RED BUCKEYE

HORSECHESTNUT

SIERRA BLADDERNUT

BARRETA

PLATE 12

TREES WITH OPPOSITE LEAVES
FEATHER-COMPOUND: ASHES I

Ashes of the Pacific states and Ariz. Leaves mostly 5–12 in. long; leaflets 3–9 (mostly 5–7), toothed or not. Flowers mostly small, clustered, dark, mostly without petals. Fruits dry, single-winged, mostly blunt-tipped. These ashes mostly with seed flattened. See also Pl. 13 and Singleleaf Ash, Pl. 16.

SPECIES AND REMARKS	Major distribution[1]	Leaflets long-pointed[2]	Leaflet length[3]	Leaflets always toothed	Leaflet stalks under 1/16 in.	Fruits winged to base	Fruit length[5]	Text page
OREGON ASH *Fraxinus latifolia* Leaves ± hairy; Pacific N.W./Calif.	P	–	L	–	+	–	L	192
TWO-PETAL ASH *F. dipetala*[6] Petals 2, white, ⅛ in. wide.	P	–	M	+	–	+	M	193
(FRAGRANT ASH *F. cuspidata*) Petals 4, white, ¹⁄₃₂ in. wide; Pl. 13.	S	+	M	–	–	+	M	196
VELVET ASH *F. velutina*[4] Leaves ± hairy; s. Calif./ sw. Utah/w. Texas.	PT	±	M	+	–	–	M	194
(CHIHUAHUA[7] ASH *F. papillosa*) Leaflets whitish beneath; Pl. 13.	S	–	M	–	+	–	M	197
LOWELL ASH *F. lowellii*[6] Twigs 4-lined; n. Ariz.	S	–	M	+	±	+	M	194
GOODDING ASH *F. gooddingii*[8] Leaves 1–3¼ in.	S	–	S	+	+	±	S	196

[1] P = Pacific states, S = Southwest, T = Texas.
[2] – = tips short-pointed.
[3] L = long, 3–5 in.; M = medium, 1–3 in.; S = short, ⅜–1 in.
[4] Seeds swollen, plump, not flattened.
[5] L = long, 1–2 in.; M = medium, ½–1¼ in.; S = short, ½–1 in.
[6] Twigs ± 4-lined or 4-angled.
[7] chee-WAH-wah.
[8] Evergreen; leafstalk and midrib winged (use lens), se. Ariz.

PLATE 12

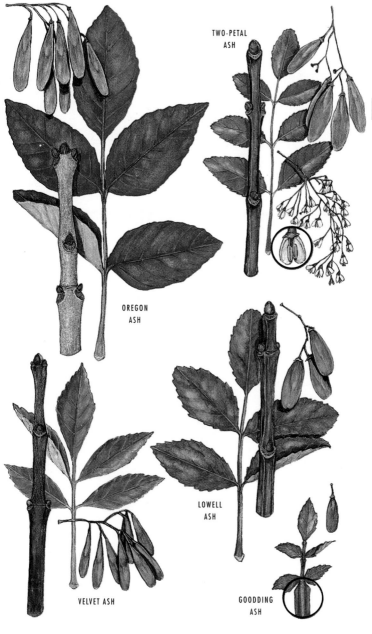

TWO-PETAL
ASH

OREGON
ASH

LOWELL
ASH

VELVET ASH

GOODDING
ASH

PLATE 13

TREES WITH OPPOSITE LEAVES
FEATHER-COMPOUND: ASHES II

Ashes of the Mexican border region (Ariz. to Texas) and Great Plains. Leaves mostly 5–12 in. long; leaflets 3–9 (mostly 5–7), toothed or not. Flowers mostly small, clustered, dark, without petals. Fruits dry, single-winged, mostly blunt-tipped. See also Pl. 12 and Singleleaf Ash, Pl. 16.

SPECIES AND REMARKS	Major distribution[1]	Leaflets long-pointed[2]	Leaflet length[3]	Leaflets always toothed	Leaflet stalks under 1/16 in.	Fruits winged to base	Fruit length[5]	Text page
(VELVET ASH *Fraxinus velutina*, Pl. 12) Leaves ± hairy; s. Calif. to w. Texas.	PT	±	M	+	–	–	M	194
FRAGRANT ASH *F. cuspidata*[4] Petals white, 1/32 in. wide.	S	+	M	–	–	+	M	196
CHIHUAHUA ASH *F. papillosa*[4,6] Leaflets whitish beneath.	S	–	M	–	+	–	M	197
(GOODDING ASH *F. gooddingii*)[4,7] Leaflets 1–3¼ in., tips pointed, se. Ariz.; Pl. 12.	S	–	S	+	+	±	S	196
GREGG ASH *F. greggii*[7] Leaflets ½–1¼ in., tips blunt; w. Texas.	T	–	S	–	+	–	S	197
TEXAS ASH *F. texensis* Leaflets 1–3 in. long; s. Okla./ cen. Texas.	T	–	M	+	–	–	M	197
BERLANDIER ASH *F. berlandierana* Leaflets 3–4 in. long; s./cen. Texas.	T	+	L	–	–	±	M	198
GREEN ASH *F. pennsylvanica*[8] Leaflets 4–6 in.; plains, Alta. to Texas.	E	+	L	–	±	–	L	198

[1] E = e. U.S. to Great Plains, P = Pacific area, S = Southwest, T = Texas.
[2] – = tips short-pointed.
[3] L = long, 3–6 in.; M = medium, 1–3 in.; S = short, under 1 in.
[4] Seeds somewhat flattened, not plump.
[5] L = long, 1–2 in.; M = medium, ¾–1¼ in.; S = short, ½–1 in.
[6] chee-WAH-wah.
[7] Leafstalk and midrib winged (use lens).
[8] Leaflet stalks winged.

PLATE 13

FRAGRANT
ASH

CHIHUAHUA
ASH

GREGG
ASH

TEXAS
ASH

BERLANDIER
ASH

GREEN
ASH

PLATE 14

ELDERBERRIES AND OTHER TREES WITH OPPOSITE FEATHER-COMPOUND LEAVES

Leaflets 3–16, mostly toothed;[1] twigs mostly ringed at nodes, hairless. Elderberries have pith large, mostly white; flower/fruit clusters mostly flat-topped; flowers white; fruits mostly fleshy, small.

SPECIES AND REMARKS	Major distribution[2]	Leaflets per leaf	Leaflet bases uneven	Leaflet stalks under 1/16 in.	Leaflets hairy beneath	Fruit color and type[3]	Text page
FERNLEAF LYONTREE *Lyonothamnus floribundus*[1] Evergreen, bark shreddy.	P	3–7	±	+	±	D	198
ASHLEAF MAPLE *Acer negundo* Leaf scars meet at raised points.	w	3–5	−	−	−	G	199
RED ELDERBERRY *Sambucus racemosa* Leaflets 2–6 in., pith brown, flower clusters cone-shaped.	P	5–7	±	±	−	R	201
BLUE ELDERBERRY *Sambucus caerulea* Leaflets 2–6 in., pith white/brown, flower clusters flat.	w	5–9	+	−	−	U	201
VELVET ELDERBERRY *Sambucus velutina* Leaflets 1–1½ in., velvet-hairy, pith white; mostly Calif., 3000–8000 ft.	P	3–5	+	+	+	UK	202
MEXICAN ELDERBERRY *Sambucus mexicana* Leaflets 1–1½ in., hairless, pith brownish; n. Calif. to sw. N.M., to 4000 ft.	PS	3–5	±	+	−	K	202
COMMON ELDERBERRY *Sambucus canadensis* Leaflets 2¼–5 in., west to w. Kansas and nw./s. Texas; pith white.	E	5–11	−	±	±	K	203
TEXAS LIGNUMVITAE *Guaiacum angustifolium* No end leaflet, tiny leaflets fold.	T	8–16	+	+	−	D	203

[1] Fernleaf Lyontree (var. *asplenifolius*) leaflets are variously described as toothed or lobed; note simple leaves of Santa Catalina I. variety (see Pl. 16).
[2] E = e. U.S., P = Pacific states and B.C., S = Southwest, T = Texas, w = widespread.
[3] D = dry, brownish capsules; G = green, paired maple keys; K = black, juicy; R = red, juicy; U = blue, juicy.

PLATE 14

(CATALINA LYONTREE)

FERNLEAF
LYONTREE

ASHLEAF MAPLE

RED
ELDER-
BERRY

BLUE
ELDER-
BERRY

VLEVET
ELDER-
BERRY

COMMON
ELDERBERRY

MEXICAN
ELDER-
BERRY

TEXAS
LIGNUMVITAE

PLATE 15

TREES WITH OPPOSITE SIMPLE LEAVES LOBED: MAPLES

The only U.S. trees with such foliage. Leaves of Western Mountain and Canyon maples may be in 3 leaflets (see Pl. 11). First 5 species: buds mostly red and pointed; flower clusters mostly pendent, fruits mostly forming U- and V-shaped pairs. Ashleaf Maple (Pl. 14) has compound leaves. Last 4 species: buds blunt.

SPECIES AND REMARKS	Major distribution[1]	Leaf length (in.)	Leaf lobes	Leaf teeth sharp	Bud scales only two	Flower/fruit cluster slim[2]	Single fruit length (in.)	Text page
BIGLEAF MAPLE *Acer macrophyllum* Leafstalks 8–12 in., milky sap.	P	16–24	5	−		−	+	1½–2	206
WESTERN MOUNTAIN MAPLE *A. glabrum* Twigs hairless; north to s. Alaska.	w	4–7	3–5	+	+	−	¾–1	206
(EASTERN MOUNTAIN MAPLE *A. spicatum*) Twigs ± fine-hairy, flower cluster erect.	C	4–10	3–5	+	+	+	½–¾	207
CANYON MAPLE *A. grandidentatum* Bud scales 4; Idaho to Texas/Okla.	R	2–4½	3–5	−		−	−	½–1	207
VINE MAPLE *A. circinatum* Leaves circular, fruit pairs horizontal.	P	3–6	7–9	+	±	−	½–¾	208

PLANTED TREES FROM EASTERN U.S. AND EUROPE (*see p. 208*)

SPECIES AND REMARKS								
(NORWAY MAPLE *A. platanoides*)[3] Leafstalk sap milky.	I	5–9	5–7	+		−	−	1½–2	208
(SYCAMORE MAPLE *A. pseudoplatanus*)[3] Leafstalk sap clear.	I	5–9	5	−		−	+	2–4	208
(SILVER MAPLE *A. saccharinum*)[4] Leaf lobes deep; base of end lobe narrow.	I	4–8	5	+		−	−	1½–3	208
(RED MAPLE *A. rubrum*)[4] Leaf lobes shallow, base of end lobe wide.	I	4–8	3–5	+		−	−	½–1	208

[1] C = Canada, Sask. and East; I = foreign, introduced; P = Pacific states and B.C.; R = Rocky Mts.; w = widespread.
[2] Flowers/fruits in finger-shaped cluster along central, mainly unbranched axis.
[3] Buds green.
[4] Leaves whitish below.

PLATE 15

BIGLEAF
MAPLE

III

CANYON
MAPLE

VINE MAPLE

WESTERN MOUNTAIN MAPLE

PLATE 16

TREES WITH OPPOSITE SIMPLE LEAVES TOOTHED OR WAVY-EDGED

A miscellaneous group, mostly with shiny leaves 2–7 in. long. Some with 4-sided twigs. Leaf tips mostly pointed. These viburnums have winged leaf-stalks. Pacific Dogwood (Pl. 17) has leaves sometimes toothed. Camphor-tree (Pl. 30), Cascara Buckthorn (Pl. 43), and California Buckthorn (Pl. 45) may have some leaves opposite.

SPECIES AND REMARKS	Major distribution[1]	Leaf edge type[2]	Twigs 4-lined	Flowers[3]	Fruits[4]	Text page
WAVYLEAF SILKTASSEL *Garrya elliptica*[5] Leaves woolly; coastal, cen. Ore./s. Calif.	P	W	+	C	H	209
WESTERN BURNINGBUSH *Euonymus occidentalis* Twigs green; coastal mountains.	P	T	+	P	D	209
(CATALINA LYONTREE *Lyonothamnus floribundus*[5]**)** Simple-leaf form, Santa Catalina I., illus. on Pl. 14.	P	TS	–	W	C	210
SINGLELEAF ASH *Fraxinus anomala* Leaves ± circular, 1–3 leaflets.	RS	TS	+	G	W	210
NANNYBERRY *Viburnum lentago* Buds long, slender, brown; west on Great Plains.	E	T	–	W	F	210
RUSTY BLACKHAW *Viburnum rufidulum* Midribs red-hairy, buds short.	T	T	–	W	F	211

[1] E = eastern species ranging west to Black Hills, S.D., P = Pacific states, R = s. Rocky Mtns., S = Southwest, T = Texas and se. U.S.
[2] S = smooth, without teeth; T = toothed; W = wavy-edged.
[3] C = catkinlike string of small flowers; G = greenish, small; P = purple, small; W = white, clusters nearly flat-topped.
[4] C = capsules, dry, in flat-topped clusters; D = dry capsule, opening to show fleshy red fruits; F = fleshy, dark, single-seeded clusters; H = white-hairy; W = winged, dry.
[5] Var. *floribundus* Gray.

PLATE 16

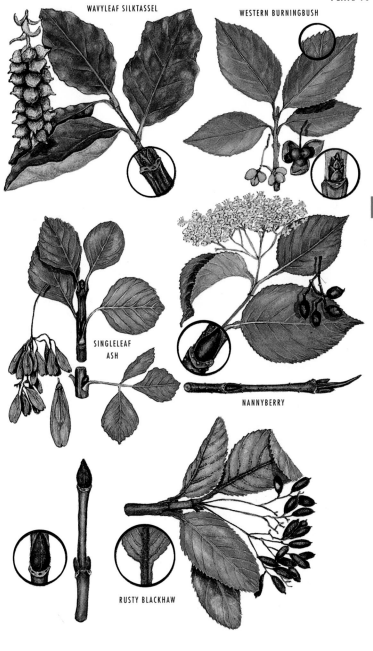

WAVYLEAF SILKTASSEL

WESTERN BURNINGBUSH

SINGLELEAF ASH

NANNYBERRY

RUSTY BLACKHAW

PLATE 17

TREES WITH OPPOSITE OR WHORLED SIMPLE LEAVES NOT TOOTHED

Dogwoods: Veins tend to follow leaf edges, twigs mostly red-purple, leaf scars raised, bundle scars 3, pith brown or white, flowers white or greenish and mostly in round or flat-topped clusters. Others: Not as above, bundle scars 1. See also Pl. 16. Species on Pls. 39, 45, and 46 have some leaves opposite.

SPECIES AND REMARKS	Major distribution[1]	Color of pith[2]	Bud scales two	Color of mature fruits[2]	Text page
PACIFIC DOGWOOD *Cornus nuttallii* Leaves ± hairy,[3] vein pairs 4–6, flowers showy, fruits stalkless.[5]	P	B	+	R	212
SMOOTH DOGWOOD *Cornus glabrata* Leaves smooth, vein pairs 3–4; coastal.	P	B	+	W	213
WESTERN DOGWOOD *Cornus occidentalis* Leaves ± hairy, vein pairs 4–7.	P	WB	+	W	214
(BLACKFRUIT DOGWOOD *Cornus sessilis*) Vein pairs 4–5; n. Calif.	P	W	+	K	214
RED-OSIER DOGWOOD *Cornus stolonifera* Twigs bright red, vein pairs 4–7.	w	W	+	W	215
ROUGHLEAF DOGWOOD *Cornus drummondii* Sandpapery, vein pairs 3–4; s. plains.	TE	B	+	W	215
DESERT-OLIVE FORESTIERA *Forestiera phillyreoides* Leaves 5x width, edges rolled.	S	B	–	K	216
(TEXAS FORESTIERA *Forestiera angustifolia*) Leaves 8x width; s. and w. Texas.	T	B	–	K	216
SILVER BUFFALOBERRY *Shepherdia argentea* Leaves/twigs silver-scaly, ± thorny.	w	B	+	R	217
BUTTONBUSH *Cephalanthus occidentalis* Leaves often in 3s–4s, buds embedded.	PT	B	±	D	217
(CRAPEMYRTLE *Lagerstroemia indica*) Trunk yellow-green, mottled.[4]	PT	B	+	B	218
(BLACK MANGROVE *Avicennia germinans*) Coastal, evergreen, erect breather roots.	T	W	+	G	218

[1] E = e. U.S.; I = introduced, planted; P = Pacific states and B.C.; S = s. Ariz.; T = Texas; w = widespread.
[2] B = brown; D = dry, ball-shaped; G = green; K = black; R = red; W = white.
[3] Leaves occasionally fine-toothed.
[4] Bark resembles that of Texas Persimmon.
[5] Other dogwoods have stalked flowers/fruits.

PLATE 17

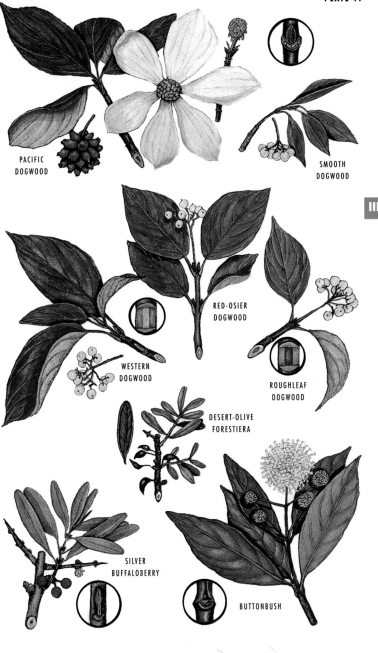

PACIFIC
DOGWOOD

SMOOTH
DOGWOOD

RED-OSIER
DOGWOOD

WESTERN
DOGWOOD

ROUGHLEAF
DOGWOOD

DESERT-OLIVE
FORESTIERA

SILVER
BUFFALOBERRY

BUTTONBUSH

PLATE 18

THORNY SOUTHWESTERN TREES WITH ALTERNATE ONCE-COMPOUND LEAVES

Southwestern trees plus Black Locust. Leaflets mostly under 2 inches long. Coralbean often leafless. Fruit pods beaded in first two species. Prickly-ash leaflets wavy-toothed. *Robinia* buds hidden beneath leaf scars. Honey Locust may have some or all leaves once-compound. Several species evergreen[3]. Littleleaf Sumac (Pl. 23), though mostly thornless, has stiff thornlike twigs. Leaves of some species on Pls. 19–20 may appear to be once-compound.

SPECIES AND REMARKS	Major distribution[1]	Thorns paired	Leafstalks thorny	Leaflets per leaf	Twigs hairy	Flower color[2]	Text page
SOUTHWESTERN CORALBEAN *Erythrina flabelliformis* Leaflets 2–4 in. long, triangular.	S	±	+	3	±	R	220
DESERT IRONWOOD *Olneya tesota*[3] Leaves dense, clustered, gray-green.	S	±	–	8–20		P	221
LIME PRICKLY-ASH *Zanthoxylum fagara*[3] Leaves thin, midribs winged.	T	±	–	5–11		G	222
TEXAS PRICKLY-ASH *Zanthoxylum hirsutum*[3] Leaves crinkled, leathery.	T	–	+	3–7	+	G	222
(SOUTHERN PRICKLY-ASH *Zanthoxylum clava-herculis*)[3] Leaflet halves unequal.	TE	±	+	7–17	–	G	223
NEW MEXICO LOCUST *Robinia neomexicana* Leaflets with tiny bristle tips.	S	+	–	9–21	±	P	223
BLACK LOCUST *Robinia pseudoacacia* Escaped widely; no leaflet tips.	E	+	–	7–19	–	W	224
(HONEY LOCUST *Gleditsia triacanthos*) Thorns 2–10 in. long; Pl. 20.	E	–	–	8–16		W	235

[1] E = e. U.S., planted in West; S = Southwest; T = Texas.
[2] G = greenish, P = purplish, R = red, W = white.
[3] Evergreen or nearly so; crushed leaves of prickly-ashes have a lemon odor.

PLATE 18

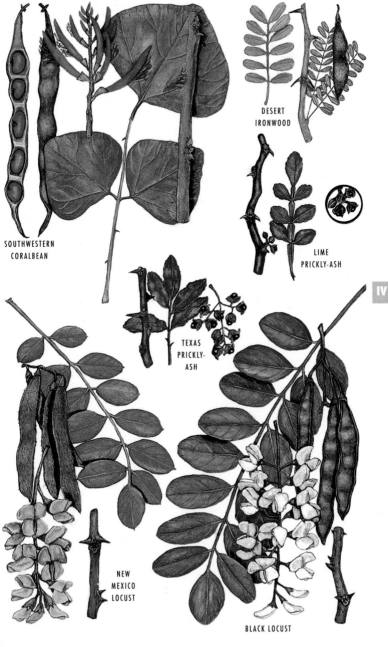

SOUTHWESTERN
CORALBEAN

DESERT
IRONWOOD

LIME
PRICKLY-ASH

TEXAS
PRICKLY-
ASH

IV

NEW
MEXICO
LOCUST

BLACK LOCUST

PLATE 19

SOUTHWESTERN TREES WITH ALTERNATE LEAVES TWICE-COMPOUND AND THORNS PAIRED

Pea-group plants with leaflets not toothed. Spur branches present (especially obvious in mesquites). Thorns straight or slightly curved; single or in 3s in Jerusalem-thorn. Roemer Catclaw (Pl. 20) and mesquites may have some single thorns. First 4 species evergreen.

SPECIES AND REMARKS	Major distribution[1]	Major leaflet pairs	Minor leaflet pairs per major	Minor leaflet width[2]	Flower clusters[3]	Fruit pod type[4]	Text page
HUISACHE[5] *Acacia farnesiana* Leaves 2–4 in. long, pods hairless.	PT	4–8	10–25	T	BY	C	225
(HUISACHILLO[6] *Acacia tortuosa*) Leaves 1–1½ in. long, pods hairy.	T	4–8	15–20	T	BY	C	226
TENAZA[7] *Pithecellobium pallens* Minor leaflets medium green, narrow.	T	4–6	8–20	N	BW	F	226
TEXAS EBONY *Pithecellobium flexicaule* Minor leaflets dark, wide.	T	1–3	3–6	M	SW	C	227
HONEY MESQUITE[8] *Prosopis glandulosa*[9] Leaflets hairless, ¾–1½ in. long.	ST	1	10–20	M	SY	C	228
VELVET MESQUITE *Prosopis velutina*[9] Leaflets hairy, ¼–½ in. long.	S	1	15–20	N	SY	C	229
SCREWBEAN MESQUITE *Prosopis pubescens*[9] Leaflets ± hairy, ¼–⅜ in. long.	BT	1	5–9	M	SY	S	229
JERUSALEM-THORN *Parkinsonia aculeata* Midribs grasslike, leaflets fall.	ST	1–3	20–30	N	LY	B	229

[1] BT = Great Basin to Texas, PT = s. Calif. to Texas, S = Southwest, T = s. Texas.
[2] T = thin, $\frac{1}{32}$ in., N = narrow, $\frac{1}{16}$ in., M = medium, $\frac{1}{8}$–¼ in.
[3] B = ball-shaped, L = loose, S = slim spike, W = white, Y = yellow.
[4] B = beaded, C = cylindrical, F = flat, S = spiraled.
[5] weesah-chay.
[6] weesah-CHEE-yoh; fruit pods slightly beaded.
[7] ten-AH-za.
[8] mes-KEET or, more properly, mes-keetay.
[9] Major leaflet pairs rarely 2 (or 2–3 in Honey Mesquite).

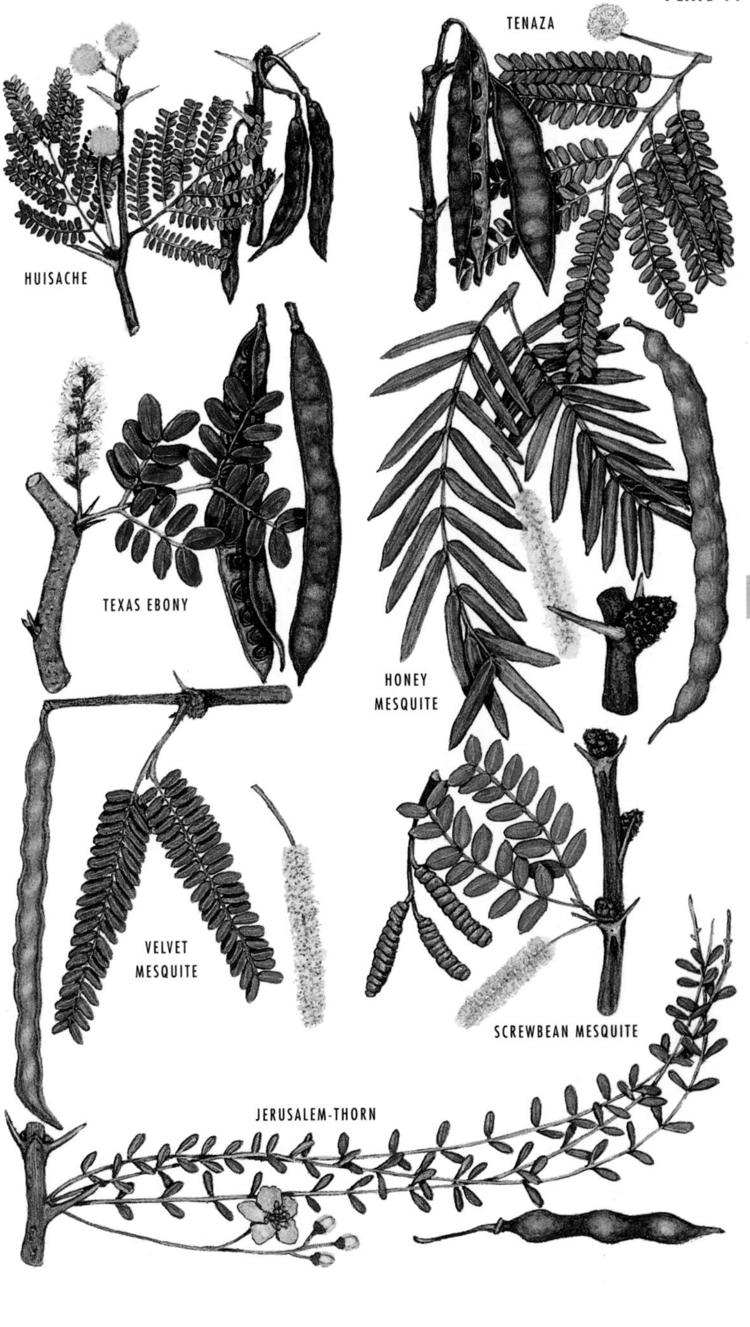

PLATE 19

HUISACHE

TENAZA

TEXAS EBONY

HONEY MESQUITE

IV

VELVET MESQUITE

SCREWBEAN MESQUITE

JERUSALEM-THORN

PLATE 20

MOSTLY SOUTHWESTERN TREES WITH ALTERNATE LEAVES TWICE-COMPOUND AND THORNS SINGLE

More pea-family plants, mainly of the Mexican border and Southwest. Fruit pods flat. Paloverdes have tiny leaves present only briefly in spring (see Pl. 26). These acacias have single hooked thorns. All have leaves with no teeth, except some Honey Locusts. Jerusalem-thorn and mesquites (Pl. 19) may have some single thorns.

SPECIES AND REMARKS	Major distribution[1]	Thorn length[2]	Major leaflet pairs	Minor leaflet width[3]	Flower cluster[4]	Fruit pod length[5]	Text page
BLUE PALOVERDE[6] *Cercidium floridum* Trunk blue-green.	S	M	1	N	LY	±	231
(YELLOW PALOVERDE[6] *Cercidium microphyllum***)** Trunk yellow, twig tips spiny; Pl. 26.	S	L	1	N	LY	±	262
TEXAS PALOVERDE[6] *Cercidium texanum* Trunk gray-green.	T	M	1–3	M	LY	−	231
GUAJILLO[7] *Acacia berlandieri* Pods velvety, flat.	T	M	5–12	T	BW	+	232
GREGG CATCLAW *Acacia greggii* Pods hairless, twisted.	ST	M	1–3	N	SY	±	233
ROEMER CATCLAW *Acacia roemeriana* Pods hairless, flat.	T+	S	1–3	M	BW	±	233
WRIGHT CATCLAW *Acacia wrightii* Pods hairless, flat.	T	S	1–2	M	SY	±	234
DWARF POINCIANA[8] *Caesalpinia pulcherrima* Leaflets blunt, flowers red.	ST	M	5–10	W	LR	+	234
HONEY LOCUST *Gleditsia triacanthos* Thorns ± branched, leaves large, 6–15 in. long.	E	L	4–8	W	LW	++	235

[1] E = e. U.S. west to Great Plains, S = s. Ariz./s. Calif., T = Texas, T+ = e. N.M. to cen. Texas.
[2] S = under ¼ in., M = ¼–⅜ in., L = over 2 in.
[3] T = thin, ¹⁄₃₂ in., N = narrow, ¹⁄₁₆ in., M = medium, ⅛–¼ in., W = wide, ³⁄₁₆ in. or more.
[4] B = ball-shaped, L = loose, R = red, S = slim spikes, W = white, Y = yellow.
[5] − = 1–3 in., ± = 2–4 in., + = 3–6 in., ++ = 8–18 in.
[6] pay-low-VEHR-deh.
[7] wah-HEE-yo.
[8] poin-see-AHN-ah.

PLATE 20

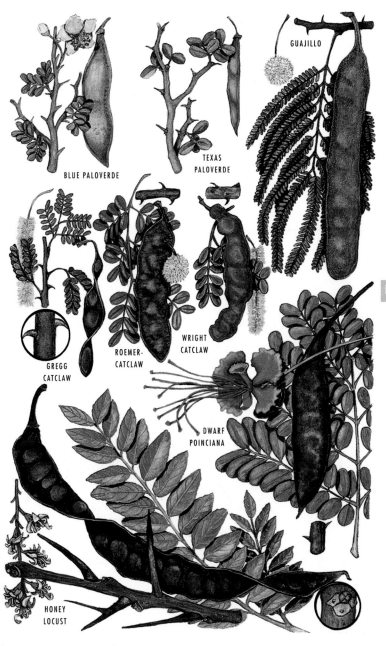

BLUE PALOVERDE

TEXAS PALOVERDE

GUAJILLO

GREGG CATCLAW

ROEMER-CATCLAW

WRIGHT CATCLAW

DWARF POINCIANA

HONEY LOCUST

IV

PLATE 21

THORNLESS TREES WITH ALTERNATE LEAVES ONCE-COMPOUND AND TOOTHED: I

Trees with feather-compound leaves and large shield-shaped leaf scars, buds hairy, spur branches absent. Walnuts:[3] branchlets with pith chambered, buds gray, bundle scars 3 or in 3 groups, nut husks do not split. Hickories: pith solid, buds yellow or rusty, bundle scars many, nut husks 4-parted. Tree-of-heaven: pith yellowish, large; buds brown-hairy; teeth only 2–4, glandular; fruits papery. See Silk-oak.[4]

SPECIES AND REMARKS	Major distribution[1]	Leaflets per leaf	Fruit length (in.)	Nut (not husk)[2]	Text page
HINDS WALNUT *Juglans hindsii* Leaflets 2½–4 in.; native cen. Calif.	P	15–19	1½–2	NG	237
CALIFORNIA WALNUT *Juglans californica* Leaflets 1–2½ in. long; native coastal s. Calif.	P	7–17	½–1	SG	237
ARIZONA WALNUT *Juglans major* Leaflets long-pointed; n. Ariz. to cen. Texas.	S	9–15	1–1½	DG	237
TEXAS WALNUT *Juglans microcarpa* Leaflets slim, teeth few; N.M. and Kansas to Mexico.	T	15–25	¾–1	DG	238
BLACK WALNUT *Juglans nigra* Leaflets wide; west to Texas/w. Okla.	E	15–23	1¼–2½	DG	238
BLACK HICKORY *Carya texana* Buds/twigs rusty-hairy.	E	(5–)7	1¼–2	RA	239
PECAN *Carya illinoensis* Buds yellow-hairy, twigs hairless.	E	9–17	1½–3	LS	239
TREE-OF-HEAVEN *Ailanthus altissima* Basal leaf glands; invades cities.	w	11–41	1–2	WD	240

[1] E = e. U.S., west to cen. Texas; P = Pacific area (Calif.); S = Southwest; T = Texas and nearby; w = widespread.

[2] DG = deep grooves; LS = longer than wide, smooth; NG = not grooved; RA = round, 4-angled; SG = shallow grooves; WD = fruits winged, dry, papery, in large clusters.

[3] For note on English Walnut, see pp. 236, 237.

[4] Lobed leaves of Silk-oak (Pl. 24) are sometimes described as toothed.

PLATE 21

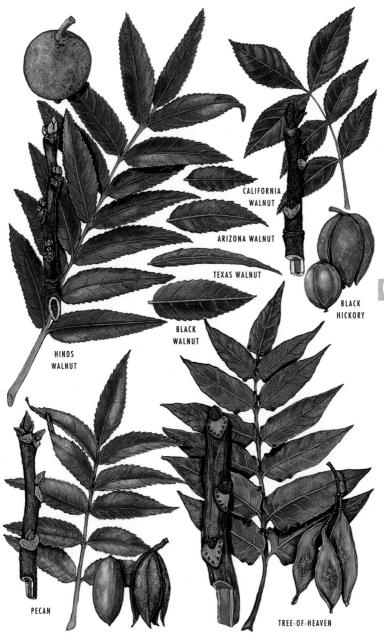

CALIFORNIA WALNUT

ARIZONA WALNUT

TEXAS WALNUT

BLACK WALNUT

BLACK HICKORY

HINDS WALNUT

IV

PECAN

TREE-OF-HEAVEN

PLATE 22

THORNLESS TREES WITH ALTERNATE LEAVES ONCE-COMPOUND AND TOOTHED: II

Deciduous trees with leaf scars not shield-shaped. Pith continuous. Spur branches present in Mountain-ashes. See also Pl. 21. Some species of Pls. 23 and 24 occasionally with some toothed leaflets. Other sumacs are on Pls. 23, 24, 45, and 46.

SPECIES AND REMARKS	Major distribution[1]	Leaf length (in.)	Leaflets per leaf	Leaflet tips[2]	Bud type[3]	Leaf scars[4]	Bundle scars[5]	Fruit type[6]	Text page
(CALIFORNIA HOPTREE *Ptelea crenulata***)** Calif. only; see related species, Pl. 24.	P	4–6	3	BS	WW	U	3	DC	241
SITKA MOUNTAIN-ASH *Sorbus sitchensis* Basal ⅓ of leaflet without teeth; trunk smooth.	P	4–8	7–11	BS	RH	N	5	OA	242
EUROPEAN MOUNTAIN-ASH *Sorbus aucuparia* Leaflets white-hairy beneath; trunk with horizontal streaks.	C	4–8	9–15	S	WW	N	5	RA	242
GREENE MOUNTAIN-ASH *Sorbus scopulina* Leaflets toothed nearly to base, trunk smooth.	w	4–9	11–15	L	RN	N	5	RA	243
SMOOTH SUMAC *Rhus glabra* Twigs 3-sided; east from B.C./N.M.	w	12–24	11–31	L	WW	U	m	RH	243
MEXICAN-BUCKEYE *Ungnadia speciosa* Several stems normal; se. N.M./Texas.	T	5–12	5–7	L	DB	L	m	3C	244

[1] C = Canada and n. U.S., P = Pacific states and B.C., T = Texas/s. N.M., w = widespread.
[2] B = blunt, L = long-pointed, S = short-pointed.
[3] DB = dark, blunt; RH = red-hairy; RN = red, not hairy; WW = white, woolly.
[4] N = narrow, L = lobed, U = U-shaped.
[5] m = many.
[6] DC = dry, circular; OA = orange, applelike, over ⅜ in.; RA = red, applelike, under ⅜ in.; RH = red-hairy; 3C = 3-lobed capsule.

PLATE 22

SITKA MOUNTAIN-ASH

EUROPEAN
MOUNTAIN-ASH

GREENE
MOUNTAIN-ASH

IV

SMOOTH
SUMAC

MEXICAN-
BUCKEYE

PLATE 23

THORNLESS SOUTHWESTERN TREES WITH ALTERNATE ONCE-COMPOUND LEAVES MOSTLY NOT TOOTHED: I

Arid-zone trees with leaflets narrow (under ⅛ in. wide) and (except Peru Peppertree) under ¾ in. long. The last 2 species are evergreen. See also Pl. 24. Other sumacs on Pls. 22, 24, 45, and 46.

SPECIES AND REMARKS	Major distribution[1]	Leaflets per leaf	Shape of leaflet tips[2]	Crushed leaves aromatic	Side twigs spiky[3]	Flower color[4]	Mature fruits[5]	Fruit size[6]	Text page
ELEPHANT-TREE *Bursera microphylla* Trunk short, massive, peeling.	S	20–40	R	+	+	W	DA	±	245
FRAGRANT BURSERA *Bursera fagaroides* Mexico north to Pima Co., Ariz.	S	5–11	RL	+	+	W	DA	+	246
WESTERN KIDNEYWOOD *Eysenhardtia polystachya* Flower spikes 2–3 in. long.	S	20–56	RS	+	–	W	FP	+	246
TEXAS KIDNEYWOOD *Eysenhardtia texana* Flower spikes to 3½ in. long.	T	15–30	R	+	–	W	FP	+	247
LITTLELEAF SUMAC *Rhus microphylla* Leafstalks winged, twigs stubby.	S	5–9	RS	–	+	G	RH	±	247
TEXAS PISTACHIO *Pistacia texana* Leaflet halves unequal.	T	9–21	T	–	–	–	RN	–	247
PERU PEPPERTREE *Schinus molle* Leaflets ± toothed; s. Calif. to s. Texas.	PT	17–41	LS	+	–	W	RF	–	248

[1] P = Pacific coast, S = Southwest, T = s. or w. Texas.
[2] L = long-pointed, R = rounded, S = short-pointed, T = tiny sharp tips present.
[3] Short, stiff, and somewhat pointed; spur branches also present.
[4] G = greenish, W = white, – = no petals or sepals.
[5] DA = dry, angled, 3-sided; FP = flat pod; RF = red, fleshy; RH = red-hairy; RN = red nut.
[6] – = ⅛–¼ in., ± = ⅛–3⁄16 in., + = ¼–½ in. long.

PLATE 23

ELEPHANT-TREE

FRAGRANT
BURSERA

LITTLELEAF
SUMAC

WESTERN
KIDNEYWOOD

TEXAS
KIDNEYWOOD

IV

TEXAS
PISTACHIO

PERU
PEPPERTREE

PLATE 24

THORNLESS SOUTHWESTERN TREES WITH ALTERNATE ONCE-COMPOUND LEAVES MOSTLY NOT TOOTHED: II

Arid-zone trees with leaflets relatively wide and mostly over 1 in. long. Winged Sumac, Prairie Sumac, and Brazilian Peppertree have winged midribs. Several have evergreen foliage;* others may have some leaves toothed. See also Pl. 23.

SPECIES AND REMARKS	Major distribution[1]	Leaflets per leaf	Leaflet tips[2]	Leaf scars U-shaped	Flower color[3]	Mature fruits[4]	Fruit size[5]	Text page
TEXAS SOPHORA *Sophora affinis* Leaves not leathery, buds hidden.	T	13–15	RS	±	W	BP	+	248
***MESCALBEAN SOPHORA** *Sophora secundiflora* Leaves leathery, buds visible.	T	5–9	RN	±	P	bP	+	249
***EVERGREEN SUMAC** *Rhus choriophylla* Mostly 3–5 leaflets.	S	3–7	SR	−	W	RH	o	250
PRAIRIE SUMAC *Rhus lanceolata* Leaflets 4x–8x width, much curved.	T	11–23	L	+	G	RH	o	250
WINGED SUMAC *Rhus copallina* Leaflets 2x–4x width; west to w./cen. Texas.	E	11–23	LS	+	G	RH	o	251
COMMON HOPTREE *Ptelea trifoliata* West to Utah/Ariz.; see Pl. 22.	ES	3	SL	+	G	bC	±	251
WESTERN SOAPBERRY *Sapindus drummondii* Leaflet halves unequal; east to sw. Mo.	ST	8–18	L	−	W	YB	−	252
***BRAZILIAN PEPPERTREE** *Schinus terebinthefolia* Aromatic, leafstalks red.	PS	3–11	RS	−	W	RF	o	253
***SILK-OAK** *Grevillea robusta* Leaflets lobed, ± hairy.	PS	3–16	D	−	RY	SP	±	253

[1] E = e. U.S., P = Pacific coast, S = Southwest, T = Texas and (often) bordering states.

[2] D = leaf divided into lobes, L = long-pointed, N = notched, R = rounded, S = short-pointed.

[3] G = greenish, P = purple, R = red, W = white, Y = yellow.

[4] BP = black-beaded pod; bP = brown, somewhat beaded pod; bC = brownish, circular, dry, winged; RF = red, fleshy; RH = red-hairy heads; SP = stalked pods; YB = yellowish, berrylike.

[5] o = $\frac{1}{8}$–$\frac{3}{16}$ in., − = $\frac{3}{8}$–$\frac{1}{2}$ in., ± = $\frac{3}{4}$–1 in., + = 1–5 in. long.

PLATE 24

TEXAS SOPHORA

MESCALBEAN SOPHORA

WINGED SUMAC

EVERGREEN SUMAC

PRAIRIE SUMAC

COMMON HOPTREE

WESTERN SOAPBERRY

BRAZILIAN PEPPERTREE

SILK-OAK

IV

PLATE 25

THORNLESS SOUTHWESTERN TREES
WITH ALTERNATE LEAVES TWICE-COMPOUND

Leaves 2–12 in. long; leaflets ±blunt or appearing so, mostly not toothed, evergreen; flowers/fruits at twig ends; fruits flattened and mostly hairless pods. All members of the pea group. Chinaberry is an exception to many items above. Thorny species on Pls. 19–20. Brazilian Peppertree (Pl. 24) may be wavy-toothed.

SPECIES AND REMARKS	Distribution in Texas[1]	Pairs of major leaflets	Minor leaflet width (in.)	Flower clusters[2]	Fruit pod length (in.)	Text page
GREAT LEADTREE *Leucaena pulverulenta* Leaves large, fernlike.	s	14–20	$\frac{1}{32}$	BW	4–12	254
PARADISE POINCIANA *Caesalpinia gilliesii* Twigs hairy; to s. Calif.	s	6–12	$\frac{1}{16}$	LY	2–4	255
LITTLELEAF LYSILOMA *Lysiloma microphylla* Rincon Mts., se. Ariz.	S	4–9	$\frac{1}{16}$	BW	4–8	255
MEXICAN LEADTREE *Leucaena leucocephala* Leaflets only pointed.	s	4–8	$\frac{3}{16}$	BW	4–6	256
GOLDENBALL LEADTREE *Leucaena retusa* Tiny leaflet tips.	w	2–4	$\frac{7}{16}$	BY	3–10	256
MEXICAN POINCIANA *Caesalpinia mexicana* Leaflet tips rounded.	s	2–5	$\frac{5}{16}$	LY	1–3	257
(DWARF POINCIANA *Caesalpinia pulcherrima***)** S. Calif. to Texas; rarely tree size; Pl. 20.	s	5–10	$\frac{5}{16}$	LR	3–5	234
(CHINABERRY *Melia azedarach***)**[3] Leaflets 1–3 in. long, long-pointed, coarse-toothed.	E	5–9	H	LP	$\frac{1}{2}$	257

[1] E = e. U.S. west to s. and cen. Texas, s = s. Texas, w = w. Texas, S = se. Ariz.
[2] B = ball-like; L = longer, loose; P = purple; R = red; W = white; Y = yellow.
[3] Fruits not pods but clustered, yellow, poisonous balls ¼ in. in diameter.

PLATE 25

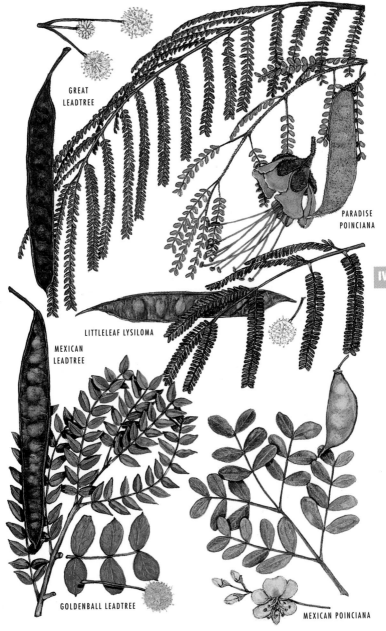

GREAT
LEADTREE

PARADISE
POINCIANA

IV

LITTLELEAF LYSILOMA

MEXICAN
LEADTREE

GOLDENBALL LEADTREE

MEXICAN POINCIANA

PLATE 26

LEAFLESS DESERT TREES WITH TWIGS SPINE-TIPPED BUT OTHERWISE THORNLESS

Trees of the southwestern deserts. Leaves tiny but usually absent except briefly in spring, mostly simple.[1] Twigs greenish and function as foliage. Twig ends sharp; small side thorns absent. Flowers clustered. Top 3 species all sometimes called Crucifixion-thorn. See also Jerusalem-thorn (Pl. 19), other paloverdes (Pl. 20), and leafy spine-tipped trees (Pl. 28). Leaves are alternate.

SPECIES AND REMARKS

Species and Remarks	Twigs mostly at right angles	Twigs stout, stiff	Twigs fine-hairy	Trunk bark[2]	Flower color[3]	Fruit type[4]	Text page
ALLTHORN *Koeberlinia spinosa* Twigs 1–2 in., green; se. Calif. to s. Texas.	+	+	−	G	G	B	259
CRUCIFIXION-THORN *Holacantha emoryi* Fruits dry, starlike; se. Calif./s. Ariz.	−	+	±	G	R	D	260
CANOTIA *Canotia holacantha* Twigs yellow, fine grooves,[5] tiny leaf scars black; Ariz./s. Utah.	−	−	−	G	G	D	260
SMOKETHORN *Psorothamnus spinosa* Twigs gray, "smoky," tiny leaf scars brown; se. Calif./w. Ariz./ s. Nev.	−	−	+	Gr	P	O	261
YELLOW PALOVERDE *Cercidium microphyllum*[1] Twigs yellow, leaflets 8–16; se. Calif./Ariz.	−	±	−	Y	Y	P	262

[1] Yellow Paloverde has small feather-compound leaves in season (see also Pl. 20).
[2] G = greenish, Gr = gray, Y = yellow-green.
[3] G = greenish, P = purple, R = reddish purple, Y = yellow.
[4] B = blackish berry; D = dry brownish capsule; O = one-seeded, tiny pea-pod; P = pea-pod, beaded.
[5] Use lens.

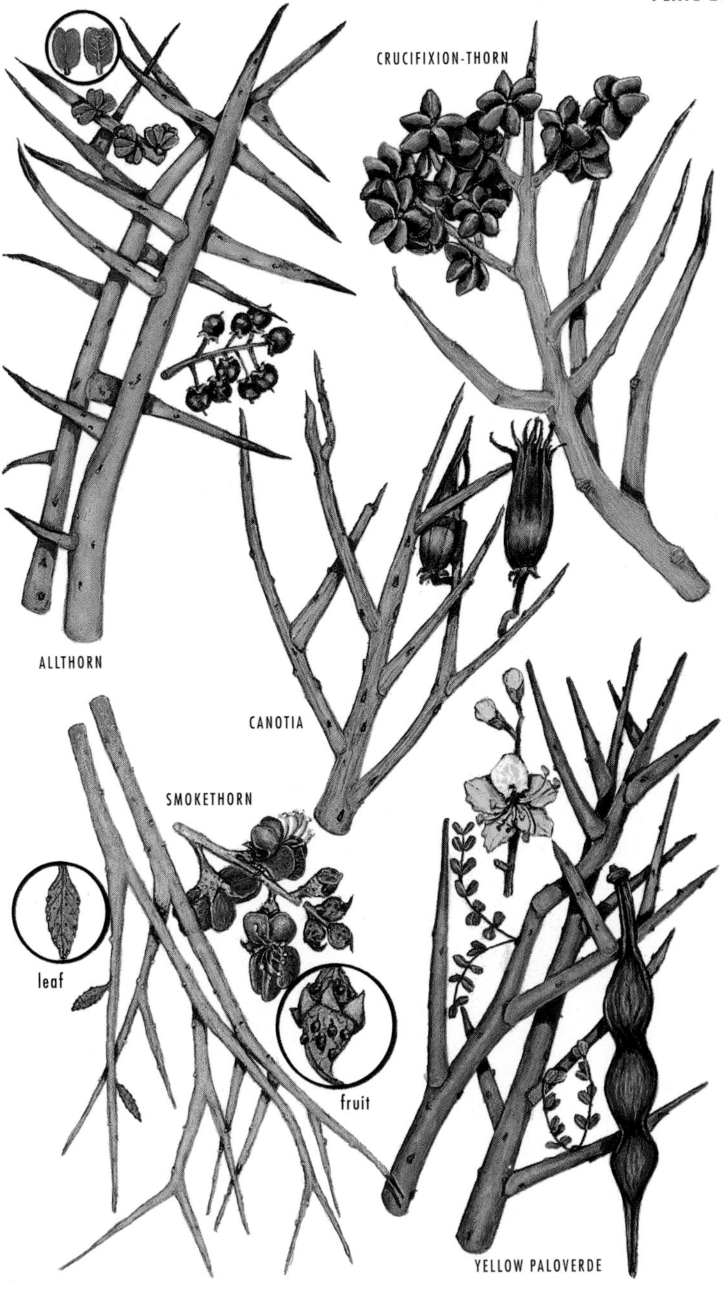

PLATE 26

CRUCIFIXION-THORN

ALLTHORN

CANOTIA

SMOKETHORN

leaf

fruit

YELLOW PALOVERDE

V

PLATE 27

THORNY TREES WITH ALTERNATE SIMPLE LEAVES TOOTHED

Long bare spines in hawthorns; paired thorns in Jujube; sharp short branches in others. Leaves mostly over 1 in. long with sharp teeth; mostly deciduous. No twigs alternate at right angles and no species with milky sap (see Pl. 28). Spur branches present. Bundle scars 3 (1 in *Ziziphus* and this *Rhamnus*). Species sometimes thorny on Pls. 39, 42, 43, and 44.

SPECIES AND REMARKS

SPECIES AND REMARKS	Major distribution[1]	Leaf characteristics[2]	Leaf bases with glands[3]	Twigs hairy	Trunk w/ horizontal lines	Flower color/location[4]	Fruit color/type[5]	Text page
BLACK HAWTHORN *Crataegus douglasii* — Trees variable, fruits red to dark.	w	L	–	–	–	WE	VA	264
OREGON CRABAPPLE *Malus fusca* — Leaves ± hairy; Pacific Northwest.	P	L	–	+	–	WS	RA	264
(PRAIRIE CRABAPPLE *Malus ioensis*) — Leaves/twigs woolly; to cen. Texas.	E	L	–	+	–	WS	GA	265
KLAMATH PLUM *Prunus subcordata* — Leaves ± round; Calif./Ore. mts.	P	W	±	±	±	WS	DP	266
DESERT APRICOT *Prunus fremontii* — Leaves to 1 in.; s. Calif. area.	P	W	±	–	–	WS	YP	266
AMERICAN PLUM *Prunus americana* — Leaves wide; west to Sask./N.M.	E	D	–	±	+	WS	RP	266
CHICKASAW PLUM *Prunus angustifolia* — Leaves narrow; west to Colo./N.M.	E	S	+	–	+	WS	RP	267
HOLLYLEAF BUCKTHORN *Rhamnus crocea* — Leaves to 1½ in., spiny, evergreen.	PS	E	–	±	–	YS	RB	267
JUJUBE *Ziziphus jujuba* — Leaves fan-veined, one thorn larger.	T	V	–	+	–	GS	DF	268

[1] E = e. U.S. to plains, P = Pacific states, S = Southwest, T = Texas, w = widespread.
[2] D = double-toothed, E = evergreen, L = ± lobed, S = single-toothed, V = 3-veined, W = wide, blunt.
[3] Raised dots on lower leaf edge or leafstalk.
[4] E = at twig ends, G = greenish, S = at side buds/spurs, W = white, Y = yellow.
[5] A = applelike, B = berrylike, D = dark, F = fleshy, G = green, H = hairy, P = plum, R = red, V = variable, Y = yellow.

PLATE 27

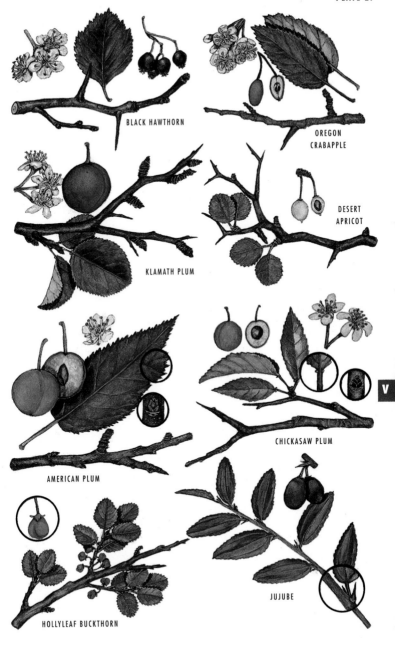

BLACK HAWTHORN

OREGON CRABAPPLE

KLAMATH PLUM

DESERT APRICOT

AMERICAN PLUM

CHICKASAW PLUM

V

HOLLYLEAF BUCKTHORN

JUJUBE

PLATE 28

THORNY TREES WITH ALTERNATE SIMPLE LEAVES NOT TOOTHED[1]

Except for Osage-orange, all occur wild only in the Southwest. Thorns single, mostly leafy; leaves mostly rounded at tips. Spur branches with clustered leaves often present. All but Osage-orange have spine-tipped twigs, often stiff and alternating.[2] *Bumelia* and *Maclura* have milky sap. See also Russian-olive (Pl. 39), sometimes thorny.

SPECIES AND REMARKS	Major distribution[3]	Leaf length (in.)	Leaf base shape	Flower clusters[4]	Fruit type/color[5]	Text page
GREENBARK CEANOTHUS *Ceanothus spinosus*[2] Evergreen, tiny leaf tips;[6] sw. Calif.	P	³/₈–1¼	U	BE	BC	269
BITTER CONDALIA *Condalia globosa*[2] Very spiny; sw. Ariz./se. Calif.	S	¼–½	V	WA	BB	270
BLUEWOOD CONDALIA *Condalia hookeri*[2] Tiny leaf tips;[6] cen. and s. Texas.	T	½–1½	V	GA	BB	270
GUM BUMELIA *Bumelia lanuginosa* Leaves/twigs ± hairy; Texas/se. Ariz.	ES	1–4	V	WA	BB	271
SAFFRON-PLUM BUMELIA *Bumelia celastrina* Twigs hairless; s. Texas and s. Fla.	T	½–2	V	WA	BB	272
(LONGLEAF PEPPERTREE *Schinus longifolius*[2]**)** Spiny twigs to 5 in. long, leaves slim, s. Texas.	T	1–2	V	WA	LB	272
OSAGE-ORANGE *Maclura pomifera* Thorns bare, leaves long-pointed.	ET	1–8	U	GA	GW	272

[1] Seldom with a few teeth.
[2] Twigs in two planes, alternating at right angles; rows of twigs forming a + when the branch is viewed from its end.
[3] E = e. U.S., P = Pacific Slope, S = Southwest, T = Texas.
[4] A = at leaf angles, B = pale blue to white, E = at twig ends, G = greenish, W = white.
[5] BB = black, berrylike; BC = black, dry capsules; GW = green, grapefruit-size, much wrinkled; LB = lavender, berrylike.
[6] Use lens.

PLATE 28

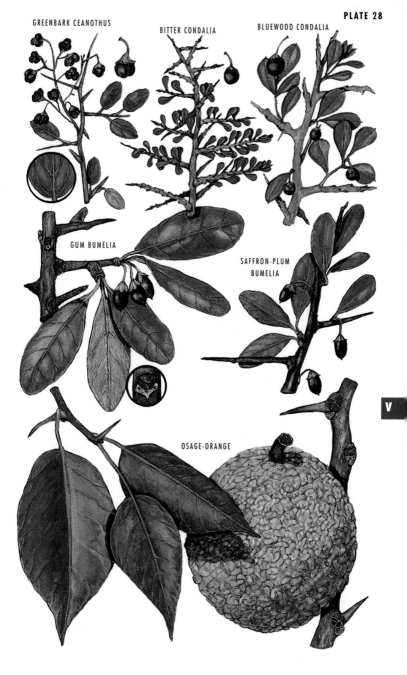

GREENBARK CEANOTHUS

BITTER CONDALIA

BLUEWOOD CONDALIA

GUM BUMELIA

SAFFRON-PLUM
BUMELIA

OSAGE-ORANGE

V

PLATE 29

THORNLESS TREES WITH ALTERNATE FAN-LOBED LEAVES

Some or all leaves lobed; 3–5 veins meet near leaf bases. Fremontia evergreen with showy yellow flowers. Mulberries with fibrous inner bark and milky sap. Sycamores with jigsawlike bark and buds covered by leafstalk bases. See also White Poplar (Pl. 31) and Cliffrose (Pl. 44). Fruits.[6]

SPECIES AND REMARKS	Major distribution[1]	Lobes toothed	Lobes per leaf	Leaves sandpapery above	Leaves hairy beneath	Bud scales per bud	Bundle scars[2]	Text page
CALIFORNIA FREMONTIA *Fremontodendron californicum*[3] Leaves 1–2 in., main veins 1–3; spur branches present.	PS	±	3–5	±	+	0	1	273
TEXAS MULBERRY *Morus microphylla* Leaves 1–3 in. long, rough both sides, scales not dark-edged.	S	+	1–5	+	+	3–5	4+	274
WHITE MULBERRY *Morus alba*[4] Buds reddish, scales not dark-edged.	E	+	1–5	–	–	5–6	4+	274
RED MULBERRY *Morus rubra* Buds green, scales dark-edged.	E	+	1–3	+	+	5–6	4+	275
PAPER-MULBERRY *Broussonetia papyrifera* Twigs hairy, pith partitioned.	E	+	1–5	+	+	2–3	4+	275
CALIFORNIA SYCAMORE *Platanus racemosa*[5] Leaf lobes halfway, fruit balls 3–7.	P	±	3–5	–	+	1	m	277
ARIZONA SYCAMORE *Platanus wrightii*[5] Leaf lobes over half, fruit balls 3–5.	S	–	5–7	–	±	1	m	277
CHINESE PARASOLTREE *Firmiana simplex* Twigs green, buds hairy.	L	–	3–5	–	±	2–3	1+	277
SWEETGUM *Liquidambar styraciflua* Crushed leaves spicy; parks.	E	+	5–7	–	–	5–6	3	278
TULIPTREE *Liriodendron tulipifera*[5] Buds spicy, pith chambered; parks.	E	–	4	–	–	2	4+	278

[1] E = e. U.S. west to cen. Texas, planted West; L = local escape from cultivation; P = Pacific region, Calif.; PS = Calif./cen. Ariz./n. Mexico; S = Southwest.
[2] m = many.
[3] See also Mexican Fremontia, p. 274.
[4] Escaped in Calif. and Wash.
[5] Twigs ringed; see also Eastern Sycamore, p. 277.
[6] Fruits — fremontia: dry 1-in. capsule; sycamores: dry 1-in.-wide brown balls; mulberries/Paper-mulberry: blackberrylike, multiple, fleshy; Sweetgum: prickly brown balls; Tuliptree: winged, dry, 1–2-in. whitish clustered keys.

PLATE 29

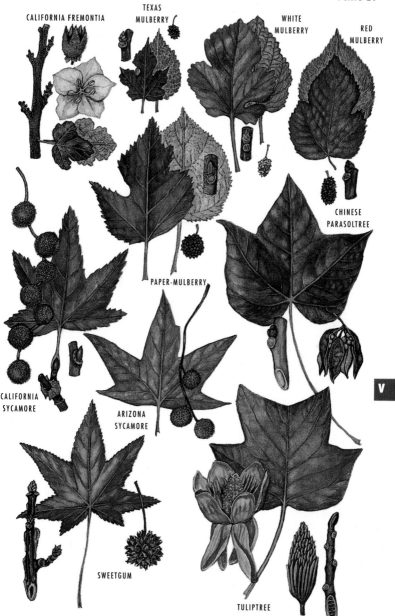

CALIFORNIA FREMONTIA

TEXAS MULBERRY

WHITE MULBERRY

RED MULBERRY

CHINESE PARASOLTREE

PAPER-MULBERRY

CALIFORNIA SYCAMORE

ARIZONA SYCAMORE

SWEETGUM

TULIPTREE

V

PLATE 30

THORNLESS TREES WITH ALTERNATE SIMPLE LEAVES FAN-VEINED

Three or more main veins meet at the leaf base. Hackberries have trunks warty, twigs hairy, pith chambered, leaves rough-hairy, mostly leathery with bases uneven. Fruits mostly wrinkled when dry; fruitstalks mostly longer than leafstalks. Ceanothuses and Camphortree evergreen. See also Jujube (Pl. 27), Greenbark Ceanothus (Pl. 28), fremontias and mulberries (Pl. 29), and poplars (Pl. 31), also fan-veined.

SPECIES AND REMARKS	Major distribution[1]	Leaves toothed	Leaf shape[2]	Bundle scars	Flowers[3]	Fruits[4]	Text page
CALIFORNIA REDBUD *Cercis occidentalis* Fruit pods more than ⅝ in. wide.	PS	—	H	3	P	P	279
(EASTERN REDBUD *Cercis canadensis***)** Fruit pods less than ¼ in. wide.	E	—	H	3	P	P	280
CAROLINA BASSWOOD *Tilia caroliniana* Buds 2–3 scales, inner bark tough.	E	+	H	4+	Y	S	280
NETLEAF HACKBERRY *Celtis reticulata* Fruits smooth when dry.	w	±	L	3	G	R	282
SOUTHERN HACKBERRY *Celtis laevigata* Fruits dry ± smooth, stalks short.	E	±	L	3	G	R	282
LINDHEIMER HACKBERRY *Celtis lindheimeri* Leaves narrow, pale-hairy beneath; s. Texas.	T	±	L	3	G	R	282
NORTHERN HACKBERRY *Celtis occidentalis* Leaves not leathery, teeth numerous.	E	+	L	3	G	R	283
BLUEBLOSSOM CEANOTHUS *Ceanothus thyrsiflorus* Twigs angled, leaves hairless.	P	+	BE	1	B	B	283
(SNOWBRUSH CEANOTHUS *Ceanothus velutinus***)** Twigs smooth, leaves hairless (at least on veins).	P	+	W	1	W	B	284
(FELTLEAF CEANOTHUS *Ceanothus arboreus***)** Twigs smooth, leaves white-hairy; islands.	P	+	W	1	B	B	284
CAMPHORTREE *Cinnamomum camphora* Spicy, glands on veins beneath.	I	—	LE	1	Y	B	284

[1] B = Great Basin, E = e. U.S. to cen. Texas, I = foreign introduction, P = Pacific Slope, S = Southwest, T = Texas, w = widespread.
[2] B = blunt, E = elliptic, H = heart-shaped, L = long-pointed, W = wide.
[3] B = blue, G = greenish, P = pink, Y = yellow.
[4] B = black, 2–3 seeds; P = pea-pods; R = round, small, brownish; S = small spheres with leaflike parachute wing.

PLATE 30

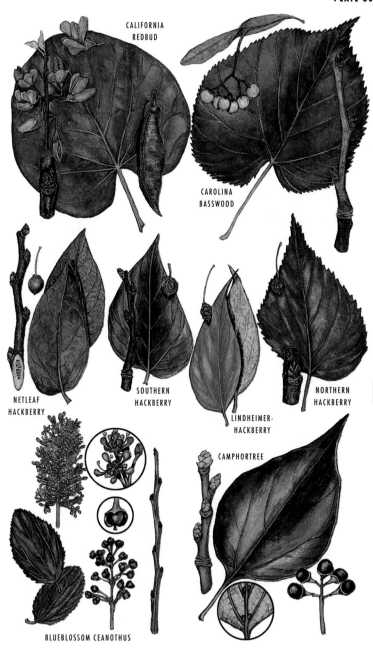

CALIFORNIA
REDBUD

CAROLINA
BASSWOOD

NETLEAF
HACKBERRY

SOUTHERN
HACKBERRY

LINDHEIMER-
HACKBERRY

NORTHERN
HACKBERRY

V

CAMPHORTREE

BLUEBLOSSOM CEANOTHUS

PLATE 31

POPLARS, INCLUDING ASPENS AND COTTONWOODS

Leaves toothed, with 3–5 main veins meeting near the leaf base; mostly triangular. Leafstalks mostly long. Lowermost bud scale exactly above the leaf scar. Bundle scars 3. Young bark smooth and yellow-green to chalky white. Fruits dry capsules, seeds hairy or fluffy. See also Tallowtree, p. 286.

SPECIES AND REMARKS	Major distribution[1]	Leafstalks flattened	Leaf length (in.)	Twig color[2]	Bud scales[3]	Mature end bud length (in.)	Text page
QUAKING ASPEN *Populus tremuloides* Leaves round, teeth small.	w	+	2–6	B	N	$1/4-3/8$	286
FREMONT COTTONWOOD *P. fremontii* Leaves wide, teeth large.	PR	+	2–5	Y	N	$3/8-1/2$	287
NARROWLEAF COTTONWOOD *P. angustifolia* Leaves narrow, stalks short, to 1 in.	R	±	3–5	Y	G	$1/4-1/2$	288
LOMBARDY POPLAR *P. nigra* var. *italica* Tree narrow, columnar, planted.	Iw	+	2–8	Y	N	$1/4-3/8$	289
BLACK COTTONWOOD *P. trichocarpa*[4] Leaves whitish beneath, buds spicy.[7]	PR	–	4–8	B	G	$3/4-7/8$	289
WHITE POPLAR *P. alba*[5] Leaves, twigs white-hairy.	Iw	±	2–6	W	H	$1/4-1/2$	290
EASTERN COTTONWOOD *P. deltoides*[7] Leaf teeth coarse; buds not spicy.	E	+	2–8	Y	G	$5/8-1$	290
BALSAM POPLAR *P. balsamifera*[6, 7] Leaf teeth fine; buds spicy.	C	–	6–10	B	G	$5/8-1$	291

[1] C = Canada/Alaska, E = e. U.S. to Great Plains, I = foreign introduction, P = Pacific states and B.C., R = Rocky Mt. region, w = widespread.
[2] B = brown, W = white-hairy, Y = yellowish.
[3] G = gummy, H = hairy, N = neither of these.
[4] Fruits 3-parted.
[5] Leaves often shallowly to deeply lobed.
[6] Fruits 2-parted.
[7] Leaf base glands present: Black Cottonwood ±, Eastern Cottonwood +, Balsam Poplar ±.

PLATE 31

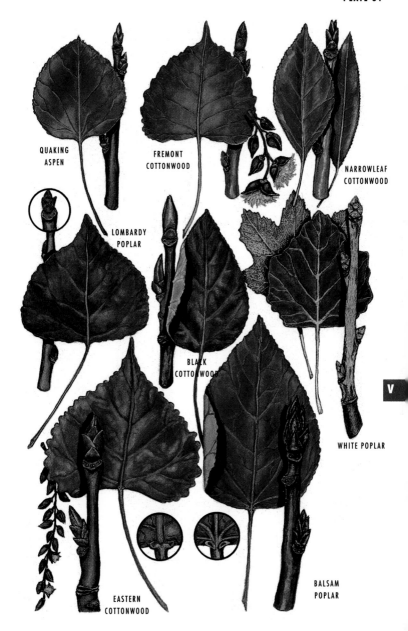

QUAKING
ASPEN

FREMONT
COTTONWOOD

NARROWLEAF
COTTONWOOD

LOMBARDY
POPLAR

BLACK
COTTONWOOD

WHITE POPLAR

V

EASTERN
COTTONWOOD

BALSAM
POPLAR

PLATE 32

OAKS I: WESTERN OAKS WITH DECIDUOUS AND MOSTLY LOBED LEAVES

Buds clustered at twig tips, flowers in catkins, fruits acorns. These oaks with leaves 2–7 in. long. Acorn cups mostly bowl-shaped. Range overlap minimal. California Scrub Oak (Pl. 33) may have some lobed leaves. Except California Black and Graves oaks, all are members of the white oak group.[1] In w. Texas, see also Lateleaf Oak (Pl. 34). In the plains states, see also Pl. 35.

SPECIES AND REMARKS	Major distribution[2]	Leaf lobe depth[3]	Leaves hairy beneath	Twigs hairy	Buds over ¼ in. long	Buds sharp	Buds hairy	Text page
CALIFORNIA BLACK OAK *Quercus kelloggii*[5] Dry slopes, Calif./Ore.	P	D	±	±	±	+	−	293
OREGON OAK *Q. garryana*[4] Leaves leathery; B.C. to cen. Calif.	P	D	+	±	+	+	+	294
VALLEY OAK *Q. lobata* Leaves thin, stalks under ¼ in.; Calif.	P	D	−	−	±	+	±	295
BLUE OAK *Q. douglasii* Leaves 1–3 in., wavy/toothed; foothills.	P	S	±	+	±	−	−	296
GAMBEL OAK *Q. gambelii* Dry slopes, Utah/s. Wyo. south.	R	D	±	−	−	+	−	296
(WAVYLEAF OAK *Q. undulata*) Hybrid; see p. 296.	R	M	±	±	−	+	−	297
HAVARD (SHIN) OAK *Q. havardii* Shrubby ±; w. Okla/w. Texas/ e. N.M.	T	S	±	±	−	−	−	298
LACEY OAK *Q. laceyi*[4] Shrubby ±; Edwards Plateau.	T	S	−	−	−	+	+	298
GRAVES OAK *Q. gravesii*[5] Mountains, w. Texas/Coahuila, Mexico.	T	M	±	−	−	±	+	298

[1] Red oaks have bristle-tipped leaves, inner shell (not cup) of acorns hairy, acorns maturing in 2 years (developing on branchlets as well as twigs), and trunk dark. White oaks have smooth-edged leaves, hairless inner acorn shells, acorns maturing in 1 year on twigs, and trunk bark gray.

[2] P = Pacific Coast region, R = Rocky Mts. and Southwest, T = Texas.

[3] D = deep, M = medium, S = shallow.

[4] Acorn cup saucer-shaped.

[5] See also Shumard Oak, Pl. 35.

PLATE 32

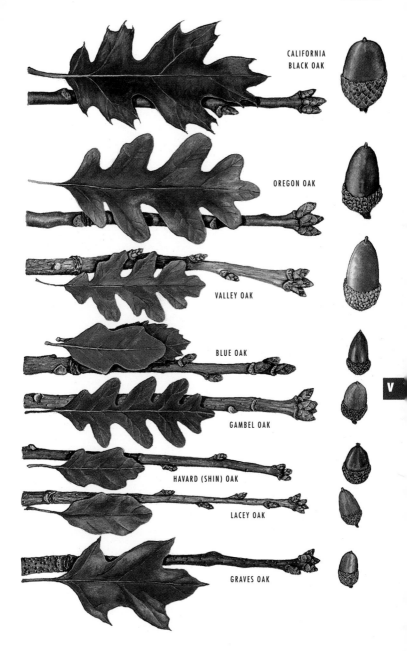

CALIFORNIA
BLACK OAK

OREGON OAK

VALLEY OAK

BLUE OAK

GAMBEL OAK

HAVARD (SHIN) OAK

LACEY OAK

GRAVES OAK

V

PLATE 33

OAKS II: EVERGREEN OAKS OF CALIFORNIA AND ITS BORDERS

Buds under ¼ in. long, clustered at twig ends; fruits acorns. Leaves leathery, toothed or not, sometimes prickly, hollylike. Hybrids common. In s. and w.-cen. Calif., see also Turbinella and Dunn oaks (Pl. 34). Twigs illustrated with leaves removed.

SPECIES AND REMARKS	Major distribution[1]	Leaf length (in.)	Leaves shiny above	Leaves hairy beneath	Buds sharp	Buds hairy	Acorns narrow	White (W) or red (R) oak[2]	Text page
CALIFORNIA SCRUB OAK *Quercus dumosa* Leaves spiny, no acorn stalks.	c	½–1¼	+	±	+	−	±	W	299
COAST LIVE OAK *Q. agrifolia* Leaves convex above, wide.	c	1–4	+	−	−	−	+	R	300
INTERIOR LIVE OAK *Q. wislizenii* Leaves flat, narrow, pointed.	v	1–2	+	−	+	−	+	R	301
CANYON LIVE OAK *Q. chrysolepis*[4] Acorn cup gold, leaf veins parallel.	m	1–2½	+	±	±	−	±	I	302
ENGELMANN OAK *Q. engelmannii* Leaves blue-green; sw. Calif.	c	1–3	−	+	−	±	−	W	302
ISLAND LIVE OAK *Q. tomentella* Leaf veins parallel, cup hairy.	i	1–4	−	±	+	+	−	I	302
TANOAK *Lithocarpus densiflorus*[3] Leaf veins parallel, cup long-scaled.	c	2–5	−	+	±	+	−	R	303

[1] c = coastal slopes and islands, i = native on s. Calif. islands only, m = mountains, v = interior slopes and valleys.

[2] Red oak group has inner shell (not cup) of acorn hairy, acorns maturing in 2 years (developing on branchlets as well as twigs), trunk dark. White oaks have smooth-edged leaves, hairless inner acorn shells, acorns maturing in 1 year on twigs, and trunk bark gray. I = intermediate oak whose acorns, like those of red oaks, have hairy inner acorn shells (not cups) and require two years to mature. They grow, however, on wood that does not normally produce new growth during the second year and thus appear mature on twigs like white oaks (see p. 299).

[3] *Lithocarpus* has all catkins erect, true oaks (*Quercus*) have drooping male catkins; also sw. Ore.

[4] Also to sw. Ore., w. Nev., w. and cen. Ariz.

PLATE 33

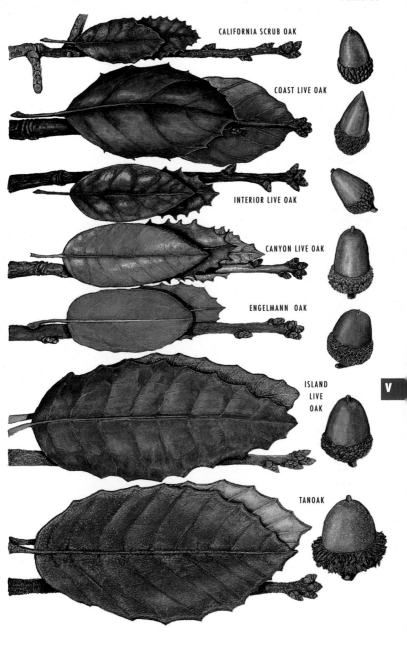

CALIFORNIA SCRUB OAK

COAST LIVE OAK

INTERIOR LIVE OAK

CANYON LIVE OAK

ENGELMANN OAK

ISLAND LIVE OAK

TANOAK

V

PLATE 34

OAKS III: EVERGREEN OAKS OF THE ARID SOUTHWEST

Trees/leaves small, leaves toothed or not. Buds clustered at twig tips. Flowers in catkins, fruits acorns (mostly short-stalked). Hybrids common. See Wavyleaf Oak (Pl. 32), Canyon Live Oak (Pl. 33), Virginia Live Oak (Pl. 35). Some twigs shown with leaves removed.

SPECIES AND REMARKS	Major distribution[1]	Maximum leaf length (in.)	Leaves often prickly	Leaf veins much raised[2]	Leaves shiny above	Leaves hairy beneath	White (W) or red (R) oak[3]	Text page
SANDPAPER OAK *Quercus pungens*[4] Leaves crinkled, rough-hairy.	aT	2	+	−	+	+	W	304
TURBINELLA OAK *Q. turbinella*[4] Leaves ± flat, acorn stalks ¼–1 ½ in.	w	2	+	−	−	+	W	304
DUNN OAK *Q. dunnii*[5] Leaves crinkled; cup gold, flared.	cn	2	+	−	±	±	R	305
GRAY OAK *Q. grisea* Leaves gray-green, mostly pointed.	At	3	−	−	−	±	W	305
NETLEAF OAK *Q. rugosa* Leaves convex; acorn stalks 1 –3 in.	At	3	−	+	+	±	W	306
ARIZONA OAK *Q. arizonica* Leaves ± blunt, widest near tip.	At	4	−	+	−	±	W	306
MOHR OAK *Q. mohriana* Leaves white-hairy beneath.	To	4	−	−	+	+	W	307
EMORY OAK *Q. emoryi* Leaves narrow, shiny both sides.	At	4	−	−	+	−	R	308
SILVERLEAF OAK *Q. hypoleucoides* Leaves narrow, woolly, edges rolled.	at	4	−	+	+	+	R	309
MEXICAN BLUE OAK *Q. oblongifolia* Leaves grayish, tips blunt.	an	2	−	+	+	−	W	309
TOUMEY OAK *Q. toumeyi* Leaves ½–1 in., branchlets flaky.	an	1	−	−	+	−	W	310
(CHISOS OAK *Q. graciliformis*) Leaves narrow, coppery, drooping.	t	4	−	−	+	−	R	310
(LATELEAF OAK *Q. tardifolia*) Leaves ± lobed, stalks short.	t	4	−	−	+	−	R	310

[1] A = Ariz.; a = se. Ariz.; c = s. Calif., local Ariz.; n = sw. N.M.; o = w. Okla.;
T = cen. Texas; t = w. Texas; w = widespread.
[2] On leaf undersides.
[3] See footnote 2, Pl. 33.
[4] Leaves bristle-tipped even though a white oak. See also Valley Oak, p. 295.
[5] Trunk bark light even though a red oak. Now a part of Palmer Oak, a shrubby intermediate oak. See p. 305.

PLATE 34

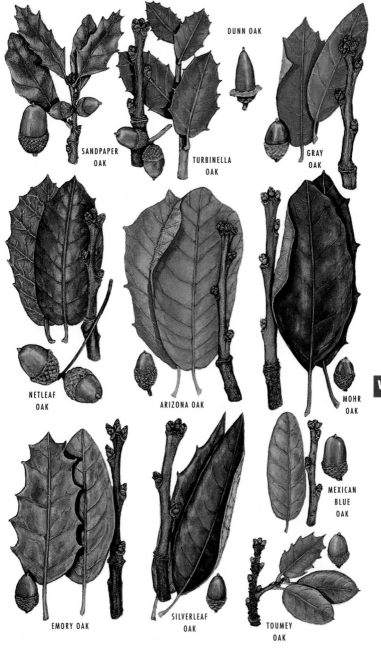

DUNN OAK

SANDPAPER
OAK

TURBINELLA
OAK

GRAY
OAK

NETLEAF
OAK

ARIZONA OAK

MOHR
OAK

V

EMORY OAK

SILVERLEAF
OAK

TOUMEY
OAK

MEXICAN
BLUE
OAK

PLATE 35

OAKS IV: OAKS OF THE GREAT PLAINS

Eastern oaks whose ranges extend west to the plains states (mainly to cen. Texas). Buds clustered at twig tips. Mostly non-evergreen. Fruits are acorns. White oak trunks mostly gray, red oaks dark.

SPECIES AND REMARKS	White (W) or red (R) oak[5]	Leaf edge type[1]	Leaves thick, leathery	Leaves hairy beneath	Twigs hairy	Buds hairy	End buds over ¼ in.[2]	Acorn cup shape[3]	Text page
EASTERN BLACK OAK *Quercus velutina* Twigs angled, bark ridged; Okla.	R	M	+	±	−	+	+	B	311
BLACKJACK OAK *Q. marilandica* Twigs angled, bark blocky.	R	S	+	±	+	+	+	B	311
SHUMARD OAK *Q. shumardii*[6] Buds pale, angled.	R	D	−	±	−	−	+	S	312
BUR OAK *Q. macrocarpa* Stipules among end buds.	W	D	±	+	±	+	−	U	312
POST OAK *Q. stellata* Leaves crosslike, bark ± blocky.	W	D	±	+	+	+	−	B	313
DURAND OAK *Q. sinuata* Leaves vary; buds round.	W	S	+	−	±	±	−	S	313
CHINKAPIN OAK *Q. muehlenbergii*[4] Teeth sharp, 8–13 pairs; buds pointed.	W	T	−	+	−	−	−	B	314
BLUEJACK OAK *Q. incana* Leaf undersides whitish; bark ± dark, blocky.	R	N	+	+	±	+	±	S	314
VIRGINIA LIVE OAK *Q. virginiana* Evergreen, acorn stalks ¾–1 in. long.	W	N	+	±	−	−	−	B	314

[1] D = deep lobes, M = medium lobes, N = neither lobed nor toothed, S = shallow lobes, T = toothed.
[2] Also angled and pointed.
[3] B = bowl-shaped, S = saucer-shaped, U = unique, cup long-fringed.
[4] Ranging west to w. Okla., se. N.M., and n. Mexico.
[5] See footnote 2, Pl. 33.
[6] See also Buckley Oak, p. 312.

PLATE 35

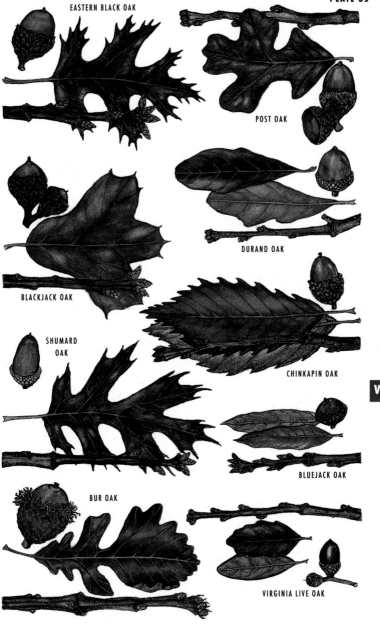

EASTERN BLACK OAK

POST OAK

BLACKJACK OAK

DURAND OAK

SHUMARD OAK

CHINKAPIN OAK

BLUEJACK OAK

BUR OAK

VIRGINIA LIVE OAK

V

PLATE 36

WILLOWS I: LEAVES VERY NARROW

Willows are catkin-bearing plants with 3 bundle scars and a single, smooth, caplike bud scale mostly with no overlap evident. Willows on this plate have leaves 8–15 times longer than wide, toothed, with V-shaped bases and without stipules or leafstalk glands (note exceptions). See also Pls. 37–39.

SPECIES AND REMARKS	Major distribution[1]	Leaves toothed	Leaves long-pointed	Leaves whitened beneath	Leaves hairy beneath	Leafstalks under 1/8 in.	Leaves shade of green[2]	Twigs hairy	Text page
YEWLEAF WILLOW *Salix taxifolia* Leaves ½–1 ¼ in. long.	S	±	−	−	+	+	G	+	317
SANDBAR WILLOW *S. exigua* Leaves to ⅜ in. wide, sides parallel.	w	+	+	±	±	+	G	±	317
HINDS WILLOW *S. hindsiana*[3] Leaves to ⅜ in. wide, mainly Calif.	P	−	−	±	+	+	G	±	317
NORTHWEST WILLOW *S. sessilifolia* Leaves wide at middle, teeth few.	P	±	−	−	+	±	G	+	317
RIVER WILLOW *S. fluviatilis* Leaves long, teeth many; Columbia R. basin.	P	+	+	+	±	+	Y	−	318
BLACK WILLOW *S. nigra*[4] Leaves green both sides.	PT	+	+	−	−	−	B	−	318
(GOODDING WILLOW *S. gooddingii)*[5] Buds show scale edge overlaps.	S	+	+	−	−	−	B	+	319
SATINY WILLOW *S. pellita* Leaves ± leathery, teeth rare; Sask. east.	C	±	−	+	+	−	B	−	319
WEEPING WILLOW *S. babylonica*[5] Glands ± present; twigs long, droop.	w	+	+	+	±	±	D	±	320

[1] C = Canada/Alaska, P = Pacific states, S = Southwest, T = Texas/Okla. and east, w = widespread.
[2] B = bright-, D = dark-, G = gray-, Y = yellow-green.
[3] Now considered part of Sandbar Willow.
[4] Twigs brittle at the base (snap with fingers).
[5] Leafstalk glands present.

PLATE 36

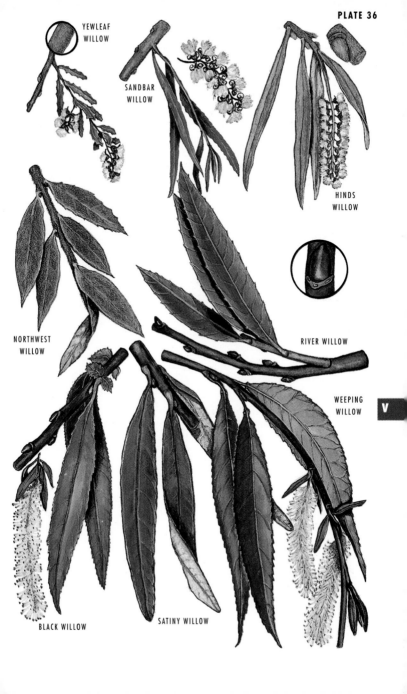

YEWLEAF
WILLOW

SANDBAR
WILLOW

HINDS
WILLOW

NORTHWEST
WILLOW

RIVER WILLOW

WEEPING
WILLOW

V

BLACK WILLOW

SATINY WILLOW

PLATE 37

WILLOWS II: LEAVES OF INTERMEDIATE WIDTH

Willows of this plate have leaves 5–7 times longer than wide, mostly deciduous, fine-toothed, whitened beneath, and without stipules, leafstalk glands, or evident bud scale overlap. Northwest Willow (Pl. 36) and Littletree Willow (Pl. 38) sometimes have medium-narrow leaves. See Pl. 36 for group characteristics and Pl. 39 for nonwillows with slim leaves. In the Rocky Mts., Narrowleaf Cottonwood (Pl. 31) is willow-like in appearance and habitat.

SPECIES AND REMARKS	Major distribution[1]	Leaves long-pointed	Leaves hairy beneath	Leaf base V-shaped	Leaves shade of green[2]	Text page
WHITE WILLOW *Salix alba* — Leaves ± whitish both sides, leafstalk glands.	w	±	+	+	G	320
MEADOW WILLOW *S. petiolaris* — Local, n. plains area; young leaves dry black.	CR	+	−	+	D	321
GEYER WILLOW *S. geyeriana* — Leaves dull, without teeth, often blunt, stalks short.	PR	−	±	+	D	321
PACIFIC WILLOW *S. lucida* — Glands on leaf bases or stalks, stalks long.	PR	+	−	−	D	322
ARROYO WILLOW *S. lasiolepis* — Leaves thick, teeth rare, tips ± rounded.	PR	−	±	+	D	322
BONPLAND WILLOW *S. bonplandiana* — Leaves thick, ± evergreen, tips pointed.	PS	±	±	±	Y	323
(RED WILLOW *S. laevigata***)** — Buds show scale edge overlap.	PS	±	±	±	R	323
MACKENZIE WILLOW *S. mackenzieana* — Leaves ± heart-based, stipules ± present.	CR	−	−	−	Y	323
COASTAL PLAIN WILLOW *S. caroliniana* — Twigs ± hairy, bases brittle; stipules ±.	TE	+	−	−	Y	324
PEACHLEAF WILLOW *S. amygdaloides* — Twigs hairless, ± droop; also n. plains and nw. U.S.	RE	+	−	−	Y	324

[1] C = Canada/Alaska, E = e. U.S., P = Pacific states and B.C., R = Rocky Mts., S = Southwest, T = cen. Texas/cen. Okla., w = widespread.
[2] D = dark green, G = gray-green, R = reddish, Y = yellow-green.

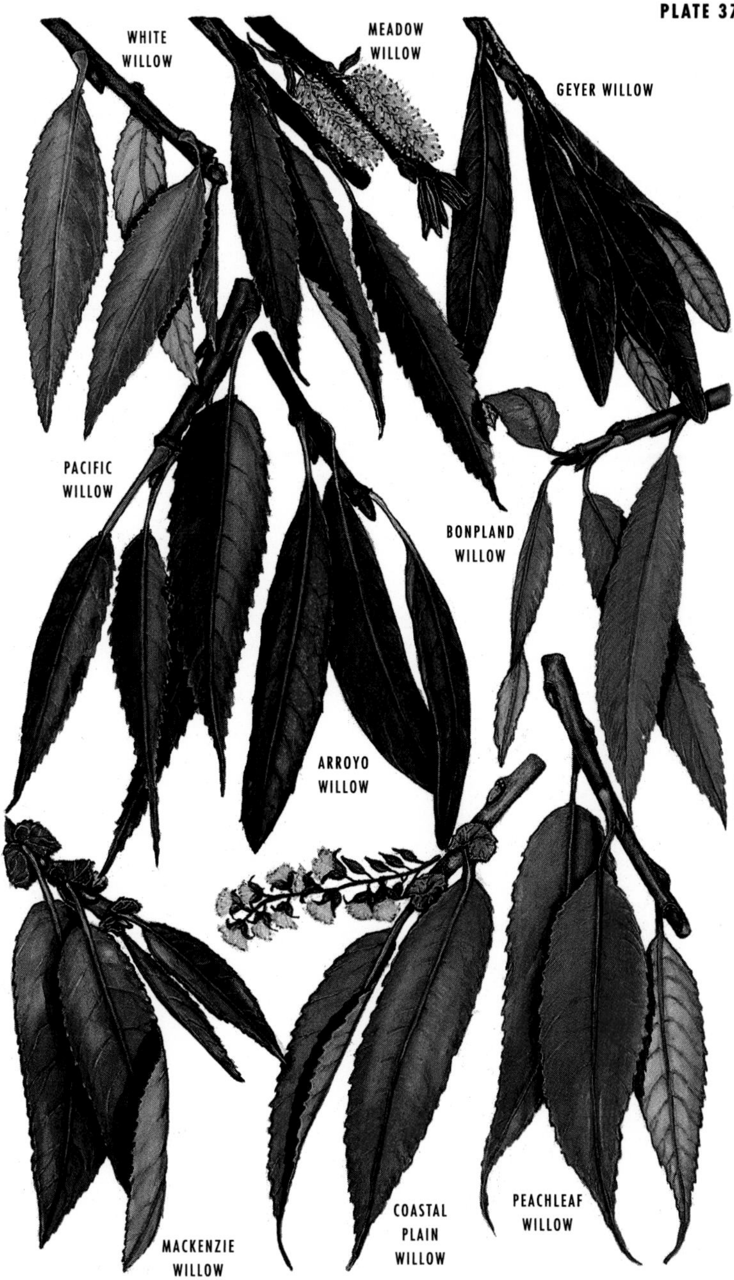

PLATE 37

WHITE WILLOW

MEADOW WILLOW

GEYER WILLOW

PACIFIC WILLOW

BONPLAND WILLOW

ARROYO WILLOW

V

MACKENZIE WILLOW

COASTAL PLAIN WILLOW

PEACHLEAF WILLOW

PLATE 38

WILLOWS III: LEAVES RELATIVELY WIDE

These willows usually have leaves 2–4 times longer than wide and mostly without leafstalk glands. Northwest Willow (Pl. 36) may have some wide leaves. See Pl. 36 for group field marks. See also Pls. 37 and 39.

SPECIES AND REMARKS	Major distribution[1]	Leaves toothed	Leaves hairy beneath	Leaf base V-shaped	Stipules usually present	Leaves shade of green[2]	Twigs brittle-based°	Text page
SHINING WILLOW *Salix lucida* Leaves long-pointed, glands present.[3, 9]	E	+	−	−	+	Y	+	325
PUSSY WILLOW *S. discolor* Leaf teeth coarse, stalks over ½ in.	CE	±	−	±	+	B	−	325
LITTLETREE WILLOW *S. arbusculoides* Leaf teeth fine, twigs ± hairy.	C	+	+	+	−	D	−	326
BALSAM WILLOW *S. pyrifolia* Leaves spicy; B.C./Yukon east.	C	+	±	−	−	D	−	326
FELTLEAF WILLOW *S. alaxensis* Twigs thick white-woolly; far north.	C	−	+	+	+	Y	−	326
SITKA WILLOW *S. sitchensis*[4, 5, 9] Leaves silver-silky beneath.	P	−	+	+	+	B	+	327
SCOULER WILLOW *S. scouleriana*[5] Leaves blunt, red-hairy, wavy-edged.	w	±	+	+	+	D	−	328
BEBB WILLOW *S. bebbiana* Leaves gray-hairy, teeth coarse.[6]	CR	±	+	+	+	G	−	328
HOOKER WILLOW *S. hookeriana*[7, 9] Leaves white-woolly; near ocean.	P	±	+	−	−	D	+	328
TRACY WILLOW *S. tracyi*[8] River sandbars; leafstalks under ¼ in.	P	±	±	+	−	B	−	329

[1] C = Canada/Alaska, E = e. U.S., P = Pacific states and B.C., R = Rocky Mts., w = widespread.
[2] B = blue-, D = dark-, G = gray-, Y = yellow-green.
[3] Species of n. plains; use lens.
[4] Also local n. Rocky Mts.
[5] Leaf edges strongly rolled under.
[6] Leafstalks ¼–⅜ in. long.
[7] S. Alaska to n. Calif.
[8] Nw. Calif./sw. Ore. Recently judged to be part of Arroya Willow (Pl. 37).
[9] Twigs snap off easily at the base.

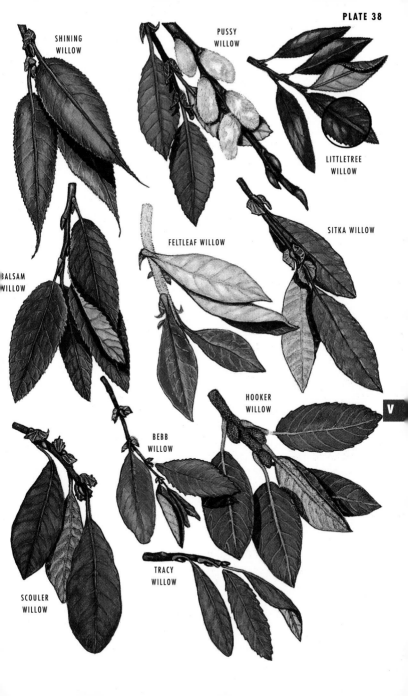

PLATE 38

SHINING WILLOW

PUSSY WILLOW

LITTLETREE WILLOW

BALSAM WILLOW

FELTLEAF WILLOW

SITKA WILLOW

HOOKER WILLOW

BEBB WILLOW

V

SCOULER WILLOW

TRACY WILLOW

PLATE 39

NONWILLOWS WITH NARROW WILLOWLIKE LEAVES

Leaf length 3–15 times width; buds lacking the single caplike scale of willows. First five species evergreen. Narrowleaf Cottonwood (Pl. 31), Fire and Black cherries (Pl. 42), Arizona Madrone (Pl. 45), and Bluegum Eucalyptus (Pl. 46) also have leaves sometimes narrow.

SPECIES AND REMARKS	Major distribution[1]	Leaf length (in.)	Leaf teeth[2]	Leaves long-pointed	Leaf base V-shaped	Flower color[3]	Fruit type[4]	Fruit length (in.)	Text page
CALIFORNIA-BAY *Umbellularia californica* Leaves spicy, no bud scales; sw. Ore./Calif.	P	3–5	N	–	±	Y	F	¾–1	330
GOLDEN CHINKAPIN *Chrysolepis chrysophylla*[5] Leaves not spicy, gold beneath; buds scaly.	P	3–5	N	±	±	W	B	1–1½	331
PACIFIC BAYBERRY *Myrica californica*[5] Leaves aromatic, resin dots beneath.[6]	P	3–4	CN	–	+	G	W	¼	332
(SOUTHERN BAYBERRY *Myrica cerifera*) Aromatic, resin dots both sides.[6]	E	2–3	CN	±	+	G	W	⅛	333
TORREY VAUQUELINIA *Vauquelinia californica* Leaves parallel-sided; Ariz./ Baja California.	S	2–4	C	–	+	W	D	¼	333
JUMPING-BEAN SAPIUM *Sapium biloculare* Sap milky, poisonous.[5]	S	1–2	F	–	–	G	D	½	334
DESERT-WILLOW *Chilopsis linearis* Leaves/fruits slim, flowers showy, pods persist.	BS	3–7	N	+	+	W	P	4–12	334
RUSSIAN-OLIVE *Elaeagnus angustifolius* Leaves, twigs, fruits silver-scaly; ± thorny.	wI	1–4	N	–	±	Y	F	½	335
PEACH *Prunus persica* Fruits velvety; Calif.	PI	3–6	F	+	±	P	F	1–4	335

[1] B = Great Basin; E = se. U.S. to Texas; I = introduced from abroad, naturalized; P = Pacific states and B.C.; S = Southwest; w = widespread.
[2] C = coarse, F = fine, N = none.
[3] G = greenish, P = pink, W = white, Y = yellow.
[4] B = bur, prickly; D = dry, brownish; F = fleshy; P = slender, dry pod; W = waxy.
[5] Leaves clustered at or near twig tips.
[6] Use lens.

PLATE 39

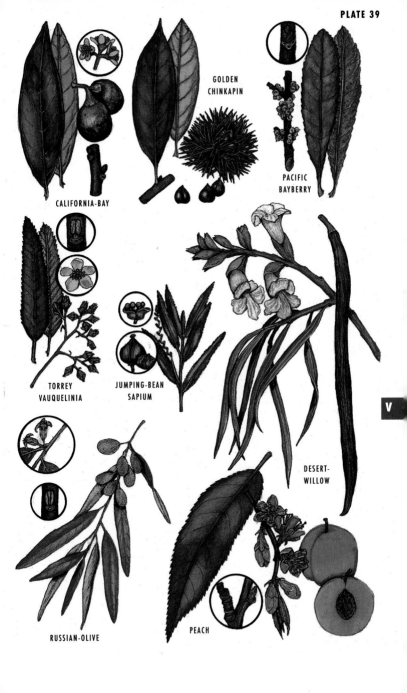

CALIFORNIA-BAY

GOLDEN CHINKAPIN

PACIFIC BAYBERRY

TORREY VAUQUELINIA

JUMPING-BEAN SAPIUM

DESERT-WILLOW

RUSSIAN-OLIVE

PEACH

V

PLATE 40

TREES WITH CATKINS THAT RESEMBLE SMALL CONES: ALDERS

Primarily northern plants, mostly of streamsides and damp soils. Leaves largely double-toothed and 2–5 in. long with main side veins parallel. Buds mostly stalked, reddish, blunt, ¼–⅜ in. and with 2–3 scales not overlapping. Bundle scars 3. Cones mostly ½–¾ in. long. California Hazelnut (Pl. 41) also has alderlike leaves.

SPECIES AND REMARKS	Major distribution[1]	Leaf teeth single/double	Leaf tooth shape[2]	Leaf vein pairs	Length of mature buds[3]	Trunk bark[4]	Text page
RED ALDER *Alnus rubra* Leaf edges rolled under.[5]	P	D	C	10–15	+	G	336
WHITE ALDER *A. rhombifolia* Leaves single-toothed, edges flat.	P	SD	F	9–12	±	G	337
SITKA ALDER *A. viridis* ssp. *sinuata*[6] Leaves shiny beneath; buds pointed.	PR	D	L	6–10	+	G	338
MOUNTAIN ALDER *A. incana* ssp. *tenuifolia* None of above; veinlets in network.[5]	PR	D	F	6–9	±	D	339
SPECKLED ALDER *A. rugosa* Veinlets parallel, ladderlike.[5]	C	D	F	9–12	±	D	339
ARIZONA ALDER *A. oblongifolia* Leaves narrow, base V-shaped.	S	D	F	9–13	+	C	340
SEASIDE ALDER *A. maritima* Bud scales separated; s. Okla.[7]	O	S	C	5–7	−	D	340

[1] C = Canada, O = Okla., P = Pacific states and B.C., R = Rocky Mts., S = Southwest.
[2] C = coarse, F = fine, L = long-pointed, very fine.
[3] − = under ¼ in., ± = ¼–⅜ in., + = over ⅜ in. long.
[4] C = checkered small plates; D = dark, usually with short whitish horizontal streaks (lenticels); G = gray.
[5] Use lens.
[6] Cone stalks as thin as leafstalks and as long as cones; buds not stalked, scales overlap.
[7] Also Md./Del.

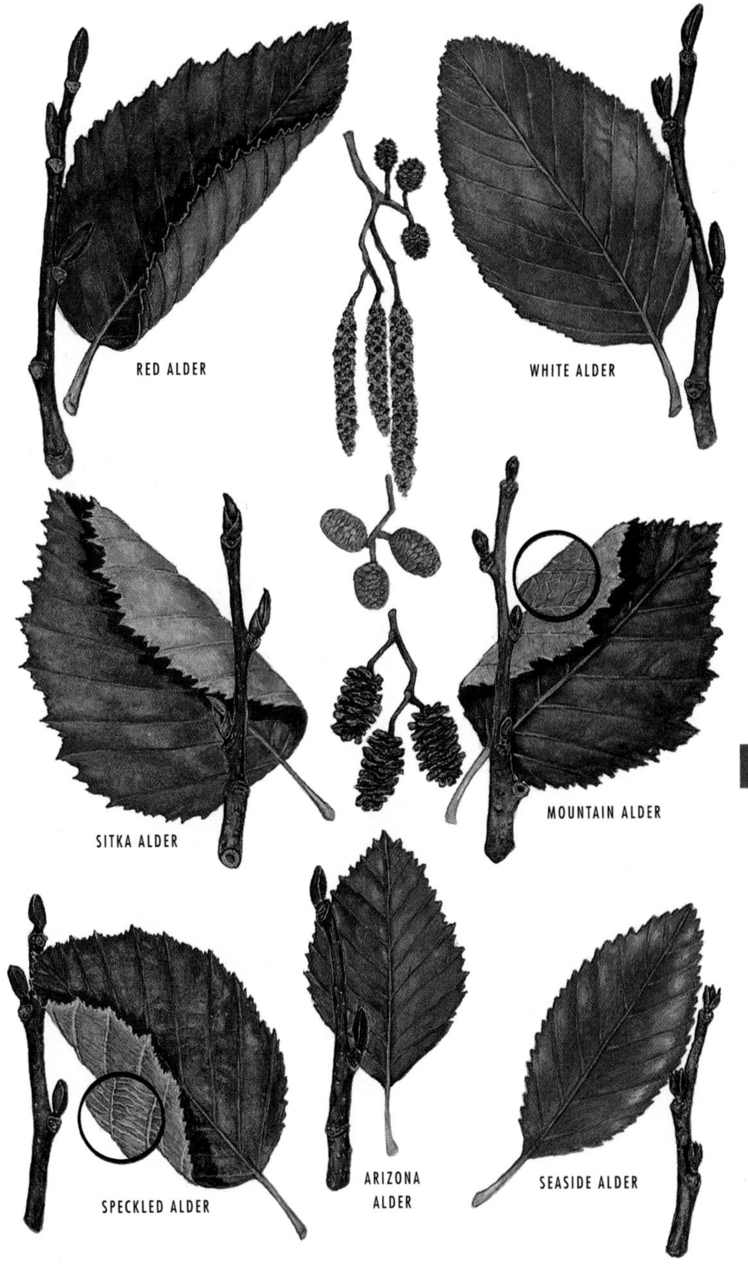

PLATE 40

RED ALDER

WHITE ALDER

SITKA ALDER

MOUNTAIN ALDER

V

SPECKLED ALDER

ARIZONA ALDER

SEASIDE ALDER

PLATE 41

OTHER TREES WITH ALTERNATE LEAVES MOSTLY DOUBLE-TOOTHED[1]

Birches have smooth bark with horizontal streaks, spur branches, and buds with 2–3 scales. Other species have dark rough bark, no spurs, and 6–8 bud scales. Elms have fibrous inner bark and mostly uneven-based, sandpapery leaves. All have 3 bundle scars and a false end bud.

SPECIES AND REMARKS	Major distribution[2]	Leaf length (in.)	Leaves long-pointed	Fruit type[3]	Text page
PAPER BIRCH *Betula papyrifera* Trunk white, peeling, dark streaks.[4]	C	2–4	±	C	341
(ALASKA WHITE BIRCH *Betula neoalaskana*) Twig resin-glands large, dense.	C	2–3	±	C	342
(KENAI BIRCH *Betula kenaica*) Twig resin-glands few.	A	1–2	–	C	342
WATER BIRCH *Betula occidentalis* Trunk brown, not peeling, white streaks.	w	2–3	–	C	343
KNOWLTON HORNBEAM *Ostrya knowltonii* Leaves egg-shaped, fruit clusters 1–2 in. long.	S	1–3	–	S	343
(CHISOS HORNBEAM *Ostrya chisosensis*) Leaves elliptic, fruit clusters ½–1 in.; Big Bend, Chisos Mts., w. Texas.	T	1–3	–	S	343
(EASTERN HORNBEAM *Ostrya virginiana*) Leaves long-pointed, fruit clusters 2–2½ in.	E	2–5	+	S	343
CALIFORNIA HAZELNUT *Corylus cornuta* ssp. *californica* Leaves hairy, round, heart-based.	P	2–4	–	B	344
AMERICAN ELM *Ulmus americana* Trunk divided, bud scales dark-edged.	E	4–6	±	W	344
(SLIPPERY ELM *Ulmus rubra*) Buds red-hairy, twigs rough-hairy.	E	4–8	±	W	345
CEDAR ELM *Ulmus crassifolia*[5] Leaves small, buds brown, fall-flowering.	T	1–2	–	W	345
(WINGED ELM *Ulmus alata*)[5] Leaves small, smooth; buds dark-edged; spring-flowering.	E	1–2	–	W	346
SIBERIAN ELM *Ulmus pumila* Leaves ± single-toothed; buds dark.	Iw	1–3	–	W	346

[1] Except Siberian Elm.
[2] A = Alaska, C = Canada; E = e. U.S. to plains; I = introduced, foreign; S = Southwest; T = Texas; w = widespread.
[3] B = beaked nuts; C = catkins; S = sacs, inflated, containing flat nuts; W = winged, flat, ± circular.
[4] Broken horizontal lines (lenticels) on bark; see also Weeping Birch, p. 342.
[5] Corky wings may occur on some branchlets.

PLATE 41

PAPER BIRCH

WATER BIRCH

KNOWLTON
HORNBEAM

CALIFORNIA
HAZELNUT

AMERICAN ELM

CEDAR ELM

SIBERIAN
ELM

V

PLATE 42

CHERRIES AND THORNLESS PLUMS

Trees with single- or double-toothed alternate leaves; leafstalks or leaf bases with tiny paired glands. Twigs mostly hairless; broken twigs with a sour almondlike odor. End buds false in plums. Bundle scars 3. Except Chokecherry and Black Cherry,[4] flower/fruit clusters umbrella-shaped on spur branches. Fruits single-seeded. Other *Prunus* species are on Pls. 27, 39, 44, and 45.

SPECIES AND REMARKS	Major distribution[1]	Leaf length (in.)	Leaves narrow[2]	Leaves double-toothed	Leaf teeth sharp	Fruit color[3]	Text page
BITTER CHERRY *Prunus emarginata* Leaves ± round-pointed.	PR	1–3	±	–	±	RB	348
CHOKECHERRY *P. virginiana*[4] Leaves wide, bud scales rounded.	w	2–5	–	–	+	P	348
BLACK CHERRY *P. serotina*[4] Leaves narrow, bud scales pointed.	SE	2–6	+	–	–	B	349
FIRE CHERRY *P. pensylvanica* Leaves/buds crowded at twig tips.	CE	2–5	+	–	+	R	350
SWEET CHERRY *P. avium* 10–14 vein pairs, spurs leafless.	IP	2–6	–	+	±	RB	350
SOUR CHERRY *P. cerasus*[5] 6–8 pairs of veins, spurs leafy.	IP	2–5	–	+	–	R	351
MAHALEB CHERRY *P. mahaleb* Leaves often round, twigs hairy.	IP	1–3	–	–	–	B	351
GARDEN PLUM *P. domestica* Leaves not round, twigs hairless.	IP	2–4	–	–	–	P	351
MEXICAN PLUM *P. mexicana* Seed round; west to cen./s. Texas.	E	2–4	–	+	+	RP	352
WILDGOOSE PLUM *P. munsoniana* Seed pointed; west to cen. Texas.	E	3–6	–	–	–	RP	352

[1] C = Canada, E = e. U.S., I = introduced from abroad, P = Pacific Slope, R = Rocky Mts., S = Southwest, w = widespread.
[2] See also Peach, Pl. 39.
[3] B = black, P = purple, R = red, Y = yellow.
[4] Flower/fruit clusters finger-shaped, spurs lacking.
[5] Main central trunk lacking.

PLATE 42

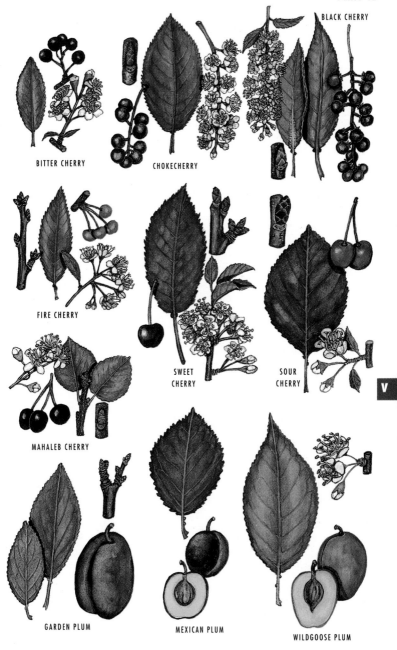

BLACK CHERRY

BITTER CHERRY

CHOKECHERRY

FIRE CHERRY

SWEET CHERRY

SOUR CHERRY

MAHALEB CHERRY

GARDEN PLUM

MEXICAN PLUM

WILDGOOSE PLUM

V

PLATE 43

MISCELLANEOUS TREES WITH ALTERNATE LEAVES THIN, NOT LEATHERY

Leaves with single teeth or none, tips ± blunt. First 5 species with parallel veins. Tree Tobacco ± evergreen. Buckthorns of this plate lack bud scales. All fleshy fruits here are several-seeded. White and Seaside alders (Pl. 40) and Siberian Elm (Pl. 41) have single teeth. Texas Persimmon (Pl. 46) is deciduous in some areas of that state.

SPECIES AND REMARKS	Major distribution[1]	Leaf length (in.)	Leaf teeth[2]	Spur branches common[3]	Flower color[4]	Fruits fleshy[5]	Text page
WESTERN (SASKATOON) JUNEBERRY *Amelanchier alnifolia* — Leaves round, stalks ½-1 in. long.	w	1–3	C	+	W	P	353
UTAH JUNEBERRY *Amelanchier utahensis* — Leaves round, stalks ¼–½ in. long.	RB	½–1¼	C	+	W	P	354
(ALDERLEAF CERCOCARPUS[6] *Cercocarpus montanus*) — Leaves resemble *C. betuloides*, Pl. 44.	RB	1–1½	C	+	G	−	354
CASCARA BUCKTHORN *Rhamnus purshiana* — Leaves hairless, vein pairs 10–15.	PR	3–6	WF	−	G	B	355
BIRCHLEAF BUCKTHORN *Rhamnus betulifolia* — Leaves ± hairy, vein pairs 7–10.	S	3–6	F	−	G	B	355
(CAROLINA BUCKTHORN *Rhamnus caroliniana*) — Leaves hairless, vein pairs 8–11.	E	2–6	F	−	G	B	356
DOMESTIC APPLE *Malus sylvestris* — Tree crown broad, thorns uncommon.	PI	1–4	F	+	WP	GR	356
DOMESTIC PEAR *Pyrus communis* — Tree crown narrow, thorns occasional.	PI	1–3	F	+	W	G	357
(INDIAN-PLUM *Oemleria cerasiformis*) — Leaf base narrowly V-shaped.	P	2–5	N	−	W	±	357
TREE TOBACCO *Nicotiana glauca* — Leaves long-stalked, white-powdered.	PT	2–8	N	−	Y	−	357
AMERICAN SMOKETREE *Cotinus obovatus* — Leaves blunt, bundle scars 3, wood yellow.	E	3–6	N	−	B	−	358
POSSUMHAW HOLLY *Ilex decidua* — Side twigs stiff, bundle scar 1.	E	2–3	W	+	G	R	358

[1] B = Great Basin; E = e. U.S. to cen. Texas; I = introduced, local; P = Pacific states and B.C.; R = Rocky Mts.; S = Southwest; T = Texas; w = widespread.
[2] C = coarse, F = fine, N = none, W = wavy-toothed.
[3] Especially on older wood.
[4] B = brownish, G = greenish, P = pink, W = white, Y = yellow.
[5] B = black; G = green; P = purple; R = red; − = small, dry, not fleshy.
[6] Rarely tree size.

PLATE 43

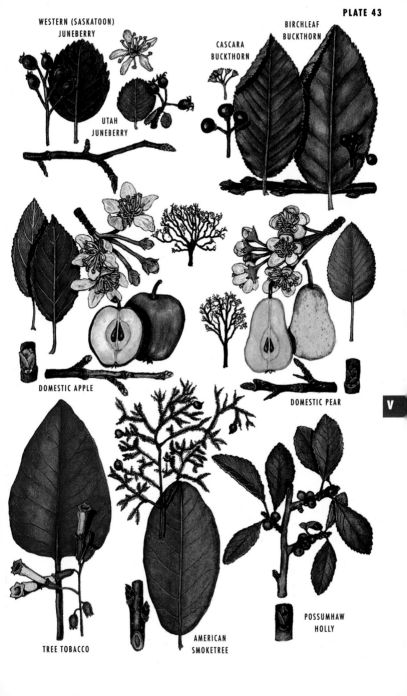

WESTERN (SASKATOON) JUNEBERRY

UTAH JUNEBERRY

CASCARA BUCKTHORN

BIRCHLEAF BUCKTHORN

DOMESTIC APPLE

DOMESTIC PEAR

TREE TOBACCO

AMERICAN SMOKETREE

POSSUMHAW HOLLY

PLATE 44

TREES WITH ALTERNATE EVERGREEN LEAVES TOOTHED

Leaves leathery, mostly with sharp teeth, some prickly. Cercocarpuses have leaf teeth near the tips, parallel veins, and fruits with 1–4-in. feathery tails. Flowers whitish and (except Cliffrose) small. Fruits mostly 1-seeded. See also ceanothuses (pl. 28, 30), Hollyleaf Buckthorn (Pl. 27), some oaks (Pls. 33, 34), narrow-leaved trees (Pl. 39), and sometimes-toothed species (Pl. 45).

SPECIES AND REMARKS	Major distribution[1]	Leaf length[2]	Leaf bases V-shaped	Leaves hairy beneath	Spur branches present	Text page
TOYON *Heteromeles arbutifolia* Not prickly; red fruits in winter, 1–4 seeds.	P	+	±	−	−	359
HOLLYLEAF CHERRY *Prunus ilicifolia* Leaves prickly, net-veined.	P	±	−	−	±	360
BIRCHLEAF CERCOCARPUS *Cercocarpus betuloides*[3] Leaf edges flat, flowers/fruits 2–5 per cluster.	PS	−	+	±	+	361
CATALINA CERCOCARPUS *Cercocarpus traskiae* Leaf edges flat, flowers/fruits 1–few per cluster.	P	±	±	+	+	361
HAIRY CERCOCARPUS *Cercocarpus breviflorus*[4] Leaf edges rolled, flowers/fruits single.	S	−	+	+	+	361
CLIFFROSE *Cowania mexicana* Leaves 3–5-lobed, white-woolly, sticky.	SR	o	+	+	+	362
BIG SAGEBRUSH *Artemisia tridentata* Leaves V-shaped, narrow, 3–5 end teeth.	w	−	+	+	−	363
AMERICAN HOLLY *Ilex opaca* Christmas holly; leaves spiny.	E	+	−	−	±	363
YAUPON HOLLY *Ilex vomitoria* Leaves small, blunt, wavy-edged.	E	−	±	−	±	364

[1] E = e. U.S. to cen. Texas, P = Pacific Slope (Calif. foothills and islands), R = Rocky Mts., S = Southwest, w = widespread.
[2] o = ¼–½ in., − = ½–1½ in., ± = 1½–3 in., + = 2–5 in.
[3] North to sw. Ore.
[4] Some leaves not toothed.

PLATE 44

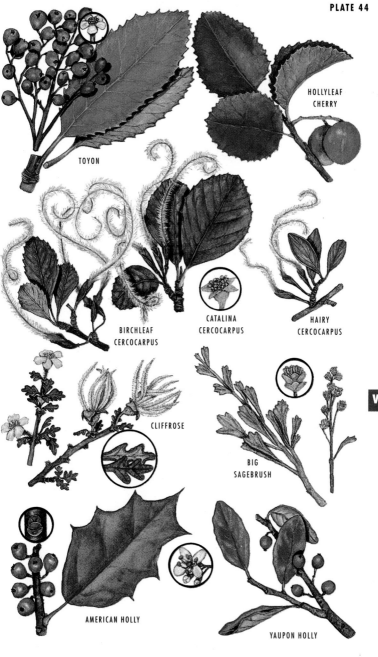

TOYON

HOLLYLEAF CHERRY

BIRCHLEAF CERCOCARPUS

CATALINA CERCOCARPUS

HAIRY CERCOCARPUS

CLIFFROSE

BIG SAGEBRUSH

AMERICAN HOLLY

YAUPON HOLLY

PLATE 45

TREES WITH ALTERNATE EVERGREEN LEAVES SOMETIMES TOOTHED

Leaves leathery or sandpaper-hairy, mostly not toothed. Flower clusters white to pink; fruits fleshy but red-hairy in sumacs. Buds of sumacs and California Buckthorn lack scales. See also Hollyleaf Buckthorn (Pl. 27), some oaks (Pls. 33, 34), and trees of Pls. 44 and 46. Mostly southwestern.

SPECIES AND REMARKS	Major distribution[1]	Leaf length (in.)	Leafstalks under 3/8 in.	Leaf edges sometimes[2]	Buds hairy	Fruits[3]	Text page
PACIFIC MADRONE *Arbutus menziesii*[8] Leaves wide.	P	4–6	–	F	–	O	365
ARIZONA MADRONE *Arbutus arizonica* Leaves narrow (1/3 length), V-based.	S	2–4	–	F	–	O	366
TEXAS MADRONE *Arbutus texana*[8] Leaves medium width, U-based.	T	2–4	–	F	–	O	366
CATALINA CHERRY *Prunus lyonii* Leaves pointed, pith slim.	P	2–4	–	W	–	B	366
SUGAR SUMAC *Rhus ovata* Leaves pointed, folding; pith wide.	PS	3–4	–	C	+	S	367
LEMONADE SUMAC *Rhus integrifolia*[4] Leaves blunt, not folding; s. Calif.	P	1–2½	+	PS	±	S	367
(CALIFORNIA BUCKTHORN *Rhamnus californica*)[5] Leaf veins parallel.	PS	2–4	–	F	+	V	368
ANACUA[6] *Ehretia anacua* Leaves rough, rounded, tiny tips.	sT	2–2½	+	C	–	O	369
ANACAHUITE[7] *Cordia boisseri* Leaves rough, pointed, white-woolly.	sT	2–8	–	W	+	R	369
SPARKLEBERRY *Vaccinium arboreum* Leaves with tiny tips; to cen. Texas.	E	1–2	+	F	–	B	370

[1] E = e. U.S., P = Pacific states, S = Southwest, T = w. Texas, sT = s. Texas.
[2] C = coarse-toothed, F = fine-toothed, P = prickly, S = smooth, W = wavy.
[3] B = black, O = orange-red, R = red, S = sticky, V = variably black or red.
[4] Leaves rarely divided into 3 leaflets.
[5] Some leaves may be opposite.
[6] ah-NAH-kwah.
[7] ahnahcah-WEE-tah.
[8] Trunk smooth, red, peeling.

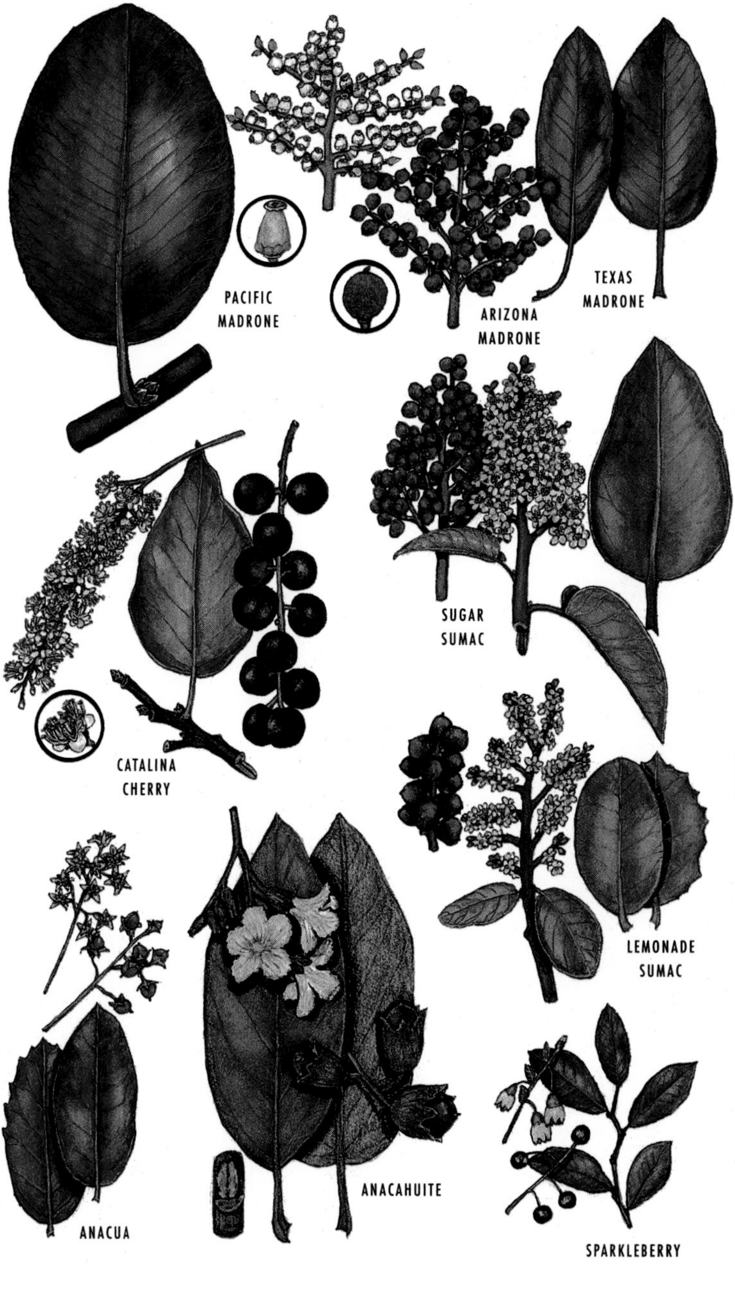

PLATE 45

PACIFIC
MADRONE

ARIZONA
MADRONE

TEXAS
MADRONE

CATALINA
CHERRY

SUGAR
SUMAC

LEMONADE
SUMAC

ANACUA

ANACAHUITE

SPARKLEBERRY

V

PLATE 46

TREES WITH ALTERNATE EVERGREEN LEAVES NOT TOOTHED

Leaves mostly leathery. See also some oaks (Pls. 33–35), Bonpland Willow (Pl. 37), and the sometimes-toothed species of Pl. 45. If leaves narrow, see also Pl. 39. If fan-veined, see also Blueblossom Ceanothus and Camphortree (Pl. 30). Twigs mostly hairless.

SPECIES AND REMARKS	Major distribution[1]	Leaf length (in.)[2]	Leaves narrow[3]	Leaf edges rolled under	Leaf bases V-shaped	Leaves long-pointed	Fruits[4]	Text page
PACIFIC RHODODENDRON *Rhododendron macrophyllum* Flowers showy; B.C. to n. Calif.	P	+	±	+	+	−	D	370
BLUEGUM EUCALYPTUS *Eucalyptus globulus* Leaves[5] hang, curved; bark peels.	PI	+	+	−	−	+	D	371
MANZANITAS *Arctostaphylos* species Trunk smooth, red-brown; shrubby.	PS	−	−	−	−	−	R	372
CURLLEAF CERCOCARPUS *Cercocarpus ledifolius*[6] Leaves clustered on spurs	w	o	+	+	+	−	F	373
LAUREL SUMAC *Rhus laurina* Leaves fold, fruits white; Calif.	P	±	±	−	−	±	S	374
KEARNEY SUMAC *Rhus kearneyi*[6] Leaves ± blunt, fruits red-hairy; Yuma.	A	−	−	+	−	−	H	374
TEXAS PERSIMMON *Diospyros texana*[6] Bark mottled; deciduous north.	T	−	+	+	+	−	J	374
REDBAY *Persea borbonia* Leaves spicy, ± hairy, twigs angled.	TE	±	±	+	+	±	J	375
POTATO-TREE *Solanum erianthum* Leaves woolly with tar odor.	T	±	+	−	±	+	S	375

[1] A = Arizona and south; E = e. U.S., I = introduced from Australia, P = Pacific states, S = Southwest, T = Texas, w = widespread in mts.
[2] o = ½–1½ in., − = 1–2½ in., ± = 2–8 in., + = 3–12 in.
[3] Length at least 3x width.
[4] D = dry capsule; F = feathery; H = hairy; J = juicy, fleshy; R = reddish; S = smooth, hairless.
[5] Juvenile leaves often shorter and opposite.
[6] Leafstalks under ⅜ in. long.

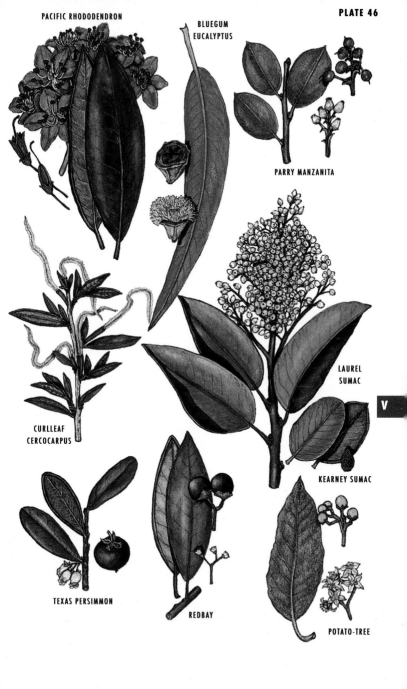

PLATE 46

PACIFIC RHODODENDRON

BLUEGUM EUCALYPTUS

PARRY MANZANITA

CURLLEAF CERCOCARPUS

LAUREL SUMAC

KEARNEY SUMAC

V

TEXAS PERSIMMON

REDBAY

POTATO-TREE

PLATE 47

PALMS AND TREE-CACTI

Southwestern desert plants with evergreen
parallel-veined leaves or succulent thorny
trunks. Palm trunks may be covered with
dead leaves under natural conditions.

SPECIES AND REMARKS	Major distribution[1]	Leaf type[2]	Flower color[3]	Color of mature fruits[4]	Text page
CALIFORNIA WASHINGTONIA *Washingtonia filifera* Trunk stout, not flared at base; Calif./Ariz.	PS	Fa	W	B	377
(MEXICAN WASHINGTONIA *Washingtonia robusta)* Trunk thinner, flared at base; planted Calif.	P	Fa	W	B	378
MEXICAN PALMETTO *Sabal mexicana* Leafstalk enters blade to 4 in.; s. Tex./Mexico.	T	Fa	W	B	378
(DWARF PALMETTO *Sabal minor)* Leafstalk enters blade to 2 in.; to cen. Texas.	E	Fa	W	B	378
DATE PALM *Phoenix dactylifera*[5] Leaves to 20 ft. long; planted.	PS	Fe	W	B	378
SAGUARO[6] *Cereus giganteus* Trunk tall, thick, thorny, often branched.	S	T	W	R	379
ORGANPIPE CACTUS *Cereus thurberi* No trunk but many branches from base.	S	T	L	R	380
INDIAN-FIG PRICKLYPEAR *Opuntia ficus-indica* Flat pads with or without bristles.	S	P	Y	R	380
JUMPING CHOLLA[7] *Opuntia fulgida* Branches segmented, rounded, thorns barbed.	S	T	P	G	381

[1] E = se. U.S., P = Pacific states (s. Calif.), S = Southwest, T = Texas.
[2] Fa = fan-shaped; Fe = featherlike; P = pads flat, bristly; T = thorny structures not flat.
[3] L = lavender, P = pink, W = white, Y = yellow.
[4] B = blackish, G = green, R = red.
[5] Leaflets close to trunk spinelike.
[6] sah-WAHR-oh.
[7] CHOY-yah.

PLATE 47

CALIFORNIA WASHINGTONIA

MEXICAN PALMETTO

DATE PALM

VI

SAGUARO

ORGANPIPE CACTUS

INDIAN-FIG
PRICKLYPEAR

JUMPING
CHOLLA

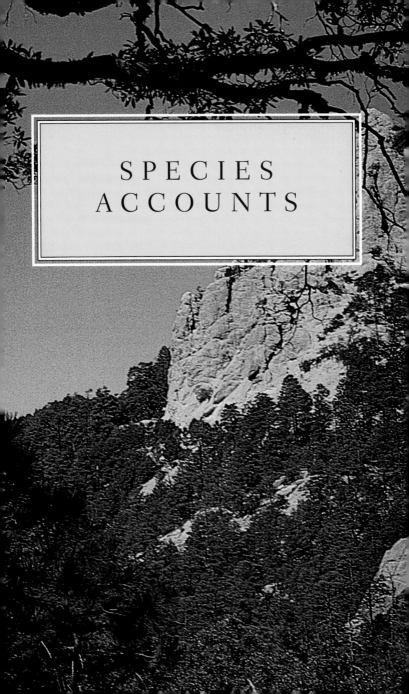

SPECIES
ACCOUNTS

TREES WITH NEEDLELIKE OR SCALELIKE LEAVES, MOSTLY EVERGREEN

PLATES 1–10

Cone-bearing trees are especially important in the West from both commercial and aesthetic standpoints. They and a few non-coniferous plants with tiny leaves make up this well-defined group. The leaves are either long and slender (needlelike) or small and overlapping (scalelike). Though individual needles and needle-clusters may drop throughout the year, most conifers are green the year around. The larches (Pl. 1) and baldcypress (Pl. 8), however, are exceptions. They drop their green foliage in autumn; their branches remain bare until spring. The deciduous tamarisks (Pl. 10) either lose their green scalelike leaves or retain them on protected branches in a dried brown condition.

Conifers are not the only evergreen trees; many broad-leaved trees (such as the madrones and live oaks) and tropical trees (like palms and yuccas) also hold green leaves throughout the year, but they are not part of this section.

The fruits of conifers typically are woody cones with seeds developed at the bases of the cone scales. The cones illustrated on the plates are the mature female cones. Male cones are small, pollen-producing organs that are obvious only during the early flowering period. Female cones usually take two years to mature. If cones are not present on the tree, old ones can frequently be found on the ground nearby.

The Pacific Yew, California Torreya, and junipers (Pls. 8, 10) have fleshy, somewhat berrylike fruits. While these bear little resemblance to the usual cones of members of the pine family, all are alike in being developed from naked ovules. Higher flowering plants have ovules enclosed in ovaries.

Foresters often refer to conifers as softwoods, in contrast to the broad-leaved trees, or hardwoods, though not all hardwoods are as hard as some softwoods.

Trees in this section can be identified by looking through Pls.

1–10 or by tracing the proper plate number using the following key:

1. Leaves ¾–18 in. long, needle-shaped. 2
1. Leaves ¹⁄₁₆–¼ in. long, mostly hugging the twigs, either blunt and scalelike or hollowed, awl-shaped. 10
   2. Needles in groups along the twigs. 3
   2. Needles 4-sided or flat, attached singly to the twigs. 8
3. Needles many, clumped on short spur branches.
                             Larches, etc., Pl. 1
3. Needles bound at the base in bundles, spur branches absent. 4
   4. Needles 1–3 per bundle. 5
   4. Needles 5 per bundle. 7
5. Needles 1–2 per bundle.   **Pines, Pl. 1**
5. Needles 3 per bundle. 6
   6. Pines of California.   **Pines, Pl. 2**
   6. Ponderosa Pine plus pines of the Mexican border.
                                Pines, Pl. 3
7. Needles 2½–13 in. long.   **Pines, Pl. 4**
7. Needles 1–2¼ in. long.   **Pines, Pl. 5**
   8. Dead twigs roughened by stiff woody pegs.   **Spruces, Pl. 6**
   8. Dead twigs smooth (hemlocks have weak pegs). 9
9. Needle scars smooth, circular; cones erect.   **Firs, Pl. 7**
9. Needle scars various; cones pendent. **Douglas-firs, etc., Pl. 8**
   10. Leaves scalelike, mostly blunt; cones woody.
                 "Cedars," Cypresses, Pl. 9
   10. Leaves both scalelike and awl-shaped; cones fleshy, solid.
                      Junipers, etc. Pl. 10

CONE-BEARING EVERGREEN TREES WITH CLUSTERED NEEDLES: LARCHES, 1- AND 2-NEEDLE PINES, AND AUSTRALIAN PINE (PLATE 1)

LARCHES

Larches are trees mostly of cold latitudes and open mountain slopes with needles clustered on short spur branches and single on longer shoots. The larches are the only northern needle-bearing species that turn golden yellow and *drop their needles* in autumn, leaving obvious warty spurs on the branchlets. The slen-

Tamarack (American Larch)

der and flexible needles are triangular (4-sided in Subalpine Larch) as seen in cross section under a microscope. Larch cones are not prickly and have fewer and mostly thinner scales than pines. Larch seeds are long-winged and dispersed mainly by winds. Larches are often called tamaracks. Lumbermen in the Northwest reportedly sometimes misname Silver Fir (Pl. 7) as "larch."

TAMARACK (AMERICAN LARCH)
Larix laricina (DuRoi) K. Koch   **PL. 1**

A medium-size tree with pointed top and slender yellow-green needles ¾–1 in. long. Twigs and branchlets *hairless, not* drooping. Cones ½–¾ in. long with no papery bracts protruding beyond the cone scales. Trunk bark dark, flaking in small scales. Height 40–80 (90) ft.; diameter 1–2 (3) ft., but in severe cold and windswept areas the species may only be a low shrub with branches flattened on the ground. Mostly wet organic soils. **SIMILAR SPECIES:** (1) European Larch has longer needles and cones, drooping branchlets, and bark divided into large plates. (2) Western and Subalpine larches also have longer needles and cones, and their cones have bracts protruding beyond the cone scales. (3) Baldcypress (Pl. 8) also loses its needles in winter, but it has flat needles and occurs in southern swamps. (4) Most tamarisks or salt-cedars (Pl. 10) are deciduous, too, but they have tiny juniperlike leaves, some of which usually remain in dried condition. **REMARKS:** Important for rough lumber (poles, posts, railroad ties). Tamarack seeds, needles, twigs, buds, and inner bark are eaten by ruffed, spruce, and sharptail grouse, red squirrels, snowshoe hares, whitetail deer, and porcupines. Grows nearly to the arctic tree line.

EUROPEAN LARCH *Larix decidua* Mill.   **NOT SHOWN**

Widely planted in N. America and sometimes spreading. Needles 1–1½ in. long; twigs and branchlets *drooping*. Cones ¾–1½ in. with pointed bracts mostly not visible beyond the cone scales. Trunk bark divided into large plates. Height to 100 ft.; diameter to 2 ft. Mostly on upland sites.

WESTERN LARCH *Larix occidentalis* Nutt.   **PL. 1**

The largest of our larches, with distribution centered in the Columbia R. basin. Tree slender, columnar with short branches and sparse foliage. Needles 1–1¾ in. and somewhat flattened or

Western Larch

WESTERN LARCH

triangular. Twigs ± *hairless*. Cones 1–1½ in. long with *pointed* bracts projecting beyond the cone scales. Mature bark thick and broken into reddish brown ridges. Height 100–180 (240) ft.; diameter 3–4 (8) ft. Mountain slopes and bottomlands, 2000–8000 ft. elevation. **SIMILAR SPECIES:** Subalpine Larch is distributed in much the same region but grows mainly near timberline and in other exposed positions. It has a broad crown plus white-hairy twigs and toothed, protruding cone bracts. **REMARKS:** A fire-resistant species protected by bark several inches thick and sometimes living 900 years. Young trees grow rapidly. Useful for poles and house construction. Twigs are an occasional food of deer, while blue and spruce grouse eat the needles.

SUBALPINE LARCH *Larix lyallii* Parl.   PL. 1

A tree of the Pacific Northwest mountains. Often a gnarled timberline plant, but less stunted specimens may occur at high sheltered locations and also as low as 5000 ft. elevation. Needles slender, 1–1½ in. long, and rounded or indistinctly 4-sided. Twigs *white-hairy.* Cones 1½–2 in. long, with *ragged* bract tips protruding between the scales. Height 30–50 (90) ft.; diameter 1–3 (6) ft. Poor soils. See Western Larch.

Subalpine Larch

SUBALPINE LARCH

TRUE CEDARS (*Cedrus* SPECIES., NOT SHOWN)

The imported Atlas (*C. atlantica* Manetti), Deodar (*C. deodara* Loud.), and Lebanese (*C. libani* Loud.) cedars resemble larches in the arrangements of needles and spurs but are *evergreen*. Introduced from N. Africa, the Himalayas, and the Middle East, respectively, they are planted in parks and gardens mainly in areas of moderate climate. Needles are ¼–2 in. long and quadrangular in cross section. Blue varieties are common. Cones are 2–5 in. long, upright, wider than those of larches and with thin, wide scales. Whereas larch cones fall as a single unit, the scales of *Cedrus* cones fall separately after the second summer. Seeds are broad-winged.

TRUE CEDARS	Needle length (inches)	Leader droops	Branchlets droop	Twigs hairy	Cone length (inches)	Cone scale tips	Scale width (inches)
ATLAS	½–1	–	–	+	2–3	SQUARE	1½
DEODAR	1–2	+	+	+	3–5	ROUND	1¼–1½
LEBANESE	1–1¼	–	–	–	3–5	BLUNT	1¾–2½

PINES (PLATES 1–5)

Pines are cone-bearing evergreen trees with slender needles mostly in clusters of 2 to 5. There are two principal groups, the white or soft pines and the yellow or hard pines. White pines have soft, clear wood and *thin, blue-green* needles in clusters of 5 (1–4 in some species), each needle with one vascular bundle. Such bundles are ducts running the length of the needle and are visible in cross section under the microscope. Members of the white pine group mostly have *lengthened* cones with *thin* scales that *lack* thorns. In contrast, yellow pines have harder and more resinous wood plus needles in clusters of 2–3 (5, in two forms). Each needle has two vascular bundles. The cones of yellow pines tend to be *short-stalked* and *egg-shaped* with *thick, thorny* scales.

SINGLELEAF
PINYON

Bark of Singleleaf Pinyon

Both groups of pines have the needle clusters wrapped in thin, papery sheaths at the base. The sheaths tend to drop early in white pines. One species, Singleleaf Pine, does not have its needles in groups (except occasionally when there are two in a bundle). Its needles, nevertheless, have a deciduous sheath around the base and other characteristics that indicate white pine relationships. Leaf sheaths are short in all pines of Pl. 1 except for Lodgepole/Shore Pine and Bishop Pine.

The cones described are the mature woody female cones. These usually take two years to mature but in some species may remain unopened on the tree for several years. The seeds of most pines are winged; the relative length of seed to wing often assists in identification. Wing lengths are measurements beyond the seed itself. Seeds are located between the cone scales. They will usually drop from dried-out mature cones. Pine branches occur in whorls around the trunk; normally one whorl is added at the tree top each year.

Pines are probably the world's most important timber trees. Mostly germinating best and growing well on bare and infertile mineral soils, they yield not only lumber but also turpentine, pitch, and various oils. Pine seeds are eaten by many birds and small mammals, while twigs and needles serve as food for deer,

Two-needle Pinyon

moose, and other browsing animals. Hybrids between species do occur and result in some specimens being difficult to identify. The two-needle Aleppo Pine (*P. halepensis* Miller) of s. Europe is planted as a landscape tree in some areas. It has very thin needles, ash-gray branchlets, and thornless cones.

SINGLELEAF PINYON *Pinus monophylla* Torr. & Frem. **PL. 1**
One of the easiest pines to recognize. The *single* (rarely 2 or 3), stout, *spine-tipped* and grayish needles, 1–2¼ in. long, are field marks. Cones 2–3 in. long and nearly globular, with thick, blunt, *thornless* scales and two nearly inch-long wingless nuts per scale. Height to 40 ft. Arid soils. **SIMILAR SPECIES:** No other pine has either single or spine-tipped needles (but see Remarks under Two-needle Pinyon). **REMARKS:** Also called Singleleaf Pine. The nuts are eaten by many birds, rodents, deer, and other wildlife. They were an important food of the early Native Americans and are still much sought after by local residents. Pine nuts are especially tasty when roasted. Two-needle Pinyon, Mexican Pinyon (Pl. 5), and Parry Pinyon (Pl. 5) are related nut pines which, though also not 5-leaved, are all considered to have had origins as members of the white pine group.

TWO-NEEDLE PINYON *Pinus edulis* Engelm. **PL. 1**

A short, round-topped, arid-zone tree mainly of the s. Rockies. Needles 2 per cluster, ¾–2 in. long, dark green, sharp but *not* spiny. Cones *short*, 1–2 in. long, somewhat spherical, with thick, blunt, *thornless* scales and 2 wingless half-inch nuts per scale. Height 15–20 (50) ft.; diameter 1–2 (3) ft. Dry sites. **SIMILAR SPECIES:** See Lodgepole Pine. **REMARKS:** Like the other nut pines (see Singleleaf Pinyon), the fruits are eagerly sought by wildlife and humans alike. Reported to be the most common tree in N.M. A single-needle population is reported to occur in cen. Ariz. Resin from trunk wounds is said to have been used by Native Americans to waterproof woven bottles and to cement turquoise jewelry.

LODGEPOLE/SHORE PINE
Pinus contorta Dougl. ex Loud. **PL. 1**

Though sufficient differences exist between the Rocky Mountain and Cascades-Sierra Nevada forms for each to be named as a separate variety, both are tall, narrow trees with somewhat sparse yellow-green needles and thin, scaly, *yellowish, cornflakelike* bark. Needle sheaths are ¹⁄₁₆–⅛ (³⁄₁₆) in. long. Both are known as Lodgepole Pine. On the Pacific slope, however, from the Alaska panhandle through nw. Calif., a third variety is a short, round-topped tree with dense dark green needles and a *blackish furrowed* trunk. It is known as Shore Pine. In contrast to the Lodgepole Pines, which seems to hold their needles for 1–2 (4) years, Shore Pine often has the previous 3–4 (7+) years' growth sheathed with needles along the branches. The several forms within the species all have 1–2 (3) in. needles with 2 per cluster. Cones 1–2 in. long,

Bark of Lodgepole Pine

usually off-center at the base, with *thin* scales tipped with *slender prickles,* usually persisting on the tree. Seed ⅛ in.; wing ½ in. Coastal trees 15–30 ft. tall and 1–2 ft. in diameter; inland specimens 60–100 (115) ft. and 1–2 (3) ft. diameter. Damp to dry sites. **SIMILAR SPECIES:** (1) Two-needle Pinyon, also with short needles and cones, has no cone prickles. (2) Bishop Pine is found only within a few miles of the ocean and has 4–6 in. needles and large, thick-scaled, heavy cones. In the Pacific Northwest and w. Canada, see (3) Austrian and (4) Jack pines. **REMARKS:** Typical Lodgepole Pine is a "fire species." Following blazes that are not so severe as to destroy all cones, massive seed releases result in dense stands of young trees, which become gradually thinned by competition. The slender trunks of these saplings once were used by Native Americans to support their buffalo-hide tepees. Nowadays, clear trunks about 8–10 in. in diameter are peeled, planed, and fitted to make attractive log homes. Wood also is harvested for paper pulp. Seeds are eaten by squirrels, chipmunks, and grouse while twigs are browsed by deer and elk. Porcupines gnaw the inner bark, damaging many trees in some areas.

AUSTRIAN PINE *Pinus nigra* Arnott   **NOT SHOWN**

A tree mainly of cen. and s. Europe but widely planted and spreading in the Pacific Northwest. Needles dark green, rather stiff, 3–6 in. long, with ¼–½ (¾) in. basal sheaths. Winter end buds *whitish.* Cones 2–3 in. long, not persistent; scale prickles ¹⁄₁₆ in. long. Seed ¼–⅜ in.; wing ½–¾ in. Mature trunk with *grayish yellow* vertical bark plates. Resistant to pollution and sea air; useful in landscaping and for windbreaks. Known also, mainly in Britain, as Black Pine. **SIMILAR SPECIES:** Lodgepole Pine has shorter needles, needle sheaths, and cones as well as a scaly yellow trunk.

JACK PINE *Pinus banksiana* Lamb.   NOT SHOWN

A shrubby, small or medium-sized tree distributed across Canada east of the Rockies and also in the ne. U.S. Needles yellow-green, *very short,* only 1–1½ in. long, with sheaths only ¹⁄₁₆–⅛ (³⁄₁₆) in. long. Cones usually curved or *bulging* on one side, 1½–2½ in. long; persistent; scales either thornless or with tiny weak prickles. Seed ³⁄₃₂ in.; wing ⅜ in. Height 15–40 (90) ft.; diameter 9–15 (24) in. with the smaller specimens widespread east of our area. Mostly poor soils. **SIMILAR SPECIES:** No other northern pine has such short needles or curved cones. Lodgepole Pine needles are somewhat longer and, though off-center at the base, the cones do not bulge unevenly. **REMARKS:** Produces poor timber. Widespread in some northern areas of dry, infertile soils that would otherwise support no tree growth. Fires cause cones to open and release seeds. Reported to intergrade with Lodgepole Pine where their ranges meet in cen. Alta. and extreme sw. N.W. Terr.

BISHOP PINE *Pinus muricata* D. Don   PL. 1

Native only within a few miles of the Pacific in scattered groves along the Calif. coastline, these are round-topped trees with dark *paired* needles 4–6 in. long. Bark brown. Cones 2–3¼ in. long and nearly as wide; *asymmetrical* at the base. The scales are massively thick, with each more or less diamond-shaped tip supporting a thorn at the center. The cones become firmly attached to the branches for some years, even becoming embedded as the branches grow. Seeds ¼ in.; wing 1¼ in. Height 40–60 ft.; diameter 2–3 ft. Sea level to 1000 ft. elevation. Fog belt from Santa Cruz, Calif., northward almost to Oregon, also Santa Cruz and Santa Rosa islands. **SIMILAR SPECIES:** (1) Ponderosa Pine usually has most or all of its needles in threes. Two-needle Ponderosa specimens have larger and more symmetrical cones. Normally they would not occur within the range of Bishop Pine. See also (2) Lodgepole Pine. **REMARKS:** The species is thought to be so-named because it was discovered by a Catholic bishop in the 19th century. According to the fossil record, the species was more widespread in earlier geologic times.

AUSTRALIAN-PINE (HORSETAIL CASUARINA)
Casuarina equisetifolia L.   PL. 1

Not a pine but resembling one. *Drooping* "needles" up to 1 ft. long attached *singly.* Each *evergreen* "needle" comprises a series of jointed, fine-grooved green sections that technically are twigs. The true leaves form whorls of 6–8 tiny gray scales fringing each joint between the sections. Fruits 1 in. long, brown, conelike but nearly ball-shaped. Height 60–90 (100) ft.; diameter 10–15 (18) in. Subtropical locations. **SIMILAR SPECIES:** No native tree has jointed "needles." **REMARKS:** The casuarinas (also called beefwoods) comprise a large group of tropical species. Unlike pines, they are true flowering plants, though the blossoms are minute. The needles resemble those of the herbaceous horsetails (*Equisetum*). Imported from Australia and planted in parks and gardens; also used in windbreaks and hedges.

THREE-NEEDLE PINES OF CALIFORNIA AND ITS BORDERS (PLATE 2)

Six of the ten 3-needle western pines occur mainly in Calif., with three of the six extending somewhat into sw. Ore. and/or w. Nev. All are members of the yellow or hard pine group, and all have evident papery *sheaths* (⅛–½ in. long) encasing the needle bases. Cones are mostly *stout, thorny,* and *short-stalked.* Probably the most abundant 3-needle species in Calif. is Ponderosa Pine (Pl. 3), which is common in mountains throughout the West. It is compared under Washoe and Jeffrey pines of this plate.

KNOBCONE PINE *Pinus attenuata* Lemm.   **PL. 2**
A tree whose unusual *1-sided, curved* cones have some scale ends prominently raised as pointed *knobs.* Needles 3–6 in., slender and yellow-green. Cones *yellow-brown,* 3–7 in. long, *narrowly pointed,* mostly paired or whorled, hugging the branches. They usually remain closed on the tree, often partly buried in the expanding branches or trunk. Scales on the outer side *very thick;* scale knobs may or may not end in stout curved prickles. Seed ¼ in.; wing ¼ in. The trunk may be *forked.* Height 20–30 (80) ft.; diameter 6–12 (24) in. Dry slopes, scattered locally in Calif.'s coastal mountains and the Sierra Nevada to Baja California Norte, with

the principal range of the species at 2000–5000 ft. elevation in the coastal mountains of nw. Calif. and sw. Ore. **SIMILAR SPECIES:** (1) Gray Pine, also with a forked trunk, has longer gray-green needles plus large, heavy, uniformly thorny cones. (2) Monterey Pine occurs naturally only south of San Francisco. Its trunk is single and cones are brown, egg-shaped, and with scales moderately or not at all knobby. **REMARKS:** Wood weak and brittle. Not a useful timber tree.

MONTEREY PINE *Pinus radiata* D. Don   **PL. 2**

With 3-needle clusters of dark needles 4–6 in. long, this species occurs locally at only a few places on the Calif. coast and on offshore Guadalupe Island, Mexico. Cones *deep brown,* 3–6 in. long, egg-shaped, *off-center* at the base. Scale tips diamond-shaped and *very thick,* some of them raised and knobby. Small straight prickles may or may not be present. Cones, often clustered, may remain closed and attached to the tree for years. Seeds ¼ in.; wing 1 in. long. Trunk normally *single* and bark dark. Height 40–60 (100) ft.; diameter 1–2 (3) ft. **SIMILAR SPECIES:** See Knobcone Pine. Other 3-needle pines have broad cone scales with stronger thorns. **REMARKS:** Not an economically important tree in its home area but widely planted in portions of Africa, South America, and the South Pacific. In the southern hemisphere, where pines are not native, Monterey Pine grows tall and straight and has excellent timber value.

WASHOE PINE *Pinus washoensis* H. Mason & Stockwell   **PL. 2**

Found to date only in the mountains of ne. Calif. and w. Nev., this 3-needle pine was not discovered until the late 1930s. It is most like Ponderosa Pine (Pl. 3), but needles are 4–6 in. long, thick, and *gray-green.* Cones only 2–3½ (5) in. long, with slender *straight-down* prickles and 160–190 total scales. Seed ⅜ in.; wing ½ in. Height 40–50 (60) ft.; diameter 1–2 (3) ft. Mature bark in yellowish plates. Established above the Ponderosa Pine belt,

WASHOE PINE

mainly at 8000 ft. and higher. Identified only on the western border of the Great Basin near Galena Creek, Mt. Rose, Washoe Co., Nev. and in the Bald (Babbitt Peak) and Warner mts., Calif. Also Blue Mts., Ore. **SIMILAR SPECIES:** (1) Ponderosa Pine (Pl. 3) has 4–10-in. yellow-green needles and 3–6-(8-)in. cones. Its cones have straight or curved-out prickles, 130–140 total scales, and seed wings more than twice as long as the seeds. (2) Jeffrey Pine has 5–10-in. needles, 6–10-in. cones with curved-in lower prickles, seed wings 3 times seed length, and mature trunk bark rosy, tight.

JEFFREY PINE *Pinus jeffreyi* Grev. & Balf. PL. 2

Much like Ponderosa Pine (Pl. 3) and at one time confused (or combined as a variety) with it. A large 3-leaved pine with blue-green needles 5–10 in. long and basal sheaths mostly ¼–½ in.

Bark of Jeffrey Pine

JEFFREY PINE

long. Cones 6–8 (10) in. long, shiny, with symmetrical bases. Cone scales stiff, flat, light brown beneath, and tipped by moderate-size prickles, at least the lower ones usually *curved in*. Seed ½ in.; wing 1¼ in. Trunk bark *firm* and furrowed, somewhat *purplish* or rosy in hue and yielding a vanilla or pineapple-like odor when one's nose is pressed into a deep furrow. This pleasant scent also may be given off by broken twigs. Height 100–130 (180) ft.; diameter 2–4 (6) ft. Mountain slopes, mostly between 6000–9000 ft. elevations. **SIMILAR SPECIES:** In contrast to (1) Ponderosa Pine (Pl. 3), Jeffrey Pine has bark with tight texture and fruity odor as well as cones that are larger, rigid, and shiny. It mostly occurs at elevations somewhat higher and drier than those occupied by Ponderosa Pine. See also (2) Washoe Pine. **REMARKS:** An important timber tree often marketed with Ponderosa Pine as Yellow Pine. The seeds are eaten by squirrels, chipmunks, grouse, and quail. Named after an early Scottish botanical explorer, John Jeffrey. Known to hybridize with Ponderosa and Coulter Pines.

COULTER PINE *Pinus coulteri* D. Don PL. 2

A 3-needle tree with the heaviest and most thorny cones of all western pines. Needles blue-green, 6–12 in. long, stout and tufted near the ends of the branches. Twigs ½–1 in. thick. Cones massive, 10–14 in. long and often weighing 4–5 lbs. They are long-stalked and *yellowish,* with thick scales ending in curved *outward-pointing,* spiky *claws* up to 1¼ in. long. Cones obvious, remaining on the tree for years. Seed ½ in.; wing 1 in. Trunk *single;* bark dark, furrowed. Height 40–60 (80) ft.; diameter 1–2 (2½) ft. Dry slopes. **SIMILAR SPECIES:** Gray Pine also has large and heavy cones. Its forked trunk, slender twigs, somewhat smaller and less thorny brownish cones, and markedly gray-green drooping foliage distinguish it where the two species overlap in range.

COULTER PINE

GRAY PINE

Gray Pine

REMARKS: The seeds once were eaten by Native Americans. Thomas Coulter, an early 19th-century medical doctor, discovered the species. Hybrids with Jeffrey Pine have been recorded.

GRAY PINE *Pinus sabiniana* Dougl. ex D. Don   **PL. 2**
Needles 3 per cluster, distinctly *gray-green,* 7–14 in. long, *drooping,* and with ¼–½ in. sheaths. Twigs ⅛–½ in. in diameter. Cones 6–10 in. long and weighing one or more pounds. They are *brown,* long-stalked, uneven-based, and equipped with strong, *downward-pointing,* ¼–¾-in. thorns. Cones usually remain attached to the tree for some years. Seed ¾ in.; wing ⅜ in. Trunk usually *forked,* grayish, furrowed. Height 40–50 (90) ft.; diameter 2–3 (4) ft. Occurs at low elevations (1000–3000 ft.) from n. Calif. to n. Los Angeles Co. **SIMILAR SPECIES:** See (1) Knobcone and (2) Coulter pines. **REMARKS:** The seeds were once an important food of Native Americans, though they are more resinous than those of the pinyon (nut) pines. It is reported that the buds and soft green cones of this pine also were eaten. The seeds are consumed, too, by squirrels and other rodents. Named after Joseph Sabine, a London lawyer and naturalist who supported botanical studies in the early 19th century. Also called Digger Pine.

PONDEROSA PINE PLUS 3-NEEDLE PINES OF THE MEXICAN BORDER (PLATE 3)

Ponderosa Pine is the most widely distributed and important pine in the West. In addition to it and the several 3-needle pines of the California region (Pl. 2), three others occur along the border with Mexico. These can be seen at Chiricahua Nat'l. Monument in se.

Ariz. and on Mt. Lemmon, just ne. of Tucson, Ariz. Mexican Pinyon and Chihuahua Pine have deciduous needle sheaths. A 3-needle pine of the se. United States, Loblolly Pine (*P. taeda* L.) with 6–9 in. needles and dark trunk bark, ranges west to near Austin, Texas.

PONDEROSA PINE *Pinus ponderosa* Dougl. ex Laws. **PL. 3**
The most common and widespread western conifer, the distribution of Ponderosa Pine is sometimes said to outline the American West. It occurs mostly in mountains from s. B.C., sw. N.D. and cen. Neb. to s. Calif., w. Texas, and n. Mexico. Typically, Ponderosa Pine is a 3-needle species, sometimes with a few 2-needle clusters present. Needles 4–10 in., yellow-green, with basal sheaths ¼–1 in. long. Twigs ¼–½ in. thick. Cones egg-shaped, 3–6 *in.* long, *dull brown,* short-stalked, and with bases symmetrical. Scales rather flexible, dark brown beneath, and tipped with a slender, ⅛–3⁄16 in. prickle often *curved out*; total scales 130–140. Seed ⅜ in.; wing 1 in. Mature specimens have trunks with bark in flaky *yellow* plates from which jigsawlike pieces can easily be removed. Younger trunks are dark, furrowed. Trunk bark and broken twigs have a *resinous* odor. Height 60–130 (230) ft.; diameter 2–4 (8) ft. Mostly 3000–5000 (9500) ft. elevation. Specimens in the Rocky Mts. region have darker bark, needles mostly 3–6 in. long and more often in twos, plus cones smaller. **SIMILAR SPECIES:** See (1) Jeffrey and (2) Washoe pines (Pl. 2), and (3) Apache Pine (below). For Arizona Pine, a 5-needle variety, see p. 141 and Pl. 4. **REMARKS:** The most economically important pine in the West. Over large regions, it is the only 3-needle pine, the only pine with long needles, and the only tree of significant commercial value. It

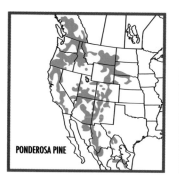

PONDEROSA PINE

MEXICAN PINYON

forms pure or nearly pure stands in many areas, mostly on dry soils and at lower elevations than many pines. Like most pines, it is a sun-loving species. It grows rapidly and shows considerable ability to survive surface fires. Sooty grouse, California quail, and both red and gray squirrels eat the seeds; porcupines feed on the inner bark; deer browse the twigs and needles. Native Americans are reported to have used the seeds for food and the trunk resin to waterproof fiber and wicker containers.

MEXICAN PINYON *Pinus cembroides* Zucc.   **PL. 3**
A 3- (occasionally 2–4-) needle nut pine with both short needles and short cones. Needles *1–2½ in.,* blue-green, thin, with leaf sheaths soon shed. Cones *1–2 in.* long, short-stalked, at least as wide as long, with broad scales and no prickles. Trunk gray-brown, furrowed. Nuts dark, wingless, ¼–¾ in. long. Height 15–20 (30) ft.; diameter to 1 ft. Dry slopes. **SIMILAR SPECIES:** No other 3-needle pine has such short needles. **REMARKS:** Sometimes called Three-needle Pinyon. It would be convenient if the species could be more widely known by that name. Then, if Parry Pinyon (Pl. 5) could be known as Four-needle Pinyon, there would be a nice set beginning with Singleleaf and Two-needle pinyons (Pl. 1). The nuts of all are excellent eating, especially when roasted.

CHIHUAHUA PINE *Pinus leiophylla* Schiede & Deppe   **PL. 3**
This small tree, though a white pine, has 3-leaved needle clusters *2¼–4 in.* long. Needles are *slender,* blue-green, double white-striped (use lens), and with *deciduous* leaf sheaths *under ⅟₁₆ in.* long. The 1¼–3 in.-long cones are only very slightly prickly. They are *long-stalked* (½ in.) and, atypically, may *remain* on the tree for several years. Trunk nearly black, often with light tan underbark in vertical fissures. Stumps may *sprout.* Seed ⅛ in.; wing ⁵⁄₁₆ in.

CHIHUAHUA PINE

APACHE PINE

Height 35–50 (80) ft.; diameter 1–2 ft. Dry slopes, 5000–8000 ft. elevation, cen. Mexico to cen. and se. Ariz.and sw. N.M. **SIMILAR SPECIES:** (1) Mexican Pinyon foliage is shorter and more dense while (2) Apache and (3) Ponderosa pines have longer needles and needle sheaths. No other tree of this plate has long-stalked cones or ones that remain on the tree for very long. **REMARKS:** The name of the Mexican state and of this pine is pronounced chee-WAH-wah.

APACHE PINE *Pinus engelmannii* Carr.   **PL. 3**

A medium-size tree of limited U.S. distribution with long needles in large clusters at the ends of thick twigs. The dark green 3-needle clusters (rarely twos or fives) are 8–15 in. long, with durable basal sheaths 1–1¼ in. long. Mature trees with few branches. Twigs dark, *thumb-wide,* very stout as seen against the sky. Cones short-stalked, 4–6 in. long, often in pairs and threes, scales light brown beneath, and with short, sometimes-curved prickles. Seed ⁵⁄₁₆ in.; wing 1 in. Mature bark in yellow plates. Height 50–60 (75) ft.; diameter 1–2 (3) ft. Found between 6000 and 8000 ft. elevations. **SIMILAR SPECIES:** Ponderosa Pine has shorter needles (usually only 4–8 in. in Ariz.), shorter leaf sheaths, thinner twigs, and darker cones. **REMARKS:** Native Americans made wicker canteens and waterproofed them with the resin that oozed from the trunks after the bark was removed. Early peoples are reported to have chewed the inner bark when other foods were scarce.

5-NEEDLE PINES WITH NEEDLES 2½–13 IN. LONG (PLATE 4)

The white (or soft) pines have 5 *blue-green* needles per cluster, each cluster bound at the base by a papery sheath. Unlike the yel-

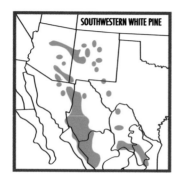

SOUTHWESTERN WHITE PINE

low pines, this sheath is *soon shed,* leaving only a remnant $\frac{1}{32}$–$\frac{1}{16}$ in. long. The needles of white pines also are more *slender* than those of yellow pines, and the branches are whorled at regular annual intervals along the trunk. Typically, cones of white pines are long-stalked, slender, and drop soon after maturity. They can usually be found beneath the parent tree and provide a good clue to identification. They have thin scales ending in slender prickles or none.

Atypically, Southwestern White Pine has short-stalked cones, while Arizona and Torrey pines, although members of the yellow pine group, have 5 needles per bundle. The needles of the species of this plate rarely are as short as those of the pines on Pl. 5.

SOUTHWESTERN WHITE PINE   PL. 4
Pinus strobiformis Engelm.

Found from the mountains of cen. Mexico north to cen. Ariz., cen. N.M., and w. Texas, this pine has thin needles 2½–3 in. long. The best field mark is provided by the short-stalked, moderately heavy, and *elongate* 5–9 in. cones whose blunt scale tips are *bent back.* Seed ⅜ in.; wing ⅛ in. or less. Bark brownish. Height 60–80 (100) ft.; diameter 1–2 (3) ft. Dry slopes, 5000–10,000 ft. elevation. **SIMILAR SPECIES:** The only white pine in its region (Limber Pine. Pl. 5, comes close in cen. N.M.). Slender needles, long cones, and reflexed cone scale tips are distinctive. Arizona Pine has long needles and needle sheaths plus short prickly cones. **REMARKS:** Sometimes classed as a variety of Limber Pine (Pl. 5). Though edible, the nuts have shells that are thick and hard to crack. Also known as Mexican White Pine, but so are other species of Mexico. Common at the ski lodge and other high elevations on Mt. Lemmon, just east of Tucson, Ariz.

SUGAR PINE   *Pinus lambertiana* Dougl.   PL. 4
The world's largest pine and the one with the longest cones. Needles are blue-green, 2½–4 in. long, mostly with needle tips long-pointed (use lens). Cones long-stalked, 11–20 *in.* long, slender, with mature scales 1–1½ in. wide. Seed ⁹⁄₁₆ in.; wing 1 in. and *wider* than seed, with tip broadly *rounded.* Mature trunk bark brown or gray, in vertical *ridges.* Height 180–200 (250) ft.; diame-

SUGAR PINE

Bark of Sugar Pine

ter 3–6 (8) ft. Cool slopes and deep soils from w. Ore. to Baja California Norte, mostly at 4000–9000 ft. elevations in the Sierra Nevada and s. Cascades. **SIMILAR SPECIES:** Western White Pine has finely checkered bark and a pointed seed wing. **REMARKS:** A tall, columnar tree of great beauty. Its soft, clear wood has value in cabinetwork, veneer backing, house interiors, and shingles. Longevities of 300–600 years have been reported. The common name derives from sweet exudations that occur at the edges of wounds. These, as well as the seeds, were eaten by Native Americans and early settlers.

WESTERN WHITE PINE PL. 4
Pinus monticola Dougl. ex D. Don

Distributed mainly as scattered specimens in mountains of the Pacific Northwest, this 5-leaved pine has blue-green needles 2½–4 in. long and tips short-pointed (use lens). Cones usually hang from tips of high branches and on the ground nearby. They are long-stalked, 5–10 in. long, *narrowly cylindrical,* and with mature scales ½–¾ in. wide. Seed ⅜ in.; wing 1 in. and not much wider than the seed, with tip pointed. Mature trunk bark gray or brown, finely fissured or in distinctive small *square plates.* Height 100–165 (225) ft.; diameter 3–5 (7) ft. Heavy snowfall areas at

Bark of Western White Pine

medium elevations in the n. Rockies and Cascades to the cen. Sierra Nevada and w. Nev. **SIMILAR SPECIES:** (1) Sugar Pine has ridged mature trunks, much longer cones, wider cone scales, and a rounded seed wing. Difference in shape of needle tips may require direct comparison. Sugar Pine does not occur in the n. Cascades or Rocky Mt. portions of the Western White Pine range. (2) Limber and (3) Whitebark pines (Pl. 5) have shorter cones and thicker cone scales and occur mostly at higher elevations. **REMARKS:** A large tree and an important timber species, but generally uncommon. The source of most wooden matches. Like other 5-needle pines, it is susceptible to blister rust (transmitted via currant and gooseberry shrubs) but being controlled. Seeds consumed by squirrels and chipmunks. May live 200–500 years.

TORREY PINE *Pinus torreyana* Parry ex Carr.   **PL. 4**
This localized 5-leaved member of the yellow pine group is native only on about 2 square miles of coastal hills in San Diego Co., Calif., and again 175 miles northwest on Santa Rosa I. Needles *8–13 in.* long, dark green, and with *persistent* needle sheaths. Twigs ¼–½ in. thick. Cones 4–6 in. long, *long-stalked,* dark brown, with *thick* pointed *closed* scales sometimes tipped with small

prickles. Cones sometimes persistent. Seed ¾–1 in.; wing ⅓ in., nearly surrounding the edible nut. Bark dark, furrowed. Height 20–30 (50) ft.; diameter 1–2 ft. **SIMILAR SPECIES:** Arizona Pine occupies a different area. It has smaller cones and thicker twigs. **REMARKS:** Often dwarfed and twisted by ocean winds. More widespread in earlier geological times; now the pine with the most limited natural range. Common, however, at Torrey Pines State Reserve north of San Diego. Planted in some California parks and reportedly introduced into New Zealand and Kenya. Seeds said to be edible.

ARIZONA PINE
PL. 4

Pinus ponderosa var. *arizonica* (Engelm.) Shaw

Like typical Ponderosa Pine (Pl. 3) but with 5 needles and short-stalked *open* cones only 2–3¼ *in.* long. Some 2- and 3-needle clusters may be present. As one of the yellow pines, the leaf sheaths are long and *persist* at the bases of the needle bundles. Twigs ¼–1 in. thick. Height 80–100 ft.; diameter 2–3 (4) ft. Canyon slopes, 6000–8000 ft. elevation, from nw. Mexico north to se. Ariz. and sw. N.M. **SIMILAR SPECIES:** See (1) Southwestern White and (2) Torrey pines.

5-(OR 4-)NEEDLE PINES WITH NEEDLES 1–2½ IN. LONG (PLATE 5)

Like the three members of the white pine group on Pl. 4, these species have short (½–⅟₁₆ in.) needle sheaths and early-falling cones with prickles small or or lacking. The cones of these several species, however, have *short* stalks. All except Parry Pinyon grow mainly at rather high elevations and have 5 needles per cluster. The needles are only 1–2¼ in. (sometimes 3 in.) long.

Three small subgroups of white pines are involved here. Bristlecone Pine and Foxtail Pine together are called foxtail pines. While in most pines the needles are bunched at or near the branch ends, in these two species the needles are retained along the last 10 years or so of branchlet growth, giving the appearance of a long furry fox tail to the outer branch. The needle sheaths of these two species are more persistent than for the following three. Parry Pinyon, like the other pinyons (Pls. 1 and 3), is a nut pine with short, wide-scale, open cones that produce tasty and nutritious nuts. Whitebark and Limber pines, in the third group, are high-elevation and timberline species that resemble the Swiss Stone (Arolla) Pine (*P. cembra* L.) of central Europe. The group is known as stone pines.

Pinus longaeva D. K. Bailey

The oldest Bristlecone Pines display gnarled and often bare trunks; they seem to be more dead than alive. Yet, after living for more years before the time of Christ than have elapsed since then, some of these venerable trees still survive in the dry, desert mountains of the Great Basin region. Needles in clusters of 5, dark green, only 1–1½ in. long, and held for 10–20 years in bushy *foxtails*. Cones cylindrical, thin-scaled, 3–3½ in. long, and with *rounded* bases. Cone scales slender, mostly with straight, barely prickly *bristles* ¹⁄₁₆–¼ in. in length. Seed ⅜ in.; wing 1 in. Bark brownish. Trunk often forked. Height 15–40 ft.; diameter 1–2½ ft. Near timberline, rocky ridges, scattered locations. **SIMILAR SPECIES:** (1) Foxtail Pine occurs only on high mountains in n. Calif. and again in the s. Sierra. Its foliage is similar, but the cones have narrow bases and very small incurved prickles or none. (2) Limber Pine has needles in short tufts, not foxtails. **REMARKS:** Found to outclass both Redwood (Pl. 8) and Giant Sequoia (Pl. 10) as the longest living trees; the oldest surviving specimen has been dated as at least 4600 years of age. A scattered forest of these trees, including the oldest known, can be seen on the White Mountains at about 8500 ft. elevation in the Inyo Nat'l. Forest east of

Colorado Bristlecone Pine

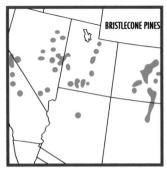

FOXTAIL PINE

PARRY PINYON

Bishop, Calif. The history of past climates has been recorded in the trees' growth rings, giving rise to the science of dendrochronol-ogy. Bristlecone growth rings of known age have enabled improved precision in the radiocarbon dating of ancient organic materials found elsewhere. But see Quaking Aspen, p. 286.

COLORADO BRISTLECONE PINE NOT SHOWN
Pinus aristata Engelm.

Also called Rocky Mountain Bristlecone Pine and found in Colo., n. N.M. and n. Ariz. (San Francisco Mt.), this tree is distinguished from *P. longaeva* by needles strongly grooved and bearing a "dandruff" of tiny resin spheres on fresh foliage. It also has cone prickles ¼–⅜ in. long.

FOXTAIL PINE *Pinus balfouriana* Grev. & Balf. PL. 5

Closely related and with foliage lacking a strong groove but otherwise much like that of the bristlecone pines. Cones 3–4 in. long with *tapered* bases and prickles *absent* or under ¹⁄₁₆ in. long. This species occurs only in the s. Sierra (Tulare and Inyo counties) and again in the Klamath Mts. (Trinity and Siskiyou counties) of n. Calif. It is not reported from the White Mts. of Inyo Co., the most westerly location of Intermountain Bristlecone Pine. Longevity is believed not to exceed 350 years. A high-elevation tree, mostly at 6500–7500 ft. Distributed more widely in earlier geologic time. John H. Balfour, a 19th-century botany professor, sponsored John Jeffrey in his California botanical explorations.

PARRY PINYON *Pinus quadrifolia* Parl. ex Sudw. PL. 5

A localized nut pine with mostly *4-leaved*, yellow-green needle clusters and short cones with a *few* thick scales. Leaves 1–1½ in. long; cones 1½–2½ in., sometimes with a small prickle. Nuts ¾ in.

Bark of Parry Pinyon

long and wingless or nearly so. Trunk gray to brown and scaly. Height 15–30 ft.; diameter 1–1½ ft. Dry slopes at 4000–6000 ft. elevation, native in Riverside and San Diego counties, sw. Calif., and in Baja California Norte. **SIMILAR SPECIES:** This species may occasionally have 3-leaved needle clusters, but the only other pine in the area with short needles is the 1-needle Singleleaf Pinyon. **REMARKS:** Like the Singleleaf, Two-needle (Pl. 1), and Mexican (Pl. 3) pinyons, this species produces delicious nuts.

WHITEBARK PINE *Pinus albicaulis* Engelm. PL. 5

A tree of high elevations, often with several trunks and frequently windblown and shrubby. Needles yellow-green in 5-leaved bundles, 1½–2½ *in.* long. Twigs very flexible. Cones 1–3 *in., dark purple,* and with scales *thick* and *pointed* (but not prickly). Cones may disintegrate on the tree or may remain *closed* whether or not they fall. The presence of purplish brown cone fragments scattered by seed-eating wildlife may identify the tree as a Whitebark Pine even if whole cones are absent. Seed ½ in., dark brown; wing small or absent. Trunk bark not distinctive, rather smooth, in gray or whitish plates. Height 15–30 (60) ft.; diameter 1–2 (3) ft. Rocky slopes at 5000–12,000 ft. elevations. **SIMILAR SPECIES:** Limber Pine is best separated by its larger, light brown, open cones. Both it and Whitebark Pine have highly flexible twigs that withstand winter winds and the weight of timberline snow. Limber Pine is absent from the Pacific Northwest west of the Continental Divide, while Whitebark Pine does not occur in the s. Rocky Mts. **REMARKS:** Squirrels, chipmunks, and birds (especially Clark's nutcracker) often harvest the cones before they can be examined by the naturalist. Believed to live 250–350 years.

LIMBER PINE *Pinus flexilis* E. James **PL. 5**

Like Whitebark Pine, a 5-leaved high-altitude pine with flexible twigs and yellow-green needles 1½–2½ in. long. Limber Pine cones, however, *open* readily at maturity to allow the seeds to fall. Cones are 3–6 *in.* long, *light brown,* with scales only somewhat thickened and tips *rounded.* Seed ⅜–½ in., red-brown, and *dark-mottled;* wing small or lacking. Mature trunk bark brownish to black, furrowed. Height 35–50 (80) ft.; diameter 1–2 (3) ft. Dry ridges 5000–12,000 ft. elevation, mainly in Rocky Mts. **SIMILAR SPECIES:** See (1) Whitebark Pine in areas where the ranges of the two species overlap, mainly in the n. Rockies and s. Sierra. In cen. N.M. see also (2) Southwestern White Pine (Pl. 4). **REMARKS:** Though the flexible twigs of this species give it its name, those of Whitebark Pine seem equally capable of being tied in knots. Some few Limber Pines are reported to live as long as 2000 years. Limber Pine is common and is the only pine in Craters of the Moon Nat'l. Monument near Arco, Idaho.

CONIFERS WITH SINGLE NEEDLES ON WOODY PEGS: SPRUCES (PLATE 6)

Spruces have single needles, not clustered. When spruce needles fall, the twigs and branchlets remain *rough* from the small but stout persistent *woody pegs* that support the needle bases. Hemlocks (Pl. 8) have only weak pegs. Other conifers lack these pegs.

Spruces are ornamental, sharply steeple-shaped evergreen trees of cold climates whose needlelike leaves are mostly more or less 4-sided and can easily be twirled between the fingers. In two species, however, they are rather flattened and cannot easily be twirled. Needles are more broadly white-striped in these two species. Spruce needles are short and tend to be stiff and some-

Bark of Sitka Spruce

what sharp. They grow all around the twigs. Like firs, spruce branchlets are tipped with twigs arranged in the shape of Christian crosses.

Spruce cones are brown and woody when mature. Unlike fir cones, those of spruces hang pendent and do not fall apart on the tree. Spruce cone scales are *thin*, not heavy or thorny as in pines. Trunk bark is brown and often *scaly*.

Spruces grow north to the limit of trees, forests thinning to dwarf specimens extending far into the tundra. To the south, some species persist on high mountains as far south as s. N.M. They are absent, however, from the Sierra Nevada proper.

Spruces do not make satisfactory Christmas trees: their needles fall quickly upon drying. The wood is soft, light, resinous, and straight-grained. It provides a principal source of pulp for making paper and is valuable for construction work, interior finishing, and boatbuilding. Tannin and "burgundy pitch," used in varnishes and medicinal compounds, come from the bark of certain species. In Europe some spruces are tapped for turpentine, and in times of food shortage the inner bark has been ground and added to flour. Spruce beer, it is reported, is made from fermented needles and twigs that have been boiled with honey. Several spruces are of value in landscaping.

SITKA SPRUCE *Picea sitchensis* (Bong.) Carr. **PL. 6**
Distributed from s. Alaska to n. Calif., this coastal fog-belt species has needles sharp, *flattened*, dark green, white-striped, and ¾–1

SITKA SPRUCE

WEEPING SPRUCE

in. long. Twigs *droop* and are *hairless*. Cones 2–4 in. long with scale tips *narrowed* and somewhat ragged. Trunk base of large trees often enlarged and *buttressed*. Shrubby at its northern limits but may become 100–160 (215) ft. tall and 3–4 (17) ft. in diameter elsewhere. **SIMILAR SPECIES:** Resembles (1) Douglas-fir at a distance, but trunk is scaly rather than furrowed. Flat needles occur also in Douglas-firs and (2) some true firs, but their dead twigs lack stout woody needle bases and their cones differ. (3) Weeping Spruce, also with flattened needles, has twigs and branchlets usually hanging "weeping" to 4–8 ft., twigs hairy, and cone scales broad, not ragged. Our other spruces have 4-angled needles. **REMARKS:** Our largest spruce and a valuable lumber species. In 1841, members of the Charles Wilkes' American exploring expedition found logs 300 ft. long and 20 ft. in diameter. Certain logs have resonant qualities and are of value for musical instruments. Native Americans wove baskets of the rootlets. Some trees live to be 700–800 years old. Fine stands can be seen in the Hoh Valley at Olympic Nat'l. Park, Wash. Widely planted for timber in Great Britain.

WEEPING SPRUCE *Picea breweriana* S. Wats.   **PL. 6**
Native only near the Calif.-Ore. border. This uncommon spruce has needles *flattened*, ¾–1 in. long, somewhat blunt, yellow-green, white-lined, and spreading in all directions. Branches and thin branchlets hang *pendent* up to 8 ft. in length. Twigs *hairy.* Cones 2–4 in. with *broadly rounded* and *even-edged* scales. Trunk base often enlarged. Height 80–100 ft.; diameter 1–2 ft. High, dry slopes of the Siskiyou Mts. and nearby. **SIMILAR SPECIES:** See Sitka Spruce. **REMARKS:** Also called Brewer Spruce. William H. Brewer, a Yale University professor, discovered the species during the 1800s. Tree may not weep strongly until mature.

Engelmann Spruce

ENGELMANN SPRUCE PL. 6
Picea engelmannii Parry ex Engelm.

As the principal spruce of inland western mountains, Engelmann Spruce has dark- to blue-green, 4-sided, rather *flexible* needles mostly ¾–1 in. long, not very sharp to the touch. Twigs mostly *fine-hairy.* Cones ½–2 (3) in. with middle scales usually *diamond-shaped* and scale tips *ragged* and *narrowed.* The tip of the seed wing impression on the cone scale is *less than* ³⁄₁₆ in. from the end of the scale. Light brown cones often crowded at tree top and numerous beneath the tree. Trunk bark of large trees *light brown, thin* (¼–⅓ in.), and *scaly,* often resembling that of Lodgepole Pine (Pl. 1). Height 80–120 (180) ft.; diameter 1–3 (8) ft. and crown narrow. Moist slopes and canyons from cen. B.C. and sw. Alta. to n. Calif. and s. N.M. at 5000–11,000 ft. elevations. **SIMILAR SPECIES:** (1) Blue Spruce has a more restricted range, darker and thicker trunk bark, somewhat stiffer and sharper needles, usually hairless twigs, mostly larger cones with rounded middle scales, and a more-distant seed wing impression. See also (2) White Spruce and (3) Subalpine Fir (Pl. 7). **REMARKS:** A major lumber tree. Wood is made into boxes and construction timber but also is reported, like Sitka Spruce, to have resonant qualities of value in making

pianos and violins. Paper pulp is an important product. Where ranges overlap in the n. Rockies, intergradation with White Spruce has been found. One study determined that natural hybrids with Blue Spruce do not occur. Blacktail and whitetail deer and bighorn sheep browse the twigs, porcupines feed on the growing layers beneath the outer bark, and dusky grouse and red squirrels eat the seeds. Trees over 500 years old have been recorded. George Engelmann was a midwestern 19th-century physician and botanist who specialized in conifers.

BLUE SPRUCE *Picea pungens* Engelm.   **PL. 6**
A tree of the central Rocky Mts. with needles *stiff, sharp* to the touch, ¾–1¼ in. long, and green to *blue-green.* Twigs mostly *hairless.* Cones 2½–4 *in.* long, with central scales mostly *rounded,* and scale tips *ragged* and *narrowed.* The seed wing impression ends ⁵⁄₁₆–¹³⁄₃₂ in. from the cone scale tip. Trunk bark of large trees *dark, thick* (¾–1½ in.), and *furrowed* rather than scaly. Height 80–100 (150) ft.; diameter 1–2 (3) ft. Stream bottoms and other moist soils at 6000–11,000 ft. elevations from sw. Montana, e. Idaho and w. Wyo. to s. N.M. **SIMILAR SPECIES:** See Engelmann Spruce, from which it is not always distinguishable with certainty. **REMARKS:** Widely used in landscaping. Wild trees seldom as markedly blue as cultivated varieties.

WHITE SPRUCE *Picea glauca* (Moench) Voss   **PL. 6**
A northern transcontinental species. Needles ⅜–¾ in. long, yellow- to blue-green and often massed on the twig tops by means of twisted lower needles. Twigs *hairless* (use lens after removing needles). Cones *cylindrical,* 1½–2 *in.* long, *dropping* soon after maturing; scales rounded and *flexible* with edges nearly *smooth.* In the far north and on high mountains a low matlike form occurs in

BLACK SPRUCE

White Spruce

exposed locations. Height 50–60 ft.; diameter 1–2 ft. Upland tundras and forests from the northern limit of trees south to the Black Hills of S.D. and ne. U.S. **SIMILAR SPECIES:** (1) Black Spruce has hairy twigs and shorter needles. Its cones, which accumulate on the tree, are smaller with rigid and ragged-edge scales. It occurs more common in swamps. In the Canadian Rockies, (2) Engelmann Spruce has longer needles and cones, the latter also with ragged cone scale tips. **REMARKS:** Trees 200 years old are not unusual. Twigs browsed occasionally by whitetail deer, moose, and bighorn sheep. Red squirrels and crossbills eat the seeds; porcupines gnaw the inner bark.

BLACK SPRUCE *Picea mariana* (Mill.) BSP.   **PL. 6**

Also a wide-ranging subarctic species. Needles *short,* mostly 1/4–7/16 in. long, green or sometimes blue-green with a white powder. Twigs *hairy* (use lens after removing needles). Cones ± *spherical,* only 3/4–1 1/4 *in.* long, somewhat gray-brown, with scales *stiff* and tips rather *ragged.* Cones usually *remain* on tree for several years. Low matlike forms are known from northern mountains, especially where exposed to severe winds and cold. Height 25–30 ft.; diameter 1–2 ft. Tundras, bogs, and wet soils from the arctic limit of trees s. to cen. B.C., s. Man., and ne. U.S. **SIMILAR SPECIES:** See

White Spruce. **REMARKS:** Some trees survive for 250 years. Snow-shoe hares, porcupines, and crossbills have been recorded as feeding on parts of this spruce.

CONIFERS WITH NEEDLES SINGLE AND FLAT (OR 4-SIDED): FIRS (PLATE 7)

Like spruces (Pl. 6), firs of the genus *Abies* are evergreen trees of cold climates. These are *true firs,* as distinct from Douglas-firs (Pl. 8). Needles are short and mostly *flat, blunt,* grooved above, white-striped beneath and sometimes above. (Note: Weather and drying both weaken white lines; these are best seen [use lens] on fresh needles at twig ends.) Needles on upper (cone-bearing) branches tend to be more sharply pointed than those on lower branches. Unless otherwise noted, the lower needles are those described here. At least one species has low 4-sided needles, which, in contrast to flat ones, can easily be twirled between the fingers.

The needles of true firs are unlike those of other conifers (except Douglas-firs, see below) in that when plucked they leave smooth *circular scars* on the twig. Newly grown needles are bluish in several species. The winter buds are mostly *blunt* and resin covered.

The cones of true firs are unique but not long-lasting. They mature in late summer and are mostly gone by late September. While immature, they are green to purple and stand *erect.* Their fleshy scales *fall apart* upon ripening, leaving upright but unob-trusive spikelike cores. Cones and their spikes are most frequent on the highest branches. Sometimes cones (or piles of their remains) can be found on the ground after squirrels have cut the small branches that hold them. Cone bracts protrude from between the scales in two firs (and also in Douglas-firs, see below). Young trunks of true firs are pale and mostly smooth, with resinous blisters. Older trees mostly have dark, scaly, or furrowed bark. Topmost leader twigs are erect. The ranges of the several species do not much overlap. Especially in nw. Calif./sw. Oreg., however, hybrid intergrades between species may occur.

Firs are important more for pulpwood than timber, but most species are also widely planted in landscaping. As for many other conifers, effective seedling survival usually requires sunlight. Firs make good Christmas trees, holding their needles even when dry.

True firs and Douglas-firs (Pl. 8) are alike in having circular leaf scars. Douglas-firs differ from true firs, however, in that their needles have thin stalks, their buds are pointed, and their cones

GRAND FIR

Grand Fir

are brown with woody, persistent scales and protruding 3-pointed bracts. Cones are usually abundant on the ground beneath Douglas-firs.

Fir species are most numerous in the Pacific Northwest, especially Ore. In addition to wild populations, the Hoyt Arboretum, Washington Park, Portland, Ore., offers a complete and well-marked display.

GRAND FIR *Abies grandis* (Dougl. ex D. Don) Lindl.   **PL. 7**
A large tree of the Pacific Northwest and n. Rockies whose flat ¾–1-in. (2-in.) needles are of *different lengths* and occur in *flat sprays* on the lower branches. They are medium-dark green above, white-lined beneath, and with tips mostly notched (use lens). Twigs clearly *visible* from above. Twigs hairless; buds resin-covered. Cones green and 2–4 in. long. Height 150–200 (250) ft.; diameter 2–3 (5) ft. Moist bottomlands and slopes from sea level to 6000 ft. elevation, s. B.C. and w. Mont. to nw. Calif. **SIMILAR SPECIES:** (1) White Fir has needles whitish above and often curved upward in a broad, shallow U. (2) Silver Fir has needles not in flat sprays. Though its needles sometimes may appear to be of two lengths, they are quite dark above and so dense as usually to hide the twig top. (3) Noble Fir needles are quite thin, all of equal

length and with two white lines above as well as below. Of the several other lowland conifers that have flat needles green above and white-striped below (Pl. 8), the (4) Douglas-firs also display circular leaf scars on dead twigs, but these species, as well as (5) hemlocks have stalked needles and brown, woody, pendent cones. (6) Redwood, (7) California Torreya, and (8) Pacific Yew (all of Pl. 8) have needle bases which extend downward along the twig. **REMARKS:** Rather tolerant of shade and a fast-growing tree, some surviving to about 280 years. The wood is reported to repel insects and sometimes is called Stinking Fir because of an odor that is unpleasant to some people. Hybridizes with White Fir.

WHITE FIR   PL. 7
Abies concolor (Gord. & Glend.) Hildebr.

A common tree of mountain slopes in the s. Rockies, the Sierra Nevada, and some coastal range locations. The *flat* needles are 1½–2½ in. long, whitish on both sides, mostly blunt, and with a ± narrowed base. The upper surface is smooth, blue-green, *un-grooved,* and white-powdered; there are double white lines beneath. Some needles spread to the sides; others curve upward to form a U. Twigs *hairless;* buds resin-covered. Cones 3–5 in. long, greenish becoming purple or brown at maturity. Trunk bark

White Fir

smooth ash-gray when young. Height 100–180 (210) ft.; diameter 2–5 (6) ft. Middle elevations. **SIMILAR SPECIES:** Grand Fir has needles green above, of two lengths, and not U-curved. **REMARKS:** Some specimens live to be 350 years old. Twigs are eaten by blacktail and mule deer, buds and needles by sooty grouse, and seeds by chipmunks and squirrels. Wood, lacking odors, once much used for butter tubs. The specific name refers to the uniformity of color on both surfaces of the needles. Called Concolor Fir in some areas. Hybrids with the following species and with Grand Fir are common where they occur together. Specimens from the Sierra Nevada and n. Calif. are often distinguished as Sierra White Fir, *A. lowiana* (Gordon) A. Murry. They have needles less whitened above, the low needles with tips weakly notched (use lens).

SILVER FIR *Abies amabilis* Dougl. ex J. Forbes   PL. 7

A coastal tree, ranging from extreme se. Alaska to nw. Calif. Needles not in flat sprays except as seen from beneath. Rather with bases *J-curved,* many needles tend to grow upward and become massed on the tops of twigs and branchlets, *hiding* them from above. Individual needles ¼–1 in. long, *flat, very dark green above,* silvery white beneath, and notch-tipped (use lens). Twigs hairy or not; buds resin-covered. Cones purplish, 3½–6 in. long. Trunk bark smooth, gray, fissured. Height 75–100 (245) ft.; diameter 2–4 ft. Coastal fog belt and high rainfall areas; mountain slopes at 2000–6000 ft. elevations. **SIMILAR SPECIES:** Within the range of Silver Fir, only (1) Grand Fir and (2) Western Hemlock (Pl. 8) also have flat needles green above and whitened below. Both of those species have needles in flat sprays and twigs easily visible from above. **REMARKS:** A beautiful tree, but shallow rooted and subject to windthrow. It is capable of growing in deep shade, unlike most other firs. A few specimens become 500 years old. Blue and

spruce grouse as well as Clark's nutcracker and various squirrels are reported to eat the seeds. Sometimes misnamed "larch" in the timber trade. There are nice stands of Silver Fir near the high end of the road on Mt. Baker, Wash. Sometimes named Pacific Silver Fir.

NOBLE FIR *Abies procera* Rehd.   PL. 7
This tall fir of the Pacific Northwest has slender blue-green needles (under ¹⁄₁₆ in. wide), not in flat sprays but mostly with *J-curved* bases to become massed on twig and branchlet tops. Needles mostly *short*, ½–1 in. long, blunt, marked *above and below* by *double* lines of white (use lens on fresh needles). Low branches bear flat needles that do not twirl between the fingers; needles on high (cone-bearing) branches mostly 4-sided. Twigs sometimes slightly hairy; buds mostly *not* resin-covered. Cones 4–7 in. long with long-pointed bracts extending beyond the scales and *folded downward* at right angles so as to nearly hide the scales. Often cone scales and angled bracts can be found in piles beneath the trees where squirrels have left them. Trunk purplish gray to red-brown, becoming much fissured and scaly with age. Height 150–200 (275) ft.; diameter 3–5 (9) ft. Mountain slopes at 1500–8000 ft., mainly Cascades south to nw. Calif. SIMILAR SPECIES: Three other firs have needles whitened on all surfaces. (1) White Fir has longer, wider, and flatter needles in more or less flat sprays with a U-curved pattern. (2) Subalpine Fir has needles longer with a single white stripe above, and buds resinous. (3) Red Fir has 4-sided (twirlable) needles. All of these species have cone bracts hidden between the scales. REMARKS: Noble Fir trees in dense stands often grow with few low branches. They may live to be 600–700 years old. The timber has the highest value of any fir. It is used for exterior siding and for house interiors including sash, moldings, doors, and floors.

RED FIR *Abies magnifica* A. Murr.   PL. 7
A handsome fir mainly of the Sierra Nevada and s. Cascades. Needles ¾–1¼ in. long, ± *4-sided,* and *can* be twirled between the fingers. They are whitened on all surfaces, blunt tipped and *ridged* above. Most are *J-curved* at the base and massed on the tops of the twigs and branchlets. Twigs often hairy, with buds resin covered. Cones 6–8 in. long, purplish brown, with the bracts *hidden* between the scales. At high elevations the tree top is very narrow, steeplelike. Trunk bark deeply furrowed and reddish brown. Cones 6–8 in. long with bracts hidden between the scales. Height 80–120 (175) ft.; diameter 2–4 (8) ft. Areas of heavy snow at 5000–9000 ft. elevations. SIMILAR SPECIES: See Noble

RED FIR

BRISTLECONE FIR

Fir. **REMARKS:** Red firs 200 years old are not uncommon. Sooty grouse and pine grosbeaks are among the consumers of seeds. Shasta Red Fir (var. *shastensis* Lemm.), with pointed visible cone bracts, occurs from Lassen Peak, Calif., into sw. Ore. It is generally considered to be a hybrid with Noble Fir.

SUBALPINE FIR *Abies lasiocarpa* (Hook.) Nutt. PL. 7

A tree of high elevations on coastal mountains from sw. Yukon to n. Calif., often at timberline and sometimes shrublike in exposed situations. A narrow *steeple-shaped* crown, though sometimes also seen in other firs (and spruces), is typical of this species. Needles *flat, ¼–1½ in.* long, with bases *J-shaped* so that they are mostly erect and *bunched* on the upper sides of twigs and branchlets. Needles whitened *above and below,* either ridged or grooved with a single undivided white stripe *above* (use lens on fresh needles). Needle tips rounded or sometimes notched. Twigs sometimes slightly hairy; buds resin-covered. Cones purple and 2½–4 in. long, with bracts hidden between the scales. Trunk bark grayish-white, smooth, with resin blisters when young. Height 20–100 (140) ft.; diameter 1–2 (7) ft. Rocky soils. Trees of the Rocky Mountains from e. Yukon to s. N.M. have isosceles-shaped basal bud scales, red (rather than tan) fresh leaf scars, and chemical differences. They have been differentiated as *A. bifolia* A. Murray Hybrids occur at interior locations. **SIMILAR SPECIES:** See (1) Noble Fir. Where they occur in the same habitat, (2) Engelmann and (3) White spruces (Pl. 6) often may be distinguished at a distance by the brown cones clustered near the tree top, while (3) Mountain Hemlock (Pl. 8) usually has a drooping leader shoot. **REMARKS:** Trees may reproduce vegetatively by layering, where low branches

Subalpine Fir

touch the soil and take root. Formerly called Alpine Fir, but only tundra plants found above timberline are now regarded as "alpine." Trees may reach 250 years of age. Mountain sheep and deer browse the twigs.

BRISTLECONE FIR *Abies bracteata* (D. Don) Poiteau   **PL. 7**

Rare in the wild and native only in the Santa Lucia Mts. of Monterey and nw. San Luis Obispo counties, Calif. Needles *wide* (to ⅛ in.), stiff, *spiny-tipped*, shiny, *dark green above*, white-striped beneath, and 1¾–2½ in. long. Foliage in flat sprays on the low branches, but higher on the tree may be somewhat mixed. Twigs hairless, *drooping*; buds ½–1 in. long, *pointed*, scaly, and *not* resinous. Cones are purplish and 2½–4 in. long, with bracts *bristle-pointed* and extending ½–1¾ in. beyond the scales. Trunk brown and thin, usually with branches to the ground. Tree crown narrow and sharp, steeplelike. Canyon bottoms and slopes, mostly at 2000–5000 ft. elevations. **SIMILAR SPECIES:** No other fir has such wide and decidedly prickly needles or pointed buds. California Torreya (Pl. 8) also has flat, rigid, pointed needles that are white-striped beneath. They are not truly prickly, though, and the needle bases are slender, extending along the twigs.

BALSAM FIR   *Abies balsamea* (L.) Mill.   **NOT SHOWN**

A species of e. Canada and ne. U.S. and the only fir that extends westward across the prairie provinces to ne. and cen. Alta. Needles flat, *dark green* above, white-striped below, blunt, ⅜–1 in. long and the lower ones in *flat* sprays. Twigs *hairless*; buds resin-covered. Cones purplish to green and 1–3 in. long. Bark gray and rather smooth with resin blisters. Height 40–60 (75) ft.; diameter 1–2 (3) ft. Moist soils, low elevations. **SIMILAR SPECIES:** Only in w.-cen. Alta. is there a chance of overlap with Subalpine Fir. That species, however, mostly occurs at high elevations and is narrowly steeple-shaped, with needles whitened above and the bases J-shaped. **REMARKS:** An important pulpwood species occasionally reaching 200 years of age. Canada balsam, obtained from the bark blisters, has been used by woodsmen as a wound plaster and as chewing gum. Before the invention of modern materials, it was employed in cementing lenses and mounting specimens on microscope slides. Resinous knots have been used as torches. Seeds eaten by ruffed, spruce, and sharptail grouse; twigs browsed by snowshoe hares, whitetail deer, and moose; inner bark gnawed by porcupines.

OTHER CONIFERS WITH SINGLE FLAT NEEDLES (Plate 8)

Though most are not closely related to each other, these trees tend to be evergreen, with flat needles in flat sprays and with brown, woody, pendent cones. Yet Baldcypress is non-evergreen, California Torreya and Pacific Yew have fleshy fruits, and Mountain Hemlock needles spread in all directions. Fresh needles of the first five species are white-banded beneath. The first six species have needles on thin, almost hairlike stalks.

BALSAM FIR

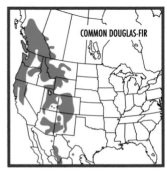

COMMON DOUGLAS-FIR

Pseudotsuga menziesii (Mirb.) Franco

A widely distributed western tree with needles ¾–1½ in. long, blunt, white-striped beneath, and *thin-stalked*. When needles fall or are plucked, they leave rather smooth *circular* leaf scars on the twigs as in true firs (Pl. 7). Twigs mostly hairless and *drooping*; buds *sharp*, hairless, reddish. Mature cones, usually common beneath even medium-size trees, are brown, woody, pendent, thin-scaled, and with peculiar and obvious *3-pointed bracts* that extend well beyond the cone scales. Cones are 1½–2¾ (4) in. long, coastal populations having shorter cones. Trunk bark dark, thick, and furrowed. Height 80–100 (300) ft.; diameter 2–5 (14) ft. Moist but well-drained soils from sea level in sw. B.C. to about 9500 ft. in the s. Rockies. Occurs locally south to cen. Mexico. **SIMILAR SPECIES:** The unique cone bracts easily separate the Douglas-firs from other conifers. (1) Big-cone Douglas-fir (cones 4–7 in.) is known only from the coastal and central mountains of sw. Calif., mostly outside the range of Common Douglas-fir. In the rare absence of cones, the stalked needles and pointed buds distinguish both species from (2) true firs (Pl. 7). Of the several other conifers with needles stalked, (3) hemlocks have short needles, weak woody needle-pegs, and small cones without evident bracts, (4) California Torreya has stiff, spicy-scented foliage, and olive-like fruits, while (5) American Yew has green twigs, needles green on both sides, and fruits red and fleshy. (6) On the northwest coast, see Sitka Spruce (Pl. 6). **REMARKS:** The nation's most important timber species and a top producer

Common Douglas-fir

BIGCONE DOUGLAS-FIR

of plywood veneer. A very popular Christmas tree. Archibald Menzies, a Scottish medical doctor, discovered this tree in 1791 but it became better known after it was later collected by David Douglas, another early Scottish botanical explorer. Its scientific and common names honor both scientists. The stalked needles and brown pendent cones of Douglas-firs are not like those of true firs. Since hemlocks do have stalked flat needles, the false-hemlock meaning of *Pseudotsuga* may be more suitable than that implied by the Douglas-fir name. Coastal and Rocky Mt. populations are recognized as varieties of the species, the inland form being less tall and with smaller cones and more blue-green foliage. A fast-growing invader of forest openings. Seedlings require some shade at first but later grow best in open sunlight. Capable of surviving both drought and forest fires, Douglas-firs more than 1 000 years old have been found. Red squirrels, chipmunks, deer mice, and birds eat the seeds. Deer browse the twigs, and black bears sometimes strip the bark to consume the inner growing layer. Old-growth stands, as at Cathedral Grove Provincial Park on Vancouver I., B.C., are most impressive.

BIGCONE DOUGLAS-FIR   NOT SHOWN
Pseudotsuga macrocarpa (Vasey) Mayr
Found in mountains of sw. Calif. from Kern and Santa Barbara counties south. Distinguished from the Common Douglas-fir mainly by cones 4–7 in. long with bracts extending conspicuously beyond the cone scales. Needles ± pointed. Forests, canyons, and slopes at 1 500–8000 ft. elevations. Height 40–50 (85) ft.; diameter 1–3 (4) ft.

WESTERN HEMLOCK *Tsuga heterophylla* (Raf.) Sarg.   PL. 8
An attractive tree of the Pacific slope and n. Rockies. Topmost leader shoot usually 1–3 ft. long with a characteristic *droop*. Needles ¼–¾ in. long, of *different* lengths, blunt, dark green above, white-striped below, with thin *stalks* attached to *weak* pegs. If the leaves are plucked, these pegs tend to be removed with the needles. Where branches die naturally, however, it is evident that the twigs are roughened by *slender* needle pegs. Needles are in flat

WESTERN
HEMLOCK

Bark of Western Hemlock

sprays. Twigs hanging, usually fine-hairy. Buds globular, hairless. Cones delicate, only ¾–1 *in.* long, thin-scaled, pendent. Trunk brown to gray with scaly ridges. Height 75–120 (150) ft.; diameter 1–3 (4) ft. **SIMILAR SPECIES:** (1) Mountain Hemlock has thicker needles not in flat sprays and cones 1¼–3 in. long. (2) Douglas-firs have stalked needles all of equal length and 3-pronged cone bracts. (3) Grand Fir and other true firs (Pl. 7) have smooth twigs with circular leaf scars and needles not stalked. (4) California Torreya and (5) Pacific Yew have fleshy fruits and needle bases which follow along the twigs. (6) Spruces (Pl. 6) have stout woody needle-base pegs. Leader shoots that lean also occur in Western Redcedar, Alaska-cedar, and Port Orford-cedar (Pl. 9), but those trees have scalelike leaves and their leaders are usually short. **REMARKS:** Wood is superior to that of Eastern and other hemlocks and is used in building construction as well as for paper pulp. Because hemlocks soon drop their needles, they do not make good Christmas trees. Bark was once extensively used in tanning leather. It is reported that Native Americans used the inner bark as food. They collected it in the spring, ground it into pulp, and baked it into cakes that were kept until needed in winter. Trees browsed somewhat by deer and elk. Hemlocks thrive on shaded sites to a greater extent than most other conifers. Though more slow-growing, they may eventually overtop and dominate other species. They may rarely live to be 500 years of age. Beautiful large specimens are common in Olympic Nat'l. Park, Wash.

MOUNTAIN HEMLOCK
Tsuga mertensiana (Bong.) Carr.   **PL. 8**

Distributed much like Western Hemlock but more alpine. Unlike the other members of this group, this species has needles *not* in flat sprays but spreading in all directions from the branchlets and forming starlike clusters on the twigs. Needles ¼–¾ in. long, tend to be *thick,* somewhat rounded in cross section, thin-stalked and whitened on *all* surfaces, appearing blue-green. Topmost leader shoot usually *droops,* 1–3 ft. long. Cones narrow, 1½–2 (3) in. long. Height 30–100 (150) ft.; diameter 1–3 (6) ft. Often growing at timberline but best developed at sheltered locations in mountainous areas of heavy snowfall. **SIMILAR SPECIES:** See (1) Western Hemlock. (2) Subalpine Fir (Pl. 7) has its leader shoot erect and needles not stalked. **REMARKS:** The narrow crown of young Mountain Hemlocks and many high-elevation tree species is believed to be an adaptation to shed snow and thus avoid breakage. Like some other species, reproduction also may occur by vegetative means when the lower branches become rooted and eventually

Bark of Mountain Hemlock

Mountain Hemlock

grow into separate trees. Fine
stands of Mountain Hemlocks
can be seen at Crater Lake
Nat'l. Park, Ore.

CALIFORNIA TORREYA *Torreya californica* Torr. **PL. 8**
With relatives occupying comparatively small areas in China,
Japan, and Florida, this species is a survivor of a group that in earlier geologic times occurred in what are now arctic regions. Needles are stalked, stiff, *spine-tipped*, flat, white-striped beneath,
and 1–3 in. long. They have a strong *odor* when crushed and
bases that *extend* along the twig. Stump sprouts occur. Sexes are
separate. Fruits fleshy but woody, *olivelike*, green with purple
lines, *closed* at the end, one-
seeded, and 1–1½ in. long.
Height 15–70 (100) ft.; diameter 1–2 (4) ft. Canyons and
streamsides to 4000 ft. elevation, cen. Calif. **SIMILAR SPECIES:**
(1) Pacific Yew has needles
shorter, softer, and not odorif-
erous. Also, its fruits are bright
red and open at the end.
(2) Redwood, which similarly
sprouts readily, has flexible,
nonstalked needles with no
marked odor. (3) Bristlecone

CALIFORNIA TORREYA

Bark of Pacific Yew

Fir (Pl. 7) has dark, spiny-tipped needles that have circular attachments to the twig. **REMARKS:** The wood has some local value in furniture making and is durable as fence posts. A member of the yew family.

PACIFIC YEW *Taxus brevifolia* Nutt.   **PL. 8**

A shrubby to medium-size tree of the Pacific slope and n. Rockies. Needles ½–1 *in.* long, thin-stalked, short-pointed, flexible, and green on both sides. Needle bases *follow* along the twigs. Twigs *green;* buds brown, hairless, pointed. On female trees, fruits are ⅜–½ in. in diameter, soft, berrylike, *bright red* when ripe, and with an *open* end revealing the single dark seed. Trunk twisted, fluted, with bark thin and peeling. Stumps can produce sprouts. Height 25–50 (75) ft.; diameter 1–2 (4) ft. A shade-loving species occurring locally within coniferous and other forests. **SIMILAR SPECIES:** None when the unique fruits are present. (1) California Torreya and (2) Redwood also have needle bases that extend along the twigs, but both have needles white-striped beneath. Those of the former are longer and stiff with pointed tips; the latter species has more fernlike foliage with needles not stalked. **REMARKS:** The drug Taxol, first discovered in the bark of this plant, has proven useful in the treatment of some cancers.

Pacific Yew

Mature foliage is poisonous to most livestock. The reddish wood is reported to take a high polish. English and Japanese yews are much used in landscape plantings.

REDWOOD *Sequoia sempervirens* (D. Don) Endl. **PL. 8**
Probably the most impressive tree in N. America. The California groves of straight and immensely tall specimens are world renowned. Large specimens are recognizable by size and beauty. For smaller plants, the needles of low branches are ½–1 ¼ in. long and in *flat* sprays. They are flexible, white-banded beneath, *not* stalked, and with bases *following* along the twig. On high branches and at some twig ends, needles are ¼–½ in. long, slender, sharp, *awl-shaped,* and *not* in flat sprays. Twigs *green;* buds scaly, hairless, blunt. Cones woody, brown, ¾–1 in. long, and with thick scales. Trunk often swollen and buttressed at the base; bark red-brown, furrowed, fibrous, and often a foot thick. Sprouts frequent at trunk bases and may occur elsewhere on the trunk, especially after damage by forest fire. Height 150–325 (365) ft.; diameter 10–18 (21) ft. Bottomlands and moist soils in the narrow *coastal* fog belt from sw. Ore. to cen. Calif. **SIMILAR SPECIES:** The related (1) Giant Sequoia (Pl. 10) grows locally above 5000 ft. in the Sierra. All of its needles are awl-shaped, and its buds lack scales. (2) Pacific Yew and the other coastal species of this plate have stalked needles. In landscaped areas, see also (3) Dawn-redwood (under Baldcypress, next). **REMARKS:** Magnificent trees, the world's tallest, providing some of the continent's most scenic and memorable vistas. No one should miss seeing them at their best in Redwoods Nat'l. Park and along the Redwoods Highway, both in n. Calif. Redwoods may live to be over 2000 years old. Despite their mas-

sive size and age, it is impressive to realize that they spring from a seed weighing only ⅟₆₀₀₀ of an ounce. The wood is termite resistant, straight-grained, usually free of knots, and highly valuable. Trunk swellings known as burls yield fine table tops and other polished articles.

Intensive lumbering has depleted Redwood stands over much of their former range. Reproduction occurs rapidly after cutting, however, originating even within 2 or 3 weeks as stump and root sprouts. Though depleted, fine virgin stands remain under protection. Fossil remains indicate that Redwoods ranged over most of the northern hemisphere in earlier geologic times. The genus was named after a prominent Cherokee chief whose name is often spelled Sequoyah.

BALDCYPRESS *Taxodium distichum* (L.) Richard   **PL. 8**
A handsome non-evergreen tree of swamps in the southeast U.S. ranging west to cen. and s. Texas. Needles ¼–⅞ in. long, green on both sides, flat or sometimes rather 3-sided; arranged alternately along slender greenish twigs that do not droop markedly. Needles and most twigs *fall in winter,* leaving branchlets roughened by small, few-scaled buds. Leaf scars lacking; twig scars similar to leaf scars are present but without bundle scars. Bark brown, rather smooth but fibrous. Trunk base often *enlarged* and deeply ridged. When growing in water, *peculiar root growths* called "cypress knees" grow upward to and above the surface. Cones ball-shaped, ¾–1 in. across, with thick scales. Height 80–120 (140) ft.; diameter 3–4 (20) ft. Swamps and streambanks. **SIMILAR SPECIES:** (1) Larches, the only other non-evergreen conifers in the West, do not occur south of the Canadian prairie provinces and n. Rockies. They have needles in clusters and cones with thin scales. (2) Dawn-redwood (*Metasequoia glyptostroboides* Hu & Cheng.),

REDWOOD

BALDCYPRESS

found in China in 1944 and regarded as a living fossil, is often seen in parks. It, too, is deciduous but the needles, buds, twigs, and cone scales are in opposing pairs. **REMARKS:** In the southeastern states, wading or boating into quiet, mature stands of Baldcypress gives one an impression of grandeur similar to that experienced amid the Redwood groves of California. Also a valuable lumber tree whose soft but durable wood is used for railroad ties, posts, and shingles. Grows on uplands even in northern states, if planted. Seeds eaten by cranes and some songbirds. Montezuma Baldcypress of Mexico is now considered of doubtful validity. True cypresses (Pl. 9) are evergreen and are in a different plant family.

CONIFERS WITH SMALL SCALELIKE LEAVES: "CEDARS" AND CYPRESSES (PLATE 9)

The "cedars" of this plate are magnificent tall trees of the Pacific Northwest. They form some of our most beautiful forests and serve as some of our most valuable timber species. No American conifer, however, is a true cedar, a fact indicated by the "cedar" name being hyphenated or otherwise linked to a prefix. For true cedars, see p. 124.

The species of this plate have twigs covered by scalelike, often aromatic, evergreen leaves mostly under ¼ in. long. The tiny leaf-scales occur mostly in pairs that alternate at right angles (use lens). Often they have a small gland dot that may require 10x magnification to detect. Several species show white markings on fresh needles. Only rarely are small pointed needles also present.

Junipers (Pl. 10) also have foliage scalelike but they usually also have some awl-shaped leaves present. Since some juniper specimens may lack these pointed needles, however, it is best to locate fruits in order to distinguish between cypresses and junipers with certainty.

In contrast to the fleshy blue or reddish fruits of junipers, the cones of "cedars" and cypresses are woody, brown, and (except for Incense-cedar and Western Redcedar) nearly globular. In cypresses, old cones tend to remain on the trees.

In both groups, branchlets and their scaly leaves may be shed together after several years on the tree. Cypress twigs tend to be 4-angled.

Most of the several American cypress species tend to occur naturally over only relatively small areas in Ariz., Calif., and Ore. In identifying these cypresses, judgments based on locality may be helpful, but plantings beyond the native range are likely. Cypresses are often difficult to name. Final identification of some specimens may require expert opinion.

Incense-cedar

INCENSE-CEDAR *Calocedrus decurrens* (Torr.) Florin **PL. 9**
A large, handsome tree of the Sierra Nevada, coastal ranges, and Cascade Mts. north to Ore. An inverted cone in shape and usually perfectly erect. Foliage in *flat* sprays. The paired scalelike leaves are *longer* (¼–½ in.) than those of other members of this group and are arranged along the twigs in slender *vase-shaped* whorls. The foliage is *neither* whitened nor gland-dotted but is smooth, *glossy*, and aromatic when crushed. It does *not* droop. Topmost leader shoot erect. Cones ¾–1 in. long, pendent, slender, with *six* scales, of which four are full-length. Wood is pale brown and aromatic. Mature trunk bark reddish brown, thick, furrowed. Height 60–80 (150) ft.; diameter 3–4 (7) ft. Moist to dry mountain slopes at 2000–8000 ft. elevation; also in Baja California Norte. **SIMILAR SPECIES:** Vase-shaped alternating pairs of elongated leaf scales and smooth, slender, few-scaled cones are unique. **REMARKS:** Formerly assigned to the genus *Libocedrus*, the species is now regarded by botanists as sufficiently different from relatives in Chile, the South Pacific, and China to deserve a different name. Trees over 500 years old have been recorded. Wood durable and fragrant; used for fencing, shingles, cedar chests, and wooden pencils.

INCENSE-CEDAR

WESTERN REDCEDAR

Bark of Western Redcedar

WESTERN REDCEDAR   PL. 9
Thuja plicata D. Don ex Lambert

An important tree of the coastal Northwest and n. Rockies. Foliage in ± flat sprays along the branches. Scaly leaves ¹⁄₁₆–¹⁄₈ in. long, paired, flat, and *broadly whitened* beneath in a so-called butterfly pattern (use lens). The tiny leaves mostly without gland dots and tips *pressed against* the scale-covered twigs. Foliage *droops,* forming inverted Us or Vs along the branches. Leader shoot short, may droop. Cones ¹⁄₂–³⁄₄ in. long, *upright,* light brown, not globular, and with 8–12 smooth pointed scales. Wood light brown. Trunk bark shreddy, reddish brown, with *vertical grooves;* trunks sometimes with buttressed bases. Height 60–130 (180) ft.; diameter 1–2 (20) ft. Mostly bottomlands and moist sites, sea level to 6000 ft. elevation. **SIMILAR SPECIES:** (1) Incense-cedar also has wood brownish and cones not ball-shaped. Its foliage does not droop, however, and its leaf scales are slender, not whitened, and form vase-shaped whorls. In addition, its cones are pendent. (2) Alaska-cedar has leaf sprays tending to hang vertically, the leaf scales pointed outward and not whitened beneath (use lens). It also has bark flaky and not furrowed plus cones globular. (3) Port Orford-cedar has ball-shaped cones, leafy twigs more slender, and leaf scales with thin white lines on the undersides (use lens on fresh needles). (4) Drooping leader shoots of hemlocks (Pl. 8) are longer, often to 1 ft. or more in length. **REMARKS:** An important decay-resistant and durable timber tree used for fences, shingles, barrels, and furniture. Native Americans used the trunks for totems and for war canoes that could hold up to 40 people. They also made the trunks into planks for constructing lodges and employed the fibrous inner bark in making ropes, fish nets, blankets, baskets, and roof thatch. Wood cut from stumps or logs makes excellent kindling even in wet weather. Western Redcedar is shade-tolerant and lives to be 450 years of age or older. Deer browse the foliage. Frequently planted in landscaping; a "golden-foliage" variety is in cultivation. The generic name is pronounced, and occasionally improperly written, *Thuya*. Western Redcedar and Eastern Redcedar (Pl. 10), despite similar common names, are in different genera. An older name, Canoe-cedar, might well be resurrected.

ALASKA-CEDAR   PL. 9
Chamaecyparis nootkatensis (D. Don) Spach.
   Also thriving on the cold and foggy northern Pacific slope, this "cedar", too, has leaves in *flat* sprays that *droop* strongly, often

Bark of Alaska-cedar

hanging vertically. Scalelike leaves 1/16–1/8 in. long, without distinct glands, and with *no whitish markings* (use lens on fresh needles). Especially on vigorous shoots, its leaves have pointed scale-tips *spreading outward* (use lens). Leader short, may lean or droop. Cones *ball-shaped*, 3/8–1/2 in. in diameter, dark, the centers of the 4–6 scales generally with prominent 1/16–1/8-in. points. Wood durable, yellow with resinous scent. Trunk bark gray or reddish and somewhat *flaking*. Trunk base often swollen or buttressed. Height 50–100 (175) ft.; diameter 1–3 (10) ft. Moist soils. Also local inland in se. B.C. and cen. Ore. **SIMILAR SPECIES:** See (1) Western Redcedar and (2) Port Orford-cedar. **REMARKS:** Also known as Yellow-cedar or Yellow-cypress. It was discovered in 1793 at Nootka, Vancouver I., B.C., by Archibald Menzies. Somewhat tolerant of shaded conditions for germination and growth. Alaska-cedar can readily be seen at middle elevations on the Hurricane Ridge road in Olympic Nat'l. Park, Wash.

PORT ORFORD-CEDAR PL. 9
Chamaecyparis lawsoniana (A. Murr.) Parl.

This scaly-leaved tree with foliage in *flat* sprays is native to restricted areas in sw. Ore./nw. Calif. and on Mt. Shasta, n. Calif., but is also planted elsewhere. Leaves about 1/16 in. long on *narrow* scale-covered twigs; marked with *conspicuous glands* and thin, white *X-like* lines beneath. Leaf scales hug the twigs and do *not* point outward. Foliage does *not* droop conspicuously. Topmost leader may lean. Cones as in Alaska-cedar but 1/4–3/8 in. in diameter, with 7–10 cone scales with or without tiny central points. Wood pale yellow. Trunk bark dark red-brown, ridged. Height 110–175 (200) ft.; diameter 1–3 (6) ft. Moist but well-drained soils. **SIMILAR SPECIES:** Related to Alaska-cedar and with similarly globular cones, but foliage more like Western Redcedar. (1) Alaska-cedar has branchlets and twigs drooping, leaf-scale points angled outward, scales not whitened, and cones larger with points centered on the scales. (2) Western Redcedar has somewhat wider scaly twigs with broad white markings beneath plus small, slender, upright cones. **REMARKS:** This is the tallest member of the cypress family. Lumber is in demand for boats, building construction, fence posts, and

PORT ORFORD-CEDAR

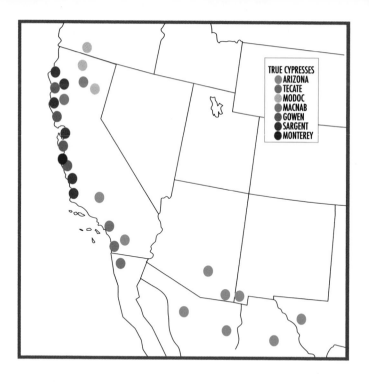

TRUE CYPRESSES
- ARIZONA
- TECATE
- MODOC
- MACNAB
- GOWEN
- SARGENT
- MONTEREY

matchwood. A large number of ornamental varieties are cultivated in Europe and around the world. Often called Lawson-cedar or Lawson-cypress. Charles Lawson was an early 19th-century Scottish nurseryman and botanist.

TRUE CYPRESSES

A number of different trees around the world, including the Bald-cypress (Pl. 8), go by the name cypress. Only those of the genus *Cupressus,* however, are true cypresses. They look much like junipers (Pl. 10) since both groups have tiny, twig-hugging leaves that mostly are *not* in flat sprays. Tree-size specimens of true cypresses, however, tend to have *only* scalelike leaves and produce

Bark of Arizona Cypress

brown, *woody,* mostly spherical cones with flat-topped scales. Cones of true cypresses take two years to reach maturity and tend to remain on the tree for some months thereafter. Furthermore, both sexes are present on the same tree. In contrast, although junipers may display *both* scalelike and awl-shaped leaves, they have *fleshy* fruits, found mainly on separate female trees. Juniper berries fall when mature (in 1–2 years) and disappear when eaten by wildlife. A tree with only scalelike needles and with brown woody cones, therefore, is a true cypress. Except for MacNab Cypress, none has needles in flat sprays.

ARIZONA CYPRESS *Cupressus arizonica* Greene   **PL. 9**
This, the most wide-ranging of our true cypresses, occurs near the border with Mexico from sw. Calif. and cen. Ariz. to w. Texas (Big Bend Nat'l. Park). Leaf scales *tiny,* 1/16 in. long, angled, somewhat *whitened* and mostly with a gland dot, rather pointed and closely *hugging* the twigs. The *blue-* or *pale green* needle-covered twigs are 4-sided, *slim,* and branched at *wide angles.* Branchlets often grayish. Cones woody, *ball-shaped,* 3/4–1 1/4 in. in diameter, with 6–8 short-pointed, red-brown or gray scales. Old cones often remain on the tree. Wood yellowish. Mature trunk bark gray to black, thin, occasionally in squarish plates, and sometimes red and smooth. Height 40–70 ft.; diameter 1–3 ft. Gravelly slopes and bottomlands; also n. Mexico. **SIMILAR SPECIES:** The trunk bark of (1) Alligator Juniper (Pl. 10) is thick and deep, and the segments are in more regular squares. In sw. Calif., see (2) Tecate Cypress.

TECATE CYPRESS *Cupressus guadalupensis* Wats. **NOT SHOWN**

A rare and local small tree with many of the characteristics of Arizona Cypress but with *smooth,* reddish brown bark *peeling* in patches and revealing orange and/or green underbark. Branchlets bright *red.* Height 20–30 ft.; diameter 1–2 ft. Cones ¾–1¼ in. in diameter. Rocky slopes and canyons, 1500–5000 ft. elevation in Orange and San Diego counties, sw. Calif. Also in nw. Baja California Norte and on Guadaloupe I., Mexico. Pronounced teh-KAH-tay.

MODOC CYPRESS *Cupressus bakeri* Jeps. **NOT SHOWN**

A scarce cypress of local, rather infertile sites in n. Calif. and sw. Ore. Leaves ¹⁄₁₆ in. long, *dark green,* each with an evident *gland dot.* Twigs 4-angled and slender. Cones ⅜–¾ in. in diameter with 6–8 *warty* scales. Seeds light brown. Bark grayish, rather smooth, often with thin curls. Height 30–80 ft.; diameter 1–2 ft. Dry inland slopes, mainly Siskiyou Mts. **SIMILAR SPECIES:** MacNab Cypress has prominent cone scale projections, foliage in flat sprays, trunk bark more furrowed. **REMARKS:** Milo Baker was a California botanist who discovered this species late in the last century. Often called Baker Cypress.

MACNAB CYPRESS *Cupressus macnabiana* A. Murr. **NOT SHOWN**

Found locally through the nw. foothills of the Sierra Nevada and the se. slopes of n. Calif. coastal ranges. Marked by glandular, dark green leaf scales mostly in *flat sprays* and by *prominent* projections of the cone scales. Cones ½–1 in. in diameter, red- or gray-brown, with 6–8 scales, each with a ⅛–³⁄₁₆-in.-long, *hornlike* cone scale protuberance. Trunk bark gray and furrowed. Height 20–30 (130) ft.; diameter 1–2 (3) ft. Dry rocky soils to 5500 ft. elevation. **SIMILAR SPECIES:** See Modoc Cypress. **REMARKS:** Used occasionally for fence posts. Named for James MacNab of the Edinburgh Botanic Garden, Scotland, who collected plants in North America in the early 1800s.

GOWEN CYPRESS *Cupressus goveniana* Gord. **NOT SHOWN**

An uncommon *coastal* species found from Mendocino Co. to Monterey. Often associated with Redwood forests. The dark green, *pointed* leaf scales are much like those of other cypresses, but, like those of Monterey Cypress, they *lack* a gland dot. Cones ½–¾ in. in diameter with 6–8 warty scales. Seeds brown to *black.* Bark gray, rough, furrowed. Height 15–25 (75) ft.; diameter 1–2

(3) ft. From sea level to 3000 ft. elevation. **SIMILAR SPECIES:** Monterey Cypress has leaf scales more obtuse and cones 1–1½ in. in diameter with 8–14 scales. **REMARKS:** Often shrubby. Named after Robert Gowen, a British botanist of the last century. Trees known as Mendocino and Santa Cruz cypresses are local varieties of this species.

SARGENT CYPRESS *Cupressus sargentii* Jeps. **NOT SHOWN**
Separated from Gowen Cypress by the usual *presence* of a leaf scale gland and cones ¾–1 in. in diameter. Seeds dark *brown*. Height 15–30 (50) ft.; diameter 1–2 (3) ft. Dry slopes of cen. and n. Calif. coastal ranges, to 3000 ft. elevation. **SIMILAR SPECIES:** (1) Gowen Cypress has smaller cones with black seeds. (2) Monterey Cypress has larger cones with more scales. Both lack leaf glands. **REMARKS:** Sometimes regarded as a variety of Gowen Cypress. Named to honor Charles Sprague Sargent, the founder of Harvard University's Arnold Arboretum and student of North American trees.

MONTEREY CYPRESS **NOT SHOWN**
Cupressus macrocarpa Hartw.
Differs from the previous two species in having cones 1–1½ *in.* in diameter with 8–14 scales. Scalelike leaves rather *blunt,* mostly *without* a gland dot. Seeds dark brown. Height 40–70 (80) ft.; diameter 1–3 (5) ft. Coast near Monterey, Calif. **REMARKS:** Much photographed, especially along the sea cliffs of Monterey Bay, where it thrives despite sea spray and onshore winds. Widely planted in Calif. and in temperate climates around the world.

TREES WITH SCALELIKE AND/OR AWL-SHAPED LEAVES: JUNIPERS, GIANT SEQUOIA, TAMARISK, REDSHANK (PLATE 10)

Junipers are small, slow-growing trees, most common in dry climates. The junipers of Pl. 10 are like the "cedars" and cypresses of Pl. 9 in having small (1/16–⅛-in.-long), scalelike leaves often marked with a gland dot. The junipers (also frequently called cedars) in addition, however, typically display small, sharp *needle-shaped* leaves ¼ (½) in. long. These are usually present on at least some of the quickly growing twigs. As in cypresses, the leaves and twigs of junipers fall together as they age.

In addition to the two types of leaves usually present, junipers can be recognized by their sometimes hard but basically fleshy fruits, which, berrylike, contain 1–12 seeds. Juniper berries are considered to be cones in which the relatively soft and thick

Bark of Rocky Mountain Juniper

scales have fused. The fruits are blue when young, maturing to be either blue or reddish brown. They are more or less ball-shaped, mostly about ¼ in. in diameter, and often covered with a powdery whitish bloom. Where the mature fruits are blue to blue-black, they usually also are juicy and resinous. The mature red-brown fruits of other species tend to be more dry and fibrous. Where a specimen has only scalelike leaves, an effort should be made to find fruits to determine whether it is a cypress (Pl. 9). Since the sexes of junipers are mostly on separate plants, female trees may have to be located in order to secure fruits. In season, developing flowers may give a brownish or yellowish cast to male trees. Junipers, like cypresses, often are difficult to identify.

Native Americans and early pioneers ate the raw fruits of some junipers and also made them into a flour, perhaps cooked with other foods to make them more palatable. They used the dried shreddy bark of many species for beds and padding. The berries have been used to flavor gin.

Juniper berries often show a whitish "bloom." They are eaten and the seeds spread by many birds, including ruffed and sharp-tail grouse, wild turkeys, and Mearns quail. Mammals that consume the fruits include black bears, three species of deer, gray foxes, coyotes, various chipmunks and squirrels, armadillos, and opossums. Deer sometimes browse the twigs.

Junipers are slow to grow but have long lives. The wood is durable and usually aromatic. It is favored for fence posts and, where large trees are available, for "cedar" chests.

Giant Sequoia has only awl-shaped leaves, and the tamarisks have only scaly, juniperlike needles. The former is the world's largest tree in terms of total bulk; the latter group comprises imported species that are naturalized in southwestern states.

ROCKY MOUNTAIN JUNIPER PL. 10
Juniperus scopulorum Sarg.

The most wide-ranging of western junipers, with thin *threadlike* scaly twigs. Often tall and usually pointed-topped but sometimes shrubby. Twigs rather obviously slender, being only about $\frac{1}{32}$ in. thick. They tend to be 4-sided and often *droop*. Leaves small, bluish- to *dark green* and somewhat long-pointed. Leaf scales mostly in pairs, alternating at right angles (use lens). A tiny gland pit usually present. Mature fruits $\frac{1}{4}$ in. across, fruits bright *blue*, with 1–3 (usually 2) seeds. Trunk usually *single*, with bark red-brown and shreddy. Height 15–30 (40) ft.; 1–2 (9) ft. Dry slopes and canyons, 5000–8000 ft. elevations mainly in the Rocky Mts. and outlying ranges. **SIMILAR SPECIES:** Our other junipers have wider ($\frac{1}{16}$ in.) scale-leaved twigs. Range overlap with (1) Western Juniper occurs only in the area where Idaho, Ore., and Wash. meet. Its foliage is gray-green with leaf scales blunt, and leaves are largely in 3-needle whorls rather than being paired, though the difference is not always easy to detect. (2) Oneseed Juniper, in the s. Rockies, usually has several trunks and only one seed per fruit. In the Great Basin, (3) Utah Juniper has blunt, yellow-green leaves without gland dots. (4) Alligator Juniper is a southwestern species with a deeply check-

Rocky Mountain Juniper

ered trunk. **REMARKS:** One specimen in Logan Canyon, Utah, is estimated to be 1500 years old, but a 200–300-year longevity is more frequent. Hybridizes with Eastern Redcedar in the plains states. Bighorn sheep and Townsend's solitaires have been recorded feeding on this juniper.

WESTERN JUNIPER *Juniperus occidentalis* Hook. **PL. 10**

A pointed-top tree mostly of the dry slopes and high country of the Sierra Nevada and Cascades. Leafy twigs about 1/16 in. thick with leaf scales *gray-green,* rather blunt, and with a distinct gland

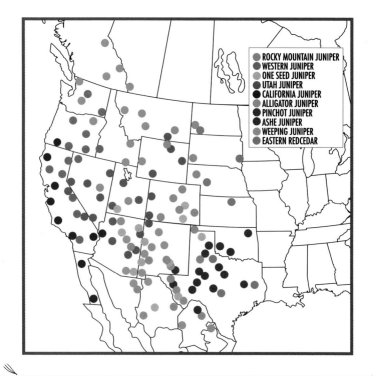

ROCKY MOUNTAIN JUNIPER
WESTERN JUNIPER
ONE SEED JUNIPER
UTAH JUNIPER
CALIFORNIA JUNIPER
ALLIGATOR JUNIPER
PINCHOT JUNIPER
ASHE JUNIPER
WEEPING JUNIPER
EASTERN REDCEDAR

Western Juniper

dot. Leaves are frequently in whorls of three rather than in opposite pairs, though this is not always readily evident (use lens). Trunk is usually *single.* Mature fruits, ¼ in. diameter, *blue-black,* with 2–3 seeds. Bark red-brown and shreddy. Height 10–25 (85) ft.; diameter 2–3 (14) ft. Dry, rocky soils to 10,000 ft. elevation, also local in sw. Idaho, nw. and s. Calif. **SIMILAR SPECIES:** Within the range of Western Juniper, (1) Utah and (2) California junipers both have yellow-green foliage and mostly bushy growth forms. Utah Juniper leaves are without gland dots, while California Juniper has bigger reddish fruits. See (3) Rocky Mountain Juniper. **REMARKS:** In Calif., often called Sierra Juniper. Thought occasionally to live over 3000 years.

ONESEED JUNIPER

PL. 10

Juniperus monosperma (Engelm.) Sarg.

A tree of the s. Rockies to cen. Ariz., w. Texas, and n. Mexico. Scalelike leaves *gray-green, long-pointed,* and mostly *with* a gland. Twigs stout, about ¹⁄₁₆ in. thick and 4-sided. Trunks usually *several,* yielding a round-topped tree. Bark shreddy. Mature fruits ⅛–¼ in. in diameter, dark blue; seed *single.* Height 10–20 (40) ft.; diameter 1–2 ft. Dry rocky soils, 3000–5000 ft. elevations. **SIMILAR SPECIES:** (1) Rocky Mountain Juniper, also blue-fruited, has fine (¹⁄₃₂ in.) twigs, usually a single trunk, and mostly 2 seeds per fruit. (2) Utah Juniper has blunt yellow-green leaf scales without glands. (3) Ashe Juniper is not associated with Oneseed except in parts of

cen. Texas. Ashe Juniper has dark green foliage and fruits ⁵⁄₁₆ in. in diameter. Other junipers within the distributional limits of Oneseed Juniper have reddish fruits. Beyond fruit color, (4) Alligator Juniper has distinctive alligatorlike trunk bark while (5) Weeping Juniper has unique drooping foliage. **REMARKS:** Fruits are eaten by Gambel quail, gray foxes, coyotes, raccoons, ground squirrels, chipmunks, and, occasionally, humans. Deer browse the twigs.

UTAH JUNIPER *Juniperus osteosperma* (Torr.) Little   PL. 10

A mostly round-topped and several-trunked tree of the Great Basin mountains and high plains. Leaf scales yellow-green, short-pointed, *lacking* a gland. Leaves basically in alternating pairs. Twigs relatively stout (¹⁄₁₆ in.) and ± 4-sided. Trunk usually single, the bark gray-brown, shreddy, sometimes weathering to nearly white. Mature fruits red-brown, ¼–½ (¾) in. in diameter, and with 1 (seldom 2) seeds; young fruits bluish. Height 15–20 (40) ft.; diameter 8–12 (36) in. Rocky hillsides and canyons, 4000–9000 ft. elevation south to s. Calif., cen. Ariz., and w. N.M. **SIMILAR SPECIES:** Mainly on the edges of Utah Juniper range: (1) Rocky Mountain and (2) Oneseed junipers have dark- or gray-green foliage and smaller mature fruits. The former species also has thin (¹⁄₃₂ in.) twigs that often droop; the latter has long-pointed leaf scales. (3) Alligator Juniper has gland-dotted, long-pointed leaf scales and a unique checkered trunk. (4) California and (5) Western junipers have gland-dotted leaves. **REMARKS:** Believed to be the most common tree in Nevada and Utah. Often associated with Oneseed Juniper, Singleleaf Pine, and Two-needle Pinyon. Chipmunks eat the seeds, and deer sometimes browse the twigs.

CALIFORNIA JUNIPER *Juniperus californica* Carr. **NOT SHOWN**
Mainly a shrubby tree of deserts and foothills from n. Calif. to w.
Ariz. and Baja California Norte. Leaf scales yellow-green, mostly
paired, *blunt,* and *with* a gland dot. Twigs tend to be *rounded*
rather than 4-sided. Fruits ⅜–⅝ in. in diameter and reddish with a
white bloom when mature, though sometimes bluish at first.
Berries have 2 (sometimes 1) seeds. Trunks several, brown to gray
and shreddy. Height 10–20 (40) ft.; diameter 1–2 ft. Dry soils
below 5000 ft. elevations south to Baja California Norte and
Guadaloupe and Cedros Is., Mexico. **SIMILAR SPECIES:** In the same
region, (1) Western Juniper has smaller blue-black fruits, gray-
green foliage, and mostly a single reddish trunk. (2) Utah Juniper
foliage lacks gland dots. **REMARKS:** Eaten by mule deer.

ALLIGATOR JUNIPER *Juniperus deppeana* Steud. **NOT SHOWN**
Mainly common in areas from cen. Ariz. and cen. N.M. south
through w. Texas to cen. Mexico. The single, *heavily checkered*
mature trunk resembles the thick square scales of an alligator
hide. Leaves blue-green, long-pointed, glandular, and often resin-
dotted. Twigs relatively thick and 4-sided. Mature fruits ⅜–⅝ in.,
reddish, with 2–5 (*usually 4*) seeds. Height 20–40 (60) ft.; diameter 1–3 ft. Dry slopes, mostly at
4000–8000 ft. elevations. **SIMI-
LAR SPECIES:** Mature trunk bark
distinctive among conifers (but
see under Arizona Cypress,
p. 173). In w. Texas, Pinchot
Juniper has smaller, brown to
red fruits with only 1–2 seeds.
REMARKS: An important food
plant for wild turkeys and several herbivorous mammals of
the region. Named in honor of
Ferdinand Deppe, a German

Bark of Alligator Juniper

Bark of Pinchot Juniper

botanist of the 1800s. A rare
variety in w. Texas is reported
to have only furrowed scaly
bark and drooping branchlets
but to retain the mostly 4-seed-
ed fruits of the parent species.

PINCHOT JUNIPER *Juniperus pinchotii* Sudw.   **NOT SHOWN**
A juniper with fruits brownish red or often *bright red* when fully
ripe. Leaves yellow-green, more or less long-pointed, and with a
prominent gland dot. Twigs slender and tend to curve *upward*.
Clumped appearance, with several stems. Bark furrowed. Often
sprouts from cut or burned stumps. Fruits ¼–⅜ in. in diameter;
seeds 1–2. Height to 20 ft. Open flats and canyons mostly from
sw. Okla. and n. Texas to sw. Texas and se. N.M. **SIMILAR SPECIES:** (1)
Ashe Juniper has blue fruits, shreddy bark, and twigs that are
thicker, somewhat stiff, and curve downward. (2) Alligator
Juniper has checkered trunk bark. **REMARKS:** Also called Redberry
Juniper. Another red-berried juniper, *J. erythrocarpa* Cory, with
the same common name, rarely attains small-tree size. It is recognizable mainly by its dark-banded and pitted seeds. Gifford Pinchot was the first chief of the U.S. Forest Service.

ASHE JUNIPER *Juniperus ashei* Buchholz.   **NOT SHOWN**
This species ranges east from w. Texas to the Arbuckle and Ozark
mts. of Okla., Ark., and Mo. Leaves dark green, long-pointed, and
with a gland dot. Twigs somewhat stout and tending to curve
down at the tips. Stems several, plant bushy. Bark shreddy.
Mature fruits about ⁵⁄₁₆ in. across, dark *blue* with a whitish bloom;

seeds 1–2. Height to 20 ft. Also ne. Mexico. **SIMILAR SPECIES:** See (1) Pinchot and (2) Oneseed junipers and (3) Eastern Redcedar. **REMARKS:** Often forms thickets on overgrazed and eroded soils. Valuable for fence posts. Also called Mountain-cedar. Named for William Ashe, an early U.S. Forest Service forester.

WEEPING JUNIPER *Juniperus flaccida* Schlecht.   NOT SHOWN

With its main distribution in Mexico, this juniper also occurs in the Chisos Mts. of sw. Texas. Leaf scales yellow-green, long-pointed, with a gland dot. Twigs 4-sided, slender, *drooping markedly*. Trunk usually single. Mature fruits red-brown with 4–12 seeds, ⅜–½ in. diameter. Height to 30 ft. Hillsides. **SIMILAR SPECIES:** No other wild juniper has such a strongly weeping habit.

EASTERN REDCEDAR *Juniperus virginiana* L.   NOT SHOWN

A medium-sized tree of the e. U.S. ranging west to the Great Plains. Leaves ¹⁄₁₆–¼ in. long, yellow-green, in pairs along 4-sided twigs and branchlets. Awl-shaped leaves ⅛–⁵⁄₁₆ in. long, sometimes with a gland. Heartwood reddish. Fruits hard, whitish- to blackish green berries about ¼ in. in diameter, with 1–2 seeds. Bark dry, shreddy, not ridged. Rarely (in severely windswept locations) shrubby and creeping. Height 40–50 (62) ft.; diameter 1–2 (4) ft. Old fields and dry soils. **SIMILAR SPECIES:** (1) Ashe Juniper has darker foliage and usually several trunks. In the West, (2) Common Juniper occurs mainly in Canada. Its awl-like needles are white above; scaly leaves are lacking. (Eastern Redcedar is a juniper, not closely related to Western Redcedar, Pl. 9.) **REMARKS:** Heartwood is aromatic and of rose-brown color. It is light, strong, durable, and widely used for cedar posts. The outer bark, when stripped, dried, and rubbed between the hands, provides excellent tinder and is used in flint-and-steel and sunglass fire sets. A volatile oil derived from juniper leaves is used in perfumes, and dried berries are used as a cooking spice. In the wild, the fruits are consumed by well over 50 species of birds, including bobwhites, sharptail grouse, ringneck pheasants, and mourning doves, and also by opossums. See Remarks under Rocky Mountain Juniper.

COMMON (DWARF) JUNIPER   NOT SHOWN
Juniperus communis L.

Rarely a tree of northern and mountain areas, more commonly a shrub. It has sharp, hollowed, 3-sided needles that occur in *whorls of 3, whitened above*, and ¼–⅞ in. long. Twigs, or at least branchlets, are *3-sided*. Fruits rather hard, blue-black, ⅜–½ in. in diameter, and with a white powder. Seeds 1–3, usually 3. Height 1–4 (35) ft.; diameter 1–6 (12) in. Pastures and infertile soils

Common Juniper

COMMON JUNIPER

from the northern limit of trees south to cen. Calif., cen. Ariz., cen. N.M., s. S.D., and e. U.S. **SIMILAR SPECIES:** Our only juniper with awllike needles strongly whitened and scaly leaves lacking. **REMARKS:** The plant supplies food for ruffed and sharptail grouse, bobwhite, European partridge, pheasant, whitetail deer, moose, and smaller birds and mammals. Grows also throughout Europe and all of n. Asia. Oil from leaves and wood is used in perfumes, and the aromatic foliage is burned as an incense in India.

NON-JUNIPERS

GIANT SEQUOIA   PL. 10
Sequoiadendron giganteum (Lindl.) J. Buchholz

Mature specimens of this huge tree are unmistakable, and young plants can usually be recognized in association with their parents. Leaves *all* narrowly awl-shaped, blue-green, and overlapping but with tips spreading. Leaves without gland dots and mostly ⅛–¼ in. long but to ½ in. on vigorous shoots. Twigs green, round in cross section. Sprouts do *not* occur. Cones *woody* and brown, ½–2½ in. long, with scales thick at the edge. Trunk single and often buttressed at the base; bark red-brown and up to 24 in. thick. Height 100–250 (295) ft.; diameter 10–20 (35) ft. Isolated groves, w.

GIANT SEQUOIA

Giant Sequoia

slopes of the Sierra Nevada at 5000–8200 ft. elevations. **SIMILAR SPECIES:** The related Redwood (Pl. 8) occurs naturally only along the Calif. coast. It has small cones, leaves both fernlike and awl-shaped, and sprouts frequently present at the trunk base and from roots. Low foliage is in flat sprays. **REMARKS:** Not reaching the height attained by some Redwoods and not as old as some Bristlecone Pines (or possibly Quaking Aspens, p. 286), but the most massive tree in the world and perhaps the world's largest organism (though Australians claim the Great Barrier Reef). Some Giant Sequoias have been estimated to be 3500 years old. One tree, cut down prior to national park establishment, is reported to have required 22 days to fell. It produced 537,000 board feet (1 ft. x 1 ft. x 1 in.) of lumber or "about as much as a portable Rocky Mountain mill [of the 1930s] would cut in five years." Called Wellingtonia in the United Kingdom, from an early scientific name that honored the Duke of Wellington.

FIVE-STAMEN TAMARISK *Tamarix chinensis* Lour. **PL. 10**
A *non-evergreen* tree with *true flowers* but with tiny, overlapping juniperlike leaves. Leaves 1/32–1/16 in. long, yellow-green, pointed, *not* gland-dotted, and dropping with the twigs in autumn. Twigs cylindrical rather than 4-sided, slender, and *without* a resinous

odor when broken. In winter, some dead foliage usually present and leaf scars lacking (branchlets may show twig scars). Trunk single; bark brown, smooth to furrowed. Flowers ⅛ in. long, *pink or white,* crowded in finger-shaped twig-end clusters, spring and summer. Petals wider toward the tip. Fruits 3–5-part dry *capsules,* brown, and only ⅛ in. long, summer. Height to 20 ft.; diameter 4 in. Moist sites, mainly dry areas in Southwest. **SIMILAR SPECIES:** Junipers have evergreen foliage with a resinous odor and bluish or reddish, mostly globular, fleshy fruits. **REMARKS:** Introduced as an ornamental, this Eurasian tree has spread to the wild. It reproduces by seeds and rooted twigs throughout much of the Southwest. Provides nest sites for doves and other birds. Often called Salt-cedar. French Tamarisk (*T. gallica* L.) is a European import established mainly in the e. U.S. but reported sometimes to grow wild in California. It closely resembles Five-stamen Tamarisk, but its pink flower petals are wider near the base. Athel Tamarisk (*T. aphylla* [L.] Karst.), a dense *evergreen* tree, is established locally near the Mexican boundary from s. Texas to s. Calif.

REDSHANK *Adenostoma sparsifolium* Torr.   **NOT SHOWN**
Another woody plant with true flowers and ± coniferlike foliage. The plant is *evergreen* with leaves thin, rounded, scattered, nearly linear, and ¼–⅝ in. long. Flowers without stalks in showy, white, terminal clusters, July–Aug.; fruits small, dry, one-seeded. Mostly shrubby, occasionally 16–30 ft. tall. Chaparral, dry slopes below 6000 ft.; s. Calif. **REMARKS:** Also called Ribbonwood. Greasewood (*A. fasciculatum* H. & A.), a related shrub, has similar, but clustered, leaves and stalked flowers and fruits.

BROAD-LEAVED TREES WITH OPPOSITE COMPOUND LEAVES
PLATES 11–14

Only a few plants bear leaves of this type. All have once-compound foliage; none has leaves twice-compound. The identification of plants in this group is comparatively simple when foliage is present. Until one becomes experienced, however, the leaflets of compound leaves may appear to be simple leaves. A review of pp. 2–5 is recommended.

In southern locations, several tropical species are evergreen. In winter in cold climates and during dry seasons in arid locations, though, leaves may be absent from deciduous trees. Unless complete dead leaves are attached to the twigs, there is no indication of whether a plant once bore compound or simple leaves. This section of the book must then be considered in conjunction with the next, in which trees whose twigs also bear opposite (or occasionally whorled) leaf scars and buds are discussed. The twigs of a leafless unknown plant with opposite leaf scars may be compared with the illustrations in Sections II and III, or "keyed out" using the leafless key of Appendix A.

Trees of this section are shown on four plates:

1. Leaves fan-compound or trifoliate.   **Buckeyes, etc. Pl. 11**
1. Leaves feather-compound. 2
    2. Ashes of the Pacific states and Ariz.   **Ashes I Pl. 12**
    2. Ashes of the Mexican border region and Great Plains.
                                                 Ashes II Pl. 13
    2. Other species.   **Elderberries, etc. Pl. 14**

Many alternate-leaved plants bear stubby, scarred, leaf-crowded *spur* branches. Care should be taken that their leaves and leaf scars are not assumed to be opposite or whorled because of this crowding. Of the plants in our area with true opposite or whorled leaf scars, only a few species in the Southwest (Texas Lignumvitae, Pl. 14, plus Desert-olive and Texas Forestiera, Pl. 17) develop ✎

spur branches. In other areas and for other species, trees with spur branches are alternate-leaved plants of Sections IV and V. Wherever possible, twigs with uncrowded leaves or leaf scars should be selected for identification.

TREES WITH OPPOSITE LEAVES FAN-COMPOUND OR TRIFOLIATE (Plate 11)

The buckeyes, which in the West occur mainly in California and Texas, have 5–9 toothed leaflets arranged like the spokes of a wheel. They also have a large end bud, upright clusters of showy flowers, and large, mostly poisonous nuts encased in heavy husks.

Two western trees, Sierra Bladdernut and Barreta, regularly have opposite three-parted leaves. Several ashes (Pls. 12, 13, 16), two maples (Pls. 14, 15), an elderberry (Pl. 14), and Fernleaf Lyontree (Pl. 14) have opposite leaves that sometimes are trifoliate. Barreta may no longer exist as a tree north of Mexico.

BUCKEYES

These are our only trees with opposite *fan-compound* leaves. End buds much *larger* than side buds and with 4 or more scales. Leaf scars large, with bundle scars several, usually in 3 groups. Flowers in large *upright* clusters at twig ends. Fruits with thick 3-part husks that contain 1–3 large shiny brown nuts. The calyx (the circle of sepals immediately exterior to the petals) is tubular and tends to be colored like the petals. The calyx tube is short (¼–⅜ in.) in most species but longer (⅜–1 in.) in Red Buckeye. The stamens (threadlike filaments tipped by pollen-bearing anthers) are longer than the petals in most species. Seeds, young twigs, and leaves of all buckeyes sometimes are toxic to livestock. The nectar has been suspected of killing bees. The seeds are poisonous, but Native Americans rendered them edible by grinding them and passing hot water through the flour. Crushed fruits and branches have been used to kill fish for food, a practice that is now illegal.

CALIFORNIA BUCKEYE   PL. 11
Aesculus californica (Spach) Nutt.

Found only in the Calif. mountains at low elevations. Prominent blossom clusters render the species highly visible between May and July. Leaves 4–8 in. long with 5 (7) fine-toothed and *long-pointed* leaflets, each 2–5 in. long. Leaflets *long-stalked*, the stalks ¼–⅝ in. long. Twigs and buds hairless; winter end bud quite *sticky*. Pith white. Flower clusters 4–8 in. long; individual blossoms 1–1¼ in. long, white to rose-colored, with 4–5 petals, May–June. Fruits 2–3 in. long, somewhat pear-shaped, husks

CALIFORNIA BUCKEYE

California Buckeye

without prickles and containing 1 or 2 large, smooth, brownish nuts. Height to 30 ft.; diameter to 6 in. Canyons and foothills to 4000 ft. elevation, coastal ranges and Sierra. **SIMILAR SPECIES:** No other tree with such fan-compound foliage grows wild in Calif. Horsechestnut, a planted ornamental, has leaflets without stalks, flowers with 5 petals, and nut husks prickly.

TEXAS BUCKEYE   PL. 11
Aesculus glabra var. *arguta* (Buckl.) Robins.

Extending west from w. Mo. and e. Texas to the e. plains and the Edwards Plateau of cen. Texas, this buckeye has leaves only 4–8 in. long. Leaflets 7–11, *narrow, long-pointed,* each 4–6 in. long, with stalks *lacking.* Bud scales *weakly* ridged (mainly at the tip), not sticky. Pith pale brown. Flowers regularly yellowish; the calyx tube only ⅛–¼ *in.* long, March–April. Fruits with *weak* prickles, occasionally none, May–June. Often shrubby but sometimes a tree to 35 ft. tall. Mature soils. cen. Texas. **SIMILAR SPECIES:** See Red Buckeye. **REMARKS:** To the east, the range of this form is contiguous with that of the Ohio Buckeye (*A. glabra* Willd. var. *glabra*), which typically has larger leaves with only 5 leaflets. Though listed as a variety of that species, the more numerous leaflets of Texas Buckeye tend to be a distinctive characteristic, and the plant is frequently classified as the full species *A. arguta* Buckl.

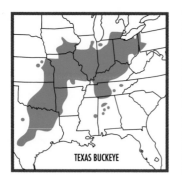

TEXAS BUCKEYE

RED BUCKEYE

RED BUCKEYE *Aesculus pavia* L.   **FLOWER, PL. 11**
A shrub or small tree of the se. U.S. Leaves 7–13 in. long with 5
leaflets narrow to elliptic and hairless when mature. Leaflets
1¼–4 in. long, *short-stalked* or without stalks, and mostly *short-
pointed.* Mature flowers and buds about ½ in. long. Bud scales
with a *central* ridge and *not* sticky. Pith brown. Flower clusters
4–8 in. long, individual blossoms bright *red* with a *calyx tube* ½ in.
long or more, April–May. Fruits not prickly. Height to 30 ft.;
diameter to 10 in. Distributed west to Edwards Plateau of cen.
Texas, where it may be *yellow*-flowered. **SIMILAR SPECIES:** Texas Buckeye leaflets are more narrow, more long-pointed, and without
stalks. Its calyx tube is short and nut husks mostly with weak
prickles.

HORSECHESTNUT *Aesculus hippocastanum* L.   **PL. 11**
A large imported tree with leaves 4–15 in. long, leaflets 7–9, each
4–10 in. long, wedge-shaped, and *stalkless.* Winter end bud over ½
in. long, very sticky. Pith white. Height 60–75 (80) ft.; diameter
1–2 (3) ft. Flowers white, with 5 petals; clusters 6–12 in., May.
Fruits with *strongly thorny husks,* Sept.–Oct. European, planted
in parks and gardens. **SIMILAR SPECIES:** See California Buckeye.
REMARKS: True chestnuts (*Castanea*) do not grow wild in the West.
They are found in e. N. America and in the Old World.

SIERRA BLADDERNUT *Staphylea bolanderi* Gray   **PL. 11**
A shrub or small tree of the central Sierra and Mt. Shasta regions
of Calif. Leaves 2–5 in. long with stalks 1–2¼ in. long. Leaflets 3,
each 1–2½ in. long, very *fine-toothed,* hairless, egg-shaped to
nearly *circular* with a small *pointed tip,* and the end one *long-
stalked.* Twigs greenish, slender, and hairless. End buds mostly
paired, the central one missing. Bundle scars 3. Flowers white,
rather showy, in drooping clusters, April–May. Fruits *inflated*

papery capsules, 1–2 in., summer. Height to 20 ft. Foothills,
to 5000 ft. elevation. SIMILAR
SPECIES: None of our other
woody species has such fruits.
Ashleaf Maple (Pl. 14) in
Calif. commonly has opposite
trifoliate leaves, but the
leaflets have large jagged teeth.
Other opposite-leaved trees
with 3-parted foliage (see
chart, Pl. 11) have either
coarsely toothed or wavy-edged leafage. The hoptrees (Pls. 22,
24), have alternate trifoliate leaves and the end leaflet short-
stalked.

BARRETA *Helietta parvifolia* (Gray) Benth.   PL. 11
A shrub or small tree of extreme s. Texas and ne. Mexico. Leaves
evergreen, only ½–2 in. long, with 3 blunt, hairless, *smooth-edged*
leaflets and narrowly winged leafstalks. Leaflets with tiny, pitted
gland dots (use lens), long-tapered at the base, mostly without
stalks, and yielding a *citrus odor* when crushed. Flowers small,

greenish white, in twig-end or near-end branched clusters, April–May. Fruits dry but resinous, with ¼–½-in. wings, Oct. Height to 25 ft. Dry hills. SIMILAR SPECIES: Gregg Ash (Pl. 13) growing in the same region has quite similar foliage, but its 3–7 leaflets lack both gland dots (use lens) and citrus odor. REMARKS: There is concern that Barreta may have been exterminated in Texas as a result of brush-clearing operations. The species may attain tree size only in Mexico.

TREES WITH OPPOSITE LEAVES
FEATHER-COMPOUND: ASHES I
ASHES OF THE PACIFIC STATES AND
ARIZONA (PLATE 12)

The ashes (Pls. 12, 13, 16) are the largest group of trees with foliage of this type. Ash leaves are mostly deciduous, 5–12 in. long and with 3–9 (usually 5–7) leaflets, which may or may not be toothed. Leaf scars are large and shield-shaped; bundle scars are numerous, mostly in a U-shaped group; buds are mostly brown, with a somewhat granular texture. The flowers of most ashes are small, often dark, without petals and in tight groups. Two species, however, have white petals in showy clusters. Flowering is in early spring, mostly ahead of the leaves. The sexes are on separate trees in most species. The one-seeded, winged fruits of all ashes look like the blades of miniature canoe paddles. Ash trunks tend to be gray with fine fissures. Singleleaf Ash, found from the s. Rockies westward, is on Pl. 16.

The ashes yield lumber for furniture, tool handles, baseball bats, and baskets. Twigs are browsed by deer and other herbivorous animals. Flowers provide pollen for bees. Native Americans once made a dark bitter sugar from the sap of some species.

Only a few ash species can be expected to be found in a particular region. The ashes of this plate occur in the Pacific states or are mainly restricted to Ariz. The species of Pl. 13 are those that range along the Mexican border from Ariz. to Texas or on the Great Plains. Four species with ranges overlapping the two plates are cross-referenced on the charts. Species that produce 3-parted leaves also are compared on the identification chart at Pl. 11. European Ash (*F. excelsior* L.), sometimes planted, has 7–13 leaflets *not* toothed and buds *black*. *Fresno* is the Spanish name for ash.

OREGON ASH *Fraxinus latifolia* Benth.   PL. 12
The only ash found wild in the Pacific Northwest and an important tree in Calif. Leaves 5–12 in. long with 5–7 mostly short-pointed leaflets 3–5 in. in length. Leaflets mainly *without stalks*,

variously *hairy* beneath, and slightly toothed. Twigs usually hairy, not 4-lined. Fruits 1–2 in. long, the wing extending over ¼ or ½ the length of the ± *flattened* seed. Height to 80 ft.; diameter to 4 ft. Mature soils, mainly valleys and lower slopes, w. Wash., w. Ore., and n. coastal ranges, the Sierra, and San Bernadino Mts., Calif. **SIMILAR SPECIES:** There are only three native Pacific Coast ashes. (1) Two-petal Ash is more shrubby and has mostly angled or 4-lined twigs, distinctly toothed leaflets and white flowers. (2) Velvet Ash has smaller leaflets with evident stalks and a different fruit wing. It does not occur north of cen. Calif. **REMARKS:** The only western ash whose lumber is harvested commercially. Native Americans used the wood for canoe paddles. Frequently planted along streets and in parks. May be evergreen in some areas.

TWO-PETAL ASH *Fraxinus dipetala* Hook. & Arn.   **PL. 12**

An attractive white-flowered shrub or small tree that ranges through Calif. and south into Baja California Norte. Leaves 3–6 in. long with 3–7 *sharply toothed* hairless leaflets. Each leaflet 1–2 in. long, *short-pointed* or blunt, and with stalk ⅛–¼ in. long. Twigs usually somewhat *4-angled* or 4-lined. Flowers in loose, drooping, branched clusters and with *two wide white petals* 3/16 in. long and about ⅛ in. across, *not* fragrant. Fruits ¾–1¼ in. long, *flattened* and winged *to the base* of the seed. Height to 20 ft. Dry slopes, foothills. **SIMILAR SPECIES:** The only Calif. ash with either white flowers or 4-angled twigs. (1) Oregon and (2) Velvet ashes, also occurring in Calif., are larger trees with leaves not sharply toothed and fruits not winged to the base. Oregon Ash has larger leaves and leaflets without stalks, while Velvet Ash has foliage ⤳

Bark of Two-petal Ash

sometimes hairy. (3) Fragrant Ash (Pl. 13), the only other ash with white blossoms, occurs from Ariz. eastward. It has long-pointed leaflets and 4 longer and narrower flower petals. **REMARKS:** Planted for ornament. Browsed by mule deer.

VELVET ASH *Fraxinus velutina* Torr.   **PL. 12**

A variable southwestern ash found from cen. Calif., s. Nev., sw. Utah, and w. Texas to n. Mexico. Leaves 4–6 in. long with 3–5 leaflets, each 1–3 in. long, pointed at both ends, mostly wavy-toothed toward the tip and either hairless or velvet-hairy beneath. May display some simple leaves (see Singleleaf Ash, Pl. 16). Leaflet stalks often ⅛–¼ in. long. Twigs hairless or long-hairy and without lines. Fruits ¾–1¼ in. long, the wing blunt, no longer than the plump seed, and extending along the seed less than ¼ the seed length. Height to 40 ft.; diameter to 1 ft. Watercourses to 6500 ft. elevation. **SIMILAR SPECIES:** Distinctive when hairy or plump seeds present. Otherwise, in Calif. see (1) Two-petal Ash and (2) Oregon Ash. Eastward, see (3) Fragrant and (4) Chihuahua ashes (Pl. 13). **REMARKS:** Velvet Ash is a rapidly growing tree frequently used in landscaping in the Southwest. In the wild, an indicator of underground water.

LOWELL ASH *Fraxinus lowellii* Sarg.   **PL. 12**

Reported only from n. and cen. Ariz. Leaves 3–6 in. long, with 3–7 short-pointed, hairless, and somewhat leathery leaflets each 2–3 in. long. Leaflets *toothed,* egg-shaped or elliptical, and often *without* leafstalks. Twigs hairless and 4-angled or *4-lined.* Fruits ¾–1¼ in. long and *flattened;* the wing broad, blunt, about as long as the seed and extending to the seed base. Height to 25 ft. Canyons and watercourses. **SIMILAR SPECIES:** (1) Two-petal Ash has 4-lined twigs but grows wild only in Calif. (2) Singleleaf Ash (Pl. 16), likewise with 4-lined twigs, occurs in Ariz. but normally has only simple leaves. In either its simple or 3-leaflet form, however, the end leaflet tends to be circular in outline. Its fruits, in addition, are under ¾ in. long. (3) Fragrant Ash (Pl. 13), also in Ariz., has leaflets long-pointed and stalked plus twigs unlined. **REMARKS:** A close relative of Singleleaf Ash and considered by some botanists to be only a variety of it. Discovered by Percival Lowell (1855–1916), an American astronomer.

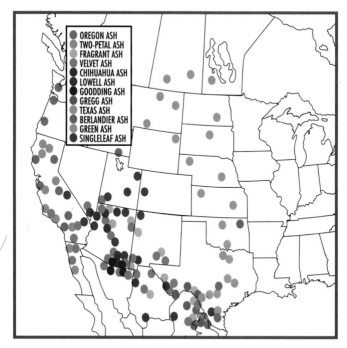

Legend:
- OREGON ASH
- TWO-PETAL ASH
- FRAGRANT ASH
- VELVET ASH
- CHIHUAHUA ASH
- LOWELL ASH
- GOODDING ASH
- GREGG ASH
- TEXAS ASH
- BERLANDIER ASH
- GREEN ASH
- SINGLELEAF ASH

GOODDING ASH *Fraxinus gooddingii* Little   **PL. 12**
   A *small-leaved* shrub or small tree known only from the mountains of se. Ariz. and nearby Sonora, Mexico. Leaves only 1–3¼ in. long and with leafstalk and midrib narrowly *winged.* Leaflets 5–9 (mostly 7), *short-pointed,* ⅜–1 in. long, stalkless, and sometimes *partly fine-toothed.* Twigs and leaflet undersides somewhat brown-hairy. Fruits ½–1 in. long; the wing broad, *blunt,* longer than the *flattened* seed, and extending *almost* to the seed base. Height to 20 ft. Rocky slopes and ridges. **SIMILAR SPECIES:** Among American ashes, only this species and Gregg Ash (Pl. 13) have such small leaves. Gregg Ash, found eastward, has shorter hairless leaves that generally are not toothed. Its fruit wing, too, is more pointed. **REMARKS:** The Peña Blanca and Sycamore Canyon areas in the Coronado Nat'l. Forest west of Nogales, Ariz., are sites for this tree. The tree is named for Leslie N. Goodding, an American botanist who discovered the species in 1934.

TREES WITH OPPOSITE LEAVES
FEATHER-COMPOUND: ASHES II
ASHES OF THE MEXICAN BORDER REGION
AND THE GREAT PLAINS (Plate 13)

These species, plus Velvet Ash and Goodding Ash (Pl. 12), occur mostly from Ariz. to Texas in the region bordering Mexico. Green Ash, primarily of the e. U.S., ranges westward through the n. plains states and has been planted elsewhere in the West. Where leaves are 3-parted, see also chart opposite Pl. 11.

FRAGRANT ASH *Fraxinus cuspidata* Torr.   **PL. 13**
   A white-flowered ash found in scattered localities from n. Ariz. to Texas and south into n. Mexico. Leaves 3–6 in. long, with leaflets 3–7, each 1½–3 in. long, stalked, hairless, usually sharply toothed, and *long-pointed.* Twigs hairless, neither angled nor marked with lines; buds sticky. Flowers *fragrant,* each with *4 narrow white petals* about ⅝ in. long and 1/32 in. wide, in loose, drooping, branched clusters. Fruits ¾–1¼ in. long, *flattened,* and *winged to the seed base.* Height to 20 ft. Dry slopes. **SIMILAR SPECIES:** The only ash with white petals found east of Calif. and our only ash with petals only 1/32 in. wide and with flowers strongly scented. When flowers are absent: (1) Velvet Ash (Pl. 12) has leaves sometimes hairy beneath and fruits with plump seeds not winged to the base, (2) Chihuahua Ash has leaflets whitened beneath and without stalks, (3) Lowell Ash (Pl. 12) and (4) Singleleaf Ash (Pl. 16) have twigs 4-angled or 4-lined. (5) Goodding Ash (Pl. 12) has leaves only 1–3¼ in. long with winged midribs and leafstalks.

CHIHUAHUA ASH *Fraxinus papillosa* Lingelsh. **PL. 13**

Localized in the n. Mexican mountains of Sonora and Chihuahua plus se. Ariz., sw. N.M., and w. Texas. Leaves 3–6 in. long, somewhat leathery, with 5–9 leaflets. Leaflets 1½–2½ in. long, short-pointed, *hairless,* essentially *stalkless,* with fine teeth or none, and *whitish* beneath. Twigs hairless and unlined. Fruits 1–1¼ in. with tips blunt, wing longer than the *flattened* seed and *not* extending to the seed base. Height to 20 ft. Rocky slopes. **SIMILAR SPECIES:** (1) Velvet Ash has leaves hairy and/or green beneath, leafstalks over ⅛ in. long, and seeds plump. See (2) Fragrant Ash. **REMARKS:** The name of the Mexican state and of this ash is pronounced chee-WAH-wah.

GREGG ASH *Fraxinus greggii* Gray **PL. 13**

Like Goodding Ash (Pl. 12), a small-leaved ash with *winged* leaf-stalk and midrib (use lens). Leaves only 1–2½ in. long, and with 3–7 leaflets, each ½–1¼ in. long, hairless, often leathery, and with tips somewhat *rounded.* Leafstalks short or lacking. Sometimes wavy-toothed. Twigs hairless or slightly gray-hairy. Fruits ½–¾ in. long with the wing *narrowed* at the tip, longer than the *plump* seed and extending *partly* toward the seed base. Height to 20 ft. Rocky soils, Big Bend National Park to Del Rio, Texas, and over much of ne. Mexico. **SIMILAR SPECIES:** No other Texas ash has such small leaves or winged leafstalks. (1) Barreta (Pl. 11) has 3 leaflets, pitted gland dots (use lens), and a citrus odor when crushed. See (2) Texas Lignumvitae (Pl. 14). In Ariz. and adjacent Mexico, see (3) Goodding Ash (Pl. 12). **REMARKS:** Josiah Gregg of Independence, Mo., was active in the Southwest as a trader, author, and botanist during the early 19th century.

TEXAS ASH *Fraxinus texensis* (Gray) Sarg. **PL. 13**

A tree mainly of cen. Texas but distributed locally from s. Okla. to s. Texas. Leaves 5–8 in. long and with 5 (7) hairless, *round-toothed* leaflets. Leaflets variably short-pointed or blunt, 1–3 in. long and ¼ to ⅔ as broad. Leaflet stalks ¼–1 in. long. Twigs usually hairless; leaf scars often somewhat *notched* at the top. Fruits ¾–1¼ in. long with the wing *twice* the length of the *plump* seed and *not* extending much, if any, upon it. Height to 50 ft.; diameter to 3 ft. Shallow to deep soils, especially those derived from limestone. **SIMILAR SPECIES:** Two other ashes with large leaves occur in cen. Texas. Both have longer leaflets. (1) Berlandier Ash also has long-pointed leaflets, and (2) Green Ash also has shorter and narrowly winged leaflet stalks plus longer fruits. **REMARKS:** Considered by some to be a variety of White Ash (*F. americana* L.), a species widespread in the e. U.S.

BERLANDIER ASH *Fraxinus berlandierana* A. DC. **PL. 13**

The *long* and mostly *long-pointed* leaflets and *broad-winged* fruits of this s. Texas ash are helpful field marks. Leaves 4–1 o in. long with 3–5 hairless leaflets, each 3–4 in. long and with widely spaced small teeth or none. Leaflet stalks ⅛–¼ in. long. Fruits 1–1 ½ in. long, the wing *1–1 ½ times* the length of the somewhat *plump* seed and extends to near the seed base. Fruits sometimes 3-winged. Height to 30 ft. Along watercourses from cen. Texas to ne. Mexico. **SIMILAR SPECIES:** See Texas Ash. **REMARKS:** The Swiss botanist Jean Louis Berlandier collected plants in Texas and Mexico in the early 19th century. Also called Mexican Ash.

GREEN ASH *Fraxinus pennsylvanica* Marsh. **PL. 13**

An eastern U.S. species whose natural distribution extends west to the e. foothills of the Rocky Mts. in Alta. and Mont. and south through the Great Plains states to Texas. Leaves 8–12 in. long with leaflets mostly 7–9, hairless, 4–6 in. long, and *long-pointed*. Leaflets sharply but irregularly toothed or without teeth. Leaflet stalks *minimal* to about ⅛ in. long, with the leaflet blade tending to follow along its stalk and causing it to be somewhat *winged* (use lens). Twigs hairless. Fruits 1–2 in. long, with the wing only about as long as the seed and not bordering the seed. Height to 70 ft.; diameter to 2 ft. Alluvial and mature soils. **SIMILAR SPECIES:** (1) Ashleaf Maple (Pl. 1 4) leaflets have large jagged teeth. (2) Texas Ash has leaflets round-toothed, often short-pointed, and under 3 in. long. **REMARKS:** The most widely distributed American ash. Also planted in Utah and elsewhere west of its natural range. Often used for paddles and oars. Formerly separated into Red and Green ashes. Planted in windbreaks on the plains.

ELDERBERRIES AND OTHER TREES WITH OPPOSITE FEATHER-COMPOUND LEAVES (PLATE 1 4)

The ashes (Pls. 1 2 and 1 3) and the few species of this plate are our only trees with this type of foliage. Those on this plate have leaflets mostly toothed and 3–1 6 per leaf. Most are deciduous trees with twigs hairless and *ringed* at the nodes. The trees whose leaves may sometimes have 3 leaflets also are listed on the identification chart of Pl. 1 1.

FERNLEAF LYONTREE **PL. 14**
Lyonothamnus floribundus var. *asplenifolius* (Greene) Bdg.

An *evergreen* tree unique in foliage and natural distribution. In its compound-leaved form, the *3–9-in. fernlike* leaves have 3–7 narrow leaflets, each 3–7 in. long, unstalked, and more or less deeply divided into many *crescent-shaped* teeth or lobes. Leaflet undersides are white-hairy or hairless, while major side veins tend to be parallel (use lens). Twigs hairy. Flowers white, small (¼ in. across) in mostly flat-topped twig-end clusters, 4–8 in. broad, May–June. Fruits small, dry, brownish, sometimes partly hairy capsules. Bark thin, peeling in long strips. Height to 50 ft., often with several stems. Native on the s. Calif. islands of Santa Rosa, Santa Cruz, and San Clemente. A simple-leaved form, variety *floribundus,* is also illustrated here but is described on p. 210. It occurs naturally only on nearby Santa Catalina I. **REMARKS:** Occasionally planted in parks in frost-free areas on the mainland. Believed to have been more widespread in earlier geologic times, before sea levels rose to create islands on which the species survived. Named for William S. Lyon, a government scientist who collected plants on Santa Catalina I. in the late 1800s.

ASHLEAF MAPLE (BOX-ELDER) *Acer negundo* L.   **PL. 14**
Our only maple with invariably compound leaves. Common east of the Rockies and in Calif. Somewhat scattered through the southwestern states and becoming naturalized in the Pacific Northwest. Leaves 4–10 in. long with 3–5 (7) leaflets over most

Ashleaf Maple

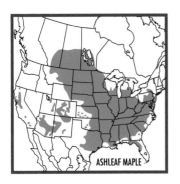

Bark of Red Elderberry

of its range and mostly trifoliate in Calif. (var. *californicum* [Torr. & Gray] Sarg.). Leaflets 2–5 in. long, usually at least half as *wide*, hairless, and mostly with teeth *large* and *jagged*. Twigs green or purplish, frequently white-powdered, sometimes glossy or even slightly hairy. Leaf scars narrow, *meeting in raised points* on opposite sides of the twigs. Pith narrow. Bundle scars 3 (or 5); buds white-hairy. Flowers small, greenish, March–April; fruits double-winged "keys," Sept.–Oct. Height 50-75 ft. **SIMILAR SPECIES:** No other ashlike tree has jagged leaf teeth and leaf scars meeting in raised points. Elderberries mostly have thicker twigs, with wide pith. **REMARKS:** In the trifoliate form the leaves often resemble those of Poison-ivy (*Toxicodendron radicans* [L.] Kuntze) or Poison-oak (*Toxicodendron diversilobium* (Torrey & Gray) Greene), shrubs or vines with alternate leaves. Box-elder, a widely used name, fails to indicate proper relationships. The soft white wood is used for boxes. Syrup can be made from the sap. Squirrels and songbirds eat the seeds.

ELDERBERRIES

Never becoming tall trees, this group includes several shrub species and some that reach small tree size. Twigs thick but weak, usually with large pithy centers. Surface wartlike lenticels common. Leaf scars large with connecting lines between pairs; bundle scars 5 (3–7). Buds small, green or brown. Unlike ashes, the central end bud is usually *missing*. Flowers small, white, in wide and (except Red Elderberry) *flat-topped* clusters at the twig ends. Fruits juicy, 3–5-seeded berries, purplish or red in color. They must be cooked but can be made into jams, jellies, and pies. The berries are eaten by many wild birds and mammals. Deer and elk browse the twigs.

RED ELDERBERRY *Sambucus racemosa* L. **PL. 14**

Alone among western tree elderberries in having fruits *bright red* and in *cone-shaped* clusters. Leaves 4–11 in. long, with 5–7 fine-toothed but otherwise variable leaflets each 2–6 in. long. Leaf bases even or not. Pith brown, sometimes pale. Flower clusters 3–4 in. across, March–July; fruits about 3⁄16 in. diameter, June–Oct. Height to 20 ft. Forest edges at low elevations, near the coast from sw. Alaska to n. Calif. **SIMILAR SPECIES:** A shrubby form (var. *microbotrys* [Rydb.] K. & P.) occurs widely through the West.

BLUE ELDERBERRY *Sambucus caerulea* Raf. **PL. 14**

Widespread in the western *mountains,* typically a *large-leaved* elderberry whose leaflets are *uneven-based* and mostly *long-stalked.* Leaves 5–8 in. long with 5–9 mostly long-pointed, *hairless,* and fine-toothed leaflets. Leaflets 2–6 in. long, the side ones with ¼–½-in. stalks. Pith white or pale brown. Flower clusters flat-topped, 2–8 in. across, June–Sept. Fruits ¼ in. across, dark *blue* to black with a *whitish coating,* the combination often resulting in a sky blue color. Height to 25 ft. Thickets to 10,000 ft. elevation. **SIMILAR SPECIES:** (1) Red Elderberry is coastal with brown pith, cone-shaped flowers, and red fruits. (2) Common Elderberry occurs east of the Rockies and has larger even-based leaflets plus dark

BLUE ELDERBERRY

VELVET ELDERBERRY

fruits without a whitish coating. **REMARKS:** Sometimes planted for ornament. Native Americans are reported to have hollowed the soft twigs to make flutes and whistles. Some authors combine Blue, Velvet, and Mexican elderberries as Blue Elderberry (*S. mexicana* C. Presl.).

VELVET ELDERBERRY **PL. 14**
Sambucus velutina Durand & Hilgard

A tree whose principal distribution is in the cen. Sierra Nevada but which also occurs in scattered localities throughout much of Calif. and adjacent portions of Nev. and Ariz. Leaves 5–7 in. long with 3–5 leaflets, each *only 1–2½ in.* long. Leaflets fine-toothed, mostly *short-pointed,* and *bases uneven.* Side leaflets *short-stalked.* Leaflets and twigs *velvet-hairy.* Pith *white.* Flower/fruit clusters 2–8 in. across. Fruits ³⁄₁₆–¼ in. in diameter and *dark blue* to black *with* a whitish waxy coating. Height to 20 ft. Slopes, 3000–8000 ft. elevation. **SIMILAR SPECIES:** See Mexican Elderberry, with leaflets also short. **REMARKS:** See under Blue Elderberry.

MEXICAN ELDERBERRY *Sambucus mexicana* C. Presl. **PL. 14**

Common in Central America and Mexico, extending north to n. Calif., w. Nev., cen. Ariz., and sw. N.M. Like Velvet Elderberry but

Mexican Elderberry

MEXICAN ELDERBERRY

hairless and with leaflets usually *long-pointed.* Leaflet bases mostly *even.* Pith *pale brown.* Fruits ³⁄₁₆–¼ in., *black, without* a whitish bloom. Height to 35 ft. Along watercourses to 4000 ft. elevation. See Remarks under Blue Elderberry.

COMMON ELDERBERRY *Sambucus canadensis* L. **PL. 14**

An eastern elderberry whose range extends west across the southern *plains* states. Leaves 5–11 in. long, with 5–11 leaflets. Leaflets 2½–5 in. long, 1–1½ in. wide and somewhat variable but usually *even-based.* Twigs stout; pith large, white. Flower clusters 4–7 in. across, June–July. Fruits mostly under ³⁄₁₆ diameter, purple-black, and *without* a whitish coating. Height to 15 ft.; diameter to 3 in. Thickets. **SIMILAR SPECIES:** No other tree-size elderberry occurs east of the Rockies.

TEXAS LIGNUMVITAE *Guaiacum angustifolium* Engelm. **PL. 14**

An *evergreen* tree of w.-cen. and s. Texas. Its distribution follows the Rio Grande in Texas and extends into ne. Mexico. A clumped species usually with many short, stout, *stiff, opposite,* spurlike side branches. Foliage often clustered at nodes but leaves clearly opposite on vigorous twigs. Leaves filmy-feathery, 1–3 *in.* long, with 4–8 pairs of thin, *stalkless, toothless,* leathery, shiny leaflets with *tiny, sharp tips.* End leaflet missing. Leaves *fold* at night and midday. Leafstalks grooved. Stipules ⅛–³⁄₁₆ in. long, spiny in appearance. Flowers a beautiful purple with yellow stamens, fragrant, ½–¾ in. across, long-stalked, at leaf angles. Fruits ½ in. long, heart-shaped, dry capsules, usually with 2 red or yellow shiny seeds. Height to 20 ft. Brushy plains and canyons. **SIMILAR SPECIES:** Dry leaves may have to be soaked to determine their nature. Once recognized as a species with opposite compound

COMMON ELDERBERRY

TEXAS LIGNUMVITAE

leaves, however, there is nothing else like it (but see Gregg Ash, Pl. 13). **REMARKS:** Useful for fence posts. An important honey species. Often placed in the genus *Porlieria*. Lignumvitae means "tree of life," reportedly carried over from the medicinal values of a related tropical species. Bark of roots sometimes used as soap. Mexican name is Guayacan (gway-ah-CAHN).

BROAD-LEAVED TREES WITH OPPOSITE SIMPLE LEAVES
PLATES 15–17

Trees with opposite simple leaves are so few as to be rather easily identified. When leafless, though, plants with opposite leaf scars may be members of either Section II or Section III. Then the illustrations for both sections must be reviewed (see also Appendix A). Care should be taken that the leaves or leaf scars on the stubby, scar-crowded spur branches (see Fig. 3, p. 6) of some alternate-leaved plants are not interpreted as opposite or whorled. Camphortree (Pl. 30), Desert-willow (Pl. 39), and Cascara Buckthorn (Pl. 43), though mainly alternate-leaved, may have some opposite foliage. In s. Texas, see Devils' Claws, p. 212.

Trees bearing opposite simple leaves may be identified as follows:

1. Leaves lobed. **Maples Pl. 15**
1. Leaves not lobed. 2
   2. Leaves toothed or wavy-edged. **Pl. 16**
   2. Leaves neither toothed nor wavy-edged. **Pl. 17**

TREES WITH OPPOSITE SIMPLE LEAVES LOBED: MAPLES (PLATE 15)

Maples are the *only* native western trees with foliage of this type. The first 5 species grow wild. These and others from the e. U.S. and from Europe and Asia are often planted in parks and gardens. Buds are reddish in western species and in Red Maple, an eastern tree often planted. In all maples, leaves are *opposite,* leafstalks are *long,* twigs are *nearly ringed* by leaf scar pairs, bundle scars are three. Flowers are small and greenish. Fruits are paired, dry, winged *"keys."* Ashleaf Maple (Pl. 14) has compound foliage; Western Mountain Maple may have some trifoliate leaves (see identification chart opposite Pl. 11).

BIGLEAF MAPLE *Acer macrophyllum* Pursh **PL. 15**

A species of the coastal ranges and Sierra Nevada with leaves *very* large. Leaves 16–24 in. in length including 8–1-in. stalks, mostly 5-lobed and with only a *few* large, *blunt* teeth. Leafstalks contain *milky* sap (best seen at the leafstalk base when newly separated from the twig). Twigs *stout;* buds *blunt,* many-scaled. Flowers in *slender,* many-flowered, drooping clusters 4–6 in. long, fragrant, April–May. Single fruits 1¼–2 in. long; paired keys narrowly V-shaped, May–July. Height to 100 ft.; diameter to 3¼ (8) ft. Low and middle elevations, deep soils, from sw. B.C. to s. Calif. **SIMILAR SPECIES:** No other far-western maple has lengthened flower/fruit clusters or such large leaves and fruits. Norway Maple of the East, sometimes planted for ornament, also has milky leafstalk sap, but its leaves are only 5–9 in. long. **REMARKS:** Wood useful for furniture, paneling, and veneer. Reported to yield sap of a quality suitable for making good maple syrup. Provides important browse for deer and elk; seeds eaten by squirrels, chipmunks, and some songbirds.

WESTERN MOUNTAIN MAPLE *Acer glabrum* Torr. **PL. 15**

A clumped shrub or small tree spread widely in the western mountains from lowlands in se. Alaska to higher elevations near

Western Mountain Maple

WESTERN MOUNTAIN MAPLE

the Mexican border. Leaves 4–7 in. long, 3 (5) lobed, with many small, coarse, *sharp* teeth. Leafstalks reddish. Sometimes the leaves are divided into three distinct leaflets (see identification chart opposite Pl. 11). Twigs slender, red-brown, *hairless;* buds *pointed,* stalked, with 2 scales. Pith *pale* brown. Flower clusters 1–3 in. long, umbrellalike, few-flowered, *drooping,* May–July. Single fruits ¾–1 in. long, the paired keys angled at about 45 degrees or less, Aug.–Sept. Height to 40 ft.; diameter to 15 in. Moist sites. **SIMILAR SPECIES:** (1) Canyon Maple has blunt leaf teeth and mostly 4 bud scales. (2) Vine Maple has nearly circular leaves with 7–9 lobes and stems that often do not stand upright. (3) Dogwoods (Pl. 17) when leafless have fleshy fruits and pith either white or darker brown. See also (4) Eastern Mountain Maple. **REMARKS:** Also called Rocky Mountain Maple or Douglas Maple. Several varieties have been recognized.

EASTERN MOUNTAIN MAPLE   NOT SHOWN
Acer spicatum Lam.

A small tree or shrub of e. Canada and ne. U.S. whose range extends west across s. Man. to s.-cen. Sask. Differs from Western Mountain Maple in having leaves 4–10 in. long, single fruits ½–¾ *in.* long, twigs mostly with *fine hairs* (especially toward the tips), and *slender* flower clusters *upright.* Height to 20 ft. Moist sites.

CANYON MAPLE *Acer grandidentatum* Nutt.   PL. 15

With its range centered in Utah's Wasatch Mts., this species is established locally from ne. Idaho to sw. Okla., cen. and sw. Texas, and n. Mexico. Leaves *small,* 2–4½ in. long and equally wide, with a few widely spaced *blunt* teeth. Leaves with 3 (5) lobes and sometimes velvety beneath. Twigs slender; buds pointed, with *about* 4 scales. Flowers long-stalked, in short, *drooping,*

VINE MAPLE

WAVYLEAF SILKTASSEL

branched, rounded clusters, April–May. Single keys ½–1 in. long, in U-shaped pairs, June–Sept. Height to 40 ft.; diameter to 1 ft. Moist soils, 2000–7000 ft. elevations. **SIMILAR SPECIES:** The only wild western maple with small blunt-toothed leaves and pointed 4-scaled buds. **REMARKS:** Also known as Bigtooth Maple. Related to Sugar Maple (*A. saccharum* Marsh) of the East and, like it, often tapped to secure sap for boiling and syrup preparation. Sometimes known as Sugar Maple. That name is better reserved, however, for the eastern species that yields the maple sugar and maple syrup of commerce, two of the few foods native to North America.

VINE MAPLE *Acer circinatum* Pursh PL. 15

A maple of the Pacific Northwest whose weak and *often reclining* stem may prevent it from reaching tree height. Leaves 3–6 in. long, almost *circular* in outline. Leaf lobes 7–9, *sharply toothed.* Twigs slender, green or *purplish;* buds blunt, with 2–4 scales. Flowers in rounded clusters, spring. Single fruits ¼–¾ in. long; paired keys form nearly a straight line, autumn. Height to 40 ft. but stems sometimes even trailing and vinelike. Damp coastal forest to 5000 ft. elevation, from sw. B.C. to n. Calif. **SIMILAR SPECIES:** No other wild American maple has many-lobed circular leaves. **REMARKS:** May form dense thickets. Foliage turns orange and red in autumn. The specific name means "circular" or "rounded." Browsed by elk and mountain-beavers.

INTRODUCED MAPLES

Maples introduced from other areas are frequently seen in parks and along streets. Prominent among these are Norway (*A. platanoides* L.) and Sycamore (*A. pseudoplatanus* L.), maples of European origin, and Silver (*A. saccharinum* L.) and Red (*A. rubrum* L.), maples native to e. N. America. See chart opposite Pl. 15.

TREES WITH OPPOSITE SIMPLE LEAVES
TOOTHED OR WAVY-EDGED (Plate 16)

Only six trees in the West regularly have this type of foliage. In addition, Pacific Dogwood (Pl. 17) occasionally may have leaves that are either fine-toothed or wavy-edged. Also Camphortree (Pl. 30), Cascara Buckthorn (Pl. 43), and California Buckthorn (Pl. 45) may have some leaves opposite.

WAVYLEAF SILKTASSEL   PL. 16
Garrya elliptica Dougl. ex Lindl.

A shrub or small tree of coastal Ore. and Calif. whose broad *evergreen* leaves have distinctive *undulating* edges. Leaves 3–5 in. long, *leathery,* generally egg-shaped, thickly *woolly* beneath. Twigs gray-brown, 4-angled or *4-lined* (use lens), usually hairy; buds with 2–4 scales; leaf scars narrow; bundle scars 3. Flowers small, in drooping 3–6-in. catkins, Jan.–March. Fruits rounded, *white-hairy,* dry berries, in dense 3–6-in. catkins June–Aug. Height to 20 ft. Mountain slopes to 2000 ft. elevation. **SIMILAR SPECIES:** Five shrubby silktassels also occur in Calif., but their foliage is hairless or slightly woolly with leaf edges not strongly undulant. (1) Western Burningbush, (2) Two-petal Ash (Pl. 12), (3) Lowell Ash (Pl. 12), and (4) Singleleaf Ash also have 4-angled twigs, but none is evergreen or has leathery, wavy-edged foliage. **REMARKS:** Named for Nicholas Garry of the early 19th-century Hudson's Bay Co.

WESTERN BURNINGBUSH   SEE PL. 16
Euonymus occidentalis Nutt. ex Torr.

Also a shrub or small tree of the coastal ranges. Leaves 2–4 in., neither leathery nor evergreen, fine-toothed, hairless, and mostly pointed at *both* ends. Twigs *green,* 4-angled or *4-lined* (use lens); buds scaly; bundle scar 1. Flowers brown-purple, few per cluster, on long branched stems, April–June. Fruits *red,* berrylike, beneath woody, 3–5-parted bracts. Height to 20 ft. Mountain slopes and canyons to 6000 ft. elevation. **SIMILAR SPECIES:** No other western tree has opposite simple leaves and green, 4-angled twigs. See Wavyleaf Silktassel. **REMARKS:** Also sometimes called Western Wahoo.

WESTERN BURNINGBUSH

CATALINA LYONTREE
PL. 16; ILLUS. PL. 14

Lyonothamnus floribundus Gray var. *floribundus*

A simple-leaved form of a unique evergreen species that was described before the compound-leaved variety (Pl. 14) was named. Leaves fine-toothed, wavy-edged, or with small lobes. Native on Santa Catalina I. Also called Catalina Ironwood.

SINGLELEAF ASH   *Fraxinus anomala* Torr. ex Wats.   **PL. 16**

An unusual ash distributed near watercourses in the s. Rockies, s. Great Basin, and cen. Ariz. areas. Unlike other ashes, the leaves are mostly simple (occasionally compound with 2–3 leaflets, or mixed). Leaves 2–3 in. long, deciduous, hairless, often almost *circular,* and with blunt teeth or none. Twigs pale brown, 4-angled or *4-lined* (use lens); bundle scars many, often indistinct. Flowers tiny, greenish, without petals, clustered at the leaf angles, spring. Fruits dry, papery, winged to the seed base, ½–¾ in. long; seed flattened. Height to 20 ft. Mountain slopes, 2000–6000 ft. elevations south to nw. Mexico. **SIMILAR SPECIES:** In Ariz., (1) Lowell Ash (Pl. 12), also with 4-lined twigs, has leaflets 5–7 and fruits ¾–1¼ in. long. (2) Velvet Ash (Pl. 12) occasionally may have simple leaves, usually along with compound ones, but on rounded unlined twigs. See (3) Wavyleaf Silktassel. **REMARKS:** The specific name points out that the species is indeed an anomaly among its compound-leaved relatives. Common in Zion and Grand Canyon national parks.

NANNYBERRY   *Viburnum lentago* L.   **PL. 16**

A species of the ne. U.S. whose distribution westward extends to se. Sask. and locally to the Black Hills, S.D., region. Leaves 2–5 in. long, *hairless* or nearly so, fine-toothed, and short- to *long-pointed.* Leafstalks *winged.* Buds brown or gray, *long, slender,*

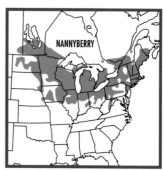

with 2 rough-granular scales. Buds of two sizes, the flower buds larger. Flowers small, white, in flat-topped clusters at the twig tips, May–June. Fruits fleshy, blue-black with one *flat* seed, Aug.–Sept. Height 9–18 (30) ft.; diameter 1–3 (10) in. Woods and thickets. **SIMILAR SPECIES:** No other western tree in its area has both paired, slender, 2-scaled buds and long-pointed leaves. Dogwoods (Pl. 17) mostly have leaves not toothed plus raised twig leaf scars and a rounded seed. **REMARKS:** Fruits are consumed by many gamebirds and songbirds as well as by rabbits and squirrels.

RUSTY BLACKHAW *Viburnum rufidulum* Raf. **PL. 16**

A small southeastern U.S. tree ranging west to cen. Okla. and cen. Texas. Leaves 2–4 in. long, elliptic to egg-shaped, sharply fine-toothed, and shiny-surfaced. Leaf undersides (at least midribs), leafstalks, buds, and sometimes twigs densely *red-hairy.* Leafstalks *winged.* Foliage may become somewhat leathery. Buds *short,* 2-scaled; leaf scars narrow; bundle scars 3. Trunk bark dark, divided into *small, squarish blocks.* Flowers and fruits similar to those of Nannyberry but flowers April–May; fruits Sept.–Oct. Height 6–18 (40) ft.; diameter 2–10 (18) in. Woods and thickets. **SIMILAR SPECIES:** Bark is similar to those of (1) Flowering Dogwood, (2) Eastern Persimmon, and (3) Sourgum, but

Bark of Rusty Blackhaw

RUSTY BLACKHAW

these species occur naturally only eastward from e. Texas. **REMARKS:** Fruits eaten by foxes, bobwhite quail, and several songbirds. Some people enjoy them, too.

TREES WITH OPPOSITE OR WHORLED SIMPLE LEAVES NOT TOOTHED (Plate 17)

In any one locality, few species have foliage of this type. Though basically alternate-leaved, Desert-willow (Pl. 39), California Buckthorn (Pl. 45), and Bluegum Eucalyptus (Pl. 46) also may have some leaves opposite and not toothed. The deciduous foliage of Desert-willow is long and slim, while the other two species have leathery evergreen leaves. Devils' Claws (*Pisonia aculeata* L.), an opposite-leaved woody vine with paired thorns, is spreading in the Lower Rio Grande Valley of Texas and sometimes grows treelike.

DOGWOODS

Of the six native dogwoods that grow to tree size in the West, only Pacific Dogwood displays showy, white, petallike bracts around its springtime blossoms. Flowers of the other species are small, mostly greenish white, and in comparatively inconspicuous clusters. The fleshy fruits are ¼–½ in. in diameter, with 1–2 *rounded*, stony seeds. Dogwoods have curved lateral leaf veins that strongly tend to *follow the leaf edges* toward the leaf tip. Leaves are elliptic to egg-shaped and short- to long-pointed. Twigs are mostly red-purple, buds with 1 pair of scales, twig leaf scars *raised* and often connected by a line, bundle scars 3, and pith white or brown. Viburnums (Pl. 16) have toothed leaves, leaf scars not raised, and dark fruits with 1–2 flat seeds. In winter, see also Western Mountain Maple (Pl. 15).

PACIFIC DOGWOOD *Cornus nuttallii* Audubon **PL. 17**
A small to large tree of the Pacific slope and the Sierra Nevada with local populations in cen. Idaho. Like other dogwoods, the flowers themselves are small. In this species, however, the tight flower heads are surrounded by 4–6 large, white or pinkish, showy, *petallike bracts* each 2–3 in. long and usually pointed. Leaves 3–5 in. long, broadly egg-shaped to almost circular, short- to long-pointed. Mostly with 4–6 pairs of side veins and often somewhat hairy beneath. Unlike other dogwoods, some specimens may have leaves raggedly fine-toothed or somewhat wavy-edged. Winter twigs display slender leaf buds and larger flower buds. Pith *brown*. Springtime flowers appear before or with the

leaves, March–May. Fruits *red* or orange, individually stalkless, and in tight heads of 30–40; Sept.–Nov. Stone smooth. Trunk divided into small squares. Height to 100 ft.; diameter to 2 ft.; usually smaller. Forest edges, to 6000 ft. elevation. **SIMILAR SPECIES:** No other wild western dogwood has such large flower structures or individual fruits without stalks. Within its range, (1) Smooth Dogwood also has brown pith, but leaves are much smaller, with only 3–4 pairs of leaf veins and the twigs/branchlets drooping. (2) Western and (3) Blackfruit dogwoods have white pith. **REMARKS:** Sometimes also flowers Aug.–Sept. Fruits eaten by bandtail pigeons and many other birds; deer browse the twigs. Native Americans are reported to have boiled the bark to make a laxative, while early settlers used the extract in place of quinine where malaria was suspected. Flowering Dogwood (*Cornus florida* L.) of e. N. America, also with showy flowers, is often planted in western parks. It is a smaller species with white pith. Its blossoms, too, usually have only 4 square-ended or notched bracts, each under 2 in. long, while the red fruits are in clusters of 4 (rarely 6–8).

SMOOTH DOGWOOD *Cornus glabrata* Benth.   **PL. 17**
This small tree or shrub, the only other Pacific slope dogwood with brown pith, occurs in coastal mountains from sw. Ore. to s. Calif. It has the smallest leaves of any western dogwood. These are only 1¼–2½ in. long, *hairless,* and with only 3–4 pairs of side veins. The brown to red-purple twigs and branchlets often *droop,* frequently taking root where they touch the ground. Flowers small, whitish, in round to nearly flat-topped clusters, *without* bracts, appearing *after* the leaves, May–June. Fruits round, *white,* with stone smooth, Aug.–Sept. Height to 20 ft. Forms thickets on moist sites to 5000 ft. elevation. **SIMILAR SPECIES:** See Pacific Dog-

wood. **REMARKS:** The common name refers to the hairless foliage. Also called Brown Dogwood.

WESTERN DOGWOOD   **PL. 17**
Cornus occidentalis (Torr. & Gray) Cov.

With foliage similar to Pacific Dogwood, this more shrubby species occupies much the same range but is absent from the Sierra. Leaves 3–5 in. long with 4–7 pairs of side veins, often somewhat *hairy*. Twigs red-purple and ± *hairy*, with pith *white* to dark tan and buds slender. Clusters of small blossoms *without* bracts appear with or *after* spring foliage. Fruits *white*; stone *grooved*. Height to 15 ft. Moist soils to 8000 ft. **SIMILAR SPECIES:** (1) Red-osier Dogwood has bright red twigs. (2) Blackfruit Dogwood is found only in n. Calif., where it can be distinguished by smaller leaves and, in season, by the presence of flower bracts and dark mature fruits. **REMARKS:** Fruits eaten by numerous songbirds; mountain beavers gnaw the inner bark. Sometimes regarded as a variety of Red-osier Dogwood.

BLACKFRUIT DOGWOOD   **NOT SHOWN**
Cornus sessilis Torr. & Durand

Found only in n. Calif., this small tree or shrub has bracts beneath the flower clusters like Pacific Dogwood. In this species, though, the bracts are brownish, often with yellow edges. Bracts are *under* ¼ *in.* long and not impressive. Leaves 2–4 in. long with only 4–5 pairs of side leaf veins. Pith *white*. Flowers small, greenish white, appearing with or *before* the leaves, April. Fruits successively white, yellow, red, and *black* on white-hairy stalks, Aug.–Sept. Height to 15 ft. Stream bank thickets to 5000 ft. elevation. **SIMILAR SPECIES:** See Western Dogwood.

WESTERN DOGWOOD

BLACKFRUIT DOGWOOD

RED-OSIER DOGWOOD

ROUGHLEAF DOGWOOD

RED-OSIER DOGWOOD *Cornus stolonifera* Michx.   **PL. 17**
Ranging from coast to coast from Alaska, across Canada and the n. U.S., this red-stemmed shrub or (rarely) small tree occurs south to cen. Mexico in scattered mountain localities. Leaves 2–4 in. long, often somewhat hairy, and with 4–7 pairs of side veins. Twigs *bright red* (occasionally green); pith *white*. Flowers *without* bracts, small, white in flat-topped clusters, appearing after the leaves, May–July. Fruits white, July–Sept. or longer; stone smooth. Height to 15 ft. Moist places. **SIMILAR SPECIES:** Western Dogwood has ± hairy foliage and grooved seeds. **REMARKS:** Fruits much sought after by songbirds and by ruffed and sharptail grouse. The twigs are eaten by deer, elk, moose, cottontail rabbits, and snowshoe hares.

ROUGHLEAF DOGWOOD   **PL. 17**
Cornus drummondii C. A. Meyer
This midwestern species ranges west into the plains states from N.D. to s. Texas. Leaves 2–4 *in.* long, with only 3–4 pairs of side veins. The upper leaf surface usually *sandpapery-rough* with short, stiff hairs and often somewhat long-pointed. Twigs slender and reddish brown. Pith *brown*. Root sprouts common. Flowers small, white, in clusters flat-topped or nearly so, with or *after* the leaves, May–June. Fruits *white,* Aug.–Oct. Height to 15 ft. Forms thickets in moist soils. **SIMILAR SPECIES:** This is the only rough-leaved dogwood and the only one that grows to tree size on the southern Great Plains. **REMARKS:** Fruits eaten by many songbirds and by prairie chickens, sharptail and ruffed grouse, bobwhite quail, and wild turkeys.

DESERT-OLIVE FORESTIERA PL. 17
Forestiera phillyreoides (Benth.) Torr.

A desert shrub or small tree found wild in s. Ariz. and Mexico. Leaves only *1 –1 ¼ in.* long, 4–5 times as long as wide, and *nearly evergreen.* They are mostly blunt-tipped, wedge-based, and with *rolled* edges (use lens). Foliage may be clustered on *spur branches* but leaves are clearly opposite on vigorous twigs. Leaf scars tiny. Buds often several above a leaf scar and with 4–8 scales; bundle scar 1; pith pale brown. Flowers small, without petals, at the leaf angles, Jan.–March. Fruits ¼–⅜ in. long, single-seeded, black, with a thin fleshy covering, summer. Height to 25 ft. Thickets, dry slopes, 2000–4500 ft. elevation. **SIMILAR SPECIES:** No other opposite-leaved tree of s. Ariz. has either such small, slender leaves or single bundle scars. **REMARKS:** The genus is named after Charles LaForestier, a French physician and naturalist of the period around 1800. *Phillyrea* is a genus of Mediterranean evergreen woody plants that the Ariz. plant was thought to resemble.

TEXAS FORESTIERA *Forestiera angustifolia* Torr. **NOT SHOWN**

Like Desert-olive Forestiera but growing in sw. and s. Texas and in ne. Mexico. Leaves ¾–1 ½ in. long and *up to 8 times* as long as wide. It is said that this species shows "conspicuous pores" on the leaf undersides. These are visible (with a lens) on some plants but do not seem to be present on all specimens. Branchlets often stiff. Height to 15 ft. **SIMILAR SPECIES:** The opposite leaves of Texas Lignumvitae (Pl. 14) are compound with tiny leaflets. Where its dried leaves are curled, however, close scrutiny may be required to recognize those distinctions. **REMARKS:** Fruits are much eaten by scaled quail.

DESERT-OLIVE FORESTIERA

TEXAS FORESTIERA

SILVER BUFFALOBERRY   PL. 17
Shepherdia argentea (Pursh) Nutt.
The *silver-scaly* twigs, buds, and leaves of this shrub or small tree
are distinctive. Leaves 1½–2½ in. long, somewhat leathery, and
wedge-based. Small leaves may be present at the leafstalk bases.
Twigs often *thorn-tipped*, bud scales 2, bundle scar single, pith
dark brown. Flowers small, without petals, greenish, at the leaf
angles, April–June. Fruits small, orange to red, berrylike, 1-seed-
ed, July–Sept. Height to 15 ft. Moist sites, mainly northern plains
but local throughout much of the West. **SIMILAR SPECIES:** (1) Russian-
olive (Pl. 39), widely planted on the prairies as a windbreak and in
gardens for ornament, also has silver-scaly foliage, but its leaves
are alternate. The opposite-leaved (2) Canada Buffaloberry (*S.
canadensis* [L.] Nutt) and the alternate-leaved (3) American Sil-
verberry (*Elaeagnus commutata* Bernh.) have brown and silver
scales, but both are shrubs. **REMARKS:** Fruits, sometimes known as
soapberries (but see Sapindus, Pl. 24), contain a bitter substance
that foams in water. Sharptail grouse and songbirds eat the fruits.

BUTTONBUSH *Cephalanthus occidentalis* L.   PL. 17
A *wetland* shrub or small tree with leaves often *whorled* in threes
and fours, elliptic and short-pointed. Leaves 3–6 in. long, stalks
often red. Twigs with side buds *embedded* in bark; bundle scar 1,
crescent-shaped; pith brown. Flowers small, white, and tubular,
densely clustered in *ball-like* heads at twig ends, May–Aug. Fruits
small, dry, brown spheres ¾–1 in. in diameter, Sept.–Dec. or later.
Height to 18 ft. Moist soils, Calif. valleys and along Mexican border to Texas and eastward. **SIMILAR SPECIES:** Dogwoods also may grow
on moist sites, but their leaf veins tend to follow the leaf edges.
They also have readily evident buds and 3 bundle scars. **REMARKS:** A
honey plant. Wilted leaves may poison livestock.

CRAPEMYRTLE *Lagerstroemia indica* (L.) **NOT SHOWN**

Not growing wild but sometimes found near old homesites. Leaves *either* alternate or opposite, 2–5 in. long, with *no* teeth, tips blunt or short-pointed, and stalks short or lacking. Evergreen in some areas. Twigs greenish and more or less *4-lined*; pith pale brown or hollow; buds with 2 scales; bundle scar 1. Flowers showy, 1–1 ¼ in. wide, pink or white in 3–6-in. end clusters, summer. Fruits dry, brown, ¼-in. capsules splitting into several parts. Trunk with vertical fluted ridges, mottled; bark peeling to leave a smooth yellowish surface. Height to 35 ft. Texas and s. Pacific Coast. **SIMILAR SPECIES:** Trunk bark similar to that of Texas Persimmon (Pl. 46), whose twigs are not 4-lined and whose leaves are sometimes evergreen, under 2 in. long and with rolled edges. **REMARKS:** Introduced from Asia.

BLACK MANGROVE *Avicennia germinans* (L.) L. **NOT SHOWN**

Standing in shallows along subtropical coasts of Fla. and La. and again in s. Texas. Numerous short, upright *breather roots* surround the plant. Leaves 2–6 in. long, *thick, leathery,* evergreen, blunt-tipped, wedge-based, with *whitish hairs* beneath, often displaying salt grains on the surface. Twigs *squarish, ringed,* bud scales 2, bundle scar 1, pith white. Wood dark brown to black. Flowers white, fragrant, at twig ends, May–July or longer. Fruits 1 in. long, yellow-green, somewhat egg-shaped but pointed, splitting, germinating while on the tree, Sept.–Oct. or later. Distributed also along both coasts of Mexico and throughout the Caribbean. **SIMILAR SPECIES:** No other mangroves occur in our region. **REMARKS:** Mangrove roots delay water movements and cause sand, silt, and debris to become deposited, extending the shoreline seaward. A good honey plant.

BROAD-LEAVED TREES WITH ALTERNATE COMPOUND LEAVES
PLATES 18–25

Trees with opposite compound leaves are described in Section II (Pls. 11–14). For trees with alternate compound leaves, care must be taken that each of the leaflets is not assumed to be a simple leaf. Also, major leaflets (pinnae) of a twice-compound leaf should not be mistaken for once-compound leaves. Major and minor leaflets attach to herbaceous leafstalks, while compound leaves attach by their leafstalks to woody twigs where buds and/or thorns are present (see Fig. 1). If in doubt whether the foliage of an unknown plant is once- or twice-compound, compare the plates and text in both categories.

When a tree has dropped its leaves, the large size of the leaf scars may sometimes indicate the former presence of compound leaves. Usually, however, the twigs of a leafless unknown plant with alternate leaf scars will have to be compared with the illustrations of both Sections IV and V or identified by means of the Leafless Key in Appendix A.

Tree species with compound leaves are most abundant in the warmer parts of our area. They are grouped as follows:

1. Trees with thorns. 2
1. Trees thornless. 4
    2. Leaves once-compound.   Pl. 18
    2. Leaves twice-compound. 3
3. Thorns in pairs.   Pl. 19
3. Thorns single.   Pl. 20
    4. Leaves once-compound. 5
    4. Leaves twice-compound.   Pl. 25
5. Leaflets toothed. 6
5. Leaflets not toothed. 7
    6. Leaf scars large.   Pl. 21
    6. Leaf scars narrow.   Pl. 22
7. Leaflets under ⅜ in. wide.   Pl. 23
7. Leaflets over ⅜ in. wide.   Pl. 24

THORNY SOUTHWESTERN TREES WITH ALTERNATE ONCE-COMPOUND LEAVES
(PLATE 18)

Throughout geologic time, arid and semi-arid areas have been a principal habitat of large grazing animals. That thorny plants were favored for survival in such an environment may be presumed. In any case, prickly species are often abundant there. Thorns are frequently located at leafstalk bases. Some desert trees may be leafless for months.

The thorny trees on this plate are those with *once-compound* leaves. In addition, Honey Locust (Pl. 20), which has mostly twice-compound foliage, may have *some* once-compound leaves. While Littleleaf Sumac (Pl. 23) has once-compound leaves and is usually thornless, it may have twigs stiff and somewhat thorny. The mesquites and Jerusalem-thorn of Pl. 19, Blue and Texas paloverdes of Pl. 20, and Yellow Paloverde of Pl. 26 are desert trees with transient twice-compound foliage whose major leaflets are joined only at the base and thus easy to mistake for once-compound leaves (see Fig. 1). Care must be taken also that once-compound leaves clustered on spur branches are not mistaken for portions of twice-compound foliage.

Except for the prickly-ashes, the plants on this plate are legumes, members of the pea-bean group. All have three bundle scars.

SOUTHWESTERN CORALBEAN PL. 18
Erythrina flabelliformis Kearney

This southwestern desert species is *leafless* for much of the year but produces a brilliant floral display in spring. Usually shrubby. Leaves 5–12 in. long with *thorny leafstalks* and 3 broad, *triangular,* smooth-edged leaflets, each 2–4 in. long and equally wide. Twigs stout, often *white-hairy,* with small single thorns; branchlets with single or paired ⅛–¼-in. thorns at the nodes. Trunk light tan. Flowers each 1–2 in. long, *bright red,* in twig-end clusters, appearing before the leaves. Fruit pods 4–10 in. long, leathery, somewhat powdery on the surface, often long-pointed, and usually *constricted* between the several ½–¾-in.-long *scarlet* seeds. Height to 15 ft.; diameter to 10 in. Dry rocky slopes, from mountains of w. Mexico north to s. Ariz. and sw. N.M. SIMILAR SPECIES: Distinctive when flowering or in leaf. When leafless, the stout, often white-hairy twigs and light tan bark are identifying characteristics. In s. Texas a shrubby relative, Southeastern Coralbean (*E. herbacea* L.) has somewhat triangular or nearly 3-lobed foliage. REMARKS: Tree-size mainly in Mexico. Wood light and sometimes made into corks. Seeds reported to be poisonous but com-

monly strung into necklaces in Mexico. Browse thought to be harmful to livestock. Sensitive to frost. Also known as Chilicote (cheelee-COAT-ay). Mescalbean Sophora (Pl. 24) has red seeds and is sometimes also called Coralbean.

DESERT IRONWOOD *Olneya tesota* Gray   **PL. 18**

A thickly leaved *evergreen* of desert washes and depressions. Leaves 2–4 in. long with dense growth of 8–20 blunt, *gray-green,* fine-hairy leaflets each ½–¾ in. long. End leaflet *often lacking.* Leafstalks not thorny. Twigs greenish, hairless; spur branches small; thorns *both* paired and single, ¼–⅓ in. long, often curved. Flowers *lavender,* ¼ in. long, pealike, in clusters to 1¼ in. long, May–June. Fruit pods 1–3 in. long, brownish, hairy, usually with *constrictions* between the 1–6 black seeds. Trunk short with stout branches; bark gray and *shreddy.* Height 25–30 ft.; diameter 1–2 ft. To 2500 ft. elevation. **SIMILAR SPECIES:** Tree presents a more solid mass of gray-green foliage than other species in its desert habitat; conspicuous in bloom. **REMARKS:** The heaviest of all American woods, except for Leadwood (*Krugiodendron ferreum* [Vahl] Urban) of s. Fla. Wood will not float. Dark heartwood is made into highly polished boxes and bowls, even though woodworking tools are dulled by it. It is outstanding for firewood and therefore becoming scarce in many places. Native Americans made arrowheads of the wood. They also ate the dried or roasted seeds and made a bread from the flour. Parts of the plant are eaten by hooded orioles, hummingbirds, deer, bighorn sheep, and horses. Gambel quail favor the plant as a roost site. The intolerance of this species to low temperatures has led to its being regarded as an indicator of climate suitable for citrus plantations. The generic name honors Stephen T. Olney, a Rhode Island naturalist of the 1800s. Also called Tesota (teh-SO-tah) and Palo de Hierro (PAH-lo day-YAIR-oh), the latter a Spanish equivalent of ironwood.

LIME PRICKLY-ASH *Zanthoxylum fagara* (L.) Sarg.   **PL. 18**

A common shrub or small tree in parts of s. Texas. Leaves 3–4 in. long, with midrib *winged*. The 5–11 leaflets are each ¼–1¼ in. long, mostly wavy-toothed, with stalks short or absent. Crushed leaves yield a lime- or *lemonlike* scent. Though mostly *evergreen*, the foliage is *not* always leathery. May show gland dots (use lens). Thorns stout, *curved*, about ⅛–¼ in. long, and paired or single. Twigs hairless. Trunk gray, often with thorn-tipped knobs. Flowers tiny and greenish, in *lateral* leaf-angle clusters. Seeds ¹⁄₁₆ in., shiny and black, within brownish 2-valved capsules. Height to 15 ft. Rio Grande plains and coastal areas. **SIMILAR SPECIES:** Our only thorny tree with compound leaves whose midribs are winged, and the only western prickly-ash with flower/fruit clusters at the leaf angles. Tenaza (Pl. 19), with thin trunk thorns, has filmy fernlike foliage. **REMARKS:** Found also from Haiti to s. Fla. and ne. Mexico and on Mexico's n.-cen. w. coast including the tip of Baja California Sur. Generic name, sometimes incorrectly spelled *Xanthoxylem*, refers to the yellow wood of some prickly-ashes. Leaves, fruits, or bark often chewed as a toothache cure. Sometimes called Toothache-tree. Also known as Colima (co-LEE-ma). In s. Fla. known as Wild-lime Prickly-ash. Not a true ash (see Pl. 12) but a member of the citrus family.

TEXAS PRICKLY-ASH *Zanthoxylum hirsutum* Buckl.   **PL. 18**

This small tree or shrub is distributed only in a narrow north-south belt from sw. Okla. through cen. Texas to ne. Mexico. Leaves 2–4 in. long and nearly *evergreen*, with 3–7 (usually 5) blunt, *wavy-toothed*, and *leathery* leaflets. Leaflets ¼–1½ in. long, undulantly *crinkled*, somewhat hairy, and with a *lemonlike* odor when crushed. Leaflets short-stalked except for the end one. Leafstalks reddish, hairy, and often *thorny*. Twigs greenish, hairy.

LIME PRICKLY-ASH

TEXAS PRICKLY-ASH

Thorns curved, single, ¼–½ in. long. Trunk bark smooth, grayish. *Trunk thorns* up to 1 in. long may be present. Flowers small, greenish, in ½–2-in. loose branched clusters at the twig *ends*. Fruits ⅛–¼ in., brown, gland-dotted capsules that split to show a shiny black seed. Height to 15 ft. Dry soils. **SIMILAR SPECIES:** (1) Lime Prickly-ash has winged leafstalks plus flowers and fruits in the leaf angles. (2) Southern Prickly-ash has leaflets not crinkled and trunk thorns with a corky base. **REMARKS:** Also known as Tickle-tongue and Toothache-tree. Chewing the leaves is said to alleviate toothache. Sometimes considered to be a variety of Southern Prickly-ash.

SOUTHERN PRICKLY-ASH **NOT SHOWN**
Zanthoxylum clava-herculis L.

A small eastern tree whose range extends west to cen. Texas. Leaves 4–16 in. long with 7–17 wavy-toothed, pointed, somewhat leathery, nearly evergreen, usually curved, and *asymmetrical* leaflets, each 1¼–3 in. long. Foliage with *lemonlike odor* when crushed, often with dark gland dots beneath. Leafstalks mostly thorny. Twigs hairless. Buds small, blunt, dark, hairless. Bundle scars 3. Flower/fruit clusters at twig *ends*. Trunk smooth and gray, with scattered *corky knobs* often thorn-tipped. Height 10–20 (50) ft.; diameter 4–8 (18) in. Poor soils. **SIMILAR SPECIES:** Texas Prickly-ash has leaves smaller, leaflets crinkled, and trunk thorns that lack corky bases. **REMARKS:** Hercules-club is an alternate name used also for another eastern species, *Aralia spinosa* L.

NEW MEXICO LOCUST *Robinia neomexicana* Gray **PL. 18**
A small tree of mountains from extreme se. Nev. and cen. Colo. to nw. Mexico and w. Texas. Leaves deciduous, 4–10 in. long with 9–21 smooth-edged, short-stalked, and *bristle-tipped* leaflets,

NEW MEXICO LOCUST

SOUTHERN PRICKLY-ASH

each ¾–1½ in. long and ½–1 in. wide. Twigs rusty-hairy or hairless; twigs and/or branchlets with ¼–½-in. *paired* thorns flanking the leaf scars. Hidden hairy buds burst *through* the leaf scars upon enlargement. Small additional buds may be present above the leaf scars. Spur branches lacking. Bundle scars 3. Bark thin, brown. *Sprouts* vigorously from stumps. Flowers attractive, *pink-purple,* fragrant, ¾ in. long, in 2–4-in. clusters drooping from the leaf bases; spring and early summer. Fruit pods 2–6 in. long, flat, and *brown-hairy;* autumn or later. Height to 25 ft.; diameter to 8 in. Forms thickets on moist sites at 4000–8700 ft. elevations. SIMILAR SPECIES: Black Locust has white flowers, hairless fruit pods, and leaflets without bristle-tips. When leafless, other trees with paired thorns have spur branches present and a single bud visible above each leaf scar. REMARKS: As in many other legumes, atmospheric nitrogen is converted to useful compounds by bacteria held in root nodules. Valuable in erosion control for this reason and because of its sprouting abilities. Trunks make durable fence posts. Deer and cattle eat the foliage and flowers. Seeds eaten by small mammals and by wild turkeys and other game birds. Native Americans, at least formerly, ate the fresh flowers and cooked the pods for food.

BLACK LOCUST *Robinia pseudoacacia* L.   PL. 18
This native of the e. U.S. is spreading rapidly in temperate zones around the world. It has been planted widely in the West and now reproduces naturally in many localities there. Leaves 8–14 in. long with 7–19 *blunt-tipped,* short-stalked, and sometimes fine-toothed leaflets, each 1–2 in. long. Twigs *hairless;* ¼-in. *paired* thorns mostly present at the leaf scars. Hidden buds break through the leaf scars. Flowers *white,* in 4–6-in. clusters. Fruits pods 2–6 in. long and *hairless.* Otherwise as in New Mexico Locust. Height 70–80 (100) ft. and diameter 2–3 (6) ft. in its native range. SIMILAR SPECIES: See New Mexico Locust. REMARKS: Wood strong and durable in soil; useful for fence posts. Young shoots and bark sometimes poisonous to livestock, but seeds eaten by many birds and by rabbits and deer. Spreading rapidly after introduction into many parts of the world. Yields a good honey.

SOUTHWESTERN TREES WITH ALTERNATE LEAVES TWICE-COMPOUND AND THORNS PAIRED (PLATE 19)

The several prickly species of this plate and the next, plus the nonthorny trees of Pl. 25, are the only trees of our area with leaves divided into major leaflets which, in turn, are divided into minor leaflets. Except for Honey Locust (Pl. 20) of the e. and cen. U.S., all are native to the Southwest.

In contrast with Pl. 20, the plants of this plate have *paired* thorns that flank the leafstalk bases or buds. The leaflets are without teeth. Knobby *spur branches* are common and often bear clusters of leaves. The pea-pod fruits are mostly hairless and variously flat, cylindrical, or beaded (with constrictions between the seeds). Roemer Catclaw (Pl. 20) may have thorns both paired and single.

The thorny plants with twice-compound leaves (Pls. 19, 20) are all members of the legume (pea-bean) group of families. They are evergreen, except for mesquites. Jerusalem-thorn sheds only its leaflets.

Legumes are of importance in that nearly all species have mutually beneficial relationships with bacteria that occupy swellings on their roots. Using nitrogen from the atmosphere, these root-nodule microorganisms manufacture compounds that enrich the soil and enable the plant to grow on an otherwise poor site. In the w. U.S., all leguminous trees except Honey Locust (Pl. 20) and the redbuds (Pl. 30) have this ability.

Many of the s. Texas species of Pls. 19 and 20 can be seen in the tree collection at the visitor center of the Santa Ana Nat'l. Wildlife Refuge south of Alamo, Texas.

HUISACHE *Acacia farnesiana* (L.) Willd.   **PL. 19**
Native from s. Texas south through much of Latin America and the Caribbean but planted and established locally from s. Calif. to Fla. An *essentially evergreen* shrub or small tree with finely divided, 2–4-in. leaves and 4–8 pairs of major leaflets. Each major leaflet divided into 10–25 pairs of minor leaflets, each only about ¹⁄₃₂ *in. wide* and ¼ in. long. Paired thorns *variable* in size, ranging from ¼–1 ½ in. long. Large thorns are usually white. Some specimens may have few or no thorns. Bundle scar 1. Trunk dark, fissured, and mostly with scattered thorns. Spur branches moderately large. Flowers crowded in *ball-shaped,* fragrant, *yellow-orange* clusters about ¾ in. wide, Feb.–April. Fruit pods *hairless,* blackish, stoutly *cylindrical,* and 2–3 in. long. They are *late* in splitting open and have blackish seeds in two rows. Height

to 30 ft. Thickets. **SIMILAR SPECIES:** (1) Huisachillo also has minor leaflets only ⅟₃₂ in. wide, but it has smaller leaves and its fruit pods are velvety, 3–5 in. long, slightly beaded, and with only one row of seeds. (2) Tenaza has minor leaflets about ⅟₁₆ in. wide, whitish flowers, and flat 3–5-in. fruit pods that split open promptly upon ripening. **REMARKS:** Pronounced weesah-chay. Also known as Sweet Acacia. Sap has been used as glue. Deer browse the foliage; bees collect the pollen. Cultivated in Europe for its flowers, used as a base for perfume. Said to have been introduced into Italy in the early 17th century by Cardinal Oduardo Farnese.

HUISACHILLO *Acacia tortuosa* (L.) Willd.   **NOT SHOWN**
Like Huisache but with many aspects reduced in size. Leaves only *1–1½ in. long* with minor leaflet pairs 15–20, and thorns ¼–¾ in. long. Flower heads *under ½ in.* in diameter, March. Fruit pods *velvety*, 3–5 in. long, slightly beaded, and with only *1* row of black seeds. Height to 20 ft. Dry soils of Rio Grande plains of s. Texas south to Guatemala. Also in s. Fla. and throughout the Caribbean. Pronounced weesah-CHEE-yoh.

TENAZA *Pithecellobium pallens* (Benth.) Standl.   **PL. 19**
A plant of s. Texas with *mostly evergreen*, fernlike foliage somewhat like that of Huisache. Leaves 2–3 in. long with 4–6 pairs of major leaflets. Minor leaflets medium green, with 8–20 pairs per major leaflet. Each minor leaflet about ⅟₁₆ in. wide. Trunk gray, mostly smooth; thorns often present, white, and to 1½ in. long. Twig and branchlet thorns brown and *only ¼ in. long*. Flowers *greenish white* in *globular* clusters about ⅜ in. in diameter. Fruit pods flat, 3–4 in. long, splitting open *promptly* upon ripening. Height to 25 ft. Rio Grande plains and ne. Mexico. **SIMILAR SPECIES:** (1) Huisache and (2) Huisachillo have narrower minor leaflets

while (3) Texas Ebony has wider ones that are a darker green. Texas Ebony also has larger thorns, only 1–3 major leaflet pairs, flower clusters in the form of slender spikes, and fruit pods that are delayed in splitting. See also (4) Lime Prickly-ash (Pl. 18) and (5) Guajillo (Pl. 20). **REMARKS:** Pronounced ten-AH-za. Reported also to be called Huajillo, pronounced essentially same as Guajillo (Pl. 20); this name is not used where the species occurs. Plants in the genus also are called blackbeads and ape's earrings; the fruits of tropical species are coiled. Browsed by sheep and goats.

TEXAS EBONY *Pithecellobium flexicaule* (Benth.) Coult. **PL. 19**
The foliage of this *evergreen* legume is markedly *darker* than its several relatives in s. Texas. Leaves 1½–2 in. long, divided into 1–3 pairs of major leaflets. Each major leaflet with 3–6 pairs of relatively wide minor leaflets. The latter mostly ³⁄₁₆–¼ in. wide and ⅜–½ in. long. Thorns ¼–½ in. long, trunk thorns lacking. Flowers *white,* in slender fragrant *spikes;* April–June. Fruit pods 4–8 in. long, flat when young, becoming cylindrical and remaining on the tree for some months before splitting open. Height 10–30 (50) ft.; diameter 1–2 ft. Roadsides and thickets, south in e. Mexico to Vera Cruz; also in Yucatan. **SIMILAR SPECIES:** See (1) Tenaza. (2) Blackbrush Acacia (*Acacia rigidula* Benth.), a shrub, has leaflet

Bark of Texas Ebony

TEXAS EBONY

tips with tiny points. **REMARKS:** Trunks are cut for fence posts. The dark heartwood is used for furniture and ornaments. The seeds are eaten as a nutritious food in Mexico and s. Texas and are also made into jewelry. A good honey species. The bark is reported to contain a yellow dye employed in tanning skins. Also called Ébano (pronounced AY-behn-oh).

HONEY MESQUITE   *Prosopis glandulosa* Torr.   PL. 19

A *deciduous* small tree or shrub with drooping foliage. Common on rangelands throughout much of the Southwest. Leaves 5–10 in. long, mostly with just *one* pair (rarely 2–3 pairs) of major leaflets. Each major leaflet with 10–20 pairs of *narrow*, hairless, minor leaflets ¾–1½ in. long and ⅛–¼ in. wide. Branchlets with *obvious* knobby spur branches, often ⅜ in. long, evident even at a moderate distance. Thorns slender, paired (sometimes single), and often 1 in. long. Bundle scars 3. Sapwood yellow; heartwood red-brown. Stumps may *sprout*. Flowers white to *pale yellow*, in slender 2–3-in. spikes, April–July. Fruit pods *cylindrical*, light brown, slightly beaded, 4–10 in. long. Trunk dark, often nearly black. Height to 20 ft.; diameter to 12 in. Grasslands and pastures, from the Great Basin, sw. Okla., and e. Texas into Mexico. **SIMILAR SPECIES:** (1) Velvet and (2) Screwbean mesquites, also mostly with one pair of major leaflets, have short (½ in.) minor leaflets. The former species has mostly velvet-hairy foliage; the latter has somewhat hairy leaflets and tightly spiralled fruits only 1–2 in. long. **REMARKS:** In grasslands, mesquites originally were restricted by wildfires and grew mainly along streambeds. Seeds are distributed by livestock and wildlife. With heavy livestock grazing and other fire-control practices, the species has spread widely into pastures. Foliage and twigs are browsed by deer; fruits are eaten by many kinds of wildlife. Excellent for fence posts, char-

HONEY MESQUITE

SCREWBEAN MESQUITE

coal, and firewood. A fine honey plant. Native Americans ground the seeds into flour for making cakes and a fermented drink. They used the inner bark in basketry and a gummy exudate of the trunk to mend pottery and as a black dye. The name mesquite is believed to have Aztec origins. Commonly pronounced mes-KEET (in Spanish, mes-keetay).

VELVET MESQUITE *Prosopis velutina* Woot.   **PL. 19**
Similar to Honey Mesquite and often regarded as a variety of it. A tree of cen. Ariz., sw. N.M., and south into Mexico. The 15–20 pairs of minor leaflets are mostly hairy, only ¼–½ in. long and ¹⁄₁₆–⅛ in. wide. Thorns sometimes few. Spur branches short. Flowers yellow-green. Height to 50 ft.; diameter to 3 ft. Streambeds and pastures.

SCREWBEAN MESQUITE *Prosopis pubescens* Benth.   **PL. 19**
A small, thorny tree with short leaves and unique fruits. Like Honey Mesquite but with both leaves and fruits only *1–2 in. long.* Minor leaflets only 5–9 pairs, more or less hairy, ¼–⅜ in. long and ⅛–³⁄₁₆ in. wide. Thorns sometimes slightly curved; spur branches small. Flower spikes pale yellow, about 2 in. long. Height to 20 ft.; diameter to 1 ft. Fruit pods light tan, tightly spiralled. Seeds eaten by Gambel and bobwhite quail, roadrunners, and other birds. Along watercourses, Great Basin to w. Texas and nw. Mexico.

JERUSALEM-THORN *Parkinsonia aculeata* L.   **PL. 19**
A thorny *green-barked* shrub or small tree whose 40–60 tiny (⅛–³⁄₁₆ in. long, ¹⁄₃₂–¹⁄₁₆ in. wide) minor leaflets drop early. This

JERUSALEM-THORN

results in 2–6 *green, grasslike* midribs, each 8–15 in. long, remaining on the tree as remnants of major leaflets of the twice-compound leaf. *Triple* or paired thorns occur at most leafstalk bases, one of these often being larger (to 1 in.). The green, drooping twigs often show fine lengthwise lines (use lens). Bundle scars 3. Flowers yellow, spring and summer. Fruits 2–4 in. beaded pods. To 35 ft. tall. Moist to dry soils, near the Rio Grande in Texas and also in s. Ariz. Planted elsewhere. Widespread in Mexico and southward. **SIMILAR SPECIES:** No other western tree has such grasslike foliage remnants. **REMARKS:** Also called Mexican Paloverde, but the paloverde name is better reserved for the *Cercidium* species of Pls. 20 and 26. The Mexican name Retama (reh-TAH-mah) is preferred in s. Texas and perhaps elsewhere in the Southwest. John Parkinson was an English botanist living between 1567 and 1650. The origin of the name Jerusalem-thorn is uncertain.

MOSTLY SOUTHWESTERN TREES WITH ALTERNATE LEAVES TWICE-COMPOUND AND THORNS SINGLE (PLATE 20)

Most of these species occur mainly along the Mexican boundary. Honey Locust is the only exception. It is an eastern tree whose natural range extends at least locally to the western portions of the plains states from S.D. to Texas. Its thornless horticultural variety is planted even more widely.

All trees on this plate are legumes, members of the pea-bean family (or group of families, according to modern botanists; see Appendix B). The thorns of these legumes are not paired. Spur branches are quite small. All have either white or yellow flowers and flat fruit pods.

In desert regions of Ariz., s. Calif., and nw. Mexico most trees are adapted to conserve moisture. In the paloverdes (*Cercidium*) this is accomplished by a reduction of leaf surface nearly to zero. Though each of the 1–3 major leaflets looks deceptively like a once-compound leaf, the leaves are twice-compound. They are extremely small and present in some areas only briefly in spring.

The smooth greenish trunk and branches largely have taken over the photosynthetic process of food manufacture. The paloverdes on this plate have side thorns at the nodes. In contrast, Yellow Paloverde (Pl. 26) is prickly at the sharp twig tips.

The catclaw acacias have sharp *hooked* thorns, which give them their well-deserved name. The Spanish name, Uña de Gato (OON-ya-deh-GAH-toh), is identical. Several shrubby acacias also occur in the region.

Honey Mesquite may have some single thorns, while Jerusalem-thorn may have one thorn larger (see Pl. 19).

BLUE PALOVERDE *Cercidium floridum* Benth. ex Gray   **PL. 20**
A tree or shrub of Ariz., Calif., and n. Mexico deserts. Leaves ephemeral, only ¾–1 in. long and with *one* pair of major leaflets. Each of these has 1–3 pairs of minor leaflets ³⁄₁₆–¼ in. long and about ¹⁄₁₆ in. wide. Twigs have a single ¼–⅜-in. *straight* thorn at each node. Flowers about ¾ in. across, yellow, in *loose* clusters, March–May. Fruit pods flat and 2–3 in. long. Young bark of trunk and larger branches smooth *blue-green*. Height to 30 ft. Drainage channels. **SIMILAR SPECIES:** (1) Yellow Paloverde (Pl. 26) has strongly spine-tipped twigs, a yellow-green trunk and branches, and 4–8 pairs of minor leaflets per major leaflet. It lacks short thorns at the nodes, and its fruit pods are beaded. See (2) Texas Paloverde. **REMARKS:** Produces masses of showy yellow blossoms. Evidently requires somewhat better water supplies than Yellow Paloverde. Native Americans cooked the young pods and also ground the ripe seeds into flour. Pronounced pah-low-VEHR-deh.

TEXAS PALOVERDE *Cercidium texanum* Gray   **PL. 20**
Similar to Blue Paloverde but found in extreme s. Texas and ne. Mexico. Reported also from Big Bend Nat'l. Park in w. Texas.

Leaves with 1–3 (*usually* 2) small major leaflets, each with 1–2 minor leaflets only ³⁄₁₆–¼ in. long and about ⅛ in. wide. Thorns rarely lacking. Flowers yellow, with *red spots* on the largest of the petals, spring. Fruit pods ½–2½ in. long. Height to 25 ft. **REMARKS:** Border Paloverde (*C. macrum* Johnst.) is included here with this species.

GUAJILLO   *Acacia berlandieri* Benth.   PL. 20

A small tree or shrub mostly with single straight or curved thorns ⅛–⅜ in. long. Ranging from the lower Rio Grande plains of s. Texas and ne. Mexico to the e. part of w. Texas, this species is unique in having nearly evergreen *fernlike* leaves 4–6 in. long, with 5–12 pairs of major leaflets. Minor leaflets are ⅛–³⁄₁₆ in. long and only about ¹⁄₃₂ in. wide, with 30–50 or more pairs per major leaflet. Twigs and branchlets occasionally thornless but usually with thorns ¹⁄₃₂–⅜ in. long. Spur branches of medium (under ¼ in.) length. Trunk gray with shallow ridges and scattered gray to black thorns ¾–1 in. long. Flowers white, in *ball-shaped* clusters about ⅜ in. across, Feb.–March. Fruit pods velvety, light brown, ½–1 in. wide and 3–6 in. long. Height to 15 ft. Limestone or sandy soils. **SIMILAR SPECIES:** A large-leaved acacia and the only one with more than three major leaflet pairs per leaf or with numerous minor leaflets. The fruits are velvet-hairy and longer than in the several other catclaws. Tenaza (Pl. 19) has 4–6 pairs of major leaflets and paired thorns, while Great Leadtree (Pl. 25) has 14–20 major leaflets and is thornless. **REMARKS:** One of several catclaw acacias. A Mexican name, pronounced wah-HEE-yo. An excellent honey plant. Foliage occasionally poisons sheep and goats. The Mexi-

can-American boundary was explored by Luis Berlandier, a Swiss botanist, in 1828.

GREGG CATCLAW *Acacia greggii* Gray **PL. 20**

The only catclaw that ranges from the Pacific Coast to the Gulf of Mexico. Leaves 1–3 in. long, only *briefly deciduous,* and with 1–3 pairs of major leaflets. Each major leaflet with 3–7 pairs of minor leaflets only ⅛–¼ in. long and 1/16 in. wide. Thorns ¼–⅜ in. long, stout, curved, and numerous. Spur branches medium-sized, under ¼ in. long. Flower clusters slim *spikes,* light *yellow,* fragrant, and 2–3 in. long. Fruit pods hairless, brown, flat but usually *much twisted,* and 2–3 in. in length, with seeds nearly circular. Height 15–30 ft.; diameter 6–12 in. Often forms thickets; arid areas. **SIMILAR SPECIES:** The only catclaw found west of Texas. (1) Guajillo and (2) Roemer Catclaw differ most markedly in having flowers in ball-shaped clusters. Guajillo has narrower minor leaflets and more numerous (5–12) major leaflets. Roemer Catclaw and (3) Wright Catclaw are both like Gregg Catclaw with 1–3 major leaflets, but they have larger minor leaflets and fruit pods not strongly twisted. **REMARKS:** The thorny thickets are widely disliked as obstacles to travel. Drought resistant and heavily browsed by livestock. Native Americans prepared the seeds as a mush. A good honey plant. Eaten by jackrabbits and Gambel quail.

ROEMER CATCLAW

Acacia roemeriana Scheele **PL. 20**

Distributed from se. N.M. through w. and cen. Texas to

Gregg Catclaw

ROEMER CATCLAW

WRIGHT CATCLAW

ne. Mexico. Like Gregg Catclaw but the leaves are larger (1½–4 in. long) and the 3–8 pairs of minor leaflets are both *longer* (¼–½ in.) and *wider* (⅛–¼ in.). Thorns under ¼ in. long, some may be paired. Spur branches inconspicuous; blossom clusters globular and whitish yellow, March–May. The dark, hairless fruit pods are 2–4 *in. long,* with seeds narrowly egg-shaped. Height 6–15 ft.; diameter to 16 in. Shrublands. **SIMILAR SPECIES:** (1) Gregg Catclaw has smaller minor leaflets plus longer and stronger thorns and twisted fruit pods. (2) Wright Catclaw usually has fewer major leaflets. Both Gregg and Wright catclaws have flowers in spikes. **REMARKS:** A valuable honey plant. Foliage consumed by whitetail deer, fruits eaten by scaled quail. Karl Ferdinand Roemer, a German scientist, collected plants in cen. Texas during the 1840s.

WRIGHT CATCLAW *Acacia wrightii* Benth.   **PL. 20**
Differs from Roemer Catclaw mainly in that the *yellowish* flowers are in slender *spikes.* Leaves 1–3 in., mainly with only 1–2 pairs of major leaflets. Minor leaflets larger than those of Gregg Catclaw and like those of Roemer Catclaw. Fruit pods 2–3 in. long with seeds narrowly egg-shaped. Height to 30 ft.; diameter to 1 ft. A good honey species. Charles Wright was a 19th-century botanist who collected plants in Texas. W. and cen. Texas to ne. Mexico.

DWARF POINCIANA *Caesalpinia pulcherrima* (L.) Sw.   **PL. 20**
Planted widely for ornament in tropical and subtropical regions and spreading to the wild from extreme s. Calif. to s. Texas and s. Fla. Leaves 5–15 in. long with 5–10 pairs of major leaflets and 6–10 minor leaflet pairs. Minor leaflets ⅜–¾ in. long and ⅙ in. wide, with *blunt* tips. Evergreen in most areas. Twigs hairless, usually with scattered *straight* thorns ¼–⅜ in. long. Flowers large,

with long red stamens, petals red sometimes bordered with yellow, in loose clusters, somewhat fragrant, blooming most of the year. Fruit pods 3–5 in. long and ½–¾ in. wide. Height to 15 ft. Disturbed soils. **SIMILAR SPECIES:** This is the only species of this group with broad blunt leaflets. When thorns are absent, other species with wide leaflets (see Pl. 25) have fewer major and minor leaflets. **REMARKS:** Leaves will stun fish. A dye can be made from the roots and flowers. Origin unknown, though sometimes called Barbados-pride. Known in Fla. as Flowerfence Poinciana. A "dwarf" in comparison with the related Royal Poinciana or Flamboyant (*Delonix regia* [Bojer ex Hook.] Raf.), a large flowering tree of Madagascar widely planted in the tropics.

HONEY LOCUST *Gleditsia triacanthos* L. PL. 20

A tall eastern tree whose range extends west to the Great Plains. Leaves *large,* 6–15 in. long, and either once- or twice-compound. Often with 4–8 pairs of major leaflets and 7–16 pairs of minor leaflets. Minor leaflets ½–1¾ in. long, ³⁄₁₆–⅜ in. wide, more or less *pointed,* and mostly finely *wavy-toothed.* Twigs hairless, stout; buds hairless, hidden by leafstalk bases in summer and nearly surrounded by leaf scars in winter. Supplementary buds may be located above the primary ones. End bud false; bundle scars 3. Flowers small, greenish white, in loose clusters, May–July. Fruits twisted flat pods, 8–18 *in.* long, Sept.–Feb. Trunk bark dark and somewhat scaly; the uncultivated wild form usually with numerous stout and often *branched* trunk thorns 2–10 in. long. **SIMILAR SPECIES:** No other American tree has such long thorns or fruits. The minor leaflets are much wider than those of Honey Mesquite (Pl. 19). **REMARKS:** Thorns have been used by woodsmen for pins, spear points, and animal traps. Heavy, durable wood used for railroad ties, fence posts, and agricultural implements. Unlike most legumes, the tree does not harbor root bacteria capable of fixing nitrogen. Pulp between the seeds has a sweet taste but, despite its common name, it does not yield a good honey. Fruits eaten by cattle, deer, rabbits, squirrels, and bobwhite quail. A thornless variety is cultivated widely.

HONEY LOCUST

THORNLESS TREES WITH ALTERNATE LEAVES ONCE-COMPOUND AND TOOTHED: I WALNUTS, HICKORIES, TREE-OF-HEAVEN
(PLATE 21)

This group is easily recognized by its 5–41 *toothed* or glandular and mostly hairless leaflets. Species on this plate have leaf scars large and shield-shaped. Tree-of-heaven usually has only one pair of gland-tipped teeth at the base of each leaflet. All are deciduous trees. Silk-Oak (Pl. 24) has leaflets deeply lobed rather than toothed.

WALNUTS

Trees with leaves 10–24 in. long and with 7–19 mostly fine-toothed leaflets that have a *spicy odor* when crushed. Twigs and branchlets stout, the latter showing *chambered* pith when cut lengthwise. Bundle scars 3 or in 3 groups. Buds gray-hairy. Flowers in spring. Male blossoms in slender hanging catkins, tiny female flowers single or in small clusters at twig ends. Fruits globular, ½–2 in. in diameter, with mostly grooved edible nuts enclosed in a smooth, fibrous, *nonsplitting* husk. The nut crop is a valuable food resource especially for squirrels and other rodents. At some seasons husks should be handled carefully to avoid staining hands and clothing. Where trees grow large, walnut lumber is highly prized for furniture. The bruised branches, foliage, and fruits of walnuts have been used to stun fish, but the practice is illegal in the U.S. The cultivated English Walnut (*J. regia* L.), originally from Asia, has *black* buds and 7–9 broad leaflets mostly *not* toothed.

HINDS WALNUT

CALIFORNIA WALNUT

HINDS WALNUT *Juglans hindsii* Jeps. ex R. E. Smith PL. 21

A Calif. species, native to the valleys east of San Francisco Bay but now planted and spreading throughout the state and northward. Leaves 7–13 in. long with 15–19 leaflets mostly 2½–4 in. long and ¾–1¼ in. wide. Twigs hairless or not. Mature fruits 1¼–2 in. in diameter with nut shell (not husk) grooved very slightly or not at all. Height 50–75 ft. Fertile, well-drained soils. **SIMILAR SPECIES:** California Walnut is a smaller coastal tree with fewer and shorter leaflets and smaller nuts shallowly grooved. **REMARKS:** Richard B. Hinds, a 19-century British botanist, discovered this species during an around-the-world voyage. Walnut Creek and Walnut Grove, towns east of San Francisco Bay, were original sites of Hinds Walnut stands. Planted as a street tree in many Calif. cities. Widely used in California's orchards as drought- and insect-resistant rootstock for grafting English Walnuts.

CALIFORNIA WALNUT *Juglans californica* S. Wats. PL. 21

Native to coastal s. Calif., this walnut has leaves 6–9 in. long with 7–17 leaflets mostly only 1–2½ *in. long* and ½–¾ in. wide. Twigs mostly hairless. Fruits only ½–1 *in.* in diameter, containing nuts whose surface is *shallowly* grooved. Trunk mostly forked. Height to 30 ft., rarely to 60 ft. Fertile soils, to 2500 ft. elevation. **SIMILAR SPECIES:** See Hinds Walnut. **REMARKS:** Hybridizes with cultivated English Walnut (*J. regia*).

ARIZONA WALNUT *Juglans major* (Torr.) A. Heller PL. 21

Mainly Mexican in distribution, this species ranges north to n. Ariz. and locally east to cen. Texas. Leaves 9–13 in. long with 9–15 *long-pointed* and *coarse-toothed* leaflets, each 2–4 in. long, ¾–1¼ in. wide and frequently curved. Twigs often velvet-hairy. Fruits 1–1½ in. in diameter, the enclosed nuts deeply grooved. Height 30–50 ft.; diameter to 4 ft. Mountain valleys, 2000– 7500 ft. elevation. **SIMILAR SPECIES:** Texas Walnut is a smaller tree with narrower and more numerous leaflets as well as smaller fruits. **REMARKS:** Intergrades with Texas Walnut and is sometimes considered a variety of it. The common name for walnut in Mexico is *nogal* (noh-GAHL). Nogales, Ariz., doubtless was named in its honor.

ARIZONA WALNUT

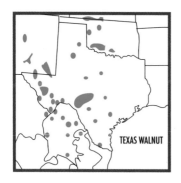

TEXAS WALNUT *Juglans microcarpa* Berlandier   **PL. 21**

The *narrow, long-pointed,* and numerous leaflets of this species are field marks. Leaves 8–16 in. long with 15–21 (25) leaflets, each 2–6 in. long, ¼–½ in. wide, often *curved,* and with *fine teeth* or none. Twigs hairy. Fruits ¾–1 in. in diameter, with nuts *deeply* grooved. Height to 20 ft.; diameter to 18 in. Along watercourses, sw. Kan. and N.M. to n. Mexico. **SIMILAR SPECIES:** See (1) Arizona Walnut. (2) Black Walnut leaflets are more broad, with the end one often lacking. It also has larger fruits.

BLACK WALNUT *Juglans nigra* L.   **PL. 21**

This valuable eastern tree extends its range west locally to the Great Plains from ne. Neb. south to cen. Texas. Leaves 8–24 in. long with 15–23 broad leaflets, each 2–4 in. long, ¾–1½ in. wide, and sharply toothed. End leaflet often absent. Twigs mostly hairless. Fruits 1¼–2½ in. in diameter with the nut deeply grooved. Height in favorable locations to 150 ft. and diameter to 4 ft. Fertile soils. **SIMILAR SPECIES:** See Texas Walnut. **REMARKS:** Black Walnut lumber is heavy, strong, durable, and takes a fine finish. It is in demand for cabinet making and interior finishing. Large roots are often sought for gunstocks. A yellow-brown dye can be made from the husks of walnuts. Toxic substances secreted from the roots are believed to be the reason that tomatoes, apples, and other species often do not survive near large walnut trees.

HICKORIES

Closely related to walnuts and, like them, with 5–17 fine-toothed, aromatic, and often long-pointed leaflets. The male flowers also occur in springtime catkins. Unlike walnuts, though, the pith is

BLACK HICKORY

PECAN

solid, bundle scars are *numerous,* and nut husks *split* into 4 parts upon ripening. Twigs and branchlets tough, difficult to break. Hickory nuts are eaten by humans and many wildlife species. Before the practice was outlawed, people crushed the green nut husks and used them to poison fish for food. The wood has some value for making tool handles, gunstocks, and baskets. It was once the best American wood for making barrel hoops. As fuel, it produces great heat and high-quality charcoal.

BLACK HICKORY *Carya texana* Buckl.   PL. 21

This hickory has its distribution centered in the Ozarks region but reaching into ne. Neb. Leaves 8–12 in. long, with 5–7 (usually 7) leaflets 2–6 in. long and 1–2¼ in. wide. Twigs/buds generally *rusty-hairy;* bud scales *overlapping,* the outer ones falling early. Fruits 1¼–2 in. long with husks yellow-scaled, ⅛ in. thick, and splitting to the base; nut nearly *globular* and slightly 4-angled with short, abrupt point. Height to 100 ft.; diameter to 3 ft. SIMILAR SPECIES: Pecan has twigs hairless plus paired, yellowish bud scales not overlapping.

PECAN *Carya illinoensis* (Wang.) K. Koch   PL. 21

An eastern tree found in the West mainly in cen. Texas and sw. Okla. Leaves 12–20 in. long with 9–17 leaflets mostly 3–5 in. long and 1–2 in. wide. Twigs *hairless;* end bud with 2–3 pairs of *yellow-hairy* scales *not* overlapping. Fruits *4-ridged;* nuts thin-shelled, 1½–3 in. long, longer than wide, Sept.–Oct. Height 100–120 (160) ft.; diameter 1–3 (6) ft. Floodplains. SIMILAR SPECIES: See Black Hickory. REMARKS: Largest of all hickories. One of the few food plants strictly American in origin. A highly valued species cultivated for its delicious nuts. Fruits of orchard varieties have thinner husks and nutshells than those of wild specimens.

Wood is of value for furniture and house construction. Wild turkeys, opossums, ringtails, and javelinas are among animals that eat the nuts.

TREE-OF-HEAVEN *Ailanthus altissima* (Mill.) Swingle   **PL. 21**
A fast-growing small to large tree with leaves 12–24 in. long and having 11–41 leaflets. Leaflets 2–6 in. long, ¾–2 in. wide, and not toothed *except* for 1–2 pairs of *gland-tipped teeth near bases*. Twigs hairless, yellow-brown, stout, with continuous yellowish pith. Buds small, brown-hairy. Leaf scars *very large*, somewhat triangular, with numerous bundle scars. Flowers small, yellowish, clustered; male blossoms with foul odor, June–July. Fruits dry, 1–2 in. long, narrow, with 1 seed centered in the papery wing, in large pale clusters on the tree, Sept.–winter. Height 80–100 ft.; diameter 1–2 ft. Widespread. **SIMILAR SPECIES:** No other tree has such basal gland-tipped leaflet teeth. In winter, stout twigs, unusually large leaf scars, and numerous bundle scars are distinctive. **REMARKS:** Imported from China by way of England, where it was first planted in 1751. The most rapidly growing woody plant in our area. Will thrive under extremely adverse conditions, growing as much as 8 ft. in a year. Sprouts 12 ft. long are not uncommon where a tree has been cut down. It is so well adapted to disturbed sites that even a crack between the bricks in an alley may provide a seedbed for this plant. Immune to dust and smoke, and may grow to a large size. Though soft, the wood has some lumber and fuel values. The common name is supposed to be of Asiatic or Australian origin, alluding to the tree's height.

Tree-of-Heaven

THORNLESS TREES WITH ALTERNATE LEAVES ONCE-COMPOUND AND TOOTHED: II (PLATE 22)

In contrast with the plants of Pl. 21, these species have narrow leaf scars. All have continuous pith. None is evergreen.

CALIFORNIA HOPTREE *Ptelea crenulata* Greene **NOT SHOWN**
Closely resembles Common Hoptree (Pl. 24) but usually shrubby and with leaf edges mostly *finely wavy-toothed.* Leaves 4–6 in. long with 3 leaflets each 1–3 in. long. Leaflet tips either blunt or short-pointed. Buds white-woolly; leaf scars *U-shaped,* bundle scars 3. Height to 15 ft. Foothill slopes, n. and cen. Calif. Lemonade Sumac (Pl. 45) occasionally has trifoliate leaves, but these are evergreen, leathery, and sometimes prickly.

MOUNTAIN-ASHES

Northern trees whose dense terminal clusters of small white blossoms, colorful autumn foliage, and groups of applelike fruits are attractive both in the wild and when planted for ornamental landscaping. Some species are hardy even in Labrador, Greenland, Iceland, and Scandinavia. The small, fleshy fruits often remain until late winter. Eaten by people and by many wild birds and mammals including ruffed and sharptail grouse, ptarmigan, fisher, and marten. Deer, elk, and moose browse the twigs. Leaves 4–9 in. long. Leaf scars crescent-shaped, narrow; bundle scars 5. Spur branches present. Trunk bark mostly smooth. Sometimes called Rowan-trees, an old Scandinavian name. True ashes (Pls. 12, 13) also have feather-compound leaves but they are opposite.

SITKA MOUNTAIN-ASH *Sorbus sitchensis* Roem. **PL. 22**
Leaflets 7–11 per leaf, *blunt-tipped* or short-pointed, and basal
⅓–½ of leaflets not toothed. Twigs and winter buds *rusty-hairy*.
Flowers about ¼ in. across, in clusters *2–4 in.* wide, June–Aug.
Fruits *orange* or red, ⅜–½ in. in diameter, Aug.–Sept. or longer.
Height to 20 ft.; diameter to 6 in. but mostly shrubby. Forest
openings. **SIMILAR SPECIES:** Leaflets of (1) European and (2) Greene
mountain-ashes are more numerous, more pointed, and ± fully
toothed. Their fruits are smaller and red; their individual flowers
larger. European Mountain-ash has short-pointed and white-
hairy leaflets, white-woolly buds, fruits ⁵⁄₁₆–⅜ in. in diameter, and
streaked bark. Greene Mountain-ash has long-pointed leaflets,
hairless buds, and fruits under ⅜ in. across. **REMARKS:** Species was
originally discovered at Sitka, Alaska.

EUROPEAN MOUNTAIN-ASH *Sorbus aucuparia* L. **PL. 22**
Native to n. Europe and Asia but introduced into N. America in
colonial times and now reproducing on its own. Leaflets 9–15,
short-pointed, toothed *nearly* to the base, and *white-hairy* beneath. Twigs ± hairless; buds white-hairy. Flowers ⅜ in. across, in
clusters *4–6 in.* wide, May–June. Fruits red, ⁵⁄₁₆–⅜ in. in diameter,
Aug.–Oct. or later. Trunk bark with rough *horizontal streaks.*
Height 20–40 ft.; diameter 6–12 in. Naturalized across s. Canada
and n. U. S. from se. Alaska and Nfld. to Calif., Iowa, and Me. **SIM-
ILAR SPECIES:** See Sitka Mountain-ash. **REMARKS:** In many areas of the
world even today, birds are caught by smearing sticky substances
from the fruits or sap (referred to as "bird lime") on favored
perches. The specific name is said to be derived from a Latin term
that relates to bird-catching. Reported to be the only tree introduced into Alaska that now grows wild there.

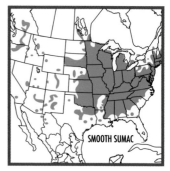

GREENE MOUNTAIN-ASH *Sorbus scopulina* Greene **PL. 22**
A widespread shrub or small tree with 11–15 *hairless, long-pointed* leaflets toothed *nearly* to the base. Twigs and buds *hairless.* Flowers ⅜ in. across, in clusters 1–3 *in.* wide, June–July. Fruits red, ¼–⅜ in. in diameter, July–Aug. Rarely to 20 ft. tall; diameter to 4 in. Forest openings. **SIMILAR SPECIES:** See Sitka Mountain-ash. **REMARKS:** The common name honors American botanist Edward L. Greene, who described the species.

SMOOTH SUMAC *Rhus glabra* L. **PL. 22**
A small tree or shrub with its principal distribution in the e. U.S. but found also in widely scattered localities throughout the West. Leaves 1–2 *ft. long,* long-pointed, and with 11–31 *coarse-toothed* leaflets whitish beneath. Twigs *stout,* pithy, hairless, and rather *flat-sided.* Sap more or less milky. Buds *hairy,* without scales, and surrounded by U-shaped leaf scars that contain *numerous* bundle scars. Flowers small, in upright, greenish white, cone-shaped clusters, June–July. Fruits each about ⅟₁₆ in. long, *red-hairy,* in tight pyramid-shaped groups, remaining on the plant for some months. Height 4–25 ft.; diameter 1–4 in. Open sites. **SIMILAR SPECIES:** The large leaves and numerous leaflets are unlike other species of this plate but resemble those of (1) Black Walnut, (2) Pecan, and (3) Tree-of-Heaven (all on Pl. 21). Those species, however, have leaf scars large and shield-shaped plus fruits other than in red-hairy clusters. **REMARKS:** Twigs cropped by deer and cottontail rabbits. Raw sprouts reported to have been eaten by Native Americans. Fruits sometimes made into "lemonade." Also eaten by ruffed and sharptail grouse, wild turkeys, ringneck pheasants, mourning doves, and many songbirds.

Smooth Sumac

MEXICAN-BUCKEYE *Ungnadia speciosa* Endl.

Found only from se. N.M., across cen. Texas and into ne. Mexico. This small tree or shrub has attractive springtime blossoms and unique 3-lobed fruits. Plants usually with *several* stems. Leaves 5–12 in. long, feather-compound with 5–7 somewhat coarse-toothed and long-pointed leaflets. Twigs *slender* and mostly short-hairy; buds dark, blunt; leaf scars 3-*lobed* with bundle scars *many,* often in three groups. Flowers pink, showy, about 1 in. across, produced from side buds often before the leaves expand. Fruits pear-shaped, dry capsules 1½–2 in. across, splitting into 3 parts to release ½-in. shiny, round, dark seeds. Height to 30 ft.; diameter to 1 ft. Limestone soils. SIMILAR SPECIES: (1) Black Hickory (Pl. 21) has leaves of similar length and leaflet number. That species is not multi-stemmed, however, and its leaflets are more fine-toothed. (2) Smooth Sumac has leaves 12–24 in. long, leaflets 11–31, twigs flat-sided, and fruits small, red. REMARKS: Though its several-stemmed growth habit could place it among shrubs, its greater size leads it usually to be called a tree. Though often leaf-less, its other characteristics cause it to be recommended for wider application in landscaping subtropical areas. The seeds, reportedly poisonous, are said to be used as marbles by w. Texas children. True buckeyes (Pl. 11) have opposite, fan-compound leaves. Also called Monilla (mo-NEE-yah) in Mexico.

THORNLESS SOUTHWESTERN TREES WITH ALTERNATE ONCE-COMPOUND LEAVES MOSTLY NOT TOOTHED: I (PLATE 23)

Trees with compound leaves are numerous in the southwestern states. This is especially true for species with leaflets not toothed. The plants of this plate have *narrow* leaflets, under ⅜ in. wide.

MEXICAN-BUCKEYE

ELEPHANT-TREE

Except Peru Peppertree, their leaflets also are *under* ¾ in. long.
The last two are evergreen. Trees with larger leaflets are shown on
Pl. 24.

ELEPHANT-TREE *Bursera microphylla* Gray   **PL. 23**

The short, stout trunk and main branches of this desert tree are
pale gray and *taper* rapidly like an elephant's trunk. Leaves only
1–1½ in. long and finely divided into 20–40 tiny leaflets. Each
leaflet ⅛–5⁄16 in. long and 1⁄32–1⁄16 in. wide with a *rounded* tip.
Midribs narrowly winged (use lens). Crushed foliage has a *spicy
aroma*. Twigs *red-brown* and hairless, tending to be *stubby* and
often with crowded leaf scars and buds. Flowers white, only ¼ in.
long, and usually 3 in a cluster at twig ends, June. Fruits about ¼
in. long, 3-*sided*, red, becoming dry and splitting, 1 gray seed,
Oct. Trunk short, massive, with thin, *peeling,* white outer bark
with green and red underlayers. Sap red. Height to 16 ft.; diameter to 2½ ft. Rocky slopes at 1000–2500 ft. elevations, extremely
hot and arid deserts of s. Calif., sw. Ariz., and nw. Mexico. **SIMILAR
SPECIES:** (1) Western Kidneywood has gray twigs, gland-dotted and
mostly larger leaflets in addition to 2–3-in. spikes of crowded
flowers. See also (2) Fragrant Bursera. **REMARKS:** Related to frankin-
cense and myrrh of Biblical fame. Aromatic resin of Elephant-tree
(both the resin and the tree are called Copal in some areas) often
is burned as incense in churches and in Native American ceremonies. Gum is also used for cement and varnish and in treating
scorpion stings. Bark is sometimes gathered for tannin. Not tolerant of cold. Joachim Burser, a German botanist, lived from 1593
to 1639.

FRAGRANT BURSERA

WESTERN KIDNEYWOOD

FRAGRANT BURSERA   PL. 23
Bursera fagaroides (H. B. K.) Engler

Though more widely distributed in Sonora, Baja California Sur, and sw. Mexico, Fragrant Bursera has been found in the U.S. only near Fresnal, Pima Co., s.-cen. Ariz. Leaves of this aromatic species are 1–2 in. long with 5–11 leaflets mostly ¼–½ in. long and ⅛–¼ in. wide. Leaflet tips often pointed. Twigs *gray-brown.* Side twigs stubby; spur branches common. Fruits about ⅜ in. long. The several 15-ft. U.S. trees found have been described as having the old bark peeling in "translucent sheets resembling parchment . . . the young bark bright green . . . and the crushed herbage (with the) odor of tangerine skin." Flowers July.

WESTERN KIDNEYWOOD   PL. 23
Eysenhardtia polystachya (Ort.) Sarg.

A tree or shrub of the higher-elevation deserts from s. Ariz. and sw. N.M. to cen. Mexico. Leaves 1¼–4 in. long with 20–56 blunt or short-pointed leaflets each ¼–½ in. long and mostly ¹⁄₁₆–⅛ in. wide. Foliage marked with dark *gland dots* beneath (use lens) and gives off a resinous odor when crushed. Twigs *gray-brown,* hairless, and mostly *flexible.* Spur branches few. Flowers small, crowded in slender, terminal and near-terminal, white spikes, each 2–3 in. long, May. Fruits tiny, flat, pealike pods only ¼–½ in. long, containing only 1–2 seeds, Sept. Trunk short; bark gray, peeling. **SIMILAR SPECIES:** See Elephant-tree. **REMARKS:** Despite an unattractive odor, the foliage is browsed by deer and livestock. Considered a good honey species. Wood yields an orange dye and is said to have both diuretic and fluorescent qualities. It has been used in some localities as a home remedy for kidney and bladder ailments.

TEXAS KIDNEYWOOD   **PL. 23**
Eysenhardtia texana Scheele
Like Western Kidneywood but with 15–30 leaflets and a more *eastern* distribution. Leaves may be absent during droughts. Flower spikes to 3½ in. long. Mainly limestone soils from s. and w. Texas to ne. Mexico.

LITTLELEAF SUMAC   *Rhus microphylla* Engelm.   **PL. 23**
A scrubby shrub or small tree found mainly from se. Ariz. to cen. Texas and locally through cen. Mexico. Side twigs often short, *stiff*, and tending to be somewhat spiky. Leaves *deciduous*, only 1–1½ in. long (small for a sumac), with 5–9 stalkless and sparsely long-hairy leaflets, each ¼–½ in. long and ⅟₁₆–³⁄₁₆ in. wide. Leaf-stalks *winged.* Flowers small and greenish, in lateral and terminal clusters, appearing before the leaves. Fruits small, *red-hairy,* clustered. Height to 15 ft. Dry slopes and plains, also recorded locally in sw. Okla., nw. Texas, and ne. N.M. **SIMILAR SPECIES:** Most other western trees have larger once-compound leaves and/or leaflets that are more numerous. Evergreen Sumac (Pl. 24) has larger, leathery foliage.

TEXAS PISTACHIO   *Pistacia texana* Swingle   **PL. 23**
Found locally on limestone cliffs and in stream bottoms, mainly along the lower Pecos R. in Val Verde Co., Texas. Leaves 2–3 in. long, normally thin but *evergreen* with *red* midribs and 9–21 leaflets each ½–¾ in. long and ¼–⅜ in. wide. The leaflets are sharply pointed with *tiny tips* and *unevenly* divided by the midrib. Flowers small, without petals or sepals and in lateral clusters. Fruits red, 1-seeded nuts similar to the commercial pistachio (*P. vera* L.) of the Middle East but smaller (⅛–¼ in.). Height to 30 ft.

Also reported near San Antonio (Bexar Co.), Texas, and in scattered localities in ne. Mexico. **SIMILAR SPECIES:** Littleleaf Sumac has fewer leaflets, winged leafstalks, stiff side twigs, and small red-hairy fruits.

PERU PEPPERTREE *Schinus molle* L.   **PL. 23**

With *evergreen* leaflets much more narrow and *long-pointed* than the Brazilian Peppertree (Pl. 24), this species has been planted from Calif. to Texas and may spread on its own. Leaves 6–10 in. long with 17–41 short- or long-pointed leaflets each 1–2 *in.* long, ⅛–¼ in. wide, and sometimes fine-toothed. Twigs *droop.* Flowers tiny, in prominent 5–12-in. branched sprays. Fruits reddish, ⅛–¼ in. in diameter, 1-seeded, aromatic, in large clusters. Height to 50 ft. **REMARKS:** Seeds reported sometimes to be crushed and used to adulterate or substitute for the (East Asian) black pepper (*Piper nigrum* L.) of commerce.

THORNLESS SOUTHWESTERN TREES WITH ALTERNATE ONCE-COMPOUND LEAVES MOSTLY NOT TOOTHED: II (PLATE 24)

Compared with the plants of the preceding plate, these species have leaflets *wider* (over ⅜ in.) and *longer* (mostly over 1 in.). The leaves of several species have winged midribs. Four species are evergreen. English Walnut (p. 236) also lacks leaf teeth. Tree-of-Heaven (Pl. 21) has only 2–4 basal leaf teeth.

TEXAS SOPHORA *Sophora affinis* Torr. & Gray   **PL. 24**

Deciduous and with thin, more or less *blunt-tipped* leaflets, this species occurs mainly from cen. to e. Texas. It barely penetrates adjacent portions of Okla., Ark., and La. Leaves 6–10 in. long

with 13–15 or more round-tipped or short-pointed leaflets ¾–1½ in. long and ¼–⅝ in. wide. Twigs green to brown; bundle scars 3. Buds *hidden,* surrounded by the leafstalk bases or erupting through the raised leaf scars. Trunk bark red-brown, scaly. Flowers white, ½ in. long, pealike, in 3–5-in. clusters, April–June. Fruit pods *beaded, black,* non-splitting, mostly 2–3 in. long, Sept.–winter. Height 18–20 ft.; diameter 8–10 in. Mostly limestone soils. **SIMILAR SPECIES:** The blunt leaflets of the *Sophoras* are distinctive among plants of this group. Though closely related, (1) Mescalbean Sophora has leathery evergreen foliage. In winter (2) Common Hoptree has evident buds, brown twigs, and a musky odor from crushed twigs.

MESCALBEAN SOPHORA PL. 24
Sophora secundiflora (Ort.) Lag. ex DC.

A *leathery-leaved evergreen* tree or shrub found mainly from w. to cen. Texas and south to cen. Mexico. Leaves 4–6 in. long with 5–9 *shiny, blunt-tipped* or notched leaflets, each ¾–2 in. long and ½–1 in. wide. Midribs *grooved.* Twigs greenish and sometimes hairy; buds hairy and *visible* in the leaf angles; leaf scars raised; bundle scars 3. Flowers purple, showy, and fragrant, March–April. Fruits stout, *brown,* rather woody, somewhat narrowed between the seeds, often hairy, 1–5 in. long and about ¾ in. wide. Seeds 3–4 (8), large, *red.* **SIMILAR SPECIES:** The shiny, wide, leathery, blunt leaflets are distinctive at all seasons. **REMARKS:** Also called Coralbean, a possible source of confusion with the thorny Southwestern Coralbean (Pl. 18). Often called Mountain-laurel in Texas, though unrelated to *Kalmia latifolia* L. of the e. U.S. The seeds, sometimes made into necklaces, can be poisonous both to people and livestock. Small amounts of powdered seeds, however, also are reported to have been added to mescal and imbibed by

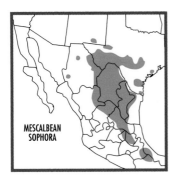

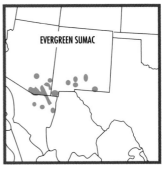

EVERGREEN SUMAC

MESCALBEAN SOPHORA

Native Americans during religious ceremonies. Mescal is an intoxicating drink made in desert areas from fermented juices of various century-plant (*Agave*) species.

EVERGREEN SUMAC *Rhus choriophylla* Woot. & Standl. **PL. 24**
A small evergreen tree or shrub of scattered localities on both sides of the international boundary from se. Ariz. to w. Texas. Leaves generally 2–3 in. long with 3–7 (usually 3–5) pointed or round-pointed, somewhat *leathery,* shiny, hairless leaflets. Leaflets 1–2 in. long, ½–⅞ in. wide, end leaflet long-stalked. Midribs *not* winged. Twigs brown or gray, hairless; leaf scars *elliptical,* raised. Flowers white or greenish, in terminal clusters, July–Aug. Fruits *red-hairy,* approx. ¼ in. in diameter, densely clustered. Height to 16 ft. **SIMILAR SPECIES:** Common Hoptree has larger and strictly 3-parted deciduous leaves, the end leaflet short-stalked and much lengthened. It also has U-shaped leaf scars. **REMARKS:** Also known as Mearns Sumac.

PRAIRIE SUMAC *Rhus lanceolata* (Gray) Britton **PL. 24**
Local throughout Texas and nearby areas. Leaves 5–10 in. long, divided into 11–23 mostly smooth-edged, *long-pointed* leaflets. Midrib *narrowly* winged (use lens). Leaflets shiny above, pale-hairy beneath, 1–3 in. long, *under ½ in. wide,* often curved. Twigs *stout,* with large pith, usually hairless. Buds hairy, partly surrounded by leafstalk bases or U-shaped leaf scars. Bundle scars many. End buds false. Flowers small, yellow-green, July–Sept. Fruits *red-hairy,* in dense upright cone-shaped clusters, present much of the year. Height 4–10 (30) ft.; diameter 1–3 (10) in. Dry, rocky soils. **SIMILAR SPECIES:** (1) Western Soapberry lacks winged midribs and has fruits yellow, single-seeded, and fleshy. (2) Com-

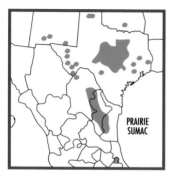

PRAIRIE
SUMAC

WINGED SUMAC

mon Hoptree has fewer leaflets, narrow pith, and only 3 bundle scars. See (3) Winged Sumac. **REMARKS:** Bark and leaves have been used to tan leather. Twigs cropped by deer and livestock; seeds eaten by bobwhite quail, prairie chickens, and many songbirds. Often considered a variety of Winged Sumac.

WINGED SUMAC *Rhus copallina* L.   **PL. 24**

Similar to Prairie Sumac but leaflets and midrib wings considerably *wider*. Leaves 5–14 in. with leaflets 2–4 in. long, *not* curved, and usually *over ½ in. wide*. Height 4–10 (30) ft. Open areas, e. U.S. west to cen. Texas. **REMARKS:** A "lemonade" can be made from the fruits. Alternate common names are Shining Sumac and Flameleaf Sumac.

COMMON HOPTREE *Ptelea trifoliata* L.   **PL. 24**

A wide-ranging shrub or small tree with thin, deciduous, 3-*parted leaves 4–10 in. long.* Foliage usually hairless but may be hairy beneath. Leaflets 1–4 in. long, ½–2 in. wide, short- or long-pointed, occasionally fine-toothed, and with pale gland dots. The end leaflet *short-stalked* with *prolonged narrow base.* Twigs brownish, hairless, with narrow pith; buds hairy and hidden in summer by

Common Hoptree

leafstalk bases; end bud false. Leaf scars *U-shaped*; bundle scars 3. Crushed leaves and twigs may emit a musky odor. Trunk bark rather smooth, light colored, shallowly grooved. Height 10–20 (25) ft.; diameter 2–10 (16) in. Flowers greenish, small, clustered, with an unpleasant scent, May–July. Fruits *flat, circular,* ¾–1 in. in diameter, papery, 2-seeded, Sept.–March. From forests of the East to mountain localities of w. Ariz., sw. Utah, and s.-cen. Mexico. **SIMILAR SPECIES:** Small specimens may be mistaken for (1) Poison-oak (*Toxicodendron diversilobium* (Torrey & Gray) Greene), but the end leaflet of that irritating shrub is long-stalked. (2) California Hoptree (Pl. 22) occurs only in that state and has round-toothed foliage. (3) Lemonade Sumac (Pl. 45) occasionally has trifoliate leaves, but these are thick, leathery, and evergreen. See also (4) Evergreen Sumac and (5) Texas Sophora. **REMARKS:** Fruits have been used as a substitute for hops (*Humulus*) in flavoring beer.

WESTERN SOAPBERRY
Sapindus drummondii Hook. & Arn. **PL. 24**

Leaves are 4–15 in. long with 8–18 *narrow, long-pointed, somewhat leathery* but deciduous leaflets, each 1–3 in. long and ¾–1 in. wide. End leaflet usually lacking but, if present, may remain in

Bark of Western Soapberry

WESTERN
SOAPBERRY

winter; leaflet halves mostly *unequal.* Twigs greenish gray and often somewhat hairy. Leaf scars triangular or 3-lobed, do not surround buds; bundle scars 3. Buds small, globose, hairy, 2-scaled, and partly embedded (use lens). Bark light gray to dark, scaly. Flowers white, clustered, May–June. Fruits ball-shaped, yellowish to white, ⅜–½ in. in diameter; Sept.–Oct. or longer. Height 20–50 (75) ft.; diameter 10–18 (24) in. Along watercourses or uplands, w. Ariz. and n. Mexico to Neb. and La. **SIMILAR SPECIES:** See Prairie Sumac. **REMARKS:** Pulp of clustered fruits forms lather in water but may act as a skin irritant yet, in Spanish it's called Jaboncillo (referring to soap). In India, the pounded fruit pulp of a related species is soaked in water and used as a shampoo. Reportedly poisonous if eaten. The buffaloberries (Pl. 17), with opposite silvery foliage, are also sometimes called soapberries.

BRAZILIAN PEPPERTREE   PL. 24
Schinus terebinthifolia Raddi

Introduced from the tropics, this ornamental tree is planted widely in warm areas. Leaves *evergreen* and 3–6 in. long with 3–11 leaflets, each 1½–3 in. long and ¾–1 in. wide. Leaflets *leathery* and rounded or short-pointed at the tip, wedge-based, sometimes wavy-toothed, increasing in width toward the leaf tips, and with a turpentine odor when crushed. Midrib *red* and narrowly *winged.* Twigs hairless, *not* drooping. Flowers small, yellow-white, in clusters at the leaf angles, summer. Fruits ⅛–³⁄₁₆ in. in diameter, *red,* 1-seeded, along the twigs, autumn–winter. Height to 20 ft. S. Calif., s. Ariz., and perhaps elsewhere. **SIMILAR SPECIES:** Peru Peppertree (Pl. 23) lacks red midribs and has drooping foliage plus leaflets shorter and less than ¼ in. wide. **REMARKS:** In s. Fla., Brazilian Peppertree is becoming a pest. Spreading vigorously from seeds and cuttings, it is displacing native species there. A popular plant for Christmas decoration.

SILK-OAK *Grevillea robusta* A. Cunn.   PL. 24

Not proven to reproduce in the wild but an attractive Australian tree planted in s. Calif., Ariz., and s. Fla. Leaves 6–12 in. long, *evergreen,* fernlike, with 3–16 *deeply lobed* leaflets usually white-silky beneath. Leaves sometimes partly twice-compound. Twigs and buds red-hairy; buds without scales. Flowers yellow and red, petals absent, in large clusters. Fruits ¾–1¼ in. long, podlike, splitting on one side. Height to 75 ft. Well-drained soils. **SIMILAR SPECIES:** The intricately lobed leaflets are unique. **REMARKS:** To 150 ft. tall and highly regarded as a timber tree in its native land. In this country, often grown as a potted plant.

THORNLESS SOUTHWESTERN TREES WITH ALTERNATE LEAVES TWICE-COMPOUND (PLATE 25)

All western trees with *twice-compound* leaves, except the introduced Chinaberry, are members of the pea-bean group of plant families. Thorny trees are shown on Pls. 19 and 20. The *thornless* species are on this plate. It should also be considered that some mesquites (Pl. 19) may have few thorns and Dwarf Poinciana (Pl. 20) is not always thorny.

Trees of this plate grow wild mainly in the southern half of Texas. Paradise Poinciana, however, and to a lesser extent Dwarf Poinciana, have escaped from plantings in the Mexican border region west to Calif. Littleleaf Lysiloma is native in s. Ariz.

Leaves large with leaflets either blunt or appearing to be. Except for Chinaberry, leaflets are not toothed, and trees are evergreen or nearly so. Twigs are hairless except for Paradise Poinciana. Flowers are either white or yellow (sometimes red in Dwarf Poinciana) and located at the twig ends. The leadtrees and Littleleaf Lysiloma have small blossoms in globular heads, while those of the poincianas are larger, showy, and in loose clusters. Fruits are flat and mostly hairless pea pods.

The first three species have markedly smaller minor leaflets than the last several.

GREAT LEADTREE
Leucaena pulverulenta (Schlecht.) Benth.

A locally common tree of extreme s. Texas with large, *fernlike* leaves. Leaves 4–10 in. with 14–20 pairs of major leaflets, each with 15–40 pairs of minor leaflets. Minor leaflets only about ³⁄₁₆

GREAT LEADTREE

LITTLELEAF LYSILOMA

in. long and $\frac{1}{32}$ in. *wide.* Twigs hairless; buds without scales. Trunk gray, scaly. Flowers *white,* fragrant, in *ball-shaped* clusters, March–June. Fruit pods 4–12 in. long. Height 40–60 ft.; diameter 12–20 in. Moist soils, lower Rio Grande Valley and south into Mexico. **SIMILAR SPECIES:** Great Leadtree has more major leaflets and the most finely divided minor leaflets of trees in this group. (1) Paradise Poinciana resembles the Great Leadtree most closely, but it has only 6–12 pairs of major leaflets, plus minor leaflets over $\frac{1}{16}$ in. wide. It also has hairy twigs and fruit pods. (2) Littleleaf Lysiloma is restricted to s. Ariz. and adjacent Mexico. (3) Guajillo (Pl. 20) is usually thorny and has only 5–12 major leaflet pairs. **REMARKS:** Common at Santa Ana Natl. Wildlife Refuge near Alamo, Texas. Local name is Tepeguaje (teh-peh-wah-hay).

PARADISE POINCIANA
PL. 25

Caesalpinia gilliesii (Hook.) Dietr.

A shrub or tree that is becoming established from s. Calif. to cen. Texas. Leaves 4–12 in. long with 6–12 pairs of major pinnae, each of which has 5–10 pairs of minor leaflets. Minor leaflets about $\frac{3}{16}$ in. long and $\frac{1}{16}$–$\frac{1}{8}$ in. wide. Twigs *hairy.* Flowers in *loose* end clusters, showy ($\frac{3}{4}$–1$\frac{1}{2}$ in. in diameter), yellow with long red stamens; summer. Fruit pods 2–4 in. long, *velvety.* Height to 15 ft. Dry soils. Also w.-cen. Mexico. **SIMILAR SPECIES:** The only member of this group with hairy twigs and fruit pods. See also Great Leadtree. **REMARKS:** Native of Argentina, widely planted and spreading along the Mexican-American border. To some people, it has an offensive odor. Also known as Bird-of-Paradise (but not the florists' Bird-of-paradise, *Strelitzia reginae* Banks, a nonwoody South African species). The genus was named after Andreas Caesalpinus, an Italian physician, while the species name honors John Gillies, an 18th-century botanist who discovered the plant.

LITTLELEAF LYSILOMA *Lysiloma microphylla* Benth.   **PL. 25**

A largely Mexican species that extends northward only to the Rincon Mts. of se. Ariz. Leaves 2–5 in. long with 4–9 pairs of major leaflets and 25–35 pairs of minor leaflets, each of the latter $\frac{3}{16}$ in. long and nearly $\frac{1}{16}$ in. wide. Flowers in globular heads, white. Fruit pods 4–8 in. Height rarely to tree size in the U.S. Rocky slopes, 3000–4000 ft. elevations from s. Mexico n. to Pima Co., Ariz. **SIMILAR SPECIES:** Among thornless Arizona trees with compound leaves, Western Kidneywood (Pl. 23) also has small minor leaflets. It has aromatic once-compound leaves, however, plus slender white flower clusters. **REMARKS:** Littleleaf Lysiloma is believed to be dying out in its American outpost because of colder winters. Sometimes called Feather-tree or Desert-fern.

MEXICAN LEADTREE

Leucaena leucocephala (Lam.) de Wit

An introduced tree with relatively wide minor leaflets and growing wild in some localities in s. Texas. Leaves 5–12 in. long with 4–8 pairs of major leaflets. Each major leaflet carries 11–18 pairs of minor leaflets ⅜–⅝ in. long, ⅛–¼ in. wide, and *pointed*. Minor leaflets are *without* abrupt leaf tip points. Flowers white, in round clusters. Fruit pods 4–6 in. long. Leaves 5–12 in. Height to 25 ft. Moist soils. **SIMILAR SPECIES:** Goldenball Leadtree has yellow blossoms and leaflets with small protruding tips. **REMARKS:** Believed to be native to the Yucatan region of Mexico but now widely established in the tropics. Known merely as Leadtree in s. Fla. Foliage is protein rich and sometimes harvested for livestock feed.

GOLDENBALL LEADTREE *Leucaena retusa* Benth. PL. 25

A plant of the mountains in w. Texas and n. Mexico and also in the western parts of the Edwards Plateau, cen. Texas. A shrub or small tree whose leaves are 3–8 in. long with only 2–4 (*usually* 3) pairs of major leaflets. Minor leaflets 4–9 (usually 3–6) pairs per pinna with each such leaflet ½–⅞ in. long and ⅜–½ in. wide. The wide minor leaflets mostly have evident *tiny tips* on the otherwise rounded foliage (use lens). Some leaflets may be notched at the end rather than with extended points. Flowers *yellow* in ball-like clusters, ¾ in. wide, April–Oct. Fruit pods dark, 3–10 in. long. Height to 25 ft., but rarely a tree in the U.S. Canyons. **SIMILAR SPECIES:** No other tree in this group has such leaflet tips or yellow, ball-shaped flower heads. **REMARKS:** Also called Littleleaf Leadtree. The leaves do tend to be shorter and the major leaflets fewer than in our other leadtrees. The minor leaflets, however, are larger.

GOLDENBALL LEADTREE

MEXICAN POINCIANA

MEXICAN POINCIANA *Caesalpinia mexicana* Gray PL. 25

Occurring in extreme s. Texas and ne. Mexico, this small tree has leaves 3–7 in. long, with 2–5 major leaflets, each divided into 3–5 pairs of minor leaflets. The minor leaflets are ½–⅝ in. long, ¼–⅜ in. wide, and *blunt-tipped.* Flowers yellow, showy, in groups of 10 to 30. Fruit pods 1–3 in. Height to 35 ft. Sandy soils. Also w.-cen. Mexico. **SIMILAR SPECIES:** (1) Goldenball Leadtree has tiny leaflet tips. (2) Dwarf Poinciana (Pl. 20) is mostly thorny, has larger leaves with more numerous minor leaflets, and longer bean pods. **REMARKS:** Sometimes cultivated as an ornamental.

CHINABERRY *Melia azedarach* L. **NOT SHOWN**

An Oriental tree typically found in dooryards in the se. U.S. west to s. and cen. Texas. It occasionally escapes to the wild. Leaves *deciduous,* 8–16 in. long, with 5–9 major leaflets and 3–7 (9) minor leaflets per major leaflet. Minor leaflets are unlike all other trees in this group, being *large, long-pointed,* and *coarse-toothed.* They are 1–3 in. long and ¼–1 in. wide. Twigs dark brown, stout with large leaf scars somewhat 3-lobed and containing 3 groups of bundle scars. Buds small and fuzzy. Flowers purplish, with an unpleasant odor, clustered, petals thin, May–June. Fruits *yellowish, ball-like,* ½ in. in diameter, usually present, internally *poisonous.* Height to 40 ft. **REMARKS:** Fruits have been used to make flea powder. They are known, too, to have paralyzed livestock and birds when eaten. Their bad taste may account for the few cases of human poisoning. The bark has been used illegally to stun fish.

BROAD-LEAVED TREES WITH ALTERNATE SIMPLE LEAVES
PLATES 26–46

About half of our trees fall in this category. Because so many species have alternate simple leaves, the group is separated into subdivisions. The outline below, which indicates the major characteristics used in dividing the group, may be used as a general guide to identification. A key to leafless plants with alternate leaf scars appears in Appendix A. Crapemyrtle (Pl. 17) has both opposite and alternate leaves. Camphortree (Pl. 30), Desert-willow (Pl. 39), Cascara Buckthorn (Pl 43), California Buckthorn (Pl. 45), and Bluegum Eucalyptus (Pl. 46) may have some opposite leaves.

1. Trees with thorny twigs or branchlets.   **Pls. 26–28**
1. Trees without thorns. 2
    2. Leaves fan-lobed or fan-veined.   **Pls. 29–31**
    2. Leaves feather-lobed or feather-veined. 3
3. End buds clustered, fruits acorns.   **Oaks Pls. 32–35**
3. End buds not clustered or, if so, then fruits not acorns. 4
    4. Buds with a single, smooth, caplike scale; leaves often narrow; bundle scars 3.   **Willows Pls. 36–38**
    4. Buds with at least 2 scales or none; leaves and bundle scars variable. 5
5. Leaves deciduous, mostly toothed.   **Pls. 39–44**
5. Leaves evergreen, mostly not toothed.   **Pls. 45–46**

LEAFLESS DESERT TREES WITH TWIGS SPINE-TIPPED BUT OTHERWISE THORNLESS (PLATE 26)

As adaptations to reduce water loss, the leaves of these arid-zone trees are tiny, mostly simple and scalelike, and they *quickly fall.* They are present only briefly, in spring. Twigs and branches are *greenish* and function like foliage in converting chemical nutrients into living materials.

This group is composed of thorny species that have only *spine-tipped* twigs. Related mostly leafless paloverdes with simple side thorns are on Pl. 20. Pls. 27–28 cover the thorny and mostly non-desert trees whose simple alternate leaves are present during much of the year.

Though this section of the book is devoted to species with *simple* leaves, Yellow Paloverde is an exception. With tiny compound leaves, it is included on this plate (as well as on Pl. 20) because its foliage is seldom present and it then resembles the simple-leaved species with thorn-tipped twigs.

ALLTHORN *Koeberlinia spinosa* Zucc. PL. 26

A species of n. Mexico that overlaps the international boundary from se. Calif. to s. Texas. Twigs *1–2 in. long, stout, greenish,* mostly *at right angles* to the branchlets, and tipped with thin *black thorns.* A variety in sw. Ariz., se. Calif., and adjacent Mexico has a more bluish green color as well as twigs longer, more slender, and arranged less regularly at right angles to the branchlets. Leaves only ¼ in. long and drop quickly. Flowers tiny, greenish white, in lateral clusters, May–July. Fruits shiny, black, ¼-in. globular *berries.* Trunk bark *greenish.* Height to 15 ft. Desert plains and slopes to 5000 ft. elevation. **SIMILAR SPECIES:** (1) Yellow Paloverde and (2) Crucifixion-thorn have dry fruits, and twigs not regularly at right angles to the branchlets. **REMARKS:** May form impenetrable thickets. Along with other prickly species, also known as Crucifixion-thorn. The generic name honors C. L. Koeberlin, a 19th-century German amateur botanist. Scaled quail eat the fruits; jackrabbits browse the twigs.

ALLTHORN

CANOTIA

Crucifixion-thorn

CRUCIFIXION-THORN *Holacantha emoryi* Gray   **PL. 26**

A small tree of desert plains and slopes to 2000 ft. elevation. Leaves very small and ephemeral. Twigs *yellow-green*, relatively stout, mostly 3–5 in. long, stiff, and sometimes fine-hairy. Leaf scars tiny, greenish white, scarcely distinguishable. Flowers reddish purple, about ¼ in. across, in dense clusters, June–July. Fruits in *starlike* rings of 5–10 flat, 1-seeded, dry bodies that remain on the plant for several years. Trunk bark greenish. Height to 15 ft. Watercourses and alluvial soils. **SIMILAR SPECIES:** Fruits are the best field mark. In their absence, the dark leaf scars usually present on (1) Canotia and (2) Yellow Paloverde twigs are lacking in this species. (3) Allthorn twigs are mostly only 1–2 in. long. **REMARKS:** Allthorn and Canotia are also frequently called Crucifixion-thorn. The age of fruit clusters often can be told by the degree of weathering. Lt. Col. William H. Emory discovered the species while in charge of the boundary survey after the Mexican war.

CANOTIA *Canotia holacantha* Torr.   **PL. 26**

The upper Mohave and Arizona deserts between 2000 and 5000 ft. elevation are the principal homes of this species. It ranges from extreme s. Utah through Ariz. to nw. Mexico. Twigs *slender, yellow-green*, 3–5 in. long, forked at *acute* angles and marked with *tiny, blackish,* mostly triangular leaf scars. The twigs also may show very *fine grooves* (use lens), often containing minute white wax particles. Flowers inconspicuous, greenish white, in small lateral clusters, May–Aug. Fruits dry, ¼ in. long, 5–10-parted capsules, remaining attached for some time. Trunk bark dark and shreddy; younger bark greenish. Height to 20 ft.; diameter to 1 ft. **SIMILAR SPECIES:** (1) Smokethorn also has slender twigs, but these are gray-green with brownish rather than black tiny leaf scars. In addition, they lack fine lines (use lens). (2) Yellow Paloverde twigs also lack fine grooves. **REMARKS:** Also called Crucifixion-thorn and Paloverde, names that are best reserved for other species.

SMOKETHORN *Psorothamnus spinosa* (A. Gray) Barnaby   **PL. 26**
Like the paloverdes, this tree is a legume. Unlike them but like the other trees of this plate, the ⅓-in. leaves are not compound. Twigs slender, densely covered with *very fine whitish hairs* (use lens), giving the plant a smoky appearance. Leaf scars *brownish.* Flowers purple, in small lateral clusters, June. Fruits tiny, 1-seeded pea pods. Trunk bark gray. Height to 25 ft. Desert washes. **SIMILAR SPECIES:** See Canotia. **REMARKS:** Conspicuous in blossom. Common in Joshua Tree Nat'l. Park, Calif. where it is called Smoketree (but see p. 358). Formerly in the genus *Dalea.*

Smokethorn

SMOKETHORN

Cercidium microphyllum (Torr.) Rose & Johnst.

Growing mainly along washes in the Sonoran desert of s. Ariz., se. Calif., and nw. Mexico, the upper trunk and branches are smooth and *yellow-green* (sometimes more green than yellow). Leaves only ¾–1 in. long with 4–8 pairs of tiny minor leaflets on each of its *single pair* of major leaflets. Twigs 3–6 *in. long,* moderately stout, *yellowish,* hairless, mostly 2–3 *in.* in length, and sharp-tipped. Dark leaf scars often sparsely dot the twigs. Flowers ⅜–1 in. across, showy, clustered, pale yellow, with the topmost petal often cream-colored, April–May. Fruits 2–4-in. *pea pods,* constricted between the seeds and with a prolonged tip. Height to 25 ft. Rocky slopes to 4000 ft. elevation. **SIMILAR SPECIES:** (1) Blue Paloverde (Pl. 20) grows in the same area but has blue-green trunk bark, thorns small and lateral, fruit pods flat and shorter. (2) Canotia, also with yellow-green bark, has flexible, fine-grooved twigs (use lens) with tiny flakes of white wax in the grooves. It differs also in having inconspicuous blossoms and 5-parted fruit capsules. **REMARKS:** Conspicuous when in flower. Also known as Foothill Paloverde. Paloverde means "green stick" in Spanish. The generic name is said to be derived from the Greek term for a

Bark of Yellow Paloverde

YELLOW PALOVERDE

weaver's spindle, based on the shape of the fruit. Native Americans have pounded the seeds into flour for food. Hybridizes with Blue Paloverde. Pronounced pay-low-VAIR-dee.

THORNY TREES WITH ALTERNATE SIMPLE LEAVES TOOTHED (Plate 27)

Most thorny species have compound leaves (Pls. 18–20). The remainder have simple leaves not toothed (Pls. 26 and 28). Only the nine trees on this plate regularly have both *thorns* and simple *toothed* leaves. In addition, however, Domestic Pear and Domestic Apple (Pl. 43) may occasionally have thorn-tipped twigs. Some oaks (Pls. 33, 34) plus Hollyleaf Cherry and American Holly (Pl. 44) have prickly leaf edges.

On this plate, the hawthorns have long single thorns seldom bearing buds or leaves. The introduced Jujube has similarly simple but paired thorns at the leaf bases. All other species have short side twigs or branches that are thorn-tipped and *also* tend to support leaves or buds. Only Hollyleaf Buckthorn is evergreen. Bundle scars are mostly 3 (1 in Jujube and Hollyleaf Buckthorn). Spur branches are frequent and occur in all species, and all have fleshy fruits, ranging from ¼ in. to 1 in. in diameter. All except Hollyleaf Buckthorn and Jujube are members of the rose family. Unlike some of the trees of Pl. 28, none of the trees of this group has either milky sap or twigs that alternate at right angles.

Hawthorns (*Crataegus* species, Pl. 27)

These plants, though distinctive as a group, tend to be indistinguishable as species except by the few botanists who have given the genus special study. Frequent hybridization complicated by great individual variation confounds accurate identification. Even the specialists vary greatly in their decisions regarding the validity of many forms. The number of species of *Crataegus* in the U.S. has been variously determined as more than 1000 and as fewer than 100. In this volume, therefore, no attempt is made to differentiate between the many hawthorn species. Thornless hawthorns are occasionally encountered.

BLACK HAWTHORN

In general, the hawthorns are a widespread group of shrubs or small trees with foliage dense, thorns ¼–2 in. long, and trunks smooth or scaly. Leaves small and coarse-toothed or shallowly lobed. Leafstalks *without* glands. Twigs hairless. Hawthorn spines are *long and slender,* mostly *without* buds or leaves. They occur on twigs as well as on older wood. Buds nearly spherical; end bud true. Bundle scars 3.

Flowers are small, white, and in twig-end clusters, spring. Fruits are small, red to nearly black, applelike, and mostly with *several* seeds. They often remain on the plants all winter, providing food for numerous birds and mammals, including ringneck pheasant, ruffed and sharptail grouse, gray fox, cottontail rabbit, and whitetail deer.

Apparently because of their density, hawthorns are much used for nesting by many songbirds. They are important honey plants but may become pests in pastures. They were formerly planted for fences in England. The name "haw" comes from the same root as *hedge.* Many varieties are used in landscaping. The species illustrated is Black Hawthorn (*C. douglasii* Lindl.), the most widespread of western hawthorns. SIMILAR SPECIES: Some crabapples and plums may have long thorns, but their thorns typically carry buds or leaves.

NATIVE CRABAPPLES (*Malus* SPECIES, PL. 27)

Crabapples have sharp leaf teeth, scaly *nonstriped* bark, blunt buds, a true end bud, 3 bundle scars, *no* glands on leafstalks, and *several-seeded* fruits. Often the leaves are somewhat *lobed.* Thorns occur on the older wood, rather than on the twigs, and usually *bear buds* or leaves. Spur branches common.

The following two crabapples are mostly thorny. They are the only native apples in our area. The domesticated apple and pear (Pl. 43) introduced from the Old World do escape to grow wild, however, and could be sharp-twigged. Hybrids between apple species are not rare and usually have intermediate characteristics. Botanists may use either *Malus* or *Pyrus* (and sometimes *Sorbus*) as the name for the genus.

OREGON CRABAPPLE *Malus fusca* (Raf.) Schneid.   PL. 27
A *coastal* species of the Northwest, extending from s. Alaska to nw. Calif. Leaves 2–3¼ in. long, egg-shaped to somewhat triangular, sharp-toothed, often shallowly *lobed* toward the tip, and leaf base U-shaped to square. Foliage usually *hairy,* at least on the midrib beneath. Twigs hairy. Flowers are white, about 1 in.

across, and clustered on spur branches, May–June. Fruits are somewhat *oblong*, ½–¾ in. long, becoming dark red, Aug.–Sept. Height to 30 ft. Forms thickets. **SIMILAR SPECIES:** Domestic Apple (Pl. 43) may be found where it appears to be wild. The leaves are more or less egg-shaped with many small rounded teeth. **REMARKS:** Oregon Crabapple fruits are eaten by ruffed grouse and by robins and other songbirds.

OREGON CRABAPPLE

PRAIRIE CRABAPPLE *Malus ioensis* (Wood) Bailey **NOT SHOWN**
Midwestern but also local on the Edwards Plateau, cen. Texas. Similar to Oregon Crabapple, but twigs and leaf undersurfaces *densely woolly.* Flowers April–May. Fruits green, ¾ in. in diameter, and bitter but make delicious jelly; eaten by many wildlife species. Thickets and open places.

WILD PLUMS (*Prunus* SPECIES, PL. 27)

Though the cherries, also in the genus *Prunus,* are never spiny, the plums are variously thorny or not. For cherries and usually thornless plums, see Pl. 42.

Some thorns of plums may be simple spines, but most are short, stiff, bud-bearing spur branches with sharpened tips. Thorns are generally present on branchlets and absent from twigs. Leaves are *fine-toothed* and hairless or nearly so. As on other species of *Prunus,* leafstalks or leaf bases of most plums (usually lacking in American Plum) bear small paired glands. The distinctive almond odor of broken twigs is less prominent in plums than in cherries. Unlike the end bud of cherries, that of wild plums is mostly regarded as *false,* though its status is not always easily determined. Bundle scars 3. Flowers white or pink, from lateral buds or spurs, in short clusters of 1–5, with or before the leaves. Wild plum fruits are small and ball-shaped, with *single,* large, and mostly somewhat flattened seeds. Bark often marked with horizontal *linelike* lenticels.

In the West, two rather *round-leaved* plums occur in coastal states while two *pointed-leaved* species extend from the e. U.S. into the plains states.

KLAMATH PLUM *Prunus subcordata* Benth. **PL. 27**

On rocky slopes from w. Ore. south to cen. Calif., this species occurs in the coastal ranges and the Sierra Nevada to 6000 ft. elevation. Leaves 1–3 in. long, egg-shaped to nearly round, leaf base often heart-shaped, glands occasional. Twigs usually hairless, with side twigs stubby and/or spine-tipped. Fruits ¼–½ in. in diameter, purple, sour, summer. Height to 25 ft. **SIMILAR SPECIES:** (1) Desert Apricot occurs southward and has leaves under 1 in. long. (2) Oregon Crabapple mostly ranges northward. It has several-seeded fruits and leaves that have rounded or square bases. (3) See Bitter Cherry (Pl. 42). **REMARKS:** Fruits may be eaten raw or made into jam and jelly. Deer and domestic sheep browse the twigs and leaves. Also called Sierra Plum.

DESERT APRICOT *Prunus fremontii* Wats. **PL. 27**

This arid-land shrub or small tree is found only in two or three of Calif.'s most southern counties and south into the Baja California states of Mexico. Leaves *fine-toothed,* hairless, ½–1¼ in. (mostly *under 1 in.*) long, often almost *circular,* and veins reddish. Twigs mostly short, stiff, and spine-tipped. Trunk mostly reddish brown, becoming grayer and scaly with age. Flowers white, Feb.–March. Fruits about ¼ in. in diameter, yellowish, *fine-hairy.* Height to 15 ft. Desert scrub and canyons to 4000 ft. elevation. **SIMILAR SPECIES:** No other thorny desert tree has fine-toothed deciduous leaves, but see Remarks on shrubby Spiny Hackberry under Jujube, p. 268. **REMARKS:** Fruits with only a thin layer of edible flesh.

AMERICAN PLUM *Prunus americana* Marsh. **PL. 27**

A somewhat *broad-leaved* shrub or small tree of the *northern* plains. Leaves 1–5 in. long, about *half* as wide as long, *dull-sur-*

faced, bases heart- to wedge-shaped, somewhat long-pointed, *sharply* and often *double-toothed.* Usually *no glands* on leafstalk or leaf base. Twigs hairy or hairless. Buds *narrow,* sometimes 2 or 3 at a node. Flowers about 1 in. across, 3–5 in clusters, April–June. Fruits red or yellow, ¾–1 in., seed somewhat *flattened,* Aug.–Oct. Height 15–30 (35) ft.; diameter 5–10 (14) in. Forms thickets, south to N.M. **SIMILAR SPECIES:** Chickasaw Plum is more southern and has leaves more narrow, finely single-toothed, shiny above, and with leafstalk glands present. Range overlap mainly Neb. and Okla. **REMARKS:** Several hundred varieties have been named. Some are cultivated. Fruits consumed by sharptail grouse, ringneck pheasants, and many songbirds.

CHICKASAW PLUM *Prunus angustifolia* Marsh.   **PL. 27**
A *narrow-leaved* shrub or small tree of the *southern* plains. Leaves 1–3 in. long, about ⅓ *as wide* as long, *shiny,* short-pointed, narrow-based with very fine, gland-tipped, *somewhat rounded single* teeth. Leafstalks bear small *glands.* Twigs *hairless;* buds about as *wide as long.* Flowers about 1 in. across, March–April. Fruits red to yellow, ½ in., seeds nearly *spherical,* July–Aug. Height to 20 ft.; diameter to 10 in. In thickets. **SIMILAR SPECIES:** See American Plum.

HOLLYLEAF BUCKTHORN *Rhamnus crocea* Nutt.   **PL. 27**
An *evergreen* shrub or small tree of Calif. and Ariz. with mostly small *prickly-edged* foliage. Leaves ¼–1 ½ in. long, almost *round, leathery,* and with the side veins rather markedly *parallel.* Side twigs often hairy, usually *spine-tipped;* side branches variably flexible or stubby. Buds scaly; bundle scar single. Flowers small, yellowish, in ¼–½-in.-long, widely branched clusters at the leafstalk bases, April–May. Fruits small, *red* at maturity, *berrylike;* seeds

AMERICAN PLUM

CHICKASAW PLUM

HOLLYLEAF BUCKTHORN

1–3; June–July. Height to 25 ft. Mountain slopes to 3500 ft. elevation. Range includes the Channel Is., s. Calif. **SIMILAR SPECIES:** (1) Hollyleaf Cherry (Pl. 44) of the coastal ranges has foliage that resembles that of this species. Its leaves, however, are more net-veined, usually larger, and mostly short-pointed. Also, woody thorns are lacking, and its flowers are white, in 2–4-in. slim clusters. (2) Prickly-leaved oak species (Pls. 33, 34) have clustered end buds, flowers in catkins, and acorn fruits. (3) Desert Apricot foliage is fine-toothed and deciduous. **REMARKS:** Browsed by mule deer and bighorn sheep. See general comments on buckthorns, p. 355.

JUJUBE *Ziziphus jujuba* Mill.   **PL. 27**

A native of s. Asia and se. Europe, escaped in states along the Gulf of Mexico west to cen. Texas. Shrub or small tree with ¼–¾-in. *paired* thorns at the leafstalk bases. Leaves 1–2¼ in. long, *shiny*, egg-shaped, short-pointed or somewhat blunt-tipped, with 3 *main veins* meeting at the leaf base. Twigs hairy, usually *green*; 1 thorn of pair generally much larger; spur branches large; bundle scar 1 or indistinct. Flowers tiny, greenish, March–May. Fruits red-brown at maturity, edible, seed single, July–Nov. Height to 50 ft. Forms thickets. **SIMILAR SPECIES:** Spiny Hackberry (*Celtis pallida* Torr.), a desert shrub also with leaves fan-veined, ranges from s. Ariz. to s. Texas and n. Mexico. It has thorns both single and paired and often at right angles. Its leaves are under 1 in. long and either without teeth or with a few wavy teeth. Bundle scars 3. Fruits dry. **REMARKS:** Sugared fruits are tasty; also known as Chinese Date. Called Granjeno (gron-HAY-no) in Spanish.

THORNY TREES WITH ALTERNATE SIMPLE LEAVES NOT TOOTHED (PLATE 28)

This distinctive group is mainly southwestern in distribution and marked by *smooth-edged* (occasionally few-toothed) and mostly *small* leaves *rounded* at the tips. They have thorns which, except for Osage-orange, often bear leaves or buds. *Spur branches* with clustered leaves are frequent. The first five species listed tend to have small, fragrant flower clusters. Of these, *Ceanothus* and

Bark of Greenbark Ceanothus

Condalia species bear stiff, spine-tipped twigs arranged in two planes to form a + when the branch is viewed from its end. The bumelias and Osage-orange have milky sap, apparent in warm weather at least, and usually seen in freshly broken leafstalks and/or twigs (caution: sap causes a rash in some people). Several desert trees of Pl. 26 also fall in this group but for most of the year are entirely leafless. Russian-olive (Pl. 39), with silvery leaves and twigs, may have spines present.

GREENBARK CEANOTHUS *Ceanothus spinosus* Nutt. **PL. 28**
Occurring naturally only in sw. Calif. and locally in nearby areas of Mexico, this is the only *Ceanothus* that is both tree-size and thorny. Leaves ⅜–1¼ in. long, *evergreen,* leathery, blunt-tipped with a *tiny point* (use lens). Foliage pale beneath; three main veins meet at the *U-shaped* leaf base. Sometimes a few teeth near the leaf tip. Side twigs short, stiff, arranged in *two planes* (alternating at right angles), and with *spiny tips.* Flowers small, pale blue or white, in elongate clusters at or near the twig ends, Feb.–May. Fruits dry, black capsules, ⅛–¼ in. across, with several seeds. Trunk bark *olive green,* smooth. Heartwood reddish. Height to 20 ft. A component of chaparral scrub on coastal mountains from San Luis Obispo Co. south to nw. Baja Califor-

nia Norte. **SIMILAR SPECIES:** This is the only thorny tree with simple fan-veined leaves not toothed. The tree-size condalias have leaves feather-veined, leaf bases wedge-shaped, flowers in small dense clusters at the leaf angles, and fruits 1-seeded, fleshy. **REMARKS:** Along with many other *Ceanothus* species, called California-lilac. Also known as Redheart. Since there are several dozen shrubby *Ceanothus* species, many of them thorny, still another common name, Spiny Ceanothus, is not distinctive. Browsed by deer. See remarks on *Ceanothus* species (p. 23).

BITTER CONDALIA *Condalia globosa* I. M. Johnst.   **PL. 28**

A *deciduous* tree of desert mountains. *Extremely spiny* with dense tangles of stiff, sharp-ended twigs. Leaves *blunt,* only ¼–½ in. long, ⅛–³⁄₁₆ in. wide, *wedge-based,* and usually hairy beneath. Branchlets with short twigs *alternating* at right angles and tipped with needle-sharp *blackish* spines. Flowers tiny, white, single or paired, at the leaf angles, March–April. Fruits black, rounded, ⅛–¼ in. in diameter. Height to 20 ft. Dry soils and near washes, to 2500 ft. elevation. **SIMILAR SPECIES:** Bluewood Condalia has larger leaves and does not range west of Texas. **REMARKS:** Often the home of nesting birds, who apparently find among the thorns both structural support for their nests and protection from predators. Fruits extremely bitter but said to be suitable for jelly. Wood yields a blue dye. Antonio Condal, a Spanish medical doctor, participated in an expedition to S. America in 1754.

BLUEWOOD CONDALIA   **PL. 28**
Condalia hookeri M. C. Johnst.

This condalia occasionally grows to tree size in cen. and s. Texas and in ne. Mexico. Leaves deciduous, ½–1½ in. long, ⅜–½ in. wide, *wedge-based,* with a *tiny point* projecting from the blunt tip

GUM BUMELIA

SAFFRON-PLUM BUMELIA

(use lens). Branchlets with twigs *alternating* at right angles. Twigs short, rather stiff, and mostly ending in sharp *spines*. Flowers greenish, in clusters of 2–4 at angles of the upper leaves, spring. Fruits dark, ³⁄₁₆–³⁄₈ in. across, not bitter, summer. Sandy soils. **SIMILAR SPECIES:** The several shrubby condalias of the area lack tiny leaf tips. See Remarks on shrubby Spiny Hackberry under Jujube (p. 268). **REMARKS:** Blue dye can be made from the wood. Also called Brazil.

GUM BUMELIA *Bumelia lanuginosa* (Michx.) Pers.   **PL. 28**
Distributed in the Miss. Valley and the se. states, this bumelia occurs also over most of Texas and ne. Mexico. A separate but more shrubby population is found in se. Ariz. and sw. N.M. Leaves *1–4 in. long,* wedge-based, leathery, and with a network of *raised* veinlets. Usually *rusty-* or *gray-hairy* beneath, but a hairless variety occurs from sw. Okla. and nw. Texas to w. and cen. Texas and n. Mexico. Foliage clustered on spurs and near twig tips. Evergreen in s. locations. Branchlets with small to medium-size spurs and usually with *both* ½–1 -in. thorns and long spine-tipped twigs. Twigs *hairy;* buds ball-shaped; bundle scars 3. Sap *milky.* Flowers small, white, in short rounded clusters at the leaf angles, April–July. Fruits ¼–½ in. long, shiny, black, fleshy, Aug.–Sept. or longer. Height to 40 ft. eastward, to 15 ft. in the Southwest. Moist to dry sites. **SIMILAR SPECIES:** Saffron-plum Bumelia has leaves less veiny, smaller, and hairless. Also, it is a fall-flowering species. **REMARKS:** Gum collected from freshly cut wood or at trunk wounds is sometimes chewed by children. Commercial chewing gum is derived from a related tropical species. Birds eat the fruits. Also called Woolly Bumelia. The word *lanuginous* means to be covered with soft hairs. Bumelia is the ancient Greek name for the European ash.

SAFFRON-PLUM BUMELIA *Bumelia celastrina* H.B.K. **PL. 28**
A tree of s. Texas, s. Fla., and the Caribbean. Leaves ½–2 *in. long,*
wedge-based, rather leathery, *evergreen,* and without a conspicuous network of small veins. Leaves often clustered on small spurs.
Branchlets with stiff, thorn-tipped side twigs. Buds hairy. Sap
milky. Flowers and fruits much as in Gum Bumelia but fruit more
edible. It blooms Oct.–Nov. with fruits maturing April–June.
Height to 20 ft.

LONGLEAF PEPPERTREE   **NOT SHOWN**
Schinus longifolius (Lindl.) Speg.
A small ornamental tree introduced from e.-cen. S. America and
naturalized in s. Texas. Also planted in s. Calif. Leaves *narrow,*
1–2 in. long, ⅛–¼ in. wide, not leathery, wedge-based, and tips
mostly blunt. Twigs *thin,* mostly 2½–5 in. long, *spine-tipped,* and
sometimes alternating in more or less right-angle planes. Flowers
whitish, in small clusters at the leaf angles. Fruits berrylike,
lavender, about ¼ in. in diameter. Height to 15 ft. **SIMILAR SPECIES:**
Twigs of the other spine-tipped species in this group are shorter
and more stout. **REMARKS:** Other peppertrees in our area have compound leaves (Pls. 23 and 24).

OSAGE-ORANGE *Maclura pomifera* (Raf.) C. K. Schneid.   **PL. 28**
A medium-sized tree. Leaves 1–8 in. long, egg-shaped, U-based,
somewhat *long-pointed.* Strong, bare, unbranched thorns ½–¾
in. long at each leaf scar. Sap *milky.* Wood *yellow.* Buds nearly
ball-shaped; end one false. Bundle scars 1 to 5. Flowers tiny,
greenish, in cylindrical leaf-angle clusters, May–June. Fruits
green, *much wrinkled, grapefruit-sized,* Oct. Bark orange-brown,
furrowed, tight, fibrous. Height 50–60 ft.; diameter 18–36 in. In
thickets; has spread widely, especially in e. and nw. U.S. **SIMILAR**

SPECIES: Osage-orange and the
bumelias are our only thorny
plants with milky sap. This
species differs from the bumelias in leaf shape and in having
bare thorns and shorter and
more rounded spur branches.
REMARKS: Once native in n.
Texas, se. Okla., and nearby
Ark., home of Osage Indians,
this species was widely planted
for living fences before the
invention of barbed wire. Because of its use in making

OSAGE-ORANGE

bows, the French name *bois d'arc* (colloquially "bodarc," "bodock") is still heard. Bark yields tannin; boiled wood chips yield yellow dye. William Maclure was an American geologist who lived from 1763 to 1840.

THORNLESS TREES WITH ALTERNATE FAN-LOBED LEAVES (PLATE 29)

There are not many thornless alternate-leaved trees with fan-lobed leaves. The mulberries (with milky sap) and fremontias (sap clear) have leaves that may be either fan-lobed or not. They are, in any case, fan-veined. White Poplar (Pl. 31) has white-woolly leaves that are often somewhat or even deeply fan-lobed. Cliffrose (Pl. 44) has tiny fan-lobed evergreen leaves, but the lobing is not obvious as such; they are here regarded as merely being toothed. The fan-lobed leaves of maples (see Pl. 15) are opposite, not alternate.

CALIFORNIA FREMONTIA PL. 29
Fremontodendron californicum (Torr.) Cov.

An *evergreen* tree or shrub principally of mountain slopes throughout Calif. but also in cen. Ariz. and Baja California Norte. Leaves only *1–2 in. long, leathery,* and with 1–3 main veins meeting at the leaf base. Usually with 3 (sometimes 5–7) lobes, occasionally with none. Lobes may be wavy-toothed. Leaf undersides *densely hairy.* Twigs stout, rusty-hairy; buds *without* scales; bundle scar 1. Flowers 1–2¼ in. across, petals absent, sepals *bright yellow* and petallike, showy, mostly on *spur branches,* May–June. Fruits 1–1¼ in. long, pointed, dry, hairy, egg-shaped capsules, Aug.–Sept. Height to 25 ft.; diameter to 12 in. **SIMILAR SPECIES:** See Mexican Fremontia. **REMARKS:** Member of the chocolate family. Some-

CALIFORNIA FREMONTIA

MEXICAN FREMONTIA

times called Flannelbush for its velvety foliage. Discovered by John C. Fremont, a 19th-century western explorer.

MEXICAN FREMONTIA   NOT SHOWN
Fremontodendron mexicanum A. Davidson
Similar to California Fremontia but leaves with 5–7 main veins and flowers *larger,* 2½–3½ in. across. Found naturally only in San Diego Co., sw. Calif., and in adjacent nw. Baja California Norte.

MULBERRIES

Leaves toothed and either lobed or not, both lobed and unlobed foliage usually present at the same time. Unlobed leaves generally heart-shaped. Three to five main veins meet near the end of the leafstalk. Sap of twigs and leafstalks *milky* (not always evident in winter twigs). More than 3 bundle scars per leaf scar, varying by species. End bud false. Fruits blackberrylike. Fibrous inner bark can be twisted into ropes and cords. Native Americans pounded the inner bark of local mulberries into bark cloth. Paper-mulberry, placed in a separate genus, has thin pith partitions at the leaf nodes.

TEXAS MULBERRY *Morus microphylla* Buckl.   PL. 29
This *small-leaved* mulberry is native from s. Okla. and Texas to Ariz. and is local in n. Mexico. Leaves *1–3 in. long,* sandpapery on *both* surfaces, often many-lobed, and sometimes heart-shaped at the base. Twigs *hairless* or nearly so; visible bud scales smooth, red-brown, 3–5; bundle scars 4 or more. Pith continuous. Flowers inconspicuous, March–April. Fruits blackish, fleshy, edible, May–June. Height to 20 ft.; diameter to 6 in. Thickets, rocky soils. SIMILAR SPECIES: Other mulberries have larger leaves not sandpapery on both sides. REMARKS: Fruits are eaten by many songbirds and by scaled, Gambel, and Mearns quail. Twigs are browsed by deer.

WHITE MULBERRY *Morus alba* L.   PL. 29
Leaves 3–10 in. long, hairless, and *not* sandpapery. Leaf bases often uneven, sometimes heart-shaped at the base. Foliage mostly 3–5-lobed but may be without lobes. Twigs *hairless* or slightly hairy. Buds *red-brown,* with 5–6 visible scales *lacking* darker scale borders. Bundle scars 4 or more. Pith *continuous.* Trunk bark *yellow-brown.* Height 30–60 (80) ft.; diameter 1–3 (4) ft. Flowers April–June. Fruits *whitish,* rather tasteless, June–July. A Chinese tree naturalized in the East and west to e. Colo. Bark *yellow-*

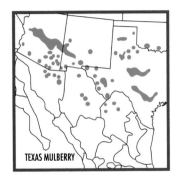

TEXAS MULBERRY

RED MULBERRY

brown. **SIMILAR SPECIES:** Other mulberries have sandpapery foliage. In winter, Red Mulberry may be separated by its greenish brown, dark-edged buds and red-brown bark. **REMARKS:** Introduced by the British in colonial times in an unsuccessful attempt to establish a silkworm industry.

RED MULBERRY *Morus rubra* L. PL. 29

Similar to White Mulberry but leaves somewhat *sandpapery* above and hairy beneath, bases usually even. Buds *greenish brown,* with 5–6 bud scales mostly *with* darker scale borders. Trunk bark *red-brown.* Fruits red-black, tasty. Lowlands, e. U.S. west to w. Okla. and cen. Texas. **SIMILAR SPECIES:** See (1) White Mulberry and (2) Paper-mulberry. **REMARKS:** Fruits eaten by squirrels and numerous song and game birds as well as by humans.

PAPER-MULBERRY *Broussonetia papyrifera* (L.) Vent. PL. 29

A medium-sized tree with *sandpapery* leaves and twigs. Leaves 4–11 in. long, fine-toothed, varying from unlobed and heart-shaped to deeply and intricately *lobed.* Leaves sandpapery above and velvety below, often with uneven bases. Twigs *rough-hairy;* buds with only 2–3 visible scales; bundle scars 4 or more. Pith blocked by a thin *woody partition* near each bud. Bark a *yellow-brown* smooth network of fine ridges. Height to 50 ft.; diameter to 4 ft. Flowers April–May. Fruits red, fleshy, barely edible, Sept. Widespread but local; found in hedgerows. **SIMILAR SPECIES:** (1) White Mulberry has smooth leaves while (2) Red Mulberry has less rough upper leaf surfaces. Both of these species have continuous pith and 5–6 bud scales. **REMARKS:** Introduced from Asia. There the inner bark once was used as paper. In the S. Pacific, the inner bark is hammered into cloth. P. M. A. Broussonet was a French naturalist of the late 18th century.

SYCAMORES (*Platanus* SPECIES)

Large floodplain and lowland trees with distinctive light green, whitish, or mottled bark that flakes off in irregular puzzlelike pieces, exposing *yellowish and whitish underbark*. Leaves 4–1 o in. long, nearly hairless, 3- *or 5-lobed,* sometimes toothed. Leafstalk bases *hollow,* covering buds; leaf scars *surround* buds. Pith continuous. Buds hairless and covered by a *single* scale; end bud false. Bundle scars many. A single, saucerlike, leafy, toothed stipule clasps and encircles twig at points of leaf attachment; stipule scars *ring* winter twigs. Flowers small, in *globose* heads, April–June. Fruits small and hairy, in tight, brown, long-stalked, hanging balls, ¾–1 ½ in. in diameter, Oct. and often through winter. Old World sycamores, often planted in cities, are called Plane-trees. They usually have 2 (London Plane, *Platanus acerifolia* Willd.) or more (Oriental Plane, *P. orientalis* L.) fruit balls per stalk and have more yellowish underbark. Hard coarse-grained wood used for boxes, barrels, butcher blocks, cabinetwork, and furniture. Native Americans in the East used trunks for dugout canoes. One such canoe reported to have been 65 ft. long and to have weighed 9000 pounds. Twigs eaten by deer and muskrats.

Bark of California Sycamore

CALIFORNIA SYCAMORE

Trunk and branch cavities sought for nests and shelter by wood ducks and raccoons.

CALIFORNIA SYCAMORE *Platanus racemosa* Nutt.   **PL. 29**
Occurs throughout Calif. and into Baja California Norte. Leaf lobes 3–5, rather narrow, sharply pointed, *mostly toothed,* and somewhat hairy beneath. Leaf sinuses extend about *halfway* to the leaf bases. Fruit balls 3–7 per stalk. Stream banks and canyons to 4000 ft. elevation.

ARIZONA SYCAMORE *Platanus wrightii* S. Wats.   **PL. 29**
Sometimes considered to be only a variety of California Sycamore but with 5–7 deep leaf lobes and *not toothed.* Leaf sinuses extend *more than halfway* to the leaf bases. Fruit balls mostly 3–5 per stalk. Trunk and large branches often almost completely white. Floodplains and valleys, at elevations of 2000–6000 ft.; in Ariz., sw. N.M., and nw. Mexico.

EASTERN SYCAMORE *Platanus occidentalis* L.   **NOT SHOWN**
Like sycamores of the Southwest but leaves *toothed,* hairless, and with 3–5 *shallow* sinuses. Fruit ball *single.* Damp soils, w. to cen. Texas. **REMARKS:** Eastern Sycamore is generally conceded to be the most massive tree of the e. U.S., but unlike the long-lived sequoias, redwoods, and bristlecone pines of Calif., it is old at 500–600 years.

CHINESE PARASOLTREE   **PL. 29**
Firmiana simplex (L.) W. F. Wight
An Asian tree of the chocolate family, planted for ornament and locally growing wild. Long-stalked leaves 6–12 in. long, *sycamore-like,* with 3–5 lobes, *shallow* sinuses, and *no teeth.* Foliage occa-

sionally somewhat hairy. Twigs *stout,* mostly *green,* and *not* ringed; pith large. Buds nearly round, hairy, with 2–3 scales, the end bud large. Leaf scars large, elliptical; bundle scars in an ellipse, single or indistinct. Flowers small, in greenish yellow clusters mostly at twig ends. Fruits leathery capsules 2–4 in., opening into 5 leaflike sections. Dark fluid released when capsule opens. Bark smooth, dark gray-green. Height to 35 ft. Thickets and woods.

SWEETGUM *Liquidambar styraciflua* L.   **PL. 29**

A tall tree of the e. U.S. and mountains of ne. Mexico. Leaves *star-shaped,* with 5–7 lobes, toothed, hairless, 5–8 in. long, pleasantly fragrant when crushed. Twigs not ringed; branchlets often *corky-winged.* Stubby spur branches densely covered by leaf scars or crowded leaves. Bud scales 6 or so, glossy and hairy-fringed; end bud true. Bundle scars 3. Pith *continuous.* Mature bark grayish, regularly grooved. Height 50–120 (140) ft.; diameter 3–4 (5) ft. Flowers in spherical heads, April–May. Fruits in brown, dry, somewhat *prickly, long-stemmed hanging balls,* Sept.–Nov. or longer. Landscape plantings in the West. **SIMILAR SPECIES:** None in summer. In winter, twigs of (1) Bur Oak (Pl. 35) and (2) some elms (Pl. 41) also may have corky wings. Bur Oak has clustered end buds. Elms have a false end bud; their bud scales often have dark borders without a hairy fringe. **REMARKS:** Both the common and scientific names allude to the sap that exudes from wounds. Hardened clumps of this gum are chewed by some people. Veneer made from Sweetgum wood takes a high polish and is widely used for furniture. Lumber also used for interiors, boats, toys, boxes, and fuel. The fruits are often painted and used to decorate Christmas trees. The seeds are eaten by many kinds of wildlife, including songbirds, bobwhite, wild turkey, chipmunks, and gray squirrel.

TULIPTREE *Liriodendron tulipifera* L.   **PL. 29**

A tall, straight tree of the e. U.S. Leaves 6–10 in. long, uniquely *4-pointed,* and hairless. Pairs of large leafy stipules attach to twigs and enclose buds. Twigs hairless, with *encircling lines* (stipule scars) at leaf scars. Only 2 bud scales cover the end bud; side buds small or indistinct. Crushed buds and leaves smell *spicy;* bundle scars more than 3. Pith *chambered.* Flowers large, *tulip-like,* orange and green, May–June. Fruits slim, dry, winged, whitish, 1–2 in., clustered upright in conelike structure about 3 in. long, Sept.–Nov. or longer; often central stalks of cones remain throughout winter, evident on higher limbs. Trunk light gray, *often whitened* in grooves and in patches on younger bark.

Height 50–100 (190) ft.; diameter 2–6 (10) ft. Plantings, Pacific coastal areas. **SIMILAR SPECIES:** None; distinctive at all seasons. **REMARKS:** Tallest and in many ways the handsomest eastern forest tree. Second only to Sycamore in trunk diameter. Wood straight-grained, fine, soft, resistant to splitting, and easily worked. Used for furniture, interiors, shingles, boats, implements, boxes, toys, pulp, and fuel. Native Americans made trunks into dugout canoes. Seeds eaten by squirrels and songbirds. Though widely known as Yellow Poplar and Tulip Poplar, this relative of magnolias is not closely related to true poplars (Pl. 31).

THORNLESS TREES WITH ALTERNATE SIMPLE LEAVES FAN-VEINED (Plate 30)

Several genera of thornless trees have alternate leaves not lobed and with 3 *or more main veins meeting at the leaf bases.* In addition to the trees of this plate, some leaves of fremontias and mulberries (Pl. 29) and poplars (Pl. 31) are of this type. Jujube (Pl. 27) and Greenbark Ceanothus (Pl. 28) are thorny trees with fan-veined foliage.

CALIFORNIA REDBUD *Cercis occidentalis* Torr. ex Gray **PL. 30**
Before the leaves appear in spring, this ornamental tree produces dense clusters of showy, ½-in.-long, red-purple, pea-type flowers that outline the twigs. Leaves heart-shaped to *nearly round,* deciduous, *without teeth,* 2–5 in. long and nearly as broad, leathery, smooth, hairless or nearly so, with 7–9 main veins meeting at the deeply notched base. Leafstalks mostly *less than 1 in. long.* Twigs hairless. Buds many-scaled, raised; end one false. Leaf scars on vigorous twigs usually with 2, sometimes 3, long descending lines. Bundle scars 3. Pith continuous. Flowers March–

May, occasionally white. Fruit pods 2–3 in. long, mostly ⅝–¾ in. wide, brown when mature, July–Aug. or longer. Height to 20 ft.; diameter to 6 in. Foothills, canyons, and slopes to 6000 ft. elevation from n. Calif. and s. Utah to s. Calif. and s. Ariz. **SIMILAR SPECIES:** Leaves distinctive. In winter, the combination of 3 bundle scars, buds with many scales, and lines on twigs distinguish it from unrelated species of this group. Eastern Redbud has long-pointed leaves, longer leafstalks, and thinner fruit pods. **REMARKS:** Blossoms, not buds, reddish. Flowers sometimes eaten in salads; red roots yield a dye. An exceptional legume species that does *not* harbor nitrogen-fixing root bacteria.

EASTERN REDBUD *Cercis canadensis* L. NOT SHOWN

A tree of the e. U.S. with range extensions into w. Texas and, locally, N.M. It is planted for ornament elsewhere in the West. The typical form is much like California Redbud but leaves are *long-pointed,* heart-shaped, and *not* leathery. Leafstalks are mostly over 1¼ in. long. A variety of the eastern species known as Texas Redbud (*C. canadensis* var. *texensis* [Wats.] Hopkins) also has leathery leaves, however, that appear remarkably like those of California Redbud. In Texas and Okla. this variety may grow along with typical Eastern Redbud. Fruit pods are *less than ½ in. wide* in both Eastern Redbud and its Texas variety but *over ⅝ in. wide* in California Redbud.

CAROLINA BASSWOOD *Tilia caroliniana* Mill. PL. 30

The basswoods are a group of eastern trees. Of these, Carolina Basswood extends west to cen. Texas. Leaves 3–6 in. long, 2–3 in. wide, *fine-toothed,* smooth, thin, deciduous, more or less *heart-shaped,* often uneven-based, and either somewhat hairy or hairless beneath. Twigs hairless; when cut with a knife, the inner bark can be pulled away in a *fibrous* strip. Buds green to red with 2–3 visible scales; end bud false. More than 3 bundle scars per leaf scar. Pith continuous. Flowers small, yellowish, fragrant, June–Aug. Fruits are small, tan, spherical nutlets clustered beneath slim, leafy wings that act as spinning parachutes when fruits are ripe, Aug.–Oct. Fertile soils. **SIMILAR SPECIES:** The few-scaled buds

CAROLINA BASSWOOD

and tough inner bark are good field marks. Basswood fruits are unique. **REMARKS:** As with mulberries, elms, and some other species, the fibrous inner bark, especially of roots, can be twisted into cords, mats, and lines. Buds and fruits eaten by prairie chickens, bobwhite quail, squirrels, and chipmunks; twigs browsed by deer and rabbits. Important honey plant.

HACKBERRIES (*Celtis* Species)

Rather distinct as a group but with such great variation between individuals that the several species often seem to merge into each other. All western hackberries tend to have triangular, *long-pointed, uneven-based,* short-stalked, and often *sandpaper-textured* leaves. Leaf edges usually lack teeth or have only a few. Pith usually *chambered* throughout the twig but sometimes partitioned only near the leaf scars. Bundle scars 3. Flowers inconspicuous, developing into small, round, brownish, 1-seeded fruits. These usually covered by a thin, sweet, somewhat edible layer; the trees consequently often called Sugarberries. Fruits of some species dry with a wrinkled surface, a feature that may reflect a thicker fleshy covering. Trunk bark has characteristic dark *warty knobs*

Bark of Netleaf Hackberry

NETLEAF HACKBERRY

and ridges. See also remarks on Spiny Hackberry under Jujube (p. 268).

Although the thornless hackberry species do not always display clear-cut identifying marks, ideally distinctions are as marked on the comparison chart opposite Pl. 30.

NETLEAF HACKBERRY *Celtis reticulata* Torr.   **PL. 30**

Like the next species with leaves *wide* (about half the leaf length), somewhat *leathery*, strongly net-veined beneath, and with *few* teeth or none. Leafstalks about ⅛–¼ in. long. In this species the leaves are 2–3 in. long and *green* beneath. Twigs hairy. Fruits remain *smooth* upon drying and fruitstalks mostly *longer* than leafstalks. Height to 50 ft.; diameter to 2 ft. A southwestern species that ranges deep into n. Mexico but apparently is not known from s. Texas. It occurs locally elsewhere in the West. Watercourses and hillsides. Fruits were formerly eaten by Native Americans.

SOUTHERN HACKBERRY *Celtis laevigata* Willd.   **PL. 30**

This species of the southeastern states ranges west through much of Texas. It differs from Netleaf Hackberry in that the leaves are mostly 2–4 *in.* long and the fruitstalks average *shorter* than the ¼–½-*in.* leafstalks. Fruits are generally *smooth* upon drying. Height to 100 ft. in favorable locations. Streamsides and moist soils. Eaten occasionally by wild turkeys.

LINDHEIMER HACKBERRY   **PL. 30**
Celtis lindheimeri Engelm. ex K. Koch

Found only in s. Texas and Coahuila, Mexico, this small tree is similar to Netleaf Hackberry but the leaves are *narrow*, about ⅓ as wide as long with *pale, soft-haired* undersides and leafstalks ¼–½

NORTHERN HACKBERRY

BLUEBLOSSOM CEANOTHUS

in. long. Fruits *wrinkled* when dry with stalks shorter than leaf-stalks. Height to 35 ft.; diameter to 6 in. Called Palo Blanco in Spanish.

NORTHERN HACKBERRY *Celtis occidentalis* L.   PL. 30
An eastern tree extending west to the Great Plains from N.D. to Okla; cultivated elsewhere. Leaves 3–5 *in. long,* usually thin and *not* leathery, with teeth *numerous.* Twigs hairless. Fruitstalks *longer* than the ¼–½-in. leafstalks, and fruits *wrinkle* upon drying. Height 20–70 (100) ft.; diameter 1–3 (4) ft. Streamsides. Fruits eaten by many songbirds and game birds.

Ceanothus SPECIES

This is a large and mainly shrubby genus, principally western in distribution. In Calif. alone, 43 species are listed, predominantly components of the brushy vegetation type commonly called chaparral. Three thornless species regularly reach tree size. Though some shrubby species have opposite and often deciduous leaves, the foliage of our trees is alternate and *evergreen.* Bundle scar 1. Flowers small, in many-flowered dense clusters. Fruits small, dark, more or less 3-lobed, several-seeded capsules. *Ceanothus* species are unusual in that, though not legumes, they nevertheless possess nitrogen-fixing root nodules. *Ceanothus* plants are often called Wild-lilac. Greenbark Ceanothus, a thorny tree, is on Pl. 28.

BLUEBLOSSOM CEANOTHUS   PL. 30
Ceanothus thyrsiflorus Eschsch.
Occurring on the outer slopes of the coastal ranges from sw. Ore. to Santa Barbara Co., Calif., this tree is a member of both forest

and chaparral plant communities. Leaves evergreen, 1–2½ in. long, fine-toothed, mostly *narrowly elliptical* in outline, often blunt, even-based, dark green, and *mostly hairless* beneath, with the 3 main veins much raised and conspicuous. Twigs green, *angled* or ridged, hairless (use lens). Flowers light to dark blue, sometimes white, April–June. Fruits black, sticky, with 2–3 seeds, July–Dec. Height to 20 ft. Forms thickets; especially invading cut-over and burned areas. **SIMILAR SPECIES:** (1) Feltleaf and (2) Snowbrush ceanothuses have wide leaves and nonridged twigs. **REMARKS:** Browsed by deer and elk. Flowers reported to wash into a soapy lather.

SNOWBRUSH CEANOTHUS   NOT SHOWN
Ceanothus velutinus var. *laevigatus* (Hook) T. & G.

Much like Blueblossom Ceanothus but with leaves 2-5 *in. long, broadly* oval, shiny above, *pale* beneath, thick, gummy, and aromatic. Twigs *rounded* and ± hairless. Flowers white. Typically a shrub throughout much of the West, this variety grows to be a tree up to 20 ft. tall in the coastal ranges from cen. Calif. to cen. B.C. Known also as Sticky-laurel, Mountain-balm, and Varnish-leaf Ceanothus.

FELTLEAF CEANOTHUS   NOT SHOWN
Ceanothus arboreus Greene

Growing wild in the chaparral of Santa Catalina, Santa Cruz, and Santa Rosa islands, offshore s. Calif., this species has *broad,* toothed leaves that are mostly *whitish and soft-hairy* beneath. Leaves 1½–3 in. long, 1–2 in. wide, and *pointed.* Twigs hairy, not angled. Flowers pale blue, Feb.–March. Fruits rough, blackish, Aug.–Sept. **SIMILAR SPECIES:** See Blueblossom Ceanothus.

CAMPHORTREE *Cinnamomum camphora* (L.) J. S. Presl.   **PL. 30**
Escaped from cultivation in s. Texas and planted for shade and ornament in s. Calif. and other warm areas. Leaves leathery, *evergreen,* 2–6 in. long, 1–2 in. wide, and wavy-edged or not toothed. Some may be opposite, but all leaves are short- or long-pointed at *both* ends and emit a *camphor odor* when crushed. *Glands* can be seen (use lens) in the vein angles on leaf undersides. There are 3 main veins from the leaf base. Leaf edges sometimes curled and wavy. Twigs *green,* buds scaly, bundle scar 1. Flowers small, yellow, 1–3-in. clusters, spring. Fruits blue-black, ⅜ in. in diameter, 1-seeded, in a greenish cup. Height to 40 ft.; diameter to 2 ft. **REMARKS:** A native of Asia. Distillation of the leaves and wood produces the oil used in medicine and industry. Becoming naturalized also in Fla. and La.

POPLARS, INCLUDING ASPENS AND COTTONWOODS (PLATE 31)

The poplars, aspens, and cottonwoods are all members of the genus *Populus*. The leaves are mostly toothed and (except Narrowleaf Cottonwood) somewhat triangular, with 3–5 *main veins meeting near the leaf base*. Most poplars tend to have unusually long leafstalks. In some species these are *flattened* near the leaf blade so that the leaves flutter even in a slight breeze.

Poplar buds are often long-pointed, and it is characteristic that the lowermost bud scale is directly above the leaf scar. The end bud is true and may have more scales than side buds. The bark of most species is distinctively smooth and greenish white when young and dark-furrowed when older. The twigs are mostly hairless and often sharply angled (somewhat ridged). Bundle scars 3 or in three groups. Spur branches occasional. Flowers of poplars are in long, clustered, caterpillarlike catkins that appear in early spring and soon release hairy, cottonlike fruits. These are "caught" by and germinate on moist soils. The sexes are separate (but female Lombardy Poplars are unknown).

Distributed widely in the northern hemisphere, trees of the poplar group may form extensive forests on barren, burned, or cleared areas. Fast-growing, mostly short-lived species, they are of most value as paper pulp, though some of their soft lumber is used in construction work and in the manufacture of boxes and woodenware. Some kinds are of value as ornamentals and windbreaks. In dry country, cottonwoods indicate the presence of underground water near the surface. Seeds, buds, and twigs are important foods of numerous birds and mammals, including ruffed, spruce, and sharptail grouse, prairie chicken, whitetail

Quaking Aspen

deer, elk, moose, porcupine, snowshoe hare, cottontail rabbit, and black bear. Beavers consume the inner bark and use the branches in dam and lodge construction.

QUAKING ASPEN *Populus tremuloides* Michx.   **PL. 31**
A medium-sized transcontinental species with the most widespread distribution of any N. American tree. Leaves 2–6 in. long, with *flattened* leafstalks. Blades nearly *circular,* without leaf-base glands and edged with 20–40 pairs of *fine teeth.* Twigs hairless and dark brown; end bud shiny, ¼–⅜ in. long. Young bark mostly *smooth, chalk white to yellow-green;* old trunks dark and fissured near the tree base. Height 20–50 (75) ft.; diameter 1–2 (3) ft. Varied open sites. **Similar species:** (1) Fremont Cottonwood has fewer and larger leaf teeth, a longer end bud, and dark furrowed bark. (2) Lombardy Poplar has dark bark, yellow twigs, leaves that are more heart-shaped or triangular, and a tall, slender silhouette. (3) Paper Birch (Pl. 41), with white trunk and often growing in the same habitat, has peeling and finely cross-striped bark. **Remarks:** Becomes golden yellow in autumn. Reproduction by root sprouts is frequent. Vegetative clones often spread over considerable areas; some groves have been calculated to live 10,000 years. Widely known as Popple and Trembling Aspen.

TALLOWTREE *Sapium sebiferum* (L.) Roxb.   **NOT SHOWN**
A Chinese tree reported to be spreading in the lower Rio Grande Valley of Texas. Leaves *aspenlike,* 2–6 in. long, pointed at both ends, and not toothed (sometimes wavy-edged). Leafstalks *not* flattened, with paired glands at the leaf base. Twigs green, bundle scars 3 or indistinct. Sap milky, *poisonous* if rubbed in the eyes or taken internally. Flowers small, greenish, at twig ends, spring; fruits ¼-in. waxy capsules splitting to show 3 white seeds on a

Fremont Cottonwood

central stalk. Introduced into se. U.S. for making soap and candles. Foliage turns red in autumn. Also called Popcorntree for the white seeds and Milktree for the white sap. Not a poplar.

FREMONT COTTONWOOD

Populus fremontii Wats.

A tree of the Southwest, growing along watercourses and on other moist sites. Leaves are 2–5 in. long, broadly *triangular, coarsely toothed, without* glands, often with a tapering point, and sometimes hairy beneath. Leafstalks are *flattened.* Twigs *yellowish,* hairless; buds also hairless, end bud ⅜–½ in. long and not gummy. Mature bark *dark,* thick, with deep furrows. Height 50–75 (100) ft.; diameter 1–3 (4) ft. Mostly below

Bark of Fremont Cottonwood

6500 ft. elevation. **SIMILAR SPECIES:** (1) Quaking Aspen has fine-toothed circular leaves and brown twigs. (2) Black Cottonwood has rounded leafstalks and gummy buds. (3) Eastern Cottonwood has coarse-toothed foliage, leaf glands, and gummy buds. (4) Lombardy Poplar has a slender, steeplelike outline. **REMARKS:** Common and scientific names both honor Col. John C. Fremont, the famous western explorer. The Spanish name for cottonwood is *alamo.*

NARROWLEAF COTTONWOOD   PL. 31
Populus angustifolia James

Willowlike in appearance and habitat but with whitish upper bark and shiny *several-scaled* buds. Mainly found in the Rocky Mts., the *slender foliage* is unique among our poplars. Leaves 3–5 in. long and only about a *third* as wide, fine-toothed, feather-veined, and without glands. Leafstalks ± rounded but *flattened* on top and only ⅜–1 *in. long.* Twigs yellowish, hairless; end bud ¼–½ in. long and quite *sticky.* Trunk bark rather smooth and whitish, becoming darker and furrowed. Height to 60 ft.; diameter to 1½ ft. Along watercourses and on other sometimes-wet sites. **SIMILAR SPECIES:** No other poplar has such narrow leaves and short leafstalks. (1) Black Cottonwood and (2) Balsam Poplar have rounded leafstalks

Narrowleaf Cottonwood

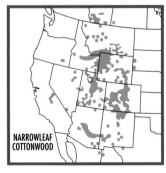

NARROWLEAF
COTTONWOOD

and buds spicy-scented when crushed, while (3) Eastern Cottonwood has glandular leafstalks and a larger end bud. (4) Quaking Aspen and (5) Fremont Cottonwood do not have sticky buds. (5) Willows (Pls. 36–38) have nonsticky single-scale buds. **REMARKS:** The most abundant tree along many central Colorado streams. Also called Lanceleaf Cottonwood. Hybridizes with Eastern Cottonwood where the ranges meet.

LOMBARDY POPLAR *Populus nigra* var. *italica* Muenchh. **PL. 31**

An imported, tall, thin, *steeplelike* tree much used to border gardens and for windbreaks. Leaves 2–8 in. long, *fine-toothed,* without glands. Leafstalks *flattened.* Twigs hairless, yellowish; end bud less than ⅜ in. long and *not* gummy. Bark furrowed, rather dark. Height 30–70 (100) ft.; diameter 1–2 (3) ft. Sometimes escapes from plantings. **SIMILAR SPECIES:** The narrow, columnar growth form is distinctive. **REMARKS:** Believed to have arisen as a genetic mutation in Italy during the 1700s. All trees are male. Reproduction is from cuttings and sprouts.

BLACK COTTONWOOD **PL. 31**
Populus trichocarpa Torr. & Gray

Ranging primarily south along the Pacific slope from s. Alaska to Baja California Norte, this species also is distributed inland to the n. Rockies. Leaves 4–8 in. long, including 1–2½-in. stalks that are *not* flattened. Leaf blades dark green above and pale to *silver-white beneath* (the contrast being especially visible during wind gusts); leaves more or less *triangular,* fine-toothed, *hairless,* and often with basal glands. Young leaves more slender. Twigs brownish, hairless; end bud ¾–⅞ in. long, *gummy* and *spicy-scented* when crushed. Fruit capsules *3-parted.* Height 60–80 (165) ft.; diameter 2–3 (9) ft. Floodplains and other moist soils. **SIMILAR SPECIES:** (1) Quaking Aspen, (2) Eastern Cottonwood, and (3) Fremont Cottonwood may have overlapping ranges with Black Cottonwood in some areas. All have flattened leafstalks, however, and end bud under ¼ in. long. (4) White Poplar has white-woolly foliage and twigs. (5) Balsam Poplar,

also with rounded leafstalks and sticky, spicy buds, overlaps only locally in the w. Rockies. It mostly has leaves only pale beneath and 2-parted fruit capsules. Hybrids with Balsam Poplar may have both 2- and 3-parted fruit capsules. **REMARKS:** The largest of our poplars and an important lumber tree in Pacific Northwest. Wood soft, useful for boxes and pulp. May live 200 years.

WHITE POPLAR *Populus alba* L.   PL. 31

European, but widely naturalized, especially in the n. U.S. A tall tree with *white-woolly* leaves, twigs, and buds. Leaves 2–6 in. long, somewhat leathery, with a few large blunt teeth. Some leaves may be shallowly notched or even deeply lobed like maples (Pl. 15). Leafstalks rounded or slightly flattened. Trunk smooth and whitish above, often thick and dark at base. Spreads by seeds and sprouts. Height 60–80 (100) ft.; diameter 2–3 (4) ft. Thickets. **SIMILAR SPECIES:** No other tree with wide leaves is as silvery white in all aspects. (1) Black Cottonwood leaves are whitened beneath but hairless. (2) Russian-olive (Pl. 39) has narrow, silver-scaled foliage.

EASTERN COTTONWOOD   PL. 31
Populus deltoides Bartr. ex Marsh

A tall tree with leaves *coarse-toothed*, triangular, 2–8 in. long, and with 2–3 *glands* (use lens) at the upper end of *flattened* leafstalks. Twigs usually hairless, *yellowish,* sometimes angled on vigorous shoots. End bud ⅝–1 in. long, *gummy* but *not* spicy-fragrant when crushed. Bark smooth, yellow-green when young but on mature trees dark and ridged. Height 40–80 (100) ft.; diameter 1–2 (3½) ft. Bottomlands, from the Rockies eastward. **SIMILAR SPECIES:** (1) Fremont Cottonwood has leaves shorter and without glands. (2) Narrowleaf Cottonwood has narrow foliage, while (3) Black Cottonwood has rounded leafstalks. All range west from the Rockies. **REMARKS:** A quick-growing but short-lived species. Made into boxes and low-quality furniture and woodenware. A yellow dye can be made from the buds. A tea made from the boiled inner bark is said to be an astringent useful in treating diarrhea.

BALSAM POPLAR *Populus balsamifera* L. **PL. 31**

A northern tree with a transcontinental distribution in Canada and the n. U.S. Leaves 6–1 o in. long, *fine-toothed, narrowly* triangular, with *rounded* leafstalks, and sometimes with glands at the leaf base. Leaves *pale* beneath, usually hairless but may be slightly hairy on veins beneath. Twigs *dark brown* and hairless. End bud ⅝–1 in. long, *gummy* and *spicy-fragrant* when crushed. Fruit capsules 2-*parted.* Mature bark dark and grooved; gray-green and smooth on younger parts. Height 3 o–8 o (1 o o) ft.; diameter 1–3 (6) ft. Local in the mountains south to cen. Colo. **SIMILAR SPECIES:** See Black Cottonwood. **REMARKS:** This species, along with a sterile form that is possibly a hybrid with another *Populus* species, is frequently called Balm-of-Gilead. Sterile plants spread mainly by sprouts and may have leaf undersides, leafstalks, and twigs somewhat *hairy.* Resident in n. Alaska and perhaps growing farther north than any tree in the United States.

OAKS I–IV (PLATES 32–35)

The oaks are a diverse and valuable group of trees. Group identification points are as follows: end buds *clustered* at tips of twigs, more than 3 bundle scars per leaf scar, and acorn fruits. A few other plants, such as Fire Cherry (Pl. 42) and Golden Chinkapin (Pl. 39), have buds clustered near the twig tips, but they lack the other characteristics. Male flowers of oaks appear in May and early June as slender drooping catkins. Female blossoms are inconspicuous. Acorns begin development shortly thereafter, becoming green at first and finally brown.

North American oaks are generally divided into two sections, red (or black) oaks and white oaks. Red oaks differ from white oaks in that leaves or their lobes or teeth have hairlike bristle tips, broken brown acorn shells (not cups) have hairy inner surfaces, and acorns require two years to mature. Tiny first-year and larger second-year acorns are usually present on the twigs *and branchlets,* respectively, of mature red oaks in summer. In contrast, white oaks have leaves that lack bristle tips, inner acorn shells that are hairless, and acorns that mature on the *twigs* during the first summer and early autumn. There are species in both groups, however, that have some characteristics not in agreement with one or more of these conditions. Some such species have been called intermediate oaks (see p. 299 and Plate 33).

In winter, white oaks normally display *no* immature acorns, although in some cases, cups of dropped nuts may remain on the twigs as remnants of the earlier crop. Red oaks, when leafless, should have growing acorns *present* on the twigs plus, perhaps, a few residual full-sized acorns (and/or their cups) that failed to fall from the branchlets. Acorns often fail to develop, however, after flowers are frozen in late spring frosts or are damaged by disease or pests. The meat of red oak acorns is yellow, bitter, and usually inedible; that of some white oaks is white, relatively sweet, and often edible. The bark of many red oaks is dark and usually furrowed; that of most white oaks is light gray and often flaky.

To provide for more simple identification, the oaks are here divided into groups by region and also according to whether the leaves are lobed, toothed, wavy-edged, prickly-edged, or none of these. Some species are deciduous, shedding their leaves seasonally; others are evergreen or hold their leaves until new ones appear. Including the closely related and acorn-bearing Tanoak (*Lithocarpus*), the tree-sized species of the w. U.S. include 22 white and 17 red oaks.

Acorns and their cups are often of assistance in identifying oak species. If none is growing on the tree, look for old ones on the ground (but try to verify that they fell from the tree being examined). Acorns always grow partly enclosed in basal growths universally called cups, but the cups are nevertheless nearly always described as saucerlike, bowllike, or otherwise uncuplike.

Not every oak specimen can be identified with certainty by the amateur. Even professional botanists are frequently puzzled by apparent hybrids and variants. Identifications of leafless specimens are often especially difficult.

Oaks provide about half the annual production of hardwood lumber in the U.S. They are slow-growing, long-lived, and relatively disease- and insect-resistant. Bark of several oaks is rich in tannin used in curing leather.

By grinding the nuts and pouring hot water through the flour to leach out the tannic acid, Native Americans converted even the bitter acorns of red oaks into a food staple. It is reported that in some parts of Mexico, roasted acorns are used as a substitute for coffee. In ancient England, oak forests were valued for fattening swine. Laws provided that anyone wantonly injuring or destroying an oak should be fined according to the size of the tree and its ability to bear fruits.

Livestock browsing on early spring foliage are sometimes poisoned. Nevertheless, deer, elk, cottontail rabbits, and snowshoe hares browse the twigs, while porcupines eat the growing layer beneath the bark. The list of species eating acorns includes many songbirds, ruffed and sharptail grouse, prairie chicken, bobwhite quail, wild turkey, ringneck pheasant, mourning dove, wood duck, whitetail deer, black bear, red and gray foxes, raccoon, opossum, and squirrels.

The Spanish name *roble* (ROHB-leh) is often applied to deciduous oaks and *encino* (en-SEEN-oh) to evergreen oaks.

OAKS I: WESTERN OAKS WITH DECIDUOUS AND MOSTLY LOBED LEAVES (PLATE 32)

There are only nine strictly western oaks with *deciduous lobed* foliage. All have leaves 2–7 in. long, and all except California Black Oak and Graves Oak are members of the white oak category. In addition, the ranges of several oaks of the e. U.S. (Pl. 35) extend westward on the Great Plains.

CALIFORNIA BLACK OAK *Quercus kelloggii* Newb.   **PL. 32**
Distributed mainly in Calif. but extending also into sw. Ore., this oak has leaves 4–7 in. long, dark green, with 5–7 *bristle-tipped lobes* often slightly hairy beneath. Leafstalks 1–2 in. long. Twigs

California Black Oak

sometimes hairy; winter buds about ¼ in. long, *hairless,* and with tips pointed. Acorns 1–1¼ in. long; cups *bowl-shaped.* Height 30–75 (95) ft.; diameter 1–3 (4) ft. Mainly mountain slopes to 9000 ft. **SIMILAR SPECIES:** No other wild oak of the Pacific Slope has deeply lobed foliage with bristle tips. Several lobed-leaved and bristle-tipped red oaks of the e. U.S. (including some on Pl. 35) may be planted, however, in western landscaped areas. Most of these have acorns under 1 in. long (see Pl. 35).

OREGON OAK *Quercus garryana* Dougl. ex Hook **PL. 32**

Distributed from extreme sw. B.C. to cen. Calif., this species has large, thick, *leathery,* dark green, *shiny* leaves 3–5 in. long, 2–4 in. wide, usually hairy beneath, with 5–9 deep lobes and leafstalks ¼–½ in. long. Twigs often hairy; buds ¼–½ in. long, sharp, and *hairy.* Acorns ¾–1¼ in. long; cups saucerlike. Height 40–65 (90) ft.; diameter 1–2 (3) ft. Mountain slopes, coastal ranges, n. and cen. Sierra Nevada. **SIMILAR SPECIES:** (1) California Black Oak has bristle-tipped leaf lobes. See (2) Valley Oak. **REMARKS:** Nicholas Garry, an officer of the Hudson's Bay Co. in the early 1800s, helped David Douglas, the Scottish botanical explorer, in his expeditions. Also known as Oregon White Oak.

Oregon Oak

OREGON OAK

The largest western oak, this *small-leaved* species mainly occurs in Calif.'s central valleys and adjacent foothills. Leaves 2–4 in. long, 1½–3 in. wide, with 7–11 deep lobes. Foliage *thin, dull,* medium green, hairless, and with stalks ¼–½ in. long. Twigs *hairless* and tending to *droop*; buds about ¼ in. long, pointed, and often hairy. Acorns 1¼–2 in. long; cups *bowl-shaped*. Height 40–100 (125) ft.; diameter 3–5 (13) ft. Fertile soils to 6000 ft. elevation. Also on Santa Catalina and Santa Cruz islands, s. Calif. **SIMILAR SPECIES:** (1) Oregon Oak has leaves larger, dark green, shiny, longer-stalked, and leathery, twigs often hairy and nondrooping, acorns smaller, and acorn cups more shallow. (2) Blue Oak has leaves smaller, blue-green, wavy-edged or toothed, and short-stalked. Also, its twigs are hairy. (3) Gambel Oak is a smaller tree of the s. Rockies. **REMARKS:** Sometimes called Weeping Oak, from the pendulous twigs. Early travelers reported that the acorns of this species was the principal food of Native Americans of the region. They were collected and stored in large quantities. On California's offshore islands, McDonald Oak, previously classed as a full species, is now regarded as a hybrid involving Valley Oak and a local shrub oak.

Valley Oak

BLUE OAK *Quercus douglasii* Hook. & Arn. **PL. 32**

An oak of the interior valleys of n., cen., and s. Calif. with *blue-green* foliage *shallowly* lobed or sometimes few-toothed (rarely without either lobes or teeth). Leaves *small,* mostly 1–3 in. long, firm but not thick or leathery, sometimes hairy beneath. Leaf-stalks *only ⅛–⅜ in. long.* Twigs *hairy;* buds about ¼ in. long, *blunt,* and *not* hairy. Acorns ¾–1¼ in. long; cups bowl-shaped. Height 25–50 (90) ft.; diameter 1–2 (3) ft. Dry slopes to 4500 ft. elevation, south to n. Los Angeles Co. **SIMILAR SPECIES:** The small blue-green leaves are readily recognized. Oaks of Pl. 33 have leathery, evergreen leaves. Except for the most northern populations of the prickly-leaved and evergreen Turbinella Oak, no species of Pl. 34 has a distribution that overlaps the range of Blue Oak. **REMARKS:** The scientific name commemorates David Douglas, the 19th-century Scottish botanist after whom the Douglas-firs (Pl. 8) also are named. In some areas, hybridization with Turbinella Oak is frequent. Intergrades involving Oregon Oak and Valley Oak also are not rare.

GAMBEL OAK *Quercus gambelii* Nutt. **PL. 32**

The only *deeply lobed* oak in the s. Rocky Mts. Leaves 2–6 in. long with 5–9 lobes, thick and *leathery,* yellow-green and mostly glossy above, somewhat hairy beneath. Leafstalks ¼–¾ in. long. Twigs hairless; buds *under* ¼ in. long, *sharp-pointed,* and hairless. Acorns ¾–1 in. long; cups bowl-shaped. Often shrubby but height to 65 ft.; diameter to 2 ft. Dry slopes to 10,500 ft. elevation. **SIMILAR SPECIES:** (1) Wavyleaf Oak, widespread in the Southwest, is interpreted as a group of hybrids involving Gambel Oak (Fig. 5). In w. Texas, (2) Graves Oak is a red oak species with bristle-tipped leaf lobes. East of the Rockies, also see Pl. 35. **REMARKS:** William Gambel collected birds and plants in the Rockies in 1844.

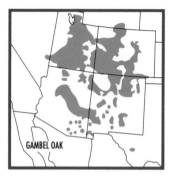

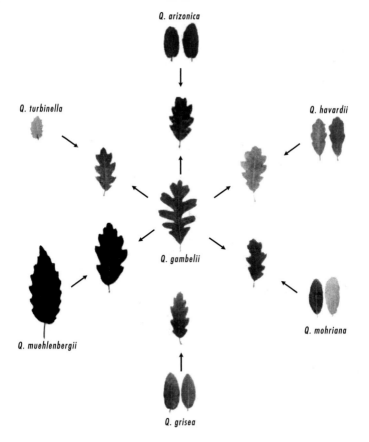

Fig. 5. Species involved in the Wavyleaf Oak (Quercus undulata) *complex (from Tucker, 1961).*

WAVYLEAF OAK

FIG. 5, ABOVE

Often termed *Quercus undulata* Torr.

A complex of apparent hybrids between Gambel Oak and other oaks common in the Southwest. Havard Oak of this plate; Turbinella, Gray, Arizona, or Mohr oaks of Pl. 34; or Chinkapin Oak of Pl. 35 may be involved. Hybrids have characteristics that are usually intermediate to those of their parents (Fig. 5). Leaves are

HAVARD OAK

1–3 in. long, either with *medium-deep lobes or large teeth.* The foliage may be deciduous or evergreen, thin or somewhat leathery. Like the twigs, leaves are sometimes hairy. The buds are short, sharp, and hairless. Hybrids may be more frequent than the parent species. Both common and scientific names may offer useful references to accounts in other books. The plants grow on dry slopes within the range of Gambel Oak.

HAVARD (SHIN) OAK *Quercus havardii* Rydb.   **PL. 32**

A frequently shrubby and highly variable species. Leaves 2–4 in. long, *shallowly lobed,* wavy-edged, or even without lobes, *leathery, bright green,* not shiny, and mostly *white-hairy* beneath. Leafstalks ⅛–⅜ in. long. Twigs sometimes hairy, buds *small, blunt,* hairless. Acorns ½–1 in. long; cups *bowl-shaped.* Height to 15 ft. Forms thickets, sandy soils. **SIMILAR SPECIES:** (1) Lacey Oak, occurring on Texas's Edwards Plateau, has hairless foliage, pointed hairy buds, and shallow acorn cups. See (2) Wavyleaf Oak. **REMARKS:** Born in France, Valery Havard was an American army physician. He collected plants while stationed in Texas in the late 1800s. Mohr Oak (Pl. 34) also is sometimes called Shin Oak.

LACEY OAK *Quercus laceyi* Small.   **PL. 32**

Similar to Havard Oak but distributed in the Edwards Plateau of cen. Texas and the mountains of ne. Mexico. Foliage *gray-green,* somewhat leathery, and mostly shallowly lobed. Leaves and twigs *hairless* with leafstalks ⅛–⅝ in. long. Buds small, hairy, *pointed.* Acorns about ¾ in. long, cups *saucerlike.* Often shrubby but sometimes a tree to 45 ft. tall. Rocky limestone soils and riverbanks. **SIMILAR SPECIES:** See several oaks of Pl. 35. **REMARKS:** Howard Lacey found the first specimen on his Texas ranch.

GRAVES OAK *Quercus gravesii* Sudw.   **PL. 32**

A member of the red oak category. Leaves 2–5 in. long, somewhat *glossy* above, *not* leathery, mostly hairless, with *pointed, bristle-tipped* lobes. Leafstalks ⅜–1 in. long. Twigs hairless, buds blunt, hairy, and more than ¼ in. long. Cups *bowl-shaped.* Height to 50 ft.; diameter to 4 ft. In canyons mostly above 4500 ft. elevation in the Chisos, Glass, and Davis mts. of Texas and in Coahuila, Mexi-

CO. **SIMILAR SPECIES:** (1) Gambel Oak has white oak characteristics. See also (2) Chisos Oak, Pl. 34. **REMARKS:** Henry S. Graves was an early chief of the U.S. Forest Service and dean of the Yale University School of Forestry.

OAKS II: EVERGREEN OAKS OF CALIFORNIA AND ITS BORDERS (Plate 33)

Called live oaks because of their *evergreen* character, the trees of this plate range mainly in Calif. and have thick and rather leathery leaves, with smooth, wavy, toothed, or prickly edges. Like all oaks, these species have leaves and buds clustered at the twig tips. Buds of this group are under ¼ in. long. Acorn cups are brownish, except in Canyon Live Oak. Tanoak differs somewhat.

While California Scrub Oak and Engelmann Oak are white oaks and Coast and Interior live oaks qualify as red oaks, Canyon and Island live oaks are among the few species termed intermediate oaks. Like red oaks, the acorns of intermediate oaks require two years to mature and have hairy inner acorn shells (not cups). These fruits grow on wood that does not normally produce new growth during the second year and thus appear to mature on twigs like white oaks.

Also with evergreen prickly leaves, Turbinella and Dunn oaks (Pl. 34) have ranges that extend into s. Calif. Golden Chinkapin and Pacific Bayberry (Pl. 39) occur in Calif. with evergreen leaves crowded toward the twig ends.

CALIFORNIA SCRUB OAK *Quercus dumosa* Nutt.   **PL. 33**
Variable in most of its characteristics and usually shrubby, this thicket-forming oak may occasionally become a small tree. Leaves mostly *under 1 in.* long, *shiny* green above, with bases ± *heart-*

Coast Live Oak

shaped. Foliage ± *hairy,* with veins raised beneath, the leaf edges often *prickly.* Twigs are brown, hairy or not; buds hairless and usually pointed. A white oak species with acorns ½–1 in. long; cups are bowl-shaped, *without* stalks, basal scales *strongly* warty, and margins *thick.* Trunk bark *grayish.* Height to 15 ft. Chaparral, coastal ranges. Also distributed in Baja California Norte. **SIMILAR SPECIES:** (1) Coast Live Oak and (2) Interior Live Oak are dark-barked and grow to a greater height. The former has markedly convex foliage, while leaves of the latter are larger, and acorns grow on both twigs and branchlets. (3) Turbinella Oak (Pl. 34) has acorn stalks ¼–¾ in. long and leaves dull gray-green with the prickly tips longer. **REMARKS:** Botanists studying this species advise that only coastal plants with heart-shaped leaf bases should be recognized under this name.

COAST LIVE OAK *Quercus agrifolia* Nee   **PL. 33**
A broad-topped tree often forming open stands on California's *coastal* grasslands to 5000 ft. elevation. Leaves usually wide and

CALIFORNIA SCRUB OAK

COAST LIVE OAK

convex, the upper surface shiny and markedly arched upward, umbrellalike. Leaves 1–4 in. long, *usually hairless* beneath except in angles of veins, edges smooth to spiny-toothed. Twigs *hairy* or not; buds blunt, hairless. Acorns of this intermediate oak (see p. 299) ¾–1½ in. long, *narrowly cone-shaped;* cups bowl-shaped. Trunk bark *dark.* Height 30–50 (90) ft.; diameter 1–2 (3) ft. Also on Santa Cruz and Santa Rosa islands, s. Calif. **SIMILAR SPECIES:** No other Calif. oak regularly has such convex arched leaves. (1) Netleaf Oak (Pl. 34) has similarly curved foliage but has other differences and occurs east from cen. Ariz. See also (2) California Scrub Oak. **REMARKS:** Acorns once much used as food by Native Americans. California quail, mule deer, and other wildlife species also use this food source. The specific name is widely presumed to have been a printer's error, probably intended to be *acrifolia,* sharpleaf, or *aquifolia,* hollyleaf.

INTERIOR LIVE OAK *Quercus wislizenii* A. DC.   **PL. 33**
Forming groves on *inland* grasslands, this is a smoothly *dark-barked* and broadly round-crowned red oak. It has *short-pointed, flat* leaves only 1–2 *in.* long, *shiny, hairless,* and either sharp-toothed or smooth-edged. Twigs usually somewhat hairy; buds hairless, pointed. Acorns ¾–1½ in. long, *narrow,* somewhat pointed; cups bowl-shaped, more or less hairless. Trunk bark *dark.* Height 30–65 ft. Dry slopes to 7000 ft. elevation. **SIMILAR SPECIES:** (1) California Scrub Oak has smaller leaves and gray bark while (2) Coast Live Oak has convex foliage. Both are white oaks. See also (3) Canyon Live Oak. **REMARKS:** Friedrich Wislizenus discovered this oak during 19th-century expeditions. A hybrid with California Black Oak (Pl. 32) has wide, toothed leaves and is known as Oracle Oak.

CANYON LIVE OAK *Quercus chrysolepis* Liebm. PL. 33

Occurring throughout Calif. and portions of adjacent states, this is a highly variable intermediate oak growing both in canyons and on exposed slopes. Frequently, it may be only a shrub. Leaves 1–2½ in., mostly pointed, smooth- or prickly-edged, *flat,* green and *shiny* above, *waxy* and either yellowish or whitish beneath, and with 6–10 pairs of *mostly parallel* veins. Twigs *flexible,* hairy; buds mostly hairless and usually blunt. Acorns ¼–1 in. long, tips rounded, maturing on the apparent (see p. 299) twigs with inner shell hairy; cups mostly bowl-shaped, often *gold-hairy,* and with thick walls and margins. Trunk bark gray. Height 20–65 ft. **SIMILAR SPECIES:** (1) Coast Live Oak and (2) Interior Live Oak have dark trunks and brownish, more thin-walled acorn cups. The leaves of (3) Engelmann Oak are dull blue-green on both sides. (4) Golden Chinkapin (Pl. 39) has clustered end buds with the leaf undersides a bright golden color and the fruits prickly burs. See also (5) Dunn Oak (Pl. 34). **REMARKS:** Wood dense, once used as wedges in splitting logs and made into mauls to hammer the wedges. Sometimes called Maul Oak.

ENGELMANN OAK *Quercus engelmannii* Greene PL. 33

A gray-barked tree of sw. Calif. with rounded crown and foliage *dull blue-green* on both sides. Leaves 1–3 in. long, *wavy-edged* or not, hairy beneath, either blunt or pointed, and with side veins not markedly parallel. Twigs *hairy;* buds blunt, sometimes hairy. Acorns ¾–1 in. long, stout; cups cover ¼–⅓ of nut. Height 15–60 (75) ft. To 4000 ft. elevation on slopes near (but not directly on) the coast, also Santa Catalina I., s. Calif. **SIMILAR SPECIES:** Most live oaks within the range of this species have shiny leaves. (1) Island Live Oak and (2) Tanoak have obviously parallel leaf veins. **REMARKS:** Hybrids with California Scrub Oak and Valley Oak are known. George Engelmann was a German-born physician and botanist of the 19th century.

ISLAND LIVE OAK *Quercus tomentella* Engelm. PL. 33

A rare California intermediate oak, growing wild only on the southern offshore islands. Leaves 1–4 in. long, mostly *wavy-toothed,* sometimes arched, densely *hairy* beneath, and with raised *parallel* veins beneath. Twigs *hairy;* buds sharp, hairy. Acorns ¾–1 in. long, stout; cups saucerlike, hairy. Trunk bark *reddish brown,* thin. Height 15–40 ft.; diameter 1–2 ft. Canyons and chaparral, Anacapa, Santa Catalina, San Clemente, Santa Cruz, and Santa Rosa islands of s. Calif., plus Guadalupe I., Baja California. **SIMILAR SPECIES:** Tanoak also is parallel-veined, but its leaf edges are sharply toothed. It occurs naturally, furthermore, only on the mainland.

ENGELMANN OAK

TANOAK

TANOAK

Lithocarpus densiflorus (Hook. & Arn.) Rehd.

Leaves 2–5 in. long, 1–2½ in. wide, usually whitish- or brownish-hairy beneath, with prominent *parallel* veins mostly ending in *sharp* teeth. Twigs and buds *yellowish-hairy.* Acorns ¾–1¼ in. long, pointed, mature in 2 years; cup saucer-shaped, covered with loose, hairy-appearing scales. Bark *dark,* thick. Height 50–100 (150) ft.; diameter 1–3 (6) ft. Mainly coastal forests, sw. Ore. to s. Calif., local in n. and cen. Sierra Nevada. **SIMILAR SPECIES:** See Island Live Oak. **REMARKS:** This is the only American tree besides the true oaks (*Quercus*) to bear acorn fruits. Male flowers are borne in dense *upright* catkins; female flowers are at the bases of male catkins. True oaks, in contrast, have drooping male catkins and female flowers in small clusters at the leaf angles. Bark heavy in tannic acid and once harvested commercially. Also called Tan-bark-oak. Native Americans pounded the acorns into flour and removed the tannin with boiling water. Several hundred *Lithocarpus* species occur in s. and se. Asia.

OAKS III: EVERGREEN OAKS OF THE ARID SOUTHWEST (PLATE 34)

The sw. U.S. is home for a large series of small, leathery-leaved, and mostly evergreen oaks. Most occur in s. Ariz. and in nearby portions of se. Calif., sw. N.M., and w. Texas. In this group, Emory, Silverleaf, Chisos, and Lateleaf oaks are in the red oak category. Canyon Live Oak (Pl. 33), found mainly in Calif., also occurs locally over much of Ariz. In the w. Texas region, Havard, Lacey, and Graves oaks (Pl. 32) may need to be considered. In cen. Texas, see also Virginia Live Oak (Pl. 35).

Many of these oaks are difficult to identify. Hybridization is common, with many resulting intermediate variations. Some ⌄

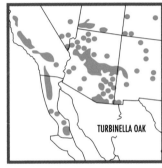

shrubby oak species also may be involved. Even experts disagree on the identity of many specimens, particularly Turbinella, Gray, and Arizona oaks but also others (see Wavyleaf Oak, Pl. 32).

SANDPAPER OAK *Quercus pungens* Liebm.   **PL. 34**

Usually a shrub but occasionally to 25 ft. tall. Leaves ¾–2 in. long, usually evergreen, 2–3 times longer than broad, light to dark green and shiny above, *rough-hairy* on both sides, and with V-shaped bases. Leaf edges markedly *crinkled*, sharply toothed, and *often prickly*, yet sometimes without teeth. Twigs hairy. Buds under ⅛ in. long, blunt, sometimes somewhat hairy. Acorns ½–1 in. long, narrowly *cylindrical*, maturing on the twigs, nuts hairless within; cups bowl-shaped on ¹⁄₁₆–⅛-in. stalks. Rocky slopes. **SIMILAR SPECIES:** Sandpapery leaf texture distinctive among oaks. (1) Turbinella Oak has flat, mostly hairless, blue-green leaves with somewhat more prolonged, hollylike leaf teeth. It has saucerlike acorn cups on ¼–1¾-in. stalks. (2) California Scrub Oak (Pl. 33) has a coastal distribution and smaller leaves. See (3) Vasey Oak. **REMARKS:** Though the leaves do not always conform, the specific name *pungens* means sharp, prickly. The name Scrub Oak is applied to this but also to several other oak species.

VASEY OAK *Quercus vaseyana* Buckl.   **NOT SHOWN**

Similar to Sandpaper Oak but often deciduous and with leaves 4–6 times longer than broad and edges ± flat. Foliage mostly short-hairy beneath and bases U-shaped. Acorn cup saucer- to bowllike. To 35 ft. tall. W. and n. Texas, n. Mexico.

TURBINELLA OAK *Quercus turbinella* Greene   **PL. 34**

Frequently shrubby and often with *prickly* hollylike leaves. Its 1–2-in. leaves are dull, *gray-green,* usually hairless above, mostly fine-hairy beneath, *flat* or with only slightly wavy surfaces, and with *spiny* leaf teeth. Foliage mostly *rounded* to heart-shaped at the base and not sandpapery, though sometimes somewhat hairy beneath. Twigs hairy. Acorns ½–¾ in. long, with characteristics of the white oak group, sometimes two or three on stalks ¼–1½ in. long; cup bowl-shaped, often with white-hairy scales. Height to 15 ft. Arid thickets to 8000 ft. elevation. **SIMILAR SPECIES:** (1) Sandpaper Oak has rough-hairy leaves with 3-dimensional undulant edges and mostly angled bases. (2) California Scrub Oak (Pl. 33) is a coastal species with small, hairless, shiny, green leaves whose teeth are not as long-pointed and whose acorn cup scales have thin margins and warty tubercles. See (3) Gray Oak. **REMARKS:** Wavyleaf Oak is a hybrid group often involving Turbinella Oak (see Fig. 5, p. 297). Hybrids with Blue Oak (Pl. 32) and California Scrub Oak (Pl. 33) are also frequent.

DUNN OAK *Quercus dunnii* Kellogg ex Curran ACORN, PL. 34
This *golden-cup* species with probable affinities to Canyon Live Oak has now been classified as a part of Palmer Oak (*Q. palmeri* Engelm.), a shrub in the intermediate oak category.

GRAY OAK *Quercus grisea* Liebm. PL. 34
A white oak species with leaves 1–3 in. long, flat, dull, *gray-green*, sometimes hairy beneath, veins *neither* sunken on top nor unusually prominent beneath. Foliage mostly U- or heart-shaped at the base, tips mostly *pointed*, and teeth few or none. Twigs *fine-hairy*. Acorns ½–¾ in. long, ± long-stalked (to 1¼ in.); cup bowl-shaped. Height to 65 ft. Rocky slopes and canyons to 8500 ft. elevation. **SIMILAR SPECIES:** (1) Turbinella Oak has smaller and spiny-toothed foliage. (2) Netleaf Oak has leaves heavily veined, shiny, and convex plus acorns on stalks 1–3 in. long. (3) Emory Oak has leaves

NETLEAF OAK

MOHR OAK

shiny green on both sides. The leaves of (4) Arizona Oak are mostly blunt, more veiny, larger, and widest near the tip. See (5) Wavyleaf Oak and Fig. 5 (p. 297). REMARKS: Both common and scientific
names refer to the gray shading of the foliage. Hybrids with Turbinella, Arizona, Gambel (Pl. 32), and Mohr oaks are frequent.

NETLEAF OAK *Quercus rugosa* Née   PL. 34
Occurs from s. Mexico north to cen. Ariz., sw. N.M., and w. Texas.
Leaves 1–3 in. long and only half as wide, *dark* green, shiny, mostly *convex* above, hairy or not, usually toothed near the *broad* tip,
veins *much raised* beneath and *sunken* above, base rounded or
heart-shaped. Twigs mostly *hairy;* buds small, blunt, hairless.
Acorns of white oak type, ¼–1 in. long and on 1–3 -in. stalks, cups
bowl-shaped. Trunk bark moderately thick. In canyons mainly
above 6000 ft. elevation, shrubby but occasionally to 15 ft. tall,
more regularly attaining tree size in Mexico. SIMILAR SPECIES: (1)
Coast Live Oak (Pl. 33) also has umbrellalike convex leaves, but it
occurs in Calif. and has short-stalked acorns with red oak characteristics. (2) Gray Oak acorns are not so long-stalked, and the
leaves are gray-green, usually with pointed tips and veins beneath
evident but not prominently raised. (3) Arizona Oak also has
prominently veined foliage, but the leaves are flat or only slightly
arched, dull gray-green, and widest near the tip. (4) Silverleaf
Oak has leaves narrow, pointed, silver-hairy, mostly with rolled
edges, and only sometimes with a few teeth.

ARIZONA OAK *Quercus arizonica* Sarg.   PL. 34
Frequent in cen. and se. Ariz. but ranging also to w. Texas and n.
Mexico. Leaves 1–4 in. long, *dull* gray-green and hairless above,
prominently veined and often *hairy beneath,* length more than
twice the width, U- or heart-based, pointed or blunt, *widest near*

ARIZONA OAK

Bark of Arizona Oak

the tip, sometimes moderately convex, and either toothed or not. Twigs hairy; buds *globular,* ¹⁄₁₆–¹⁄₈ in. across, and ± yellow-hairy. Acorns ¼–¾ in. long and with stalks to ¾ in. or none; cup bowl-shaped. Trunk bark thick. Height to 65 ft.; diameter to 3 ft. Canyons and rocky slopes mostly below 7000 ft. **SIMILAR SPECIES:** (1) Netleaf Oak leaves, also with veins much raised beneath, are usually darker, shiny, and markedly convex. Its acorns have 1–3-in. stalks. The leaves of (2) Gray Oak are pointed, smaller, and with veins subdued. (3) Emory Oak foliage is shiny on both surfaces. (4) Silverleaf Oak has narrow, silver-hairy, pointed leaves. **REMARKS:** A member of the white oak series and often called Arizona White Oak. Intergrades with Gray and Turbinella oaks are widespread (see under Wavyleaf Oak and Fig. 5, p. 297).

MOHR OAK *Quercus mohriana* Buckl.   **PL. 34**

A thicket-forming white oak species with leaves 1–4 in. long, *dark* green and *shiny* above, gray- or *white-hairy beneath,* wavy-edged or with a few teeth, and with edges *scarcely* if at all rolled under. Twigs are sometimes hairy; buds dark, ¹⁄₁₆ in. long, blunt, sometimes slightly hairy. Acorns ¼–½ in. long; cup bowllike. Height to 20 ft. Low hills and plains. **SIMILAR SPECIES:** (1) Silverleaf Oak, though mostly more western, occurs in w. Texas and also has white-hairy foliage. The leaves, however, are narrowly pointed with rolled edges and mostly have no teeth. (2) Chisos Oak has drooping coppery leaves. (3) Lateleaf Oak has dull gray-green foliage. All 3 of these species have acorns with red oak characteristics. (4) Lacey Oak (Pl. 32), a white oak species, has hairless and mostly lobed foliage. (5) Havard Oak (Pl. 32), also a white oak, has dull-surfaced, deciduous, shallowly lobed leaves and larger acorns. (6) See Wavyleaf Oak and Fig. 5, p. 297. **REMARKS:** Charles Mohr was a pharmacist and amateur naturalist who lived in Alabama in the late 1800s. This oak is reported to occur in Palo Duro Canyon, in the Texas Panhandle.

EMORY OAK *Quercus emoryi* Torr. in W. H. Emory   **PL. 34**
A common evergreen oak of the Mexican border. This species has leaves 1–3 (4) in. long, narrow, hairless, *pointed, shiny green on both sides,* toothed or not, occasionally prickly, and often with tufts of white hairs at the base of the midrib. Twigs variously hairy or not, buds about ¼ in. long, *pointed,* and somewhat hairy. Though a red oak with hairy inner acorn shells, the nuts mature in one year on the *twigs.* Fruits ½–¾ in. long; cup bowl-shaped. Height to 80 ft.; diameter to 3 ft. Canyons and slopes to 7500 ft. **SIMILAR SPECIES:** The pointed, shiny leaves, often evident even from a

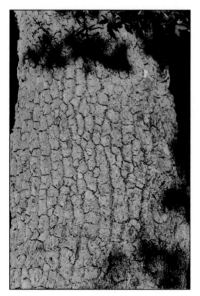

Bark of Emory Oak

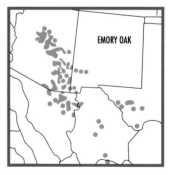

EMORY OAK

distance, are distinctive. **REMARKS:** Probably the most abundant oak of the boundary region. Hybridizes with Graves (Pl. 32) and Chisos oaks. Henry Emory was an early 19th century explorer in the Southwest.

SILVERLEAF OAK *Quercus hypoleucoides* A. Camus   **PL. 34**

A red oak with distinctive *narrow* leaves 1–4 in. long, dark green and *shiny* above, thickly *white- or silvery-hairy* and veiny beneath, *pointed* at the tip, the edges *rolled under* and with no teeth or only a few sometimes-bristly ones. Twigs hairy or not; buds small, hairless, pointed or not. Acorns ½–⅝ in. long; cup bowl-shaped. Height to 60 ft.; diameter to 3 ft. Canyons and slopes, mostly at 5000–7000 ft. elevations from se. Ariz. to w. Texas and n. Mexico. **SIMILAR SPECIES:** A rather distinctive tree, but see Mohr Oak. **REMARKS:** An attractive species used in landscaping.

MEXICAN BLUE OAK *Quercus oblongifolia* Torr.   **PL. 34**

An oak with leaves *shiny, blue-gray, blunt-tipped,* hairless, parallel-sided, only 1–2 in. long and without teeth. Twigs hairless; buds small, blunt, and hairless. Acorns ½–¾ in. long; cup bowl-like. Height to 30 ft.; diameter to 2 ft. Mountain slopes at 4500–6000 ft. elevations. **SIMILAR SPECIES:** None; foliage is unique.

Silverleaf Oak

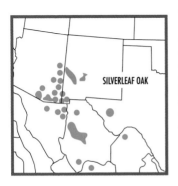

SILVERLEAF OAK

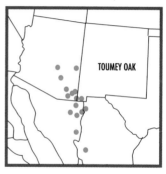

TOUMEY OAK *Quercus toumeyi* Sarg.   **PL. 34**

Localized on mountain slopes of se. Ariz., sw. N.M., and nearby n. Mexico, this species has the *smallest leaves* of any American oak. Leaves ¼–1 in. long, hairless, *shiny* above, rarely few-toothed, with *pointed tip* and rounded base. Twigs hairy; buds small, blunt, hairless. Branchlet bark flaky, *rough.* Acorns ¼–⅝ in. long; cup bowl-shaped. Height to 30 ft.; diameter to 1½ ft. At 4000–7000 ft. elevations. **SIMILAR SPECIES:** Other local white oak species have mature leaves larger and/or branchlet bark smooth. **REMARKS:** James W. Toumey discovered the species in 1894.

CHISOS OAK *Quercus graciliformis* C. H. Muller   **NOT SHOWN**

Found only in the Chisos Mts., w. Texas. Leaves *narrow,* 3–4 in. long, ¾–1¼ in. wide, thin but somewhat leathery, shiny above, hairless beneath, *drooping,* with 5–10 *large bristle-tipped teeth* or shallow lobes, or teeth lacking. Foliage hairless, long-pointed, V-based, and somewhat *copper-colored* beneath. Twigs flexible, hairy or not; buds shiny, small, hairless, and usually blunt. Acorns narrow, ⅝ in. long, ⅜ in. wide; cup saucerlike. Height to 25 ft. Rocky canyons at about 5500 ft. elevation. **SIMILAR SPECIES:** The narrow, drooping, large-toothed foliage is distinctive among Texas oaks. (1) Graves Oak (Pl. 32) has deciduous leaves with fewer and deeper lobes and hairless twigs. (2) Silverleaf Oak, also with narrow foliage, has white-hairy leaf undersides. **REMARKS:** A member of the red oak group. May hybridize with Emory Oak.

LATELEAF OAK *Quercus tardifolia* C. H. Muller   **NOT SHOWN**

With leaves thick, *leathery,* and dull blue-green, this little-known evergreen red oak was once found locally in the Chisos Mts., w. Texas. It has not been found lately and its validity is in doubt.

OAKS IV: OAKS OF THE GREAT PLAINS
(Plate 35)

Most eastern oaks are distributed in the moist regions east of the Great Plains. A few, however, also find suitable local habitats westward. The first three of these species plus Bluejack Oak are red oaks; the remainder belong to the white oak group. Only Virginia Live Oak is evergreen. In Texas and nearby, see also Lacey, Graves, and Chisos oaks, Pl. 34.

EASTERN BLACK OAK *Quercus velutina* Lam. PL. 35

Reaching westward only to cen. Okla., this tree has moderately deep leaf lobes. Leaves 4–10 in. long, *thickened,* generally *glossy* above, and mostly hairless beneath. Twigs *angled,* hairless; end buds ¼–½ in. long, pointed, densely *gray-hairy,* and *sharply angled.* Acorns ⅝–¾ in. long; cup *bowl-shaped* and finely gray-hairy, edge rough with fringelike scales. Trunk dark, ridged. Height 70–80 (100) ft.; diameter 3–4 (5) ft. Dry soils. **SIMILAR SPECIES:** (1) Shumard Oak has leaves more deeply lobed, twigs/buds hairless, and acorn cups shallow. See (2) Blackjack Oak.

BLACKJACK OAK *Quercus marilandica* Muenchh. PL. 35

A low to medium-sized tree whose range extends west to cen. Texas and w. Okla. Leaves 4–8 in. long, thick, *leathery, shallowly lobed,* bristle-pointed, shiny above, *brownish-scaly* or hairy beneath. Twigs angled, *hairy;* end buds ¼–5/16 in. long, *gray-hairy, sharp pointed, angled.* Acorns ⅝–¾ in. long. Cups somewhat hairy, *deep,* with a narrowed base, somewhat goblet-shaped, and with scales appearing loosely attached. Dark trunk bark broken into *squarish blocks.* Height 40–50 (70) ft.; diameter 1–2 (4) ft. **SIMILAR**

EASTERN BLACK OAK

BLACKJACK OAK

SPECIES: (1) Eastern Black Oak may have somewhat leathery leaves, but lobes are deeper and foliage and twigs are hairless. (2) Post Oak has leathery foliage and often grows with Blackjack, but leaves are more deeply lobed and not bristle-tipped.

SHUMARD OAK *Quercus shumardii* Buckl. **PL. 35**

Ranging west to cen. Texas, this southern tree has leaves *deeply lobed*, 6-8 in. long, shiny above, with conspicuous tufts of hair at the vein angles beneath (lens not required). Twigs hairless; end buds clay- or *straw-colored,* more than ¼ in. long, pointed, *hairless,* and *angled.* Acorns ¾–1⅛ in. long; cups *gray,* shallow, *saucer-like,* ¾–1¼ in. in diameter. Height 70–100 (120) ft.; diameter 2–3 (6) ft. Bottomlands. **SIMILAR SPECIES:** See Eastern Black Oak. **REMARKS:** Benjamin Shumard was an early state geologist of Texas.

BUCKLEY OAK *Quercus buckleyi* Nixon & Dorr **NOT SHOWN**

This recently described oak has foliage much like that of Shumard Oak but there are only *minute* hair tufts on the leaf undersides (use lens). Buds *brown,* less than ¼ in. long, and not angled. Acorn cups *bowl-shaped.* Found along the western borders of Shumard Oak distribution from ne. Okla. to s.-cen. Tex.

BUR (MOSSYCUP) OAK *Quercus macrocarpa* Michx. **PL. 35**

A tall tree found on the plains from se. Sask. to w. Okla. and cen. Texas. Though variable, foliage is usually marked by at least *1 deep pair* of indentations that divide leaves *into* 2 or more portions. Leaves 4–10 in. long, often leathery and shiny above, usually somewhat *hairy and whitish beneath.* Twigs yellow-brown, hairless to rather hairy; end buds small, hairy, blunt, not angled. Slender *stipules* commonly present in the clustered end buds. Branchlets sometimes have *corky wings.* Acorns ¾–2 in. long;

SHUMARD OAK

BUR OAK

cups bowl-shaped, with a peculiar "bur" or "mossy" *fringe* of elongate scales. Bark light *gray,* shallowly grooved. Height 70–80 (170) ft.; diameter 2–3 (7) ft. **SIMILAR SPECIES:** Fringed acorn cups and large acorns are unique. Post Oak leaves are deeply lobed but in a crosslike pattern.

POST OAK *Quercus stellata* Wangenh. PL. 35

A small eastern tree found also throughout much of Okla. and Texas. Leaves 3–8 in. long, *often leathery,* with 3–5 large lobes usually arranged so that they resemble a *cross.* Leaves typically shiny above and gray or *brown-hairy beneath.* Twigs somewhat gray-hairy; end buds less than ¼ in. long, not angled, blunt, and rather hairy. Acorns ½–1 in. long. Bowl-shaped cups cover ⅓–½ of acorn. Bark brownish, broken by long shallow cracks, and often divided into rectangular blocks. Height 50–60 (100) ft.; diameter 1–2 (3) ft. Dry soils. **SIMILAR SPECIES:** In winter, (1) Bur Oak has unique acorns, terminal stipules, and often winged branchlets. See (2) Blackjack Oak.

DURAND OAK *Quercus sinuata* Walt. PL. 35

An uncommon, medium-sized tree that grows on fertile soils of the se. U.S. west to cen. Texas. Foliage *variable* from shallow lobes to merely wavy-edged. Leaves 3–8 in. long, glossy above, hairless to silver-hairy beneath. Twigs somewhat hairy; end buds under ¼ in. long, and nearly *globular.* Acorns ½–¾ in. long; cup *saucerlike.* Bark light gray. Height 60–90 ft.; diameter 2–3 ft. Damp to dry sites. **SIMILAR SPECIES:** Blackjack Oak also may have leaves shallowly lobed, but leaves are wide and bristle-pointed, and end buds are large, sharp, gray-hairy, and angled. **REMARKS:** Previously named *Q. durandii* Buckl. after Elias Durand of Philadelphia, a 19th-century druggist and amateur botanist.

POST OAK

DURAND OAK

CHINKAPIN OAK

BLUEJACK OAK

CHINKAPIN OAK *Quercus muehlenbergii* Engelm.   PL. 35

A medium-sized *upland* tree. Leaves thin, *deciduous,* 4–9 in. long with 8–13 pairs of *sharp* teeth. Leaf undersides fine-hairy. Twigs hairless. End buds narrow, *sharp,* hairless, not angled, and mostly about ³⁄₁₆ in. long. Acorns ½–1 in. long; cups bowl-shaped, less than 1 in. across, with tight scales free only at the tips. Bark *light gray* and often flaky, not ridged. Height 20–50 (160) ft.; diameter 6–24 in. (4 ft.) West to w. Okla., se. N.M., w. Texas, and ne. Mexico. **SIMILAR SPECIES:** (1) Virginia Live Oak may have some leaves with sharp teeth, but foliage is leathery and evergreen. See (2) Wavyleaf Oak and Fig. 5, p. 297. **REMARKS:** The leaves resemble those of the chestnut-related chinkapins (*Castanea*) of the East. Also spelled Chinquapin. A white oak species. The leaf teeth, though sharp, are not bristle-tipped.

BLUEJACK (SAND) OAK *Quercus incana* W. Bartr.   PL. 35

A small tree or shrub of the southeastern states but reaching cen. Texas. Leaves smooth-edged, 2–5 in. long, and somewhat *leathery but not evergreen.* Foliage shiny and bristle-tipped, with *fine, whitish woolliness* beneath. Twigs densely woolly to nearly hairless; buds ³⁄₁₆–⁵⁄₁₆ in. long, sharp, hairless, not angled. Acorns ½–⅝ in. long, with cups saucer-shaped, ⅜–⅝ in. across, and *short-stalked.* Trunk black or gray, bark divided into squarish blocks. Height to 35 ft. Dry soils. **SIMILAR SPECIES:** Virginia Live Oak has evergreen foliage, blunt end buds, and long acorn stalks.

VIRGINIA LIVE OAK *Quercus virginiana* Mill.   PL. 35

A spreading southern *evergreen* tree of the white oak group, with *leathery* leaves. Its range extends west to cen. and s. Texas and ne. Mexico. Leaves 2–4 in. long, usually with smooth rolled edges, shiny above and mostly gray- or white-hairy beneath, sometimes few-toothed. Leaves not bristle-tipped. Twigs are hairless, rarely gray-hairy; buds under ¼ in. long, hairless, *blunt,* not angled. Acorns ⅝–1 in. long, on ¾–1 -in. stalks; cups are *bowl-shaped.* Trunk dark, bark somewhat broken into squares. Height to 60 ft.; diameter to 8 in. Mostly lowlands; sometimes thicket-forming. **SIMILAR SPECIES:** See Bluejack Oak. Many kinds of evergreen or live oaks occur farther west (Pls.

VIRGINIA LIVE OAK

33, 34). In Texas, no other oak has leathery, smooth-edged leaves and long acorn-stalks. **REMARKS:** A shade tree in towns. Once important in producing curved timbers for ships.

WILLOWS (Plates 36–38)

Many willows, but not all, are easily recognized as such by the slender leaves. The single scale of the willow bud, however, forms a complete hoodlike covering and is distinctive among plants with 3 bundle scars (use lens). Many willows are only shrubs, some far-north and high-altitude species being only a few inches tall.

The tree willows are divided here into those of Pl. 36 with leaves narrow (8–15 times longer than wide), those of Pl. 37 with leaves medium-wide (5–7 times longer than wide), and those of Pl. 38 with wide leaves (only 2–4 times longer than wide). On the vigorous shoots of some species there are also small, somewhat leaflike stipules on the twigs at the bases of leafstalks. The stipules are useful in identification but may drop early. When stated to be large, they are reasonably leafy; when reported to be small, they are not evident except upon close examination.

Mature buds are listed as small when they are less than ⅛ in. long, large if they are more than ¼ in., and medium if they are in between. The end bud is false. Twigs are said to be brittle at the base if they are easily detached, perhaps with a flick of the finger. Galls that resemble pine cones frequently grow on the twigs. The bark of tree willows is mostly yellow-ridged. Flowers and fruits are small and dry, occurring in catkins.

Identifying willows is often a difficult task even for the professional botanist. Individual variation, minute identification marks, and widespread hybridization are complicating factors. Winter characteristics are incompletely known. Final identification of willows frequently depends on examination of the tiny flowers and fruits. Some uncertain specimens may have to be identified professionally or accepted merely as willows.

As pioneer species invading moist bare soils, willows are valuable in controlling stream-bank and mountainside erosion. Stakes of green branches will often sprout if they are merely driven into damp ground. Several willows provide long twigs used in basket-making. A great many are valued as ornamental plants. Willow bark provides tannin and a medicinal substance, salicin, the basic ingredient of aspirin. Native Americans made a tough rope from the inner bark of some species.

The wood of tree species is of some commercial value but is not highly regarded even for fuel, charcoal, or posts. Willow leaves, twigs, and buds are of importance, however, as browse for livestock. The many birds and mammals eating willow twigs, buds, leaves, or fruits include ruffed and sharptail grouse, whitetail, willow and rock ptarmigans, elk, whitetail and mule deer, moose, beaver, muskrats, snowshoe hares, and porcupines. Some willows provide nectar to honeybees.

Several trees other than willows also have narrow willowlike leaves. These are mostly shown on Pl. 39. None has the single caplike bud scale of willows. While sycamores (Pl. 29) have similar single bud scales, their leaves are fan-lobed and trunks are light-barked and usually mottled.

Willows I: Leaves Very Narrow (Plate 36)

The *very narrow* leaves of these willows are 8–15 times longer than wide. They are mostly 3–5 in. long, toothed, long-pointed, deciduous, V-based, and without stipules or leafstalk glands. There are exceptions, however, as noted.

YEWLEAF WILLOW

SANDBAR WILLOW

YEWLEAF WILLOW *Salix taxifolia* H. B. H. PL. 36

An arid-zone species with *short,* gray-hairy leaves only ½–1¼ in. long, ⅛–3⁄16 in. wide, short-pointed, and generally yewlike. Foliage with few teeth or none and edges turned under. Leafstalks very short and tiny stipules often present. Twigs hairy; branchlets and twigs often drooping. Height to 40 ft., diameter to 2 ft. Moist places in deserts and grasslands, se. Ariz. and w. Texas to Guatemala. **SIMILAR SPECIES:** No other willow has such small leaves. Pacific Yew (Pl. 8) is evergreen and occurs no closer than n. Calif.

SANDBAR WILLOW *Salix exigua* Nutt. PL. 36

Very *narrow* leaves 1½–4¼ in. long and only ⅛–⅜ in. wide characterize this transcontinental species. Foliage usually has a *few* scattered tiny teeth (rarely none) and is *long-pointed,* gray-green above, hairless to white-hairy beneath. Leafstalks short (⅛ in.) or none. Twigs hairy or not; buds medium. Height to 20 ft. To 8000 ft. elevation. **SIMILAR SPECIES:** The thin parallel-sided foliage is easily recognizable. **REMARKS:** The most widely distributed of N. American willows. Also known as Narrow-leaved Willow and Coyote Willow. Used in basketry by Native Americans.

HINDS WILLOW *Salix hindsiana* Benth. PL. 36

Now considered to be a part of Sandbar Willow.

NORTHWEST WILLOW *Salix sessilifolia* Nutt. PL. 36

Found from sw. B.C. to sw. Ore., this variable species somewhat resembles Sandbar Willow. Foliage is up to 10 times as long as wide but mostly only 3–4 times as long. Leaves 1¼–4 in. long, ½–1¼ in. wide, blue-green, *hairy* on both sides, *broadest near the middle,* and short-pointed. Sometimes with a few teeth on the outer half. Leafstalks *hairy* and from *nearly absent* to 3⁄16 in. long.

HINDS WILLOW

NORTHWEST WILLOW

Twigs hairy, often whitish. Height to 25 ft. Moist soils to 1000 ft. elevation. **SIMILAR SPECIES:** (1) Sandbar and (2) River willows have leaves narrower or at least not as elliptical as in this species.

RIVER WILLOW *Salix fluviatilis* Nutt.   **PL. 36**

Reported only from the lower valleys of the Columbia and Willamette rivers in Ore. and Wash., this willow has long-pointed leaves 3–6 in. long, 5/16–1/2 in. wide, *toothed, whitened,* and *silky-hairy* to hairless beneath. Leafstalks short or lacking. Twigs essentially hairless. Height to 25 ft. **SIMILAR SPECIES:** (1) Sandbar Willow has more slender leaves usually with fewer teeth. (2) Northwest Willow has shorter and wider leaves not whitened beneath and with few teeth or none. **REMARKS:** None of our other tree willows has such a localized distribution..

BLACK WILLOW *Salix nigra* Marsh.   **PL. 36**

Distributed across the southwestern states and n. Mexico to

range widely in Texas and e. N. America. Leaves 2–6 in. long, 1/4–5/8 in. wide, *fine-toothed, green on both sides,* shiny above, paler beneath, hairless, long-pointed, V-based, with stipules usually conspicuous. Leafstalks 1/8–5/16 in. Twigs hairless and usually *brittle* at the base; buds small. Height 30–100 ft.; diameter 1–3 ft. To 5000 ft. elevation. **SIMILAR SPECIES:** In our area, only this and Goodding Willow are narrow-leaved with foliage hairless and green

on both sides. Goodding Willow has bud scales not fused. See (2) Coastal Plain Willow (Pl. 37). **REMARKS:** The largest of our willows but providing commercial lumber only in southeastern states. Wood used to make polo balls as well as barrels, doors, and furniture.

GOODDING WILLOW *Salix gooddingii* C. Ball   **NOT SHOWN**
Similar to Black Willow but with leafstalk *glands* present, the twigs yellowish and *hairy*. Also unlike most willows, the margin of the single bud scale is *not* fused but appears as a line on the surface of the otherwise smooth bud scale. A tree of the southwestern states and nearby Mexico. **SIMILAR SPECIES:** Red Willow (p. 323), also with a visible bud scale margin, has twigs reddish plus foliage less narrow and whitened beneath. **REMARKS:** Previously included as a part of Black Willow. Also called Goodding Black Willow. Native Americans are reported to have woven the twigs/branchlets into baskets that could hold water.

SATINY WILLOW *Salix pellita* Anderss. ex Schneid.   **PL. 36**
Mainly a tree of e. Canada, this willow occurs west to cen. Sask. Leaves 2–5 in. long, ¼–¾ in. wide, somewhat leathery, and mostly *without teeth.* Foliage *short-pointed,* whitened and silky-hairy beneath, with stipules small or lacking. Leaf undersides and twigs white-powdered. Leafstalks ¼-⅜ in. long. Twigs hairless; buds of medium size. Height to 30 ft. **SIMILAR SPECIES:** Sandbar Willow has leaves only ⅛–⅜ in. wide, long-pointed, and usually with a few teeth. **REMARKS:** Also called Ontario Willow.

WEEPING WILLOW *Salix babylonica* L. PL. 36

An Old World tree with *extremely long,* brittle-based twigs and branchlets that *hang vertically,* often sweeping the ground or overhanging a lake or stream. Leaves moderately narrow, 1–5 in. long, ¼–⅓ in. wide, hairless or silky, fine-toothed, long-pointed, whitened beneath. Leafstalks under ¼ in. long. Small leafstalk *glands* may be present. Twigs sometimes silky; buds of medium length. Stipules small or lacking. Height 30–50 (60) ft.; diameter 1–3 (5) ft. Flowers April–May. Planted widely. **SIMILAR SPECIES:** Short leafstalks and extreme weeping characteristics distinguish this willow from other cultivated willows with weeping growth habits. **REMARKS:** Originally from China.

WILLOWS II: LEAVES OF INTERMEDIATE WIDTH (PLATE 37)

Willows shown on this plate have *medium-wide* leaves (5–7 times longer than wide). They are mostly fine-toothed and without stipules or leafstalk glands (but see exceptions). Northwest Willow (Pl. 36) in the Pacific Northwest and Littletree Willow (Pl. 38) in Alaska and nw. Canada sometimes also have leaves of intermediate width. See Pl. 39 for similarly leaved nonwillows.

WHITE WILLOW *Salix alba* L. PL. 37

Our only willow with leaves usually *whitish above and below.* European in origin but widely planted for ornament. Leaves 2–6 in. long, ⅜–1¼ in. wide, mostly long-pointed, V-based, fine-toothed, *gray-green* above, whitened and silky-hairy beneath. Leafstalks *hairy,* glands *present* at the leaf bases, stipules mostly lacking. Twigs nearly hairless to silky; buds of medium length. Height to 80 ft.

Bark of Pacific Willow

MEADOW WILLOW *Salix petiolaris* J. E. Smith   **PL. 37**
Primarily Canadian, this shrub or tree stretches across the continent from e.-cen. Alta. to the Atlantic Ocean and occurs locally in Colo., S.D. (Black Hills), and Neb. Leaves 2–4 in. long, ⅜–¾ in. wide, toothed, V-based, *long-pointed, shiny, dark green* above, whitish and hairless beneath. Stipules small or lacking. Young leaves become *black* upon drying. Leafstalks ¼–½ in. long, *without* glands. Twigs dark, hairless, and mostly clustered near branchlet ends; buds of medium length. Height to 25 ft. **SIMILAR SPECIES:** In the prairie provinces of Canada, (1) Shining Willow (Pl. 38) has leafstalk glands present and ± wider foliage that does not blacken upon drying. See (2) Mackenzie Willow.

GEYER WILLOW *Salix geyeriana* Anderss.   **PL. 37**
A willow of the Pacific slope, Ariz., and the Rockies with leaves 1–3 in. long, ⅛–½ in. wide, V-based, mostly *without teeth,* and often *blunt-tipped.* Foliage is dull dark green above and somewhat whitened and often silky beneath. Stipules small or lacking. Leafstalks only ⅛–⅜ in. long, without glands. Twigs hairless, usually with a *white bloom;* buds small. Height to 15 ft. **SIMILAR SPECIES:** (1) The foliage of Pacific Willow bears leafstalk glands and is

toothed, long-pointed, long-stalked, and mostly U-based. (2) Arroyo Willow has thicker leaves more or less leathery. Its twigs are yellowish, somewhat hairy, and lack a powdery bloom. See (3) Scouler Willow, Pl. 38. **REMARKS:** Karl Geyer, a German botanist, collected plants from Mo. to the West Coast in the 1840s.

PACIFIC WILLOW **PL. 37**
Salix lucida ssp. *lasiandra* (Benth.) E. Murray

Ranging throughout the northern and western mountains. Leaves 2–6 in. long, ¼–1 in. wide, *finely toothed, very long-pointed, shiny* dark green above, hairless, and *whitened* beneath with a waxy bloom. *Glands* present on the upper leafstalks or on the mostly *U-shaped* leaf bases. Leafstalks ½–¾ in. long. Twigs purple to yellow, hairless; buds large. Height to 60 ft.; diameter to 3 ft. Wet to moist soils. **SIMILAR SPECIES:** Leafstalk glands, long leafstalks, and ± U-shaped leaf bases are unlike other willows of this group. See Shining Willow (Pl. 38). **REMARKS:** Once used widely to make charcoal. Formerly known as *S. lasiandra*; now classified as a subspecies of Shining Willow (Pl. 38). Also linked with Pacific Willow, ssp. *caudata* (Nutt.) Sudw.; ranges mainly in the Rockies and nearby with non-whitened foliage and other characteristics intermediate between its Pacific Willow and Shining Willow relatives.

ARROYO WILLOW *Salix lasiolepis* Benth. **PL. 37**
A variable willow with its major range along the Calif. coast but also scattered locally throughout much of the mountainous w. U.S. Leaves 2–5 in. long, ¼–1 in. wide, often thick and rather *leathery*, with few or *no* teeth, hairless or not, dark shiny green above, whitish beneath, V-based, and short-pointed to *blunt* at the tip. Leafstalks ⅛–¾ in. long, without glands, often *hairy.* Twigs yellowish, mostly hairy; buds large. Height to 30 ft. Stream banks.

ARROYO WILLOW

BONPLAND WILLOW

See Geyer Willow. **REMARKS:** Arroyo is one of the many names given to gulches, gullies, washes, wadis, dongas, etc. Also called Whiplash Willow.

BONPLAND WILLOW *Salix bonplandiana* H. B. K.   PL. 37

Distributed from coastal Calif. and sw. Utah to Baja California, se. Ariz., sw. N.M., and Guatemala. This willow has *often-evergreen* leaves 3–7 in. long, ½–1½ in. wide, *fine-toothed,* thick, firm, shiny above, distinctly whitened and sometimes hairy beneath, long- or short-pointed, and with either U- or V-shaped bases. Leafstalks ¼–½ in. long, without glands. Twigs reddish, *hairless;* buds medium. Height to 50 ft. Desert springs and moist soils to 5000 ft. elevation. **SIMILAR SPECIES:** (1) Arroyo Willow has leaves mostly without teeth and tips ± blunt. (2) Pacific Willow has leafstalk glands present. (3) Red Willow buds show a linear scale-edge overlap. **REMARKS:** A. J. A. Bonpland was a French botanist of the late 18th and early 19th centuries.

RED WILLOW *Salix laevigata* Bebb   NOT SHOWN

Similar to Bonpland Willow and also with foliage whitened beneath. Twigs *hairy,* reddish. Rather than the bud scale edges being fused as in most other willows, a margin of the single bud scale is *overlapped* on the surface. Otherwise smooth bud. Distributed much like Bonpland Willow. **SIMILAR SPECIES:** Goodding Willow (p. 319) also has buds that show a bud scale margin. Its leaves are green beneath and more slender, however, and its twigs are yellowish. **REMARKS:** Earlier accepted as part of Bonpland Willow.

MACKENZIE WILLOW   PL. 37
Salix mackenzieana (Hook.) Barrett ex Anderss.

A willow of the Canadian Rockies, ranging west to Vancouver I. and south to the cen. Sierra and n. Utah. Leaves 2½–4 in. long, ⅛–1½ in. wide, fine-toothed, *short-pointed,* yellow-green, hairless and whitened beneath, and *heart- or U-shaped* at the base. Small *stipules* may be present. Leafstalks ¼–¾ in. long, without glands. The twigs are *reddish* brown to yellowish, hairless; buds are small. Height to 20 ft. **SIMILAR**

MACKENZIE WILLOW

COASTAL PLAIN WILLOW

PEACHLEAF WILLOW

SPECIES: (1) Meadow Willow has both long-pointed and V-based leaves that, when young, turn black upon drying. (2) Pacific Willow has leafstalk glands and long-pointed foliage. See (3) Peachleaf Willow.

COASTAL PLAIN WILLOW *Salix caroliniana* Michx. **PL. 37**
Primarily an eastern tree but extending its range west to s. Okla. and to cen. Texas. Leaves 3–7 in. long, ½–1¼ in. wide, fine-toothed, *long-pointed,* bright green above, hairless and whitened beneath. Small stipules usually present, and leaf bases U-shaped. Leafstalks ¼–½ in. long with no glands. Twigs somewhat *hairy,* reddish and *brittle* at the base. They do *not* droop. Buds small. Height to 35 ft. **SIMILAR SPECIES:** (1) Peachleaf Willow is more northern and has leaves wider, twigs more firmly attached at the base and drooping moderately. (2) Black Willow (Pl. 36) is a larger tree with narrower leaves pale but not whitened beneath. Its leaf bases are V-shaped and twigs hairless. **REMARKS:** Also known as Ward Willow from an earlier scientific name.

PEACHLEAF WILLOW *Salix amygdaloides* Anderss. **PL. 37**
Primarily a Rocky Mts. and Great Plains species but with a distribution extending almost across the n. U.S. and from the prairie provinces of Canada to w. Texas. Leaves 3–7 in. long, ¾–1¼ in. wide, yellow-green, *long-pointed, U-based, dull-surfaced,* fine-toothed, hairless, somewhat leathery, whitened beneath. Leafstalks ½–¾ in. long and *without* glands. Twigs *shiny,* hairless, red-brown or *orange, drooping* moderately; buds small. Height to 40 ft. **SIMILAR SPECIES:** (1) Mackenzie Willow has short-pointed leaves and mostly red-brown twigs. (2) Pacific Willow and (3) Shining Willow (Pl. 38) have leafstalk glands and shiny foliage. See (4) Coastal Plain Willow.

These willows have moderately *broad* leaves mostly 2–4 times longer than wide. Except for Shining Willow, they are whitened beneath, mostly long-stalked, and lack leafstalk glands and long-pointed leaf tips. Several species always lack leaf teeth; others are variably without them. None is evergreen. Most are northern species. See also Pls. 36, 37, 39.

SHINING WILLOW *Salix lucida* Muhl. ssp. *lucida* PL. 38

From ne. N. America this tree ranges west to e. Sask. and, locally, in the Dakotas. Leaves 2–6 in. long, ½–1¼ in. wide, fine-toothed, shiny, hairless, *long-pointed*, mostly V-based, and sometimes pale but *not* whitened beneath. Stipules large, usually present. Leaf-stalk *glands* present. Twigs dark, hairless, and brittle-based; buds medium. Height 10–15 (25) ft.; diameter 1–6 (12) in. SIMILAR SPECIES: The only willow of this plate with either leafstalk glands or long-pointed foliage. Among willows with leaves of medium width (Pl. 37), (1) Meadow Willow has foliage becoming black on drying, while (2) Peachleaf Willow has leaves not shiny. Neither species displays leafstalk glands. REMARKS: Pacific Willow, and an associated form (p. 322), are now judged to be western sub-species of Shining Willow.

PUSSY WILLOW *Salix discolor* Muhl. PL. 38

Ornamental in spring when the furry catkin buds grow large, this willow ranges across Canada from cen. B.C. and Lab. south to Idaho, sw. S.D., e. Tenn., and N.J. Leaves 2–5 in. long, ¼–1¼ in. wide, mostly *coarse-toothed,* short-pointed, blue-green, whitened beneath, mostly *hairless,* U- or V-based, and with large stipules

SHINING WILLOW

PUSSY WILLOW

usually present. Leafstalks ½–1 in. long. Twigs purplish, hairy or not; buds large. Height to 30 ft. **SIMILAR SPECIES:** (1) Littletree, (2) Balsam, and (3) Bebb willows, also Canadian trees with toothed leaves, often have hairy foliage. Littletree Willow has small finetoothed leaves, often-hairy twigs, and stipules present. Balsam Willow has fine-toothed and fir-scented leaves. Bebb Willow has leaves with ⅛–⅜-in. leafstalks and twigs that tend to branch at wide angles.

LITTLETREE WILLOW *Salix arbusculoides* Anderss. **PL. 38**
A shrub or small tree common in Alaska and nw. Canada. Leaves dark green, 1–3 in. long, ⅜–¾ in. wide (some specimens with leaves relatively slender, 5–6 times longer than wide), *fine-toothed,* short-pointed, silver-hairy beneath, bases *V-shaped;* stipules lacking. Twigs hairy or not, red-brown. Height to 30 ft. **SIMILAR SPECIES:** See Pussy Willow. **REMARKS:** This species and Feltleaf Willow occur in Alaska but not in the lower 48 states.

BALSAM WILLOW *Salix pyrifolia* Anderss. **PL. 38**
With crushed leaves yielding a *firlike odor,* this willow occurs across Canada and the n. U.S. mainly east of the Rocky Mts. Leaves 1–5 in. long, 1–1½ in. wide, *fine-toothed,* dark green, mostly hairless, whitened beneath, short-pointed, *U-based,* and with stipules small or lacking. Twigs and buds reddish, hairless; buds medium. Height to 20 ft. **SIMILAR SPECIES:** See Pussy Willow.

FELTLEAF WILLOW *Salix alaxensis* (Anderss.) Cov. **PL. 38**
A tree of the far north with foliage and twigs *thick white-woolly.* Leaves 2–4 in. long, ¼–1½ in. wide, yellow-green, *without* teeth but with *V-shaped* bases and stipules small and slender. Height to

30 ft. in favored locations in Alaska/Yukon area. **SIMILAR SPECIES:** (1) Hooker Willow, also white-woolly, occurs only near the coast, its leaves often toothed and with U-shaped bases. (2) Bebb Willow may have leaves without teeth but foliage is gray-hairy. **REMARKS:** See under Littletree Willow. The specific name refers to Alaska.

SITKA WILLOW *Salix sitchensis* Bong.   PL. 38

A tree of northern coasts that also occurs locally inland to the n. Rockies. Leaves 2–4 in. long, ¾–1½ in. wide, *not* toothed, blue-green, V-based, *shiny, white-silky* beneath, the edges *rolled under.* Leaf tips short-pointed or blunt. Stipules usually evident. Twigs white-hairy or hairless and brittle at the base; buds large. Height to 30 ft. **SIMILAR SPECIES:** The undersides of mature leaves have a distinctive silver-satiny appearance and touch that is unlike that of other willows.

Scouler Willow

SCOULER WILLOW *Salix scouleriana* Barrett ex Hook. **PL. 38**

Widespread throughout wooded regions of w. N. America with leaves 2–5 in. long, ½–1½ in. wide, mostly *without* teeth, *widest near the tip,* short-pointed or *blunt,* more or less wavy-edged, the edges *rolled under.* Foliage V-based, dark green, whitened beneath, and often somewhat *red-hairy.* Stipules small or lacking. Twigs yellow to dark, mostly hairless, tending to *droop;* buds large. Height to 25 (40) ft. To 7000 ft. elevation; not confined to wet sites. **SIMILAR SPECIES:** (1) Sitka Willow, also with leaf edges rolled under, has distinctively silky-hairy leaf undersides. (2) Geyer Willow (Pl. 37) leaves are more narrow, widest at the middle, and short-stalked. **REMARKS:** John Scouler was a Scottish physician who collected plants along the Pacific Coast in the early 19th century. Called Fire Willow in some areas.

BEBB WILLOW *Salix bebbiana* Sarg. **PL. 38**

A common but variable willow of Alaska, Canada, and the Rockies. Leaves 2–3 in. long, ¼–1 in. wide, with coarse teeth or none. Foliage tapered at *both* ends, dull above, whitish- or *gray-hairy* on both sides. Stipules small or lacking. Leafstalks mostly under ⅜ in. long. Twigs *gray-hairy* and tending to branch at wide angles from the branchlets; buds medium. Height to 25 ft. **SIMILAR SPECIES:** See Pussy and Feltleaf willows. **REMARKS:** Like some other willows, its wood has been used for charcoal and gunpowder and its long withes (twigs and branchlets) for baskets and wickerware.

HOOKER WILLOW *Salix hookeriana* Barrett **PL. 38**

A *broad-leaved* and *woolly* willow confined to coastal lowlands from s. Alaska to nw. Calif. Leaves 2–5 in. long, 1–2 in. wide, dark green, *white-woolly beneath, widest near the tip,* short-pointed, bases mostly U-shaped, and teeth coarse or none. Heart-shaped

SCOULER WILLOW

BEBB WILLOW

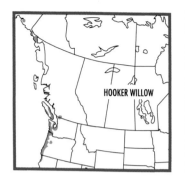

HOOKER WILLOW

TRACY WILLOW

stipules sometimes present. Leafstalks ¼–⅜ in. Twigs stout, *gray-hairy*, and easily detached at the base; buds large, dark, hairy. Height to 30 ft. Stream mouths, lagoons, and sand dunes within a few miles of the ocean, to 500 ft. elevation from near Anchorage, Alaska, to n. Calif. **SIMILAR SPECIES:** (1) Feltleaf Willow has wedge-based leaves that are not toothed. Its woolly twigs are a more brilliant white. Near the Ore.-Calif. border, (2) Tracy Willow has smaller and less hairy foliage. **REMARKS:** Rapidly invades burned areas. William J. Hooker was a British botanist who published a 19th-century book on the flora of n. North America.

TRACY WILLOW   *Salix tracyi* Ball   PL. 38

Native only in extreme sw. Ore. and nw. Calif. Leaves blue-green, 1¼–2 *in. long*, ½–¾ in. wide, mostly without teeth, *V-based, widest toward the tip*, whitened and often somewhat hairy beneath, and short-pointed or blunt-tipped. Leafstalks under ¼ in. Twigs slender, hairless. Height to 20 ft. Stream sandbars to 500 ft. elevation. **SIMILAR SPECIES:** See Scouler and Hooker willows. **REMARKS:** Recent study holds that this plant is not distinct from Arroyo Willow (Pl. 37).

NONWILLOWS WITH NARROW WILLOWLIKE LEAVES (PLATE 39)

Many willows have leaves slender or nearly so (Pls. 36, 37). Other willows have wider foliage (Pl. 38). Some plants other than willows, however, also have alternate, thin leaves 3–15 times as long as wide. These include the species of this plate as well as Narrowleaf Cottonwood (Pl. 31) plus Fire and Black cherries (Pl. 42). A few additional trees have narrow evergreen leaves that are thick, leathery, and sometimes slender (see oaks, Pls. 33, 34; Arizona Madrone, Pl. 45; and Bluegum Eucalyptus, Pl. 46). *None* of the narrow-leaved nonwillows, however, has the distinctive buds (with a single, smooth, caplike scale) characteristic of willows. The first five species of this group are evergreen.

CALIFORNIA-BAY
Umbellularia californica (Hook. & Arn.) Nutt.

Coastal Calif. and sw. Ore. plus the w. slopes of the Sierra Nevada are the home areas of this broad-leaved *evergreen* tree. Leaves 3–5 in. long, ¾–1 in. wide, short-pointed to blunt-tipped, mostly V-based, yellow-green and shiny above, *pale beneath,* hairless, leathery, *without* teeth, and strongly *spicy-scented* when crushed. Leafstalks *only* ⅛–¼ *in. long.* Twigs green and (like the leaves) aromatic when crushed. Buds small, *without* scales. Flowers small, yellow, in clusters at the leaf bases, Dec.–April. Fruits greenish purple, ¾–1 in. long, seed large, pulp thin, Oct. and later. Height 30–80 ft.; diameter 1–3 ft. Fertile soils, to 6000 ft. elevation. **SIMILAR SPECIES:** Golden Chinkapin has nonaromatic leaves with yellow undersides. **REMARKS:** The generic name refers to the umbrellalike flower clusters. Sometimes called California-laurel or Oregon-myrtle. Leaves are used in cooking to provide flavor. Wood was made into fine furniture when large trees were more available;

Bark of California-bay

CALIFORNIA-BAY

now used mostly for candlesticks and small woodenware. Squirrels and Steller's jays eat the fruits.

GOLDEN CHINKAPIN PL. 39
Chrysolepis chrysophylla (Dougl. ex Hook.) Hjelmq.

A large *evergreen* tree mostly of coastal regions from sw. Wash. to cen. Calif. and locally in the Sierra. Leaves dark green, much like California-bay but *not* spicy-scented, the tips *sharp,* short- or long-pointed, mostly V-based, and the undersides *golden yellow.* Twigs mostly yellow-scaled like the leaves; buds scaly and *clustered* at the twig ends. Flowers tiny, whitish; male blossoms in catkins, female ones in small groups, both at the leaf angles, May–June. Fruits prickly burs 1–1¼ in. long, 4-parted and containing 1–3 nuts that require two years to mature. Stumps sprout after fires. Height 50–80 (130) ft.; diameter 1–3 (4) ft. Mountain forests to 10,000 ft. elevation. **SIMILAR SPECIES:** (1) Canyon Live Oak (Pl. 33) has clustered end buds and sometimes yellow leaf undersides, but leaves are smaller, often prickly, and fruits are acorns. (2) See California-bay. **REMARKS:** Not an important timber tree, though wood is strong. Browsed by mule deer. Believed to sometimes attain an age of 500 years. Related to the Chestnut and chinkapins (*Castanea*) of e. N. America, but they have toothed deciduous leaves. This western relative is reported also to be susceptible to the chestnut blight, a fungal disease that has nearly exterminated the Chestnut (*C. dentata* [Marsh.] Borkh.) in the East. The generic name formerly was *Castanopsis.*

PACIFIC BAYBERRY *Myrica californica* Cham. PL. 39

Distributed naturally only near the coast, this species occurs from sw. Wash. to s. Calif. Leaves 3–4 in. long, ½–1 in. wide, *evergreen, coarse-toothed* (sometimes without teeth), *short-pointed, hairless,* and *crowded* toward the twig tips. Foliage also shiny above, *narrowly wedge-based,* widest above the middle, often with scattered black or *yellow resin dots beneath* (use lens), and somewhat *aromatic* when crushed. Twigs hairy or not; bud scales several, red-brown. Flowers tiny, greenish, without petals, in *catkins* about 1 in. long at the leaf angles, spring. Fruits ⅛–¼ in. in diameter,

GOLDEN CHINKAPIN

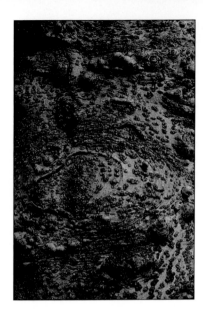

Bark of Pacific Bayberry

brownish, warty, with a thin, whitish, waxy coating. Height to 35 ft. Thickets, sand dunes, wet meadows, and hillsides; low elevations. **SIMILAR SPECIES:** In coastal areas, (1) California-bay also has evergreen foliage that is aromatic when crushed, but its odor is more strong, the leaves are without both teeth and resin dots, and the bases are not so narrow; (2) Golden Chinkapin has leaves not toothed and "solid gold" beneath. From Texas eastward, (3) Southern Bayberry has resin dots on both leaf surfaces. **REMARKS:** One of the several nonlegumes that develops root nodules to maintain nitrogen-fixing bacteria. Will grow on poor soils. Also called Waxmyrtle. California quail are among the birds that eat the fruits. In the e. U.S., early colonists dipped the fruits of the Northern Bayberry (*M. pensylvanica* Loisel.) in hot water and skimmed the melted wax to make pleasantly scented candles.

SOUTHERN BAYBERRY *Myrica cerifera* L.   **NOT SHOWN**
An *evergreen* tree or shrub of the southeastern states whose range extends west to cen. and s. Texas. Similar to the last species but leaves 2–3 in. long, ⅛ in. wide, sometimes long-pointed, with yellow resin dots on *both* surfaces. Height 10–30 (40) ft.; diameter 3–10 (12) in. Flowers April–June; fruits wax-covered nutlets, ⅛

SOUTHERN BAYBERRY

TORREY VAUQUELINIA

in. in diameter, Aug.–Oct. Damp, sandy soils. **REMARKS:** A honey plant. Leaves have been used to flavor soups and other foods. It is said that a blue dye can be made from water used to melt bayberry wax. Reportedly, this water was also used to treat dysentery. Fruits are consumed by many birds including bobwhite quail and ruffed grouse.

TORREY VAUQUELINIA   PL. 39
Vauquelinia californica (Torr.) Sarg.

Despite the specific name, only s. Ariz. and Baja California are home areas for this shrub or small tree. Leaves 2–4 in. long, ¼–½ in. wide, leathery, *evergreen, hairy* beneath, with somewhat *parallel coarse-toothed* margins, V-shaped bases, and short-pointed tips. Twigs and buds hairy. Flowers small, white, in broad twig-end clusters, June. Fruits dry, egg-shaped, hairy capsules, about ¼ in. long, Aug. Height to 20 ft. Mountain slopes and canyons, to 5000 ft. elevation. **SIMILAR SPECIES:** Desert-willow leaves are deciduous, much longer, and not toothed. **REMARKS:** Boundaries of far western states were not well defined when the species was named. Wood is heavy, close-grained, and reddish. Also called Arizona Rosewood. N. L. Vauquelin was an 18th-century French chemist.

JUMPING-BEAN SAPIUM   PL. 39
Sapium biloculare (Wats.) Pax.

Found only in sw. Ariz. and nw. Mexico. Like most other members of the Euphorbia family, the sap is *milky,* irritating to touch, dangerous to the eyes, and *poisonous* to swallow. Leaves 1–2 in. long, ⅜–⅝ in. wide, deciduous, *fine-toothed,* often *crowded at twig ends,* U-based, short-pointed or blunt, and not evergreen. Twigs hairless and often *spurlike,* roughened by crowded leaf scars; bundle scar 1. Flowers tiny, without petals, in slender spikes at twig ends,

JUMPING-BEAN SAPIUM

March–Nov. Fruits 2-lobed dry capsules about ⅓ in. long, containing a mottled seed. Height to 20 ft. Desert gullies and streambeds to 2500 ft. elevation. **SIMILAR SPECIES:** None of our other willowlike trees has roughened spur branches or milky sap. Tallowtree (p. 286) is related. **REMARKS:** One of several southwestern and Mexican plants with seeds inhabited by insect larvae whose actions may cause the seed to move. Parts of the plant have been used to anesthetize fish, but this is now illegal. Native Americans are reported also to have poisoned their arrows with the sap.

DESERT-WILLOW *Chilopsis linearis* (Cav.) Sweet   **PL. 39**

This nonwillow with long and *very narrow* leaves occurs from s. Calif., sw. Utah, and w. Texas south into n. Mexico. Leaves 3–7 in. long and *narrow*, only ⅛–¼ in. wide, *parallel-sided*, long-pointed, V-based, hairless, *deciduous*, and *without* teeth. Some leaves and leaf scars (mostly on low branches) may be opposite or in whorls of 3. Twigs long, slender, hairless; buds tiny, at right angles to twigs; end bud false. Bundle scar 1. Flowers showy, 1–1¼ in. long, white to purple, in twig-end clusters, April–Aug. Fruits slender, brown, dry, *podlike* capsules 4–12 in. long, splitting in autumn to release small winged seeds; pale capsule remnants often remain in winter. Sprouts after being cut. Height to 35 ft. Desert washes. **SIMILAR SPECIES:** (1) Russian-olive has much shorter leaves and is silver-scaled overall. (2) See also Torrey Vauquelinia. **REMARKS:** Frequently planted for ornament. Sometimes used for fence posts. Common in Joshua Tree National Park, Calif.

RUSSIAN-OLIVE *Elaeagnus angustifolius* L.   **PL. 39**

A drought-hardy species introduced from Eurasia and planted widely. Leaves 1–4 in. long, ⅓–1 in. wide, dark green above, *silver-*

DESERT-WILLOW

Desert-willow

scaled beneath, U- or V-based, short-pointed, and *without* teeth. Twigs *silver-white;* branchlets brown; bud scales 2–4; bundle scar 1. May be thorny. Root sprouts common. Flowers small, yellowish, at leaf angles, spring. Fruits ¼ in. long, egg-shaped, ± fleshy, silver-red to white in winter. Mature bark brown. Height to 25 ft. Hedgerows and ornamental plantings. **SIMILAR SPECIES:** Silver Buffaloberry (Pl. 17) also is silvery and often thorny, but it has opposite leaves. **REMARKS:** Not related to the Old World cultivated olive (*Olea europaea* L.). Often called Oleaster. Frequently planted on plains areas as a windbreak and in towns as an ornamental. Fruits are eaten by fox squirrels, sharptail grouse, ringneck pheasants, and many songbirds.

PEACH *Prunus persica* Batsch   **PL. 39**
Occasionally escaping from cultivation mainly in the e. U.S. and Calif. Leaves 3–6 in. long, ⅜–1 in. wide, *finely sharp-toothed,* hairless, variably U- or V-based, and *long-pointed.* Twigs hairless, spur branches present, buds hairy, bundle scars 3. Flowers ½–1 in. long, pink, appearing singly or in pairs along the branchlets before the leaves, spring. Fruits *velvety,* yellow, fleshy, tasty; seeds pitted. Trunk mostly marked with horizontal streaks. Height to 25 ft. **SIMILAR SPECIES:** See cherries, Pl. 42.

Alders are mainly northern plants, growing mostly in damp soils and often forming thickets along waterways. Flowers and fruits occur in catkins. The slender, drooping, male flower clusters are 1–6 in. long; female catkins develop into persistent *woody brown cones* only ⅜–1 in. long and mostly in branched groups. The immediate cone stalks of most species are thick (¹⁄₁₆ in. or more) and shorter than the cones.

The leaves are deciduous, mostly 2–5 in. long, quite wide, short-pointed, with mostly evenly U-shaped bases, *double-toothed* edges, and parallel main veins. They are mainly hairless, with teeth often glandular. Buds mostly have 2 (3) scales that meet at the edges, *not* overlapping. Buds are smooth, usually blunt, mostly *stalked* (narrow-based), and *reddish* when mature. End bud true; bundle scars 3. Most western species have light gray trunk bark. Inner bark of some species turns red-brown when exposed to air.

Alders are among the few nonlegumes that develop root swellings harboring nitrogen-fixing soil bacteria. These microorganisms convert atmospheric nitrogen into fertilizer compounds that provide nutrients for their hosts and neighboring plants. Alder foliage and bark have astringent qualities. The leaves are reported to be useful in controlling bleeding from wounds. The pulverized bark is said to be helpful in the treatment of diarrhea as well as skin irritations. Snowshoe hares, mountain-beavers, deer, moose, and elk browse alder twigs, porcupines and beavers gnaw the inner bark, and grouse eat the buds.

California Hazelnut (Pl. 41), whose foliage resembles that of alders, has soft-hairy leaves and nonstalked buds.

RED ALDER *Alnus rubra* Bong.   **PL. 40**

Our largest alder. Mostly coastal in distribution, ranging from se. Alaska to s. Calif. but also local in n. Idaho. Leaves 1½–3 in. wide, edges *narrowly rolled under* (use lens), *deeply double-toothed*, teeth rather *coarse and short-pointed*. Foliage with *10–15* pairs of side veins, whitish or sometimes reddish to reddish-hairy beneath. Mature buds ⅜–½ in. long, blunt, with 2–3 scales *not* overlapping. Cones ½–1 in. long. Trunk bark thin, *gray, mottled with white*. Height 40–60 (100) ft.; diameter 1–3 (4) ft. Damp, but not wet, alluvial soils to 2500 ft. elevation; absent from the Sierra. **SIMILAR SPECIES:** No other western alder has rolled-under leaf edges or cones over ¾ in. long. Most White Alder leaves are finely single-toothed. **REMARKS:** Abundant in its range. Intolerant of shade

Bark of Red Alder

and a rapid invader of newly exposed soils. Red alders are old at 50 years, though some individuals may reach 100. Inner bark yields a red dye. Wood becomes reddish brown; sometimes used for furniture. The whitish bark and streamside habitat often cause it to be mistaken for Paper Birch (Pl. 41).

WHITE ALDER *Alnus rhombifolia* Nutt.   PL. 40

A tree mainly of the Cascades and Sierra Nevada, ranging between Canadian and Mexican borders. Foliage *finely single-toothed* or faintly double-toothed with 9–12 pairs of side veins. Leaf edges *flat*. Mature buds ¼–⅜ in. long, blunt, with 2–3 scales whose edges meet without overlapping. Trunk bark similar in appearance to that of Red Alder but often dark and scaly. Cones ⅜–¾ in. long. Height to 80 ft., diameter

to 3 ft. Streamsides and canyons to 8000 ft. elevation; mostly absent from the coastal strip occupied by Red Alder. **SIMILAR SPECIES:** (1) Red Alder has leaves deeply and rather coarsely double-toothed with leaf edges rolled under. (2) Mountain Alder foliage also is deeply double-toothed but with only 6–9 pairs of side veins and edges flat. (3) Sitka Alder has leaves shiny beneath and buds pointed. **REMARKS:** Wood of value mainly as firewood.

SITKA ALDER
PL. 40

Alnus viridis ssp. *sinuata* (Regel) A. Löve & D. Löve

Ranging from n. Alaska to n. Calif. and nw. Wyo., this species resembles the previous two. Leaf undersides often shiny and sticky, however, and teeth *finely long-pointed* (use lens). Foliage double-toothed with 6–10 pairs of main veins. Mature buds ⅜–½ in. long, *sharp-pointed, resinous,* essentially *not* stalked, and with 4–6 *overlapping* scales. Cones ⅝–1 in. long and, unlike our other alders, mostly on *thin* (1/32 in. or less) stalks, each *as long as the cones.* Trunk bark gray. Height to 35 ft.; diameter to 10 in. Snowslide areas, stream banks and clearings to 7000 ft. elevation. **SIMILAR SPECIES:** Buds with 4–6 scales and ± not stalked, leaf undersides shiny, long-pointed leaf teeth, and thin, long-stalked cones are all unique characteristics among our tree alders. Only Seaside Alder of Okla. and Md.-Del. also has overlapping bud scales. **REMARKS:** Often confused with shrubby Green Alder (*A. viridis* ssp. *crispa* [Ait.] Turr.) at interior far-northern locations. Green Alder leaves, while also having fine long-pointed teeth, are distinguished by their single- rather than double-toothed edges. Green Alder is sometimes also called Mountain Alder (but see next species).

SPECKLED ALDER

ARIZONA ALDER

MOUNTAIN ALDER   PL. 40
Alnus incana ssp. *tenuifolia* (Nutt.) Breit.

A tree of cold climates and medium to high elevations, distributed from cen. Alaska and nw. Canada south in the mountains to cen. Calif., se. Ariz., and w. N.M. Leaves 1–3 in. wide, *finely* and often deeply *double-toothed, dull* green beneath, with 6–9 pairs of major side veins, and edges *flat*. Leaf undersides have veinlets in an irregular *network* and *not* regularly parallel (use lens). Mature buds ¼–⅜ in. long, *blunt*, slightly resinous, some with bases not stalked. Cones ⅜–⅝ in. long. Trunk brown or gray with horizontal bars (lenticels). Height to 30 ft. Wet sites, on lowlands in the north but to 10,000 ft. elevation farther south. **SIMILAR SPECIES:** Mountain Alder probably is best identified by elimination. It lacks the rolled leaf edges, more numerous veins, and whitish leaf undersides of (1) Red Alder and the shiny leaf undersides and stalkless pointed buds of (2) Sitka Alder. Unlike (3) White Alder, its leaves are more deeply double-toothed and have only 6–9 pairs of major veins. It lacks the ladderlike pattern of veinlets found in Canada's (4) Speckled Alder and the narrow foliage of (5) Arizona Alder. **REMARKS:** Also known as Thinleaf Alder, a translation of the subspecific name.

SPECKLED ALDER *Alnus rugosa* (Du Roi) Spreng.   PL. 40
Primarily a Canadian tree nearly crossing the continent from the Yukon and cen. B.C. to Lab., Nfld., and ne. U.S. Similar to Mountain Alder, but the tiny veinlets are raised, regularly parallel, and *ladderlike* on leaf undersides (use lens). Side veins are 9–12 pairs. Trunk bark brown, smooth, with horizontal marks (lenticels). Cones ½–⅝ in. Height 20–30 ft.; diameter to 6 in. **REMARKS:** See Remarks under Mountain Alder.

ARIZONA ALDER   *Alnus oblongifolia* Torr.   **PL. 40**
   Much like Mountain Alder but growing to a *larger* size. It differs
   also in that it has leaves *narrowly* egg-shaped with 9–13 side
   veins, leaf bases mostly *V-shaped,* and buds *about ¼ in. long.* Bark
   of large trees is *checkered,* broken into small plates. Cones ⅜–¾
   in. Height to 60 ft.; diameter to 3 ft. Said to be more common
   than Mountain Alder in Ariz. and w. N.M. Also extends into n.
   Mexico.

SEASIDE ALDER   *Alnus maritima* (Marsh.) Muhl. ex Nutt. **PL. 40**
   A rare tree recorded in the West only in Johnston and Pontotoc
   counties, Okla. Leaves 1–2¼ in. wide, narrowly elliptical, *pointed
   at both ends, singly and coarsely toothed,* glossy and with 5–7 pairs
   of side veins. Bud scales narrow and *distinct,* the edges *not* join-
   ing. Cones ⅜–¾ in. Flowers in *late summer.* Height to 30 ft.; diameter to 6 in. Also occurs in coastal districts of Md. and Del.
   REMARKS: Fossil evidence indicates that the separate populations
   are survivors from a more widespread distribution in earlier geologic time.

OTHER TREES WITH ALTERNATE LEAVES MOSTLY DOUBLE-TOOTHED
(PLATE 41)

   In addition to alders (Pl. 40) and some cherries (Pl. 42), the western birches, hornbeams, and elms also have deciduous, more or
   less egg-shaped, and (except for Siberian Elm) *double-toothed*
   leaves. All have 3 bundle scars (but see California Hazelnut),
   false end buds, and inconspicuous blossoms.
   These birches, hornbeams, and hazelnuts are closely related
   catkin-bearing trees with smooth, *even-based* leaves (except California Hazelnut) and *non-fibrous* inner bark. The birches have
   distinctive smooth white or brown bark with *horizontal streaks*
   (lenticels), hairless buds with only 2–3 scales, and tiny, crowded,
   dry fruits along an often persistent stem. Short *spur branches* of
   densely clustered leaves and leaf scars are usually present. Hornbeams and California Hazelnut have rough, gray-brown trunks,
   6–8 bud scales, and no spur branches. The springtime flowers of
   hornbeams develop into unusual papery, inflated, bladderlike
   fruits that contain small nutlets. Those of the hazelnut grow into
   long-beaked nuts.

   Elms have dark, furrowed trunks and generally *uneven-based,
   often sandpapery* leaves. Their buds have 6–8 scales, flowers are
   inconspicuous, and fruits are small, winged, papery, oval to circu-

Bark of Paper Birch

lar, and single-seeded. Unlike other trees with similar foliage, the inner bark of both branches and roots is tough and *fibrous*. Starting with a small cut, it can be peeled in strips to assist in identification and twisted into emergency fishlines, nets, or snares. Elm wood is difficult to split.

PAPER BIRCH *Betula papyrifera* Marsh. PL. 41

Distributed from Alaska, transcontinental across Canada and with southward extensions into the n. Rockies and nearby areas plus the ne. U.S. The *white trunk* with dull, *peeling* outer layers and thin, dark, horizontal *lines* is distinctive. Leaves 2–4 in. long, mostly *long-pointed,* and with 5–9 pairs of rather parallel and ± hairy side veins. Twigs *slightly* rough-warty or smooth. Buds *blunt.* Flowers spring. Fruiting catkins slender, ¼ in. wide, and 1½ in. long, Aug.–Sept. Height 70–80 (120) ft.; diameter 1–3 (4) ft. Open woods, cutover areas. **SIMILAR SPECIES:** See next three species. In addition, Quaking Aspen, and sometimes other poplars (Pl. 31), have yellowish to white smooth trunks. Their bark does not peel, however, or have horizontal streaks. See also Red Alder (Pl. 40). **REMARKS:** Birch bark has been used by Native Americans for canoe and wigwam coverings (tied in place with spruce rootlets), boxes, cups, makeshift shoes, and emergency snow goggles. They, as well as early French-Canadian voyageurs, used the springtime sap as a refreshing drink and also boiled it into a sweet syrup. The curled outer bark is highly flammable and provides tinder even when damp. Deeper bark should not be taken from living trees as it leaves black scars. Leaves have been used for tea but are not as peppermint-scented as those of the eastern Sweet (*B. lenta* L.) and Yellow (*B. alleghaniensis* Britton) birches. Paper birch lumber is used for woodenware, pulp, and fuel. Seeds and buds are eaten by ruffed and sharptail grouse as well as by numerous songbirds. Twigs are cropped by moose, deer, mountain goats, and snowshoe hares. Beavers and porcupines consume the inner bark. See Remarks under Water Birch.

ALASKA WHITE BIRCH *Betula neoalaskana* Sarg. **NOT SHOWN**
Otherwise resembling Paper Birch, this tree has leaves ± hairless and twigs *densely* covered with *large* resin-glands. Height to 80 ft. Distributed from n. cen. Alaska to nw. Ontario.

KENAI BIRCH *Betula kenaica* Evans **NOT SHOWN**
A northern brown- to white-barked birch with leaves less than 2 in. long, 2-6 pairs of side veins, and *few small* twig-glands. To 35 ft. tall. Ranges from w. Alaska to w.-cen. Yukon.

WEEPING BIRCH *Betula pendula* Roth **NOT SHOWN**
Much like Paper Birch but with twigs/branchlets pendent and the trunk bark *glossy* white, black-fissured at the base, sometimes peeling in lengthy strips. Leaves 1–3 in. long, ± hairless, and (like the twigs) with *small* resin-dots. Twigs hairless, ± smooth. Height to 40 ft. A landscape tree naturalized in Washington State and perhaps elsewhere. Also known as European White Birch.

WATER BIRCH

KNOWLTON HORNBEAM

WATER BIRCH *Betula occidentalis* Hook. PL. 41
Found locally from sw. Canada to cen. Calif. and n. N.M. Trunks sometimes several, *red-brown, shiny,* with *whitish horizontal streaks,* and *not* peeling. Leaves hairless, 1–3 in. long, mostly *short-pointed,* round-based, and with 4–5 pairs of side veins. Twigs mostly rough-warty; buds *pointed,* ⅛ in. long, hairless. Flowers spring. Fruiting catkins stout, often ⅜ in. wide and 1 in. long, late summer. Height to 25 (40) ft.; diameter to 6 (10) in. Thickets, streamsides to 8000 ft. elevation. **SIMILAR SPECIES:** Some cherries have spur branches and dark, birchlike trunk bark. Their broken twigs, however, have a peculiar sour odor, leaves are mostly single-toothed, leafstalks bear glands, and fruits are fleshy. **REMARKS:** Hybridizes with Paper Birch, producing specimens with intermediate characteristics. Provides food and lodge materials for beavers.

KNOWLTON HORNBEAM *Ostrya knowltonii* Cov. PL. 41
Local in the s. Rockies. Leaves 1–3 in. long, ¾–2 in. wide, *egg-shaped, and short-pointed.* Twigs hairy or not. Fruit clusters 1–2 in. long. Height to 30 ft. Moist canyons, n. Ariz. and se. Utah to Guadeloupe Mts., w. Texas. **SIMILAR SPECIES:** (1) Chisos Hornbeam has narrower leaves and shorter fruit clusters. It occurs only in the Chisos Mts., w. Texas. (2) Eastern Hornbeam has long-pointed foliage and a more eastern and northern distribution. (3) Birches and (4) cherries (Pl. 42) have distinctively striped trunk bark. The cherries also have leafstalk glands. **REMARKS:** Discovered in the Grand Canyon late in the 19th century by Frank Knowlton. Hornbeams are often known as Hophornbeams because the fruits resemble those of hops (*Humulus* spp.), a vine fruit used to flavor beer.

CHISOS HORNBEAM *Ostrya chisosensis* Correll NOT SHOWN
Similar to Knowlton Hornbeam but with leaves only ¼–1¼ in. wide and mostly *elliptical.* Fruit clusters ½–1 in. long. Height to 45 ft. Known only from canyons in the Chisos Mts., Big Bend Nat'l. Park, Texas.

EASTERN HORNBEAM NOT SHOWN
Ostrya virginiana (Mill.) K. Koch
An eastern tree occurring west to the Black Hills of sw. S.D. and ne. Wyo. Similar to Knowlton Hornbeam but leaves *long-pointed,* 2–5 in. long, and 1–2 in. wide. Fruit clusters 2–2¼ in. long, Aug.–Oct. Height 20–30 ft., diameter 1–2 ft. Fertile woods. Fruits and twigs eaten by many forms of wildlife.

CALIFORNIA HAZELNUT

PL. 41

Corylus cornuta ssp. *californica* (A. DC.) E. Murr.

Although the species is transcontinental in range, only this sub-species of the Beaked Hazelnut becomes a small tree, though often with several stems. Leaves egg-shaped to nearly *circular,* 2–4 in. across, *heart-shaped* at the base, and mostly pale and *soft-hairy* beneath. Twigs usually *hairy;* buds blunt with several scales, the lowest ones large and *paired;* bundle scars 3 or sometimes more. Fruits are edible and usually paired nuts that are enclosed in husks prolonged to form a 1–2-in. *beak.* Height to 25 ft.; diameter to 6 in. Thickets. SIMILAR SPECIES: Alders (Pl. 40) of the Pacific slope have hairless leaves and stalked buds. REMARKS: Fruits are consumed by ruffed and sharptail grouse, prairie chickens, bob-white quail, jays, and many rodents. Deer forage on the foliage and twigs.

AMERICAN ELM *Ulmus americana* L.

PL. 41

An eastern species whose range extends west to the plains states. Full-sized wild trees are becoming rare as a result of disease. When growing in the open as a large tree, however, trunk divides near the ground into large limbs, giving a *unique vase-shaped form.* Leaves 4–6 in. long, variably smooth or sandpapery above, hairless or hairy beneath. Twigs hairless or barely hairy; branch-lets *without* corky "wings." Buds more than ¼ in. long, with light brown but *dark-edged* scales. Flowers March–May. Fruits ⅜–½ in., hairless except for hairy margin, deeply notched, long-stemmed, April–May. Height 80–100 (125) ft.; diameter 2–5 (10) ft. Princi-pally bottomlands. SIMILAR SPECIES: (1) See Slippery Elm. (2) Siberi-an Elm has small single-toothed leaves. (3) Other elms have smaller double-toothed leaves and, sometimes, winged branch-lets. REMARKS: In an earlier generation, the Chestnut (*Castanea*

CALIFORNIA HAZELNUT

AMERICAN ELM

dentata [Marsh.] Borkh.), also of the e. U.S., similarly was decimated by a disease introduced from overseas. Now stands of dead American Elms occupy lowland sites in many places. "Dutch" elm disease is a fungus spread by a beetle. Seeds are eaten by bobwhite quail, European partridge, ruffed grouse, prairie chicken, gray and fox squirrels, and opossum. Cottontail rabbits, snowshoe hares, and white-tailed deer browse the twigs.

SLIPPERY ELM *Ulmus rubra* Muhl.   NOT SHOWN

An eastern species ranging west to the e. Great Plains and cen. Texas. A medium-sized tree with either single or divided trunk. Leaves 4–8 in. long, *short-stalked,* very *rough* and sandpapery above and hairy beneath. Twigs *rough-hairy;* buds prominently *red-hairy* and more than ⅛ in. long. Flowers March–May. Fruits ½ in., nearly circular, hairless except for centers of each side, slightly notched, short-stemmed, and tightly bunched, May–June. Height 40–60 (70) ft.; diameter 1–2 (3) ft. Fertile uplands. **SIMILAR SPECIES:** No other elm has rough-hairy twigs and red-hairy buds. **REMARKS:** The common name of this coarse-textured tree refers to the slimy inner bark, once well known as a scurvy preventive. It was ground into flour or chewed in pieces. Porcupines also may eat this layer. Cottontail rabbits and deer browse the twigs.

CEDAR ELM *Ulmus crassifolia* Nutt.   PL. 41

A *small-leaved, fall-flowering* tree with *sandpaper-surfaced* foliage found from the lower Miss. Valley to cen. and s. Texas. Leaves 1–2 in. Leafstalks *short,* about ⅛ in. or less in length, often nearly lacking. Narrow *corky wings* may occur on the branchlets. Twigs and buds hairless; buds ⅛–³⁄₁₆ in. long; bud scales brown *without* dark borders. Flowers *Aug.–Oct.* Fruits ³⁄₁₆–½ in. long, deeply notched, and white-hairy, Sept.–Oct. Height to 70 ft.; diameter

SLIPPERY ELM

CEDAR ELM

Bark of Winged Elm

1–2 ft. Bottomlands. SIMILAR SPECIES: Winged Elm also has small leaves with short leafstalks and may have winged branchlets. Its leaves are smooth-textured, however, and it produces flowers in spring. REMARKS: Often associated with Eastern Redcedar or Ashe Juniper (Pl. 10), both of which are locally called cedars.

WINGED ELM *Ulmus alata* Michx.   **NOT SHOWN**
Another eastern species that reaches cen. Texas. Leaves 1–2 in. long, *smooth* above, hairy beneath. Leafstalks *short.* Twigs and buds hairless or nearly so; buds less than 3/16 in. long; bud scales with dark borders. At least some of the branchlets are usually with wide, *corky wings.* Flowers March. Fruits are 1/4–3/8 in. long, deeply notched, hairy or not, with fringed edges and pointed tips, long-stemmed, March–April. Trunk single or divided. Height 40–50 (60) ft.; diameter 1–2 ft. SIMILAR SPECIES: (1) Siberian Elm has single-toothed foliage and small dark buds. (2) See Cedar Elm.

SIBERIAN ELM *Ulmus pumila* L.   **PL. 41**
A hardy shrub or small tree introduced from Asia and established from Minn. to N.M. and westward. The 1–3-in. leaves are usually narrow, only slightly uneven-based, and mostly *single-toothed.* Twigs and buds nearly hairless, twigs without wings, leaf buds small, *dark,* and *blunt.* Winter flower buds *nearly black,* enlarged,

Siberian Elm

evident even from a distance.
Fruits hairless, nearly circular,
⅜–⅝ in. long, deeply notched. Height to 80 ft.; diameter 2–4 ft.
Moist sites and hedgerows. **SIMILAR SPECIES:** Other elms have double-toothed leaves and mostly brown buds. **REMARKS:** A windbreak species on the plains. Resistant to Dutch elm disease. Often called Chinese Elm, but this name is better applied to the autumn-flowering, single-toothed, introduced ornamental (*U. parvifolia* Jacq.).

CHERRIES AND THORNLESS PLUMS (PLATE 42)

Cherries and plums (plus Peach, Pl. 39) are all members of the genus *Prunus* in the rose family. On this plate are thornless species, mostly with fine-toothed leaves. See also thorny plums (Pl. 27), since these are sometimes only slightly thorny. Hollyleaf (Pl. 44) and Catalina (Pl. 45) cherries are both leathery-leaved evergreen species.

The species of this group are mostly alike in having trunks marked with numerous *cross-streaks*, leafstalk or leaf-base *glands* present, buds with more than 3 scales, bundle scars 3, and fruits fleshy with a single seed. Leaves (with 3 exceptions) are single-toothed and mostly long-pointed. The "almond" or sour *odor* of the broken twigs is difficult to describe but once learned (by testing a known plant) is a reliable aid to the identification of many group members, especially cherries. While cherries have true end buds, those of plums are false (use lens). Indian-plum (p. 357) is not a true plum.

Except for Chokecherry and Black Cherry, which have finger-shaped flower/fruit clusters and lack spur branches, the reproductive parts are in umbrella-shaped groups borne on *spur branches*. Remnants of the calyx, the circle of sepals located just

beneath the flower petals, persist under the fruits of some species. Cherry seeds are mostly globular; those of plums often are flattened with opposite lengthwise ridges.

Although the fleshy fruits of most cherries are edible, the young leaves and twigs of these trees frequently contain hydrocyanic acid, believed to lend the characteristic odor to their broken twigs. Depending, apparently, upon the reaction of the stomach juices, the kind of feed previously consumed, and how wilted the plant is when eaten, horses, sheep, and cattle may die, become ill, or remain unaffected after browsing the foliage. Fruits of all species are eaten, however, by a large number of birds and mammals. Wood of the larger cherries is of commercial value.

BITTER CHERRY *Prunus emarginata* Dougl. ex Eaton **PL. 42**
The most western of cherries. Common in the Pacific states and n. Rockies, local in the Southwest. Leaves 1–3 in. long, half as wide, with narrow but mostly *rounded* tips, more or less *blunt* single teeth (use lens), and U- or V-shaped bases. Twigs reddish and hairless. Trunk red-brown, smooth, with horizontal streaks. Flowers in spring. Fruits red to black, calyx deciduous, late summer. To 20 ft. tall. Thickets, open sites. **SIMILAR SPECIES:** (1) Chokecherry has pointed leaves with sharp teeth. (2) Klamath Plum (Pl. 27), also often with blunt leaf tips, usually carries thorns or spine-tipped spur branches. (3) Water Birch (Pl. 41) may have similar bark, but its leaves have double teeth, pointed tips, and no leaf-stalk glands. **REMARKS:** Fruit pulp is bitter, yet eaten by many birds and mammals. Twigs much browsed by mule deer.

CHOKECHERRY *Prunus virginiana* L. **PL. 42**
Widespread over much of the U.S. and Canada. A shrub or small tree with leaves 2–5 in. long, *egg-shaped, sharply* single-toothed

(use lens), short-pointed, with U- or heart-shaped bases, *hairless* midribs, and 8–11 pairs of lateral veins. Leafstalks often reddish. Winter buds hairless, more than ³⁄₁₆ in. long; bud scales *rounded* at tips. Bark gray-brown with shallow fissures. Only this cherry and the next one have spur branches *lacking* and blossoms/fruits in *slender* clusters. Flowers April–July. Fruits purplish, *lacking* persistent calyx remnants, July–Oct. Height 6–20 (30) ft.; diameter 2–6 (8) in. Young woods and thickets. **SIMILAR SPECIES:** See (1) Bitter Cherry and (2) Black Cherry. (3) Sweet, (4) Sour, and (5) Mahaleb cherries have spur branches and fruits in short clusters. **REMARKS:** The tart fruits can be made into delicious jellies and pies. A great number of songbirds as well as ruffed grouse, sharptail grouse, prairie chickens, pheasants, raccoons, black bears, red foxes, deer, bighorn sheep, mountain goats, cottontail rabbits, and several squirrels regularly consume the fruits.

BLACK CHERRY *Prunus serotina* Ehrh.   PL. 42

Ranging in the West from cen. Ariz. and cen. Texas to Guatemala; also over most of the e. U.S. and se. Canada. A small to large tree whose leaves are 2–6 in. long, *narrow,* and *bluntly* single-toothed (use lens). Distinctive among cherries in having the midrib beneath often (especially in the n. U.S.) *prominently fringed* with brown to whitish hairs. Lateral veins more than 13 pairs. Leaf bases either U- or V-shaped. Buds less than ³⁄₁₆ in. long and hairless; bud scales *pointed;* spur branches *lacking.* Mature trunk with rough dark outer bark whose broken plates are marked with short horizontal lines and often expose red-brown underbark where cracked. Flowers in *slender* clusters, May–June. Fruits blackish, *retaining* calyx lobes. June–Oct. Height 60–80 (100) ft.; diameter 2–3 (5) ft. Woods and thickets. **SIMILAR SPECIES:** Only other tree cherry with regularly narrow leaves is (1) Fire Cherry, but it has mostly hairless leaves and buds clustered near the twig tips as well as spur branches and short flower clusters. Leaves of (2) Chokecherry are wider, hairless, bristly sharp-toothed, and with 8–11 pairs of lateral veins; its buds are somewhat longer, with rounded scale tips. Also, remnants of calyx lobes are not retained on its fruits. **REMARKS:** One of the largest cherries, this species is of value for lumber. Wood hard

BLACK CHERRY

and close-grained; used for furniture and interior furnishings. The bitter fruits are often used for jelly. Bark has been used for flavoring. Fruits and twigs eaten by many of the animals listed for Chokecherry.

FIRE (PIN) CHERRY *Prunus pensylvanica* L. f.   PL. 42
Distributed from n. B.C. across Canada to the East Coast and locally southward. A shrub or small tree with *narrow, sharply* single-toothed, hairless leaves 2–5 in. long. Buds short, nearly hairless, with pointed scales and crowded at or *near the ends* of reddish twigs (as well as on spur branches). Bark red-brown, smooth, marked with crossbars. Flowers March–July. Fruits red, calyx deciduous, July–Sept. Height 10–30 (40) ft.; diameter 2–10 (12) in. Thickets and young forests, especially after burns or land clearing. **SIMILAR SPECIES:** (1) Bitter Cherry and (2) Peach (Pl. 39) sometimes have narrow leaves, but they lack crowded end buds and produce different fruits. See (3) Black Cherry. (4) Water Birch (Pl. 41), though with similar bark, has smaller double-toothed leaves and uncrowded end buds with only 2–3 scales. **REMARKS:** Sprouts vigorously following fires. Known also as Bird Cherry. Sour fruits sometimes eaten raw or used in jellies and cough mixtures. Fruits consumed by ruffed and sharptail grouse, ptarmigan, and prairie chickens. Deer, moose, cottontail rabbit, and beaver crop the twigs.

SWEET CHERRY *Prunus avium* (L.) L.   PL. 42
A rather tall tree with a *single* main trunk. Bark *red-brown, smooth,* prominently marked with horizontal stripes, and often peeling. Leaves 2–6 in. long, egg-shaped, rather sharply *double-toothed,* hairless, and with 10–14 pairs of side veins. Buds slender, light brown, more than ¼ in. long. Flowers and fruits clustered on *leafless* spur branches. Flowers April–May. Fruits red to

FIRE CHERRY

black, with persistent calyx, sweet. June–July. Height 30–50 (75) ft.; diameter 1–2 (3) ft. Cultivated, sometimes escapes to wild. **SIMILAR SPECIES:** (1) Sour Cherry has leafy spur branches, usually lacks a central trunk, and has only 6–8 pairs of leaf veins. Blunt leaf teeth and rougher bark also are characteristic. (2) Mahaleb Cherry has often-circular aromatic leaves and hairy twigs. (3)

Chokecherry lacks spur branches and has long flower clusters. (4) Fire Cherry has narrow leaves and crowded end buds. **REMARKS:** Imported from Europe, this species is the parent of many of the sweeter garden cherries. A few ornamental varieties possess variegated foliage. Known also as Mazzard Cherry. Fruits attractive to many songbirds and to squirrels.

SOUR CHERRY *Prunus cerasus* L. PL. 42

A tree usually *without* a central trunk. Bark *grayish,* at least on older trunks *much cracked* and broken, sometimes scaly. Leaves 2–5 in. long, like Sweet Cherry but with rounded teeth and 6–8 pairs of veins. Buds stout, dark brown, and more than ¼ in. long. Flowers and fruits clustered on *leafy* spur branches. Flowers May–June. Fruits red, sour, calyx remnants persistent, July–Aug. Height 20–30 ft.; diameter 10–12 in. May escape from cultivation. **SIMILAR SPECIES:** See Sweet Cherry. **REMARKS:** Believed to have originated in w. Asia. Many cultivated varieties, principally those with tart flavor, are derived from this stock. Preferred for making pies.

MAHALEB CHERRY *Prunus mahaleb* L. PL. 42

Similar to Sour Cherry but with *hairy* twigs and small but wide, often *almost circular, hairless,* single-toothed leaves that are *aromatic* when crushed. Leaves 1–3 in. long, may be heart-shaped at base, mostly rounded, and glandular. Flowers white, in short clusters. Fruits with calyx deciduous. Established locally in the Pacific Northwest and in ne. U.S./se. Canada. **SIMILAR SPECIES:** See (1) Sweet Cherry and (2) Garden Plum. **REMARKS:** *Mahaleb* is an Arabic name. Originally imported from the Caucasus and Europe for grafting stock. Fruits inedible but yield a violet dye. Oil from seeds used to fix perfumes. Aromatic wood once fashioned into pipes and walking sticks. Also called Perfumed Cherry.

GARDEN PLUM *Prunus domestica* L. PL. 42

A small cultivated tree that has escaped to the wild in some localities in the Northwest and in ne. U.S./se. Canada. Leaves 2–4 in. long, 1–1½ in. wide, somewhat hairy beneath, short-pointed, with leaf teeth single and *rounded.* Twigs *hairless.* Flowers spring. Fruits purple, to 1½ in. diameter, calyx deciduous. Height to 25 ft. **SIMILAR SPECIES:** Mahaleb Cherry has velvety twigs and aromatic foliage. **REMARKS:** Fruits marketed fresh and as prunes. Originally native in w. Asia and e. Europe. Sometimes called Damson Plum, a name derived from its original range near Damascus, Syria. A thorny variety is sometimes called Bullace Plum.

MEXICAN PLUM

WILDGOOSE PLUM

MEXICAN PLUM   *Prunus mexicana* Wats.   **PL. 42**

Unlike other thornless plums and most cherries, this species has
foliage both *double-* and *sharp-toothed.* Leaves 2–4 in. long, to 2
in. wide and mostly short-pointed. Twigs *hairless.* Flowers March.
Fruits red to purple; stone nearly circular, not pointed. Height to
25 ft.; diameter to 10 in. Thickets and bottomlands in the Miss.
Valley and again from cen. and s. Texas to n. Mexico.

WILDGOOSE (MUNSON) PLUM   **PL. 42**
Prunus munsoniana Wight & Hedr.

A shrub or small tree with leaves 3–6 in. long, 1–1¼ in. wide,
hairless, *long-pointed,* and bluntly single-toothed. Leaf teeth may
appear to be sharp because of tiny reddish glands. Twigs hairless.
Short fruiting spurs usually present. Fruits red to yellow, stone
pointed at one end. A native species, parent of horticultural varieties. Thickets, Miss. Valley region west to cen. Texas.

MISCELLANEOUS TREES WITH ALTERNATE LEAVES THIN, NOT LEATHERY (PLATE 43)

Except for Tree Tobacco and Alderleaf Cercocarpus, which may
have persistent (evergreen) foliage, these trees have *deciduous*
leaves that are mostly finely single-toothed or smooth-edged and
often blunt-tipped. Bundle scars mostly 3. The fleshy fruits of
species in this group are several-seeded. White and Seaside alders
(Pl. 40), Siberian Elm (Pl. 41), and most cherries (Pl. 42) also
have single-toothed leaves but with associated unique features.
Texas Persimmon (Pl. 46) also may be deciduous in some areas of
that state.

Amelanchier alnifolia (Nutt.) Nutt.

A mainly northern shrub or small tree with leaf blades blunt-tipped, nearly *circular,* and *coarse-toothed* mainly above the middle. Leaves mostly hairless, 1–3 in. long with stalks ½–1 in. long and 3–20 pairs of teeth. Leaf veins 7–9 pairs, rather parallel but yet somewhat curved and branched. Twigs hairless; buds purplish; spur branches present. Flowers in attractive white clusters, petals ⅜–⅝ in. long, April–June. Fruits fleshy, reddish purple, ¼–½ in. in diameter, mostly juicy, June–Aug. Height to 22 ft. Thickets and open woods. **SIMILAR SPECIES:** Both this species and Utah Juneberry are variable. In general, however, (1) Utah Juneberry has a more southern distribution and smaller leaves, leafstalks, petals, and fruits. (2) The buckthorns have leaves more strictly parallel-veined and with fine-toothed or wavy edges. **REMARKS:** The alternate name Saskatoon Juneberry refers to Saskatoon, Sask., and reflects the important distribution of the tree in w. Canada. Also known as Alderleaf Juneberry. Plants of this genus are also called serviceberries, but the reason for that name is not clear (unless, with a European *Sorbus* [Pl. 22] being called Servicetree, it is derived from Sorbusberry). Blacktail, whitetail, and mule

Western (Saskatoon) Juneberry

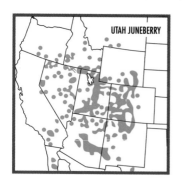

deer all browse the twigs. Sooty grouse, mountain quail, chipmunks, and other wildlife consume the fruits. People also eat them fresh, cooked, or dried.

UTAH JUNEBERRY *Amelanchier utahensis* Koehne **PL. 43**
Similar to the last species but more southern and with leaves only ½–1 ¼ in. long including ¼–½-in. stalks. Flower petals mostly under ⅜ in. long. Fruits only ⅛–¼ in. in diameter. Mountain slopes and canyons in scattered localities.

ALDERLEAF CERCOCARPUS **NOT SHOWN**
Cercocarpus montanus Raf.
Mostly shrubby, with leaves like Birchleaf Cercocarpus (Pl. 44), showing markedly *straight parallel veins, wedge-shaped* bases, and often *coarse teeth toward the tips.* Leaves 1–1 ½ in. long, hairless to hairy, with tips mostly *rounded.* Twigs generally hairless; spur branches *numerous* and buds *scaly.* Flowers greenish, single or in groups of 2–15, on the spurs, March–June. Fruits tiny, dry, and with an attractive, thin, *feathery tail* 1–3 in. long, often remaining in winter. Height to 20 ft.; rarely reaches tree size. Dry slopes. Ore. and sw. S.D. to Ariz., Colo., and n. Mexico. **SIMILAR SPECIES:** (1) Birchleaf Cercocarpus and (2) Hairy Cercocarpus (both Pl. 44) have evergreen foliage. The former occurs westward with all leaves hairless and toothed. The later is distributed in the Mexican border region with leaves silky-hairy and sometimes without teeth. (3) Curlleaf Cercocarpus (Pl. 46) is evergreen with leaf edges not toothed. (4) Juneberries and (5) buckthorns have rounded leaf bases and fleshy fruits. The buckthorns of this plate also lack bud scales and seldom have typical spur branches. **REMARKS:** An important browse species for deer, bighorn sheep and livestock. See discussion of cercocarpuses, p. 360.

A variable group that, despite the common name, has only 1 thorny-twigged species in the West. That species, Hollyleaf Buckthorn (Pl. 27), has both thorns and prickly leaves as well as buds with scales. The buckthorns of this plate and Pl. 45 are without prickles and have hairy buds *without* scales.

All western buckthorns tend to have *parallel* leaf veins. In this respect they resemble the cercocarpuses. In addition to having buds mostly without scales, these buckthorns also have *rounded,* rather than V-shaped, leaf bases. Further, buckthorns mostly *lack* spur branches and have *fine* leaf teeth or none plus *fleshy* several-seeded fruits. The buckthorns of this plate have black mature fruits. Hollyleaf Buckthorn (Pl. 27) and California Buckthorn (Pl. 45) have thick evergreen foliage.

CASCARA BUCKTHORN *Rhamnus purshiana* DC.   PL. 43

A plant of the Pacific Northwest and n. Rockies with *markedly parallel* leaf veins *enlarged* beneath. Leaves 3–6 in. long, 1–2¼ in. wide, blunt-tipped or short-pointed, nearly hairless, *wavy-edged* and/or fine-toothed, clustered at or near twig tip, where they may be nearly opposite. Side leaf veins (prominent on leaf undersides) are 10–15 pairs and *straight* until near the leaf margin. Twigs hairless; buds *rusty-hairy.* Flowers inconspicuous, greenish, clustered in the leaf angles and with stalks of individual blossoms *shorter* than the flower-cluster stalk, May–July. Fruits July–Sept. Trunk bark whitish gray, smooth. Height to 40 ft. SIMILAR SPECIES: In coastal areas of the Northwest, (1) Red Alder (Pl. 40) occurs in the same habitat and has similar bark, but it lacks the parallel-veined foliage, naked buds, and fleshy fruits of this species. (2) Birchleaf Buckthorn has fewer leaf vein pairs and comparatively longer blossom stalks. REMARKS: Young plants occasionally evergreen. Bark harvested commercially for its laxative and tonic properties. Twigs browsed by mule deer; fruits eaten by ruffed grouse, bandtail pigeons, black bears, gray foxes, raccoons, ringtails, and other wildlife.

BIRCHLEAF BUCKTHORN *Rhamnus betulifolia* Greene PL. 43

A southwestern tree. Like the last species but leaves *fine-toothed* at the rounded leaf tip. Foliage with 7–10 pairs of major leaf veins and *more or less hairy* beneath. Twigs also sometimes slightly hairy. The stalks of individual flowers are *longer* than the stalk, if any, that supports the flower cluster. This condition is like that of Carolina Buckthorn and the opposite of that in Cascara Buckthorn. Flowers May–June; fruits July–Oct. Height to 20 ft. Moist

canyons, 4000–7000 ft. elevations, s. Nev., s. Utah, and w. Texas to n. Mexico. **SIMILAR SPECIES:** (1) Western and (2) Utah juneberries and (3) Alderleaf Cercocarpus have parallel leaf veins. They have leaves under 3 in. long, spur branches present, and buds scaly. **REMARKS:** Thought by some botanists not to be clearly separable from Carolina Buckthorn.

CAROLINA BUCKTHORN
Rhamnus caroliniana Walt. **NOT SHOWN**

A small eastern tree distributed west to cen. Texas. Leaves are 2–6 in. long, elliptic, with 8–11 pairs of veins, and usually *hairless* beneath. Leaf tips usually pointed and edges mostly fine-toothed. Crushed foliage has an unpleasant odor. Twigs fine-hairy. Height to 40 ft. Flowers tiny, greenish, in the leaf angles, May–June. Fruits Aug.–Oct. Open fertile soils. **SIMILAR SPECIES:** See Birchleaf Buckthorn.

DOMESTIC APPLE *Malus sylvestris* (L.) Mill. **PL. 43**

A small tree with *rounded top*. Leaves 1–4 in. long, egg-shaped, more or less *round-toothed*, usually somewhat white- or *gray-hairy* beneath, sometimes heart-shaped at the base. Twigs short, stiff, sometimes with thorny tips, usually somewhat *hairy*. Leaf scars somewhat raised, short lines leading downward at sides. Buds usually blunt and hairy, with about 4 scales; end bud true. Flowers white or pinkish, April–June. Fruits more than 1 in. across, Sept.–Nov. Bark scaly and brownish. Height 20–30 (50) ft.; diameter 6–18 in. Hedgerows and old farms. **SIMILAR SPECIES:** Domestic Apple and Domestic Pear are the only species of this plate that usually have *large* fleshy fruits borne on spur branches. See (1) Domestic Pear. (2) Crabapples (Pl. 27) are almost always thorny and with sharp leaf teeth. **REMARKS:** The exact origin of the apple is lost in antiquity, but it is believed that the species originated in the w. Himalayas and traveled westward by way of n. Persia, Asia Minor, the Caucasus, and the Mediterranean countries. The apple of the Bible is believed to have been not our northern fruit but the apricot, still common in the Holy Land. The Domestic Apple persisting in old orchards or locally gone wild is an important food of deer, pheasant, mourning dove, gray fox, and many other animals. Botanists have also used *Pyrus* and *Sorbus* for the generic name.

DOMESTIC PEAR *Pyrus communis* L.   **PL. 43**

Similar to Domestic Apple but usually with several strong upright branches, making a *narrow-topped* tree. Twigs and branchlets nearly *hairless,* more often thorny, bearing *elongate fleshy fruits* containing *grit* cells. Leaves 1–3 in. Buds less blunt and leaf scars less raised than in Domestic Apple. Flowers white, early spring. Fruits green, autumn. Height 20–35 (60) ft.; diameter 6–15 in. Hedgerows and abandoned farms.

INDIAN-PLUM   **NOT SHOWN**

Oemleria cerasiformis (H. & A.) Landon.

Usually a shrub, occasionally treelike. Leaves 2–5 in. long, with teeth *lacking* or faintly wavy-edged, short-pointed or blunt, base *narrowly* V-shaped, fine-hairy beneath (use lens), often clustered near twig ends. Twigs purplish, hairless; pith finely *chambered;* buds ± blunt, green, usually 3-scaled, sometimes stalked; bundle scars 3. Trunk bark sometimes with horizontal markings. Flowers whitish, fragrant, in narrow, pendent clusters, March–April; fruits thinly fleshy, one-seeded, eaten by many birds and mammals. Height 5–15 (22) ft. B.C. to n. Calif. and w. slopes of the Sierra Nevada. Older generic names *Osmaronia* and *Nuttallia* are often seen. Also called Osoberry. See Appendix A for other trees with chambered pith.

TREE TOBACCO *Nicotiana glauca* Graham   **PL. 43**

A native of Argentina now established north to cen. and s. Calif. as well as east through the border states to cen. and s. Texas. Leaves 2–8 in. long, short-pointed, and hairless, with *stalks nearly as long as blades.* Leaf edges *not* toothed. Twigs hairless; bundle scars single or indistinct. Flowers 1–1¼ in. long, yellow, tubular, in large groups at twig ends. Fruits ⅜–½ in. long, dry, egg-shaped capsules. Height to 25 ft. Canyons and watercourses. Attracts hummingbirds.

AMERICAN SMOKETREE *Cotinus obovatus* Raf.   **PL. 43**

One of the rarest American trees, this relative of the sumacs is found in the West only in the Edwards Plateau area of cen. Texas. Leaves 3–6 in. long, half as wide, and usually *blunt-tipped*. Edges slightly wavy or smooth. Side buds with 2–4 scales and somewhat long-pointed. Bundle scars 3. Flowers April–May. Fruits June–Sept. Wood *yellow* and odorous; sprouts from stumps. A yellow dye can be made from the wood. Height 6–25 (35) ft.; diameter 1–12 (14) in. Name alludes to *foot-long* hazy end sprays of small, dry, feathery fruits that resemble puffs of smoke. Foliage becomes a brilliant red in autumn. The shrubby European Smoketree (C. *coggygria* Scop.) is used in landscaping. See Smokethorn, p. 261.

POSSUMHAW HOLLY *Ilex decidua* Walt.   **PL. 43**

Shrubby or growing to small-tree size, this eastern nonevergreen holly ranges west to cen. Texas. It has variable narrow to egg-shaped leaves, generally thin but sometimes somewhat thickened. Leaves 2–3 in. long, bases *narrow,* tips *blunt,* edges *wavy-toothed.* Twigs *stiff,* hairless; buds somewhat *pointed;* bundle scar 1. Spur branches *present.* Flowers short-stalked, April–May. Fruits shiny

Possumhaw Holly

POSSUMHAW HOLLY

AMERICAN SMOKETREE

TOYON

red, Sept.–March. Height 10–20 (30) ft.; diameter 2–6 (10) in. Wet sites. **SIMILAR SPECIES:** The leaves of Yaupon Holly (Pl. 44) are smaller and evergreen. **REMARKS:** Fruits attractive in winter and eaten by wildlife including bobwhite quail, opossums, and raccoons.

TREES WITH ALTERNATE EVERGREEN LEAVES TOOTHED (PLATE 44)

Trees of this group have mostly *thickened* foliage with *coarse* teeth sometimes prickly. Flowers are whitish and mostly small. Cliffrose, an exception, has showy blossoms. Fruits of the first two species are reddish and berrylike; those of the next four are small and dry, with long *feathery plumes.* None of the species of this plate occurs north of sw. Ore. and Utah. Bayberries and Torrey Vauquelinia (Pl. 39) also have toothed evergreen leaves, but their foliage is slender, willowlike. See also ceanothuses (Pl. 30).

TOYON *Heteromeles arbutifolia* (Lindl.) M. J. Roem.   **PL. 44**
An attractive tree of Calif. coastal areas and islands, the Sierra foothills, and Baja California. Leaves 2–5 in. long, sometimes narrow, mostly *pointed at both ends,* sharply toothed but *not* prickly, hairless, and with stout 1-in. leafstalks. Twigs mostly hairless; spur branches lacking. Stumps produce sprouts. Flowers ¼ in. wide, *white,* in showy end clusters 4–6 in. long, June–July. Fruits ¼–⅜ in. in diameter, applelike, *red* (or yellow), mealy, seeds 1–4, remaining through winter. Height to 35 ft. Slopes and canyons to 4000 ft. elevation. **SIMILAR SPECIES:** None. **REMARKS:** Harvested for Christmas decorations and planted as an ornamental. The supposed resemblance of the foliage to that of the madrones (Pl. 45) is said to be the basis for the specific name. Toyon is believed to

be derived from a Native American name. Also called Christmas-berry, California-holly, and Hollyberry. Fruits eaten by California quail, bandtail pigeons, and many songbirds.

HOLLYLEAF CHERRY PL. 44
Prunus ilicifolia (Nutt. ex Hook & Arn.) D. Dietr.

A *prickly-leaved* tree distributed along Calif. coastal areas from Napa Co. to Baja California Sur. Leaves 1½–2½ in. long, *round-based,* short-pointed or sometimes nearly circular, hairless, shiny, with *sharp teeth* along wavy edges. Leaf veins *not* markedly parallel. Twigs *flexible,* hairless. Flowers small, white, in slender 2–4-in. clusters from along the twigs, early spring. Fruits *juicy, red* or yellow, with a single seed, Oct.–Dec. Sprouts after fires. Height to 25 ft. Dry soils to 5000 ft. elevation. Range includes Santa Catalina and San Clemente islands, s. Calif. **SIMILAR SPECIES:** (1) Hollyleaf Buckthorn (Pl. 27) has side leaf veins parallel and twigs short, stiff, and mostly spine-tipped. (2) Prickly-leaved Calif. oaks (Pl. 33) have clustered end buds. (3) Lemonade Sumac (Pl. 45) may have prickly foliage, but the leaves are somewhat aromatic and the fruits red-hairy. **REMARKS:** Fruits eaten by songbirds, twigs browsed by mule deer. Hybrids with Catalina Cherry (Pl. 45) are known.

CERCOCARPUSES (MOUNTAIN-MAHOGANIES)

The *Cercocarpus* species are a group of trees or shrubs generally recognizable by more or less leathery leaves with straight and *markedly parallel* veins, bases mostly *wedge-shaped,* mostly hairless above, and edges toothed *above* the middle. Buds small,

HOLLYLEAF CHERRY

BIRCHLEAF CERCOCARPUS

round, scaly; bundle scars 3, sometimes obscure. Spur branches *numerous.* Flowers small, tubular, greenish white, on the spurs. Each tiny, dry, narrow, half-inch-long fruit has an attractive *feathery tail,* often several inches long.

The brown wood, the basis for the common name, is so dense that it will sink when freshly cut. Used locally in the production of handsome turned objects. Browsed by blacktail and mule deer. Porcupines feed on the inner bark.

Because the trees are not related to the tropical mahoganies, an effort is being made to encourage the use of cercocarpus as a common name. That name derives from the Greek, meaning "tailed fruit." Alderleaf Cercocarpus (Pl. 43) has mainly deciduous foliage; Curlleaf Cercocarpus (Pl. 46) has evergreen leaves not toothed. For differences between cercocarpuses and buckthorns, see p. 355.

BIRCHLEAF CERCOCARPUS   PL. 44
Cercocarpus betuloides Nutt.

Ranging from sw. Ore. through Calif. to Baja California Norte and cen. Ariz., this species is distinguished by foliage often *velvethairy* beneath. Leaves mostly ¾–1¼ in. long with *flat* edges. *All* leaves toothed. Blossoms in *clusters* of 2–5, Mar.–May; fruit plumes 1½–4 in. long. Height to 25 ft. Dry slopes, chaparral, to 10,000 ft. elevation. SIMILAR SPECIES: (1) Hairy Cercocarpus occurs from Ariz. eastward. It has slightly smaller leaves with pointed teeth or none plus rolled leaf edges and feathery fruit tails only 1–1¼ in. long. (2) See Catalina Cercocarpus. REMARKS: Regarded by some botanists as only a variety of Alderleaf Cercocarpus (Pl. 43).

CATALINA CERCOCARPUS   PL. 44
Cercocarpus traskiae Eastw.

Similar to Birchleaf Cercocarpus and often considered merely a local variety of it. Leaves 1¼–3 *in. long,* felty-hairy beneath, and often with a U-shaped base. Fruit tails 1½–4 in. long. Flowers and fruits *single* or only a few in a group. Height to 25 ft. Native to mountain slopes of Salte Verde Canyon, Santa Catalina I., Calif.

HAIRY CERCOCARPUS   *Cercocarpus breviflorus* Gray   PL. 44
A small tree of the Mexican border area. Leaves ¾–1¼ in. long, some toothed toward the apex, and *some without teeth.* Leaf surfaces *silky-hairy* at least beneath. Leaf edges *rolled under.* Flowers *single,* rarely in twos or threes; fruit plumes *short,* only 1–1¼ in. long. To 25 ft. Dry slopes at 5000–10,000 ft. elevations, from Ariz. and w. Texas to n. Mexico. SIMILAR SPECIES: See Birchleaf Cercocarpus.

CLIFFROSE *Cowania mexicana* D. Don   **PL. 44**

A distinctive small tree or shrub of Ariz., s. Rockies, and Great Basin to cen. Mexico. Leaves only ¼–½ *in. long* with *3–5 rounded lobes* whose edges are *rolled under,* somewhat *sticky,* and *gland-dotted.* Leaf undersides densely *white-woolly* (use lens). Twigs hairless; leaf bases raised; bundle scar single, indistinct. Spur branches *numerous,* with many overlapping leaf bases hiding the buds. Flowers white or cream-colored, showy, about *1 in. across,* clustered, spring. Fruits in groups of 6–10, with 1–2-in. hairy tails, autumn. Trunk shreddy. Height to 25 ft. Rocky soils from 4000–8000 ft. elevation. **SIMILAR SPECIES:** Apache-plume (*Fallugia paradoxa* [D. Don] Endl.), a shrub in the same region, has similar foliage and fruits but its leaves are not gland-dotted, the buds are visible, and the feathery plumes are in striking groups of 10–25. Antelope Bitterbrush (*Purshia tridendata* [Pursh] DC.), another closely related shrub of the region, has small gland-dotted leaves

3-toothed at the tip. Its foliage is not sticky, the flowers are single, and the fruits are not feathery-tailed. **REMARKS:** Cliffrose bark was used by Native Americans for clothing, sandals, blankets, and rope. The bitter leaves and twigs were employed to induce vomiting. Deer, nevertheless, browse the foliage. Quininebush is a local name. The plant is common on both rims of the Grand Canyon. J. Cowan was an amateur British botanist of the early 19th century.

BIG SAGEBRUSH   *Artemisia tridentata* Nutt.   PL. 44

Widespread over the semi-arid interior West. Usually shrubby but occasionally attaining tree size. Leaves ¼–2 in. long, gray-green, hairy, somewhat leathery, *narrowly wedge-shaped,* with short stalks or none, and 3 (5) distinct *teeth at the leaf end.* Leaf scars tiny; bundle scars indistinct. Flowers in small greenish clusters on long upright stems. Fruits tiny, dry, hairy. Height to 15 in. An important browse species for blacktail and mule deer, bighorn sheep, and livestock. Leaves and buds also eaten by dusky, sage, and sharptail grouse. The *sage odor* of crushed leaves is appealing to most people.

AMERICAN HOLLY   *Ilex opaca* Ait.   PL. 44

The Christmas holly of the se. U.S. grows locally west to s.-cen. Texas. It has spread to the wild in the Pacific Northwest and possibly elsewhere. The thick evergreen leaves with *long prickles* are distinctive. They are 2–4 in. long, hairless, *dull-surfaced,* and mostly with U-shaped bases. Some few leaves may be nearly smooth-edged. Twigs hairless; buds minute; spur branches usually present. Flowers greenish, May–June. Fruits fleshy, red, rarely yellow, nutlets 4, Aug.–June. Height 10–40 (100) ft. Bottom-

American Holly

YAUPON HOLLY

lands. **SIMILAR SPECIES:** English Holly (*Ilex aquifolium* L.) is often planted on landscaped areas. Its leaves are smaller (¾–1½ in. long) and shiny. It has spread to the wild in the Pacific Northwest and possibly elsewhere. **REMARKS:** Fruits are eaten by numerous songbirds and by bobwhite quail and wild turkeys. Holly lumber is ivory white and in demand for piano keys, ship models, and inlays.

YAUPON HOLLY *Ilex vomitoria* Ait.   **PL. 44**

Another distinctive plant of the southeastern states whose red-fruited branches are often gathered for decorative purposes. Ever-green leaves *small*, ¼–1½ in. long, blunt-tipped, and *wavy-edged.* Flowers May–June. Fruits red, berrylike, nutlets 4, Sept.–Oct. Height 5–15 (30) ft.; diameter 2–4 (12) in. West to s. and cen. Texas. **SIMILAR SPECIES:** Possumhaw Holly (Pl. 43) has wavy-edged leaves that are thin and nonevergreen. **REMARKS:** The caffeine-containing dried leaves reportedly make a desirable tea. As indicated by the scientific name, however, the tea taken in large amounts may act as an emetic. A strong medicinal "black drink" once brewed by Native Americans is believed to have been made from Yaupon leaves. A number of birds, including bobwhite quail, eat the fruits.

TREES WITH ALTERNATE EVERGREEN LEAVES SOMETIMES TOOTHED (PLATE 45)

Species with evergreen foliage mostly smooth-edged but some-times, especially on young plants, with the borders toothed or partly toothed. Leaves mostly thick, leathery, either smooth or rough-hairy, mostly with U-shaped bases and usually with stalks over ¼ in. long. Flowers mainly small, white to pink and clustered. Fruits red and (except sumacs) fleshy. Some bayberries (Pl. 39) have leaves of this type, but they are narrow and willowlike. See also Whiteleaf Manzanita, Pl. 40.

MADRONES

The madrones, or *madroños*, are mostly distinctively marked by *smooth reddish bark* on the trunk and large limbs. The outer bark

PACIFIC MADRONE

Bark of Pacific Madrone

is thin and typically *peels* away or flakes off to show a yellowish or gray layer beneath. The foliage of the 3 species is similar but differs in shape and size. Buds hairless. Flowers are small, white, and urn-shaped with fused petals. The blossoms resemble lilies of the valley and occur in attractive, branched, springtime clusters. Fruits are orange-red, each ¼–⅓ in. in diameter with a fleshy outer layer; often persisting into winter. They are consumed by deer, bandtail pigeons, various quails, and many songbirds. Native Americans once ate them raw or cooked. The bark and leaves have astringent properties. The wood makes good charcoal. Under favorable conditions, specimens reportedly live more than 200 years.

PACIFIC MADRONE *Arbutus menziesii* Pursh   **PL. 45**

A tree of coastal areas and the cen. Sierra with *wide* leaves 4–6 in. long and 1¼–3 in. across (sometimes more narrow than illustrated), smooth-edged or fine-toothed. Leaf bases mainly *U-shaped*. Height 25–80 (125) ft.; diameter 2–3 (5) ft. From deep moist soils to dry slopes. B.C. to s. Calif. **SIMILAR SPECIES:** Manzanitas (Pl. 46) have similar trunk bark but are only small trees or shrubs with leaves 1¼–2 in. long and somewhat round. **REMARKS:** Archibald Menzies, Scottish physician and naturalist, accompanied Capt.

George Vancouver on his early explorations. Fruits eaten by band-tail pigeons, doves, wild turkeys, raccoons, ringtails; browsed by deer. A good honey species.

ARIZONA MADRONE *Arbutus arizonica* (Gray) Sarg.   **PL. 45**
Found in the mountains of se. Ariz., sw. N.M., and nw. Mexico. Differs from the last species in having *narrow* foliage and rough bark. Leaves 2–4 in. long, ¼–1 in. wide with mostly *V-shaped* bases. Trunk bark *grayish and in furrowed plates,* unlike other madrones. Height to 30 ft.; diameter to 2 ft. Canyons and slopes at 4000–8000 ft. elevations.

TEXAS MADRONE *Arbutus texana* Buckl.   **PL. 45**
Ranging from se. N.M. east to cen. Texas and south into ne. Mexico. Leaf shape intermediate relative to the last two species. Leaves 2–4 in. long, ¾–1½ in. wide, with mainly *U-shaped* bases. Trunk *reddish, smooth.* Height to 25 ft.; diameter to 1 ft. Hills and mountains.

CATALINA CHERRY *Prunus lyonii* (Eastw.) Sarg.   **PL. 45**
A rare species native only on some of the islands offshore s. Calif. and again, some distance southward, on the mainland of Baja California Sur. The mostly pointed-tipped and U-based leaves are 2–4 in. long, ¾–1½ in. wide, and sometimes partly wavy-edged. Twigs roughened with *raised leaf scars, tough-wooded,* with *narrow* brown pith. Buds hairless, scaly. Flowers produced in slender 2–4-in.-long clusters grouped near the twig ends, March–June. Fruits about 1 in. in diameter, juicy, purple-black, and edible, with a single large stone, Aug.–Sept. Height to 50 ft. Canyon thickets. **SIMILAR SPECIES:** Sugar Sumac, with foliage somewhat similar, also occurs on some of the s. Calif. islands but has leaves that

ARIZONA MADRONE

TEXAS MADRONE

tend to fold along the midrib, smooth soft-wooded twigs with wide brown pith, and fruit clusters red-hairy. **REMARKS:** Reported to hybridize with Hollyleaf Cherry (Pl. 44) and sometimes regarded merely as a variety of it. Fruits eaten by many birds.

SUGAR SUMAC   *Rhus ovata* Wats.   **PL. 45**

Found in the mountains of sw. Calif. south through Baja California Norte and again in cen. Ariz. Leaves mostly 3–4 in. long, 1½–3 in. wide, usually short-pointed, and *tending to fold* along the midrib. Foliage sometimes sparsely coarse-toothed and with a nice resinous odor when crushed. Leafstalks ½–¾ in. long, stout. New twigs soft, easily cut lengthwise, and with *wide* brown pith. Buds small, hairy, *without* scales, and *nearly hidden* by leafstalk bases. Flowers in dense, stoutly branched, terminal clusters, March–May; fruits red-hairy, *sticky,* Aug.–Sept. Height to 15 ft. Chaparral thickets, dry slopes to 2500 ft. elevation. Also on Santa Cruz and Santa Catalina islands, s. Calif. **SIMILAR SPECIES:** (1) Catalina Cherry has scaly buds, narrow pith, and a more restricted natural range. (2) California Buckthorn leaves are marked with side veins straight and decidedly parallel. Both species have fleshy fruits. (3) Laurel Sumac (Pl. 46) foliage is more oblong and always smooth-edged, its crushed leaves are somewhat unpleasantly odorous, and fruits are smooth and white. **REMARKS:** Fruits reported to be sweet. Useful on poor soils to control erosion. Sprouts rapidly after fires. Deer may browse the plant. *Rhus* was the early Roman and Greek name for a Mediterranean sumac.

LEMONADE SUMAC   **PL. 45**
Rhus integrifolia (Nutt.) Benth. & Hook. f. ex Brewer & Watts.

A shrub or small tree growing on beaches, bluffs, and slopes of the s. Calif. coast and islands. Leaves either prickly-toothed or

SUGAR SUMAC

LEMONADE SUMAC

smooth-edged, mostly only 1–2¼ *in. long* and ⅝–¾ in. wide (sometimes to 2 in. x 1 in.), *short-stalked,* more or less *rounded* at both ends, and *not* tending to fold. Rarely with 3 leaflets. Crushed foliage pleasantly resinous. Buds hairy or not, scales lacking. Flowers small, in compact heads with *stout* branches, Oct.–May. Fruits reddish, *sticky, hairy,* Aug.–Sept. Height to 15 ft. Dense thickets. SIMILAR SPECIES: (1) Laurel Sumac (Pl. 46) and (2) Sugar Sumac have larger, pointed, folding leaves. In sw. Ariz. and Baja California, see also (3) Kearney Sumac (Pl. 46). (4) Evergreen oaks (Pl. 33) have clustered end buds and acorn fruits. (5) See Hollyleaf Cherry (Pl. 44). REMARKS: Will grow on extremely poor and saline soils. Lower branches take root. Root system extends 10 ft. or so beyond the above-ground plant. Roadrunners and other birds consume the fruits.

CALIFORNIA BUCKTHORN   NOT SHOWN
Rhamnus californica Eschsch.

With its principal range throughout Calif.'s coastal mountains and the Sierra Nevada, this shrub (rarely a small tree) occurs again from cen. and se. Ariz. to sw. N.M. and also locally in s. Nev. and sw. Ore. Leaves *variable.* Foliage ranges from narrow to wide but mostly 2–4 in. long and ½–2 in. wide with 7–11 distinctly *straight and parallel* pairs of veins. Leaves often whitish beneath, sometimes fine-toothed, with bases either U- or V-shaped. Some leaves may be opposite or nearly opposite. Twigs hairless to hairy; buds hairy, *without* scales; pith *white.* Flower clusters greenish, at the leaf angles, March–April. Fruits from green to red then black, fleshy, with several seeds, Aug.–Sept. Height to 15 ft. Canyons and slopes to 4000 ft. elevation in most of Calif.; 4000–7500 ft. elsewhere. SIMILAR SPECIES: (1) Cascara and (2) Birchleaf buckthorns (Pl. 43) and the (3) cercocarpuses (Pls. 43, 44) also have

CALIFORNIA
BUCKTHORN

straight and parallel leaf veins. The leaves of those buckthorns are larger and deciduous, however, and more regularly toothed, while the leaves of cercocarpuses mostly are smaller, wedge-based, and toothed only near the tips. See (4) Sugar Sumac. REMARKS: Also known as Coffeeberry. Fruits eaten by a number of birds and by black bears. See comments under buckthorns, p. 355

Bark of Anacua

ANACUA *Ehretia anacua* (Teran & Berl.) I. M. Johnst. **PL. 45**
A tree of cen. and s. Texas and e. Mexico. Leaves *sandpaper-rough* above, mostly 2–2¼ in. long, ¼–1 in. wide, oval, rounded at both ends, with a projecting *tiny tip*. Foliage short-stalked and sometimes with coarse teeth above the middle. Twigs and buds *hairless*. Trunk gray, deeply furrowed. Flowers white, ¼ in. across, in attractive clusters 1–3 in. long, fragrant, at twig ends, March–April. Fruits fleshy, edible, ¼ in. in diameter, orange-yellow, containing 2 seeds, June–April. Trunks several, root suckers clumped. Height to 50 ft. Dry soils. **SIMILAR SPECIES:** Anacahuite also grows in s. Texas with foliage rough-hairy above. It is white-woolly beneath, however, with twigs hairy and blossoms more showy. **REMARKS:** Also called Sandpaper-tree. George Dionysius Ehret was an 18th-century German botanical artist. Anacua is a Mexican name, pronounced ah-NAH-kwah. Birds are attracted to the fruits.

ANACAHUITE *Cordia boisseri* A. DC. **PL. 45**
Native from the lower Rio Grande Valley south into Mexico. Leaves 2–8 in. long, 2–4 in. wide, long-stalked, *rough-hairy* above and sometimes below, more or less *white-woolly* beneath, mostly short-pointed, and sometimes wavy-edged. Twigs and buds mostly

ANACAHUITE

woolly. Flowers showy, ½–1 in. across, white with yellow centers, in leaf angles and at twig ends, April–June. Fruits are 1 in. long, egg-shaped, reddish brown, single-seeded, July–Sept. Height to 25 ft. **SIMILAR SPECIES:** See Anacua. **REMARKS:** Pronounced ahnahcah-WEE-tah. Also known as Mexican-olive. Fruits are reported to be edible but to cause dizziness. Javelinas (peccaries) and other wildlife eat them readily.

SPARKLEBERRY *Vaccinium arboreum* Marsh.   **PL. 45**

A southeastern plant ranging west to se. Texas as a shrub or small crooked tree. The tallest member of the blueberry genus. Leaves elliptic, 1–2 in. long, *short-stalked,* sometimes fine-toothed, hairless, and with a slender tip. Twigs hairy or not. End bud false. Height to 30 ft. Flowers white, bell-shaped, in drooping clusters, April–June. Fruits fleshy, edible but not tasty, black, Sept.–Oct. Also called Farkleberry.

TREES WITH ALTERNATE EVERGREEN LEAVES NOT TOOTHED (PLATE 46)

Foliage of this type occurs also on the bumelias (Pl. 28), but they are thorny. It may also occur on some oaks (Pls. 33–35), but they have clustered end buds. Such leathery evergreen foliage also may be present on some California Fremontia (Pl. 29) specimens, on some narrow-leaved nonwillows (Pl. 39), and on the sometimes-toothed species of Pl. 45. Most species of this plate have hairless twigs. Texas Persimmon is deciduous in some areas.

PACIFIC RHODODENDRON   **PL. 46**
Rhododendron macrophyllum D. Don ex G. Don

A handsome shrub or small tree of nw. coastal areas and Cascades south to n. Calif. Leaves 3–6 (10) in. long, 1–2 (2½) in. wide, hairless, pointed at *both* ends, and edges *rolled under.* Flowers 1–2 in. long, showy, pink-purple (rarely white), in dense twig-end clusters, May–June. Fruits slender, dry, brownish capsules splitting into 5 parts. Trunk rough, dark. Height to 25 ft. Thickets. **SIMILAR SPECIES:** (1) Pacific Madrone (Pl. 45) has smooth, sometimes peeling, reddish bark. (2) Bluegum Eucalyptus has mostly

SPARKLEBERRY

PACIFIC RHODODENDRON

curved, flat, aromatic leaves and stout, somewhat top-shaped fruit capsules. **REMARKS:** Also called California Rosebay. Foliage poisons sheep.

BLUEGUM EUCALYPTUS *Eucalyptus globulus* Labill. **PL. 46**
Of the several introduced members of this large and mainly Australian genus, this species reproduces naturally in the warmer parts of Calif. Leaves 5–12 in. long, ¾–1 ½ in. wide, stiff, *flat*, usually *curved, long-pointed*, and *aromatic* when crushed. Foliage with U-shaped bases, dull green on both sides, and tending to *hang vertically*. Young leaves may be shorter and opposite on some twigs. Flowers white, single, at leaf angles, Dec.–May. Fruits dry, heavy, 1-in. circular or angular capsules. Trunk bark *peels* in strips; underbark gray to yellowish. Height 70–140 ft. Spreads from windbreaks and other plantings. **SIMILAR SPECIES:** See Pacific Rhododendron. **REMARKS:** Quick-growing, but wood is brittle and of little value. Falling outer bark and fruits are a nuisance in landscaped areas.

Bluegum Eucalyptus

MANZANITAS (*Arctostaphylos* SPECIES)

A large group of mainly trailing or low shrubs, yet four species occasionally grow to small-tree size in sw. Ore., Calif., and Ariz. chaparral. Trunks *smooth* and *dark red-brown,* much like those of the taller and larger-leaved madrones (Pl. 45). Leaves 1–2 in. long, mostly egg-shaped and hairless or slightly hairy. Springtime flowers ¼–⅜ in. long, pink or white, urn-shaped, and in terminal clusters. Fruits small, reddish, somewhat fleshy, with one to several seeds. Many hybrids known.

PARRY MANZANITA *Arctostaphylos manzanita* Parry   PL. 46

This species of n. Calif. has leaves *bright green,* shiny or not, with stalks ³⁄₁₆–⅜ in. long. Twigs *hairless.* Fruits smooth, hairless, ⅜–½ in. diameter. North of San Francisco Bay area, mainly in foothills of coastal ranges and Sierra Nevada to 4000 ft. elevation. Berries eaten by dusky and sharptail grouse as well as other birds. Considered a valuable honey plant.

WHITELEAF MANZANITA   NOT SHOWN
Arctostaphylos viscida Parry

Also a species mainly of n. Calif. Much like Parry Manzanita but foliage whitened (and occasionally fine-toothed). Twigs hairy or not. Fruits are *pulpy,* only ¼–⅜ in. across, and either smooth or sticky. Dry slopes, coastal ranges from sw. Ore. south to Napa Co., n. Calif. and in the Sierra Nevada to Kern Co., s. Calif.

Bark of Parry Manzanita

BIGBERRY MANZANITA
Arctostaphylos glauca Lindl.   **NOT SHOWN**

Occurring below 4500 ft. elevation in the coastal ranges and interior slopes of cen. and s. Calif. Leaves *whitened* and leafstalks ¼–½ in. long. Twigs *hairless*. Fruits sticky, ½–⅝ in. in diameter, and with *little pulp*. From San Francisco Bay south to cen. Baja California. Browsed by deer.

PRINGLE MANZANITA   **NOT SHOWN**
Arctostaphylos pringlei Parry

Similar to the last species but with foliage more *gray-green*, leafstalks ⅛–¼ in. long, and twigs *sticky-hairy*. Fruits glandular-hairy, ¼–⅜ in. in diameter. Local in mountains of s. Calif., cen. Ariz., and Baja California Norte at 4000–7000 ft. elevations. Fruits are a source of food for foxes, coyotes, and skunks as well as for Gambel and Mearns quail.

CURLLEAF CERCOCARPUS   **PL. 46**
Cercocarpus ledifolius Nutt.

This widespread cercocarpus occurs as a shrub or small tree on mountain slopes throughout much of the American West. The *small, curled-under* foliage is distinctive. Leaves ½–1½ in. long, ⅜–⅝ in. wide, pointed at both ends, hairy beneath, clustered on spur branches, and with leafstalks ⅛–3/16 in. long. Flowers inconspicuous, without petals, at leaf angles, July–Aug. Fruits attractive, with *feathery tails*, 2–3¼ in. long, Aug.–Sept. Heartwood dark brown. Height to 40 ft. Dry soils, 5000–9000 ft. elevation. **SIMILAR SPECIES:** Other evergreen cercocarpuses and the related Cliffrose (Pl. 44), all with feathery-tailed fruits, have toothed leaves. **REMARKS:** Wood so heavy that it will not float; an excellent fuel.

CURLLEAF CERCOCARPUS

LAUREL SUMAC

Browsed heavily by mule deer. Also called Curlleaf Mountain-mahogany (see discussion of cercocarpuses, p. 360).

LAUREL SUMAC *Rhus laurina* Nutt.   **PL. 46**

A shrub or small tree found from the mainland and islands of sw. Calif. to Baja California Sur. Leaves 2–5 in. long, 1–2 in. wide, with U-shaped bases, *short- to long-pointed tips,* and *tending to fold* along the midrib. Foliage with a mild and perhaps somewhat unpleasant odor when crushed. Leafstalks ¼–1 in. long. Buds small, hairless, *without* scales. Flowers small, white, in dense and finely branched end clusters, June–July. Fruits *smooth, white,* ⅛–¼ in. in diameter, persisting from Sept. into winter. Height to 15 ft. Dry slopes to 3300 ft. elevation in coastal areas, including Santa Catalina and San Clemente islands in Calif. and Cedros and Guadeloupe islands off Baja California, Mexico. **SIMILAR SPECIES:** (1) Kearney Sumac has leaves mostly blunt-tipped and fruits red-hairy. See (2) Sugar Sumac (Pl. 45). **REMARKS:** Like Sugar Sumac, this species recovers rapidly after fires and is useful in erosion control. Both common and scientific names refer to the Old World laurels, which also have leathery foliage. Fruit heads are a food source for deer and quail.

KEARNEY SUMAC *Rhus kearneyi* Barkley   **PL. 46**

A rare species of extreme sw. Ariz. and Baja California with leaves 1½–2¼ in. long, ¾–1 in. wide, and mostly *rounded* at both ends. Leafstalks under ⅜ in. long and leaf margins usually *rolled under.* Buds small, hairy, without scales. Flowers white, fruits *red-hairy.* Height to 20 ft. In the U.S., recorded only from near Tinojas Altas, Yuma Co., at 1000–1500 ft. elevation. **SIMILAR SPECIES:** See (1) Lemonade Sumac (Pl. 45) and (2) Laurel Sumac.

TEXAS PERSIMMON *Diospyros texana* Scheele   **PL. 46**

Confined to the s. half of Texas and adjacent ne. Mexico. It is deciduous on the Edwards Plateau and perhaps in other areas of the more northern parts of the range. A shrub or small tree with leaves 1–2 in. long, ¼–½ in. wide, *blunt-tipped,* V-shaped at the base, shiny, with edges rolled under and leafstalks short or *lacking.* Foliage hairless above but somewhat hairy beneath, at least on the midrib. Twigs smooth gray, sometimes spiky; winter buds small, black with some gray outer scales; bundle scar 1. Flowers ¼–½ in. long, white, April–May. Fruits black, ¾ in. in diameter, fleshy, July–Aug. Smooth gray trunk bark peels to show yellow and green underbark in a *mottled* pattern; sometimes dark gray over silver-gray over yellow-white. Heartwood dark. Height to 50

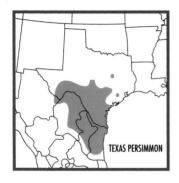

TEXAS PERSIMMON

REDBAY

ft. Rocky slopes and canyons. SIMILAR SPECIES: Bark often closely resembles that of Crapemyrtle (Pl. 17), whose leaves are both opposite and alternate and whose twigs tend to be 4-lined. REMARKS: A member of the ebony family. The heavy wood sinks in water. Unripe fruits are very "puckery" to the taste. They are edible at maturity but produce a black dye that discolors the skin. Eaten by wild turkeys, raccoons, skunks, and many other animals. The generic name translates, with uncertain veracity, into "fruit of the gods." Mexican name is Chapote (chah-POH-tay). Abundant at Enchanted Rock State Natural Area north of Fredericksburg, Texas.

REDBAY *Persea borbonia* (L.) Spreng.   **PL. 46**

A Coastal Plain tree of the se. U.S. whose range extends west to e. and s. Texas. Leaves 3–8 in. long, narrow to elliptic, shiny above, pale beneath, edges rolled under, V-based, and tip pointed or somewhat blunt. Crushed foliage with a *spicy* odor. Twigs greenish, hairy, and *angled*. Bark dark reddish, deeply grooved. Height to 50 or 70 ft.; diameter to 3 ft. Flowers May–July. Fruits blue or black, single-seeded, in red-stemmed clusters, *along* the twigs, Aug.–Sept. Dried leaves sometimes used as a substitute for commercial bay leaves (see California-bay, p. 330).

POTATO-TREE *Solanum erianthum* D. Don   **PL. 46**

An often shrubby species that occurs from extreme s. Texas south to Peru. Leaves 3–8 in. long, narrowly egg-shaped, *very woolly*, long-pointed, and with *1–2-in. stalks*. Flowers and fruits at all seasons. Flowers ½ in. wide, white; fruits green to yellow, berries resembling tomatoes. Height to 15 ft. Crushed leaves have a tar odor; broken roots smell like the closely related potato.

Palms, Cacti, and Yuccas
Plate 47

The palms, cacti, and yuccas are clearly different from other woody plants. The first and last groups have parallel-veined leaves clustered at the ends of the stems. In the palms, these are long-stalked. The tree-size cacti have unique succulent and spiny stems like those of no other trees. All are evergreen.

Palms from all over the world have been imported and planted in the subtropical portions of the Southwest. The species native to the U.S. are emphasized here. Most have single unbranched trunks with the leafy fronds of two types. They are either fan-shaped, with segments radiating from the end of a central leaf-stalk (or a quite short "partial midrib"), or they are long and featherlike with a central midrib.

Yuccas have abundant, long, sword-shaped, and usually spine-pointed leaves whose bases clasp the stem. The many western yucca species can be separated according to the identification chart on p. 384.

PALMS AND TREE-CACTI (PLATE 47)

These are evergreen plants of sw. arid regions with either parallel-veined leaves or succulent thorny joints. California Washingtonia, in s. Calif. and sw. Ariz., plus two *Sabal* species in Texas are fan-leaved and the only native palms in the Southwest. In addition, the Date Palm is listed here as an example of the feather-leaved palms and of the many foreign palms planted in the warmer parts of the region. Palm flowers are white and fragrant. As for cacti, only a few species grow to tree size. Their leaves are lacking or not readily identifiable as such.

CALIFORNIA WASHINGTONIA

California Washingtonia

CALIFORNIA WASHINGTONIA PL. 47
Washingtonia filifera (Linden ex Andre) H. Wendl.

A tall palm crowned by a cluster of *gray-green fan-shaped* leaves. Each leaf frond 3–6 ft. in diameter, divided into numerous narrow folds, and often deeply torn. Leaf edges display numerous *fibrous threads*. Leafstalks 3–6 ft. long extending well into the leaf blade, with hooked *spiny teeth* along the edges. Trunk partially or completely covered by hanging dead leaf fronds. Flowers small, in branched clusters, enclosed in a narrow, yellowish, membranous spathe 1–2 ft. long, June. Fruits spherical, fleshy, black at maturity, ¼–½ in. diameter. Height to 50 (75) ft.; diameter 2 (3) ft. Desert springs, Colo. and s. Mohave deserts, Calif., Kofa Mts., Ariz., and south in Mexico. Planted from s. Calif. to s. Texas. **SIMILAR SPECIES:** See Mexican Washingtonia. **REMARKS:** Also known as Washington Fan Palm. Named in honor of George Washington. Dead leaves often removed from planted specimens to reduce dangers of fire and rodent infestation. Leaves used for thatched roofs in some areas. An indicator of underground water. Native Americans ground the seeds into flour. They also ate the growing tip or palm heart which, like that of all palms, makes a fine salad.

MEXICAN PALMETTO

DWARF PALMETTO

Destruction of this terminal bud, however, kills the tree. California Washingtonias are easily seen at Palm Springs, Calif., and in a natural setting at nearby Palm Canyon. Twentynine Palms, Calif., also is home to this tree.

MEXICAN WASHINGTONIA   NOT SHOWN
Washingtonia robusta Wendl.

Similar to the last species but with foliage *light green*. Trunk more slender and *flaring* abruptly at the base. Leafstalks 2–3 ft. long. Native to Baja California and planted from s. Calif. to s. Texas.

MEXICAN PALMETTO *Sabal mexicana* Mart.   PL. 47

A native palm growing wild only in the lower Rio Grande Valley of Cameron Co., Texas, and south to Central America. Strong trees whose *fan-shaped* leaves are 3–7 ft. or more in diameter and with an equally long *thornless* stalk. The leafstalk penetrates the leaf blade 4 in. or more. Flowers in clusters up to 8 ft. long. Fruits ¾–1 in. in diameter, dry, black, somewhat edible. Height to 50 ft.; diameter to 2¼ ft. See next species.

DWARF PALMETTO *Sabal minor* (Jacq.) Pers.   NOT SHOWN

An eastern U.S. shrub or tree whose range extends westward to cen. Texas. Similar to Mexican Palmetto, but leafstalk penetrates the leaf blade only 2 in. or less. Also fruits *under ½ in.* in diameter. To 20 ft. tall, the most treelike specimens reportedly occur in Brazoria Co., south of Houston, Texas.

DATE PALM *Phoenix dactylifera* L.   PL. 47

An example of *feather-leaved* palms. Cultivated commercially mainly along the Mexican border for the tasty and nutritious fruits. Leaves *gray-green*, 15–20 ft. long, and somewhat erect.

Leafstalks extend the full length of the fronds; leaflets nearest trunk spinelike. Height to 35 ft. Reported sometimes to spread from plantings. The related Canary Islands Date Palm (*P. canariensis* Chaub.), with *light green* foliage and leaves more drooping, is widely planted as far north as n. Calif.

SAGUARO *Cereus giganteus* Engelm. PL. 47

A unique and widely recognized symbol of the southwestern desert. The *single,* tall, stout, thorny, green trunk is ribbed vertically and branched in maturity. Flowers white, waxy, about 2 in. in diameter, remaining open only about 24 hours, April–May. Fruits fleshy, reddish berries 2–3 in. long, with black seeds, June–July. To 50 ft. tall. Rocky soils of w.-cen. Ariz., barely into se. Calif. and south through Sonora, Mexico. **REMARKS:** Pronounced sah-WAHR-oh. Also called Giant Cactus. Sometimes placed in the genus *Carnegiea.* The corrugated trunk becomes more smooth when water is absorbed during rainy periods. The edible fruits have been gathered for centuries by Native Americans to be eaten fresh or made into preserves. The fermented fruit juice also has been made into an alcoholic drink. Fine stands of this tree can be seen at Saguaro National Park near Tucson, Ariz.

Saguaro

SAGUARO

ORGANPIPE CACTUS *Cereus thurberi* Engelm. **PL. 47**

Lacking an upright trunk, in a strict sense this cactus may not be a tree. Its many upright ribbed branches, however, are up to 20 ft. tall and quite sturdy. Flowers lavender or rose-colored, May. Rocky soils, se. Calif. and s. Ariz. **REMARKS:** Organ Pipe Cactus Nat'l. Monument, sw. Ariz., is dedicated to the preservation of this species and its habitat.

INDIAN-FIG PRICKLYPEAR **PL. 47**
Opuntia ficus-indica (L.) Mill.

A succulent cactus with *flattened joints* or pads that may bear short barbed bristles or none. Spines usually absent. Flowers yellow, up to 4 in. across, attractive. Fruits red, juicy, edible. Height to 13 ft. The origin of this pricklypear, the only one of the many *Opuntia* species that sometimes becomes treelike in our area, is not certain. It is reported that Columbus first brought this plant to Europe, calling it Indian-fig as proof that he had reached India. The species occurs frequently in Mexico and is cultivated elsewhere around the world. It sometimes escapes from cultivation in the southern parts of Calif., Texas, and Fla.

Organpipe Cactus

JUMPING CHOLLA

Jumping Cholla

JUMPING CHOLLA *Opuntia fulgida* Engelm. **PL. 47**

Though related to the flat-pad pricklypears, this cactus has more or less *cylindrical joints.* These are covered by countless inch-long *needle-sharp* and *barbed* thorns. Flowers pink, about 1 in. across, summer. Fruits 1–2 in. long, somewhat pear-shaped, green, smooth, spineless, and producing new fruits at their tips. If undisturbed, clusters of fruit chains form over months or years. Height to 15 ft. Cen. Ariz. to nw. Mexico. **REMARKS:** Pronounced CHOY-yah. Approach these plants with caution! As one author puts it: "The Cholla doesn't jump. *You* do!" Even brushing against one causes the barbed spines to penetrate the skin in large numbers. Removing the harpoon-type barbs is painful. Cholla reproduction is mainly by vegetative means; joints break off easily and take root. Thickets of shrubby chollas are impenetrable by people but are homes to rodents and nesting birds. Fruits are eaten by rodents, deer, and javelinas. A variety is known as Chainfruit Cholla. Many related shrubby species.

YUCCAS (Chart, p. 384)

A distinctive group of plants with dense clusters of evergreen, parallel-veined, *bayonet-shaped,* and *sharply spine-tipped* leaves.

Mohave Yucca (see p. 386)

The foliage in most species is stiff. Though many species are shrubby, the ones reviewed here have the height, single trunk, and branches that characterize trees. While native to warm regions throughout the Western Hemisphere, the arid Southwest (especially Texas) is home for our many yuccas. Any of the yuccas might be called Palma or Palmilla (PAL-ma/pal-MEE-ya) in Spanish.

The trunks of most tree yuccas are covered with dead brown leaves. White springtime flowers occur in showy upright clusters, the individual blossoms having 3 petals and 3 petallike sepals. The fruits are cylindrical capsules, each several inches long and clustered. For the most part, the fruits are heavy, leathery, fleshy structures that do not split open when ripe but soon droop and finally fall before winter has advanced. Two narrow-leaved species, however, have thin-walled, dry fruit capsules that mostly split open and remain on the plant for some time.

The relationship between yuccas and the *Pronuba* yucca moth has become a textbook example of mutual dependence in nature. As described by the late J. D. Laudermilk of Pomona College, Calif., the small, white, nocturnal moth visits yucca flowers to feed on nectar. When ready to lay eggs the female moth first deliberately collects pollen from several blossoms. After that act, she inserts her needlelike ovipositor through the ovary wall of a selected flower, placing an egg in each of 20–30 ovules in the flower's ovary. She then climbs to the tip of the flower's pistil (the female reproductive organ) and applies pollen to the stigma, ensuring fertilization of the ovules and their consequent seed growth. After the moth eggs hatch, the larvae feed on some of the maturing yucca seeds and develop into adults. These, in turn, visit yucca blossoms, to continue the cycle upon which the survival of both plant and animal depends.

Southwestern Native Americans ate the young flower stalks, buds, and blossoms. They used yucca leaves for thatching and leaf fibers for rope, sandals, saddle mats, baskets, and coarse blankets. Nowadays, yellow fibers from the leaf edges, green fibers from the foliage surfaces, and white fibers from the leaf interiors are woven into attractive mats and baskets. Desert rodents, rabbits, mule deer, and other wildlife consume the fleshy fruits of many yuccas. Humans also eat them raw or roasted. The word *yucca* is believed to have come from the native name of a Caribbean plant misapplied to this group. Spanish-dagger is an alternative name for many yuccas.

A desert shrub that resembles the yuccas is Bigelow Nolina (*Nolina bigelovii* [Torr.] Wats.). Its leaves are 2–6 ft. long, about 1 in. wide, often fiber-edged, and sharp pointed. The foliage is *not* spiny, however, and is more flexible and *grasslike*. The dense, whitish flower clusters are on 1–3-ft.-long stalks, but the blossoms and fruit capsules are each only ¼–⅜ in. long.

JOSHUATREE YUCCA CHART P. 384
Yucca brevifolia Engelm.
A resident of the Mohave Desert, this is the tallest and most tree-like of the yuccas. It is also the species with the *shortest leaves*. Leaves 6–13 *in.* long, only ¼–½ *in.* wide, more or less flat
(continued on p. 385)

Joshuatree Yucca

YUCCAS

Southwestern arid-zone plants with evergreen, parallel-veined, bayonet-shaped, spine-tipped leaves and upright clusters of showy white blossoms. The three sepals and three petals of the flowers are all alike. Most species with cylindrical, fleshy fruits 3–5 in. long, soon drooping, not splitting. Other yucca species are shrubby. Bigelow Nolina is similar but shrubby with leaves grasslike.

SPECIES AND REMARKS	Major distribution[1]	Leaves over 2 ft. long	Leaf width[2]	Leaf edges[3]	Leaf top flat or concave[4]	Leaf shade of green[5]	Flower stalk length (ft.)	Single blossom over 2 in. long	Text page
JOSHUATREE YUCCA *Yucca brevifolia* Trunk ± bare, leaves 5–1 3 in.; Mohave desert	PS	–	N	T	F	B	½–1	+	383
MOHAVE YUCCA *Y. schidigera* Leaves 1¼–3 ft. long; s. Calif. to s. Nev./nw. Ariz.	PS	±	M	F	C	Y	1–2	–	386
SCHOTT YUCCA *Y. schottii* Flower stalks woolly; se. Ariz./ sw. N.M.	S	±	M	N	C	B	1–3	–	386
SOAPTREE YUCCA *Y. elata*[6] Leaves thin, flexible; cen. Ariz./ sw. Utah to n. Mexico	S	±	N	F	F	Y	3–7	–	387
TORREY YUCCA *Y. torreyi* Flower parts united at base only, leaves ± rough; to s. N.M.	WT	+	W	F	C	Y	3–4	+	387
FAXON YUCCA *Y. faxoniana* Flower parts united basal ¼ in.	WT	+	W	F	C	D	3–4	+	388
CARNEROS YUCCA *Y. carnerosana* Flower parts united basal 1 in.	WT	+	W	F	C	Y	5–7	+	388
BEAKED YUCCA *Y. rostrata*[6] Only Brewster Co., w. Texas	WT	–	N	T	F	Y	1–4	+	388
TRECUL YUCCA *Y. treculeana* S.-cen. Texas	T	±	W	N	C	B	2–5	–	388

[1] P = Pacific states (s. Calif.), S = Southwest, T = Texas, wT = w. Texas
[2] M = medium, 1 –2 in.; N = narrow, ¼ in. or less; W = wide, over 2 in.
[3] F = fibrous threads frequent, T = fine-toothed, N = neither toothed nor fibrous
[4] C = concave or grooved, F = flat
[5] B = blue-, D = dark-, Y = yellow-green
[6] Fruits dry, erect, thin-walled, splitting

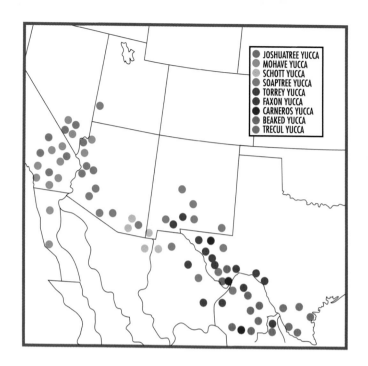

Legend	
●	JOSHUATREE YUCCA
●	MOHAVE YUCCA
●	SCHOTT YUCCA
●	SOAPTREE YUCCA
●	TORREY YUCCA
●	FAXON YUCCA
●	CARNEROS YUCCA
●	BEAKED YUCCA
●	TRECUL YUCCA

(continued from p. 383)

above, rigid, blue-green with edges *fine-toothed*. Flower clusters *short*, only 6–15 in. tall; single blossoms 2–3 in. long;March–May. Fruits 2–4 in. long, spongy at first, with walls becoming thin and *dry* but *not* splitting. Trunks and branches sometimes bare and divided into small squares. Height to 50 ft.; diameter to 3 ft. Dry soils at 2000–6000 ft. elevation, s. Calif., s. Nev., sw. Utah, and w. Ariz. **SIMILAR SPECIES:** Mohave Yucca, the only other yucca in the area, has leaves longer, wider, and with loose fibers along the edges. **REMARKS:** Wood makes poor fuel. Woodpeckers drill nesting holes in the trunk or branches. Fruits are eaten by desert rodents, rabbits, mule deer, and other wildlife. Native Americans used the rootlets to make a red dye. Common in Joshua Tree National Park, Calif., and along Joshuatree Forest Parkway, Ariz., Highway 93, between Wickenburg and Kingman.

MOHAVE YUCCA
CHART P. 384

Yucca schidigera Roezl ex Ortgies

Like the preceding yucca, a tree of the far-southwestern deserts. A smaller and less treelike species with fewer branches or none. Leaves 16–32 *in.* long (occasionally longer), 1–2 in. wide, mostly *concave* above, yellow-green, with semidetached *marginal fibers conspicuous.* Flower clusters 12–24 in. tall; single blossoms 1–2 in. long, March–May. Fruits 3–4 in. long, with thick, fleshy, nonsplitting walls. Trunk leaf-covered, sometimes bare near ground level. Height to 20 ft. Dry soils at 1000–5000 ft. elevations, s. Calif., s. Nev., and nw. Ariz. to Baja California Norte. **SIMILAR SPECIES:** See Joshuatree Yucca. **REMARKS:** The fruits were eaten raw or roasted by Native Americans. They also were dried and made into cakes to be stored for winter use.

SCHOTT YUCCA   *Yucca schottii* Engelm.
CHART P. 384

An upland yucca of se. Ariz., extreme sw. N.M., and nearby Mexico. Leaves mostly 1½–3 *ft. long,* 1–2 *in.* wide, concave above, blue-green, edges smooth without separating fibers. Flowers and stalks 1–3 ft. tall, each of the former 1–2 in. long, the latter *densely hairy,* July–Sept. Fruits 3–5 in. long, fleshy, nonsplitting, and eventually drooping. Height to 15 ft. Wooded canyons and open forests at 4000–7000 ft. elevations. **SIMILAR SPECIES:** Only Soaptree Yucca, which occurs mostly at lower elevations, shares this species' range. Its narrow leaves, long flower/fruit stalks, and dry, dehiscent fruits are distinctive. **REMARKS:** Also known as Hoary Yucca and Mountain Yucca. Arthur Schott, a German 19th-century botanist, found the species while participating in the United States–Mexico Boundary Survey.

Schott Yucca

SOAPTREE YUCCA *Yucca elata* Engelm. CHART P. 384

Occurring from Ariz. eastward, this is a very *narrow-leaved* yucca with a *long-stalked* flower cluster and *dry* fruits that split open when ripe. Leaves 12–35 in. long, ⅛–5⁄16 in. wide, flat above, yellow-green, very thin (1⁄32 in.) and *flexible,* the edges with fine *separating fibers.* Flowers and stalks combined are 3–7 ft. in length; single blossoms to 2 in. long; May–July. Fruits 1½–3 in. long, thin-walled, dry, *erect,* and *splitting open.* Height to 30 ft., usually branched. Grasslands and deserts at 1500–6000 ft. elevation. **SIMILAR SPECIES:** In w. Texas, (1) Beaked Yucca has leaves stiff and fine-toothed, without edge fibers. (2) Carneros Yucca differs in having nonsplitting fruits as well as leaves 2–3 in. wide and fruits fleshy. Westward, see (3) Schott Yucca. **REMARKS:** Native Americans used the leaves for baskets and fluids of the roots and stems for soap. During droughts, the chopped foliage sometimes is fed to livestock.

TORREY YUCCA *Yucca torreyi* Shafer CHART P. 384

This yucca occurs from s. N.M. and w. Texas into n. Mexico. Leaves 2–5 ft. long, 2–3 in. wide, thick, dull, ± *roughened* on both surfaces, *concave* above, *gray-green,* with *loose fibers* at the edge. Flower clusters *elongate* to 3–3¼ ft. long; single blossoms 2–3 in. in length, March–April. Flower segments fused only at the base.

Fruits 4–6 *in.* long, fleshy, and nonsplitting. Height to 25 ft., often not branched. Dry soils east to Devil's R., Texas. **SIMILAR SPECIES:** In w. Texas, Faxon and Carneros yuccas also have long, wide, fiber-edged leaves. (1) Faxon Yucca has dark green leaves and flower segments fused into a half-inch-long tube. (2) Carneros Yucca has yellow-green leaves and ball-shaped flower clusters on lengthy stalks. Both of these yuccas have smooth-surfaced foliage. **REMARKS:** Once described as a variety of the large-fruited but shrubby Ba-

Torrey Yucca

nana Yucca (*Yucca baccata* [Engelm.] Trel.). It is now recognized as a full species, but hybrids between these forms have been identified. Locally called Palmapita (PAL-mah-PEET-ah).

FAXON YUCCA   *Yucca faxoniana* Sarg.   CHART P. 384

A tree found only in far w. Texas and locally in adjacent Coahuila, Mexico. In this species and the next, the petals and sepals are united at the base to *form a tube* that, in this species, is ¼ in. long. Leaves much as in the last species but *dark* green and *smooth-surfaced*. Flower clusters elongate, 3–4 *ft.* long. Height to 15 ft. Desert scrub. Hybridizes with Torrey Yucca. **REMARKS:** Charles E. Faxon was a botanical artist who illustrated Charles Sprague Sargent's 14-volume *Silva of North America*, published between 1891 and 1902. He made the first drawing of this species.

CARNEROS YUCCA   CHART P. 384
Yucca carnerosana (Trel.) McKelvey

A tree of Brewster and Culberson counties, w. Texas, and adjacent Mexico. Leaves smoothly *yellow-green;* otherwise as in the two preceding species. Flower parts united to the extent of 1 *in.*; blossom cluster 5–7 *ft.* tall and *almost round,* about as wide as tall. Height to 20 ft. and mainly unbranched. Rocky slopes. **REMARKS:** First found at Carneros Pass, Coahuila, Mexico.

BEAKED YUCCA   CHART P. 384
Yucca rostrata Engelm. ex Trel.

A rare tree in the U.S., recorded only from Brewster Co. in the Big Bend country of w. Texas and in the nearby states of Coahuila and Chihuahua, Mexico. Leaves short and narrow, being only 15–24 *in.* long and ⅜–½ *in.* wide. Foliage is yellow-green, flat above, often keeled beneath, stiff, and mostly edged with *extremely fine teeth.* Flower stalks 1–4 ft. tall; single blossoms 2–2½ in. long, the parts *not* united. Related to Soaptree Yucca and, like it, with erect fruits becoming dry, durable, and *splitting open.* In this yucca, fruits often *very* numerous (about 100), 2–3 in. long, and with *slender beaks* 1–1¼ in. long. Height to 15 ft. Slopes and canyons.

TRECUL YUCCA   *Yucca treculeana* Carr.   CHART P. 384

Distributed mainly eastward of the last several species, Trecul Yucca also differs in that the smooth leaves are 20–50 in. long and blue-green. Leaf edges *neither* toothed nor fibrous. Flower stalks 2–5 *ft.* tall; individual blossoms only 1–2 *in.* long. Fruits only 2–4 *in.* long. Dry plains and slopes of s.-cen. Texas and nearby Mexico. Also called Palmapita. Hybrids with Torrey Yucca have been recorded.

APPENDIXES
GLOSSARY
REFERENCES
INDEX

APPENDIX A
KEY TO TREES
IN LEAFLESS CONDITION

The preliminary key lists the major categories into which an unknown specimen can be placed. If the specimen can be assigned to one of these sections, then proceed to that section in the main key. Otherwise, start with the main key.

PRELIMINARY KEY
- **A.** Cone-bearing trees.
- **A.** Broad-leaved trees:
    - **B.** Leaf scars opposite:
        - **C.** Bud scales 2, not overlapping.
        - **C.** Bud scales several, overlapping.
    - **B.** Leaf scars alternate:
        - **D.** Trees thorny:
            - **E.** Only paired thorns present.
            - **E.** Single thorns present, sometimes with paired thorns.
        - **D.** Trees not thorny.
            - **F.** Buds clustered at or near twig ends.
            - **F.** End bud not clustered.
                - **G.** Buds ± encircled by O-, U-, or V-shaped leaf scars.
                - **G.** Buds located above leaf scars.
                    - **H.** Leaf scars deep, either triangular or shield-shaped.
                    - **H.** Leaf scars shallow. Twigs mostly slender.
                        - **I.** Pith chambered or at least partitioned.
                        - **I.** Pith solid, continuous.
                            - **J.** Inner bark of small branches peels in fibrous strips when cut.
                            - **J.** Inner bark weak, not fibrous when cut.
                                - **K.** Spur branches present.
                                - **K.** Spur branches lacking.

Each key number is a couplet. Compare the unknown specimen with the first two choices. Select the alternative that agrees with the specimen and proceed to the couplet-number indicated. Repeat until a final determination is reached. Use a lens where necessary.

A. 1. CONE-BEARING TREES (CONIFERS) whose needles or leaf scales fall in winter; fruits are mostly dry cones over 1 in. long (Section I). **2**

A. 1. BROAD-LEAVED TREES with fruits various (Sections II–V). (The inch-long cones of alders should not be confused with the larger and much heavier cones of coniferous trees.) **4**

    2. Stubby spur branches numerous on branchlets; trees of cold climates. **LARCHES PL. 1**

    2. Spur branches absent; southern trees. **3**

3. Swamp trees of Texas and Mexico. **BALDCYPRESS PL. 8**

3. Trees of damp sites in the Southwest. **TAMARISKS PL. 10**

B. LEAF SCARS OPPOSITE:

    4. Leaf scars opposite (Sections II and III of text). **5**

    4. Leaf scars alternate (Sections IV and V of text). **19**

5. Twigs silver-scaly and/or plants thorny.
    DEVILS'-CLAWS, SILVER BUFFALOBERRY PL. 17

5. Twigs neither silvery nor thorny. **6**

    6. Buds without scales, rusty-hairy, opposite mainly near twig-tips. **CASCARA BUCKTHORN PL. 43**

    6. Buds scaly. **7**

7. Bud scales 2, not overlapping. **8**

7. Bud scales several. **11**

C. BUD SCALES 2, NOT OVERLAPPING:

8. Bundle scar one; twigs green, angled.
    WESTERN BURNINGBUSH PL.16

8. Bundle scars three. **9**

    9. Twig leaf scars raised, fruits fleshy, white or red, seed rounded. **DOGWOODS PL. 17**

    9. Leaf scars on twigs not raised. **10**

10. Fruits dry, winged, in pairs. **MAPLES PL. 15**

10. Fruits fleshy, dark, with one flat seed. **VIBURNUMS PL. 16**

C. BUD SCALES SEVERAL, OVERLAPPING:

11. Central end bud missing, a single pair of buds usually present at twig-tip; bundle scars 3 or more. **12**

11. Central end bud present, often flanked by side buds. **13**

12. Twigs slender, pith narrow. **SIERRA BLADDERNUT PL. 11**
12. Twigs stout but weak, pith wide. **ELDERBERRIES PL. 14**
13. Bundle scars more than 1 . **14**
13. Bundle scar 1 . **17**
    14. Bundle scars 3 . **15**
    14. Bundle scars many. **16**
15. End bud small, scaly or white-hairy. **MAPLES PLS. 14, 15**
15. End bud very large, scaly. **BUCKEYES PL.11**
    16. Buds scaly, bundle scars often in 3 groups.
    BUCKEYES PL. 11
    16. Buds smooth-granular. **ASHES PLS. 12, 13, 16**
17. Leaf scars often whorled; fruits dry, brown, 1-in. balls, damp sites from e. U.S. to w. Texas. **BUTTONBUSH PL. 17**
17. Leaf scars both opposite and alternate but not whorled, fruits various. **18**
18. Trunk greenish, mottled, fruits ½-in. dry capsules.
    CRAPEMYRTLE PL. 17
18. Trunk brown, ridged; fruits 4–10-in., cigar-shaped, dry capsules. **DESERT-WILLOW PL. 39**

B. LEAF SCARS ALTERNATE:
19. Twigs quite silvery, branchlets sometimes thorny.
    RUSSIAN-OLIVE PL. 39
19. Twigs not silvery, branchlets variable. **20**
    20. Trees thorny. **21**
    20. Trees not thorny. **37**

D. TREES THORNY:
21. Green grasslike streamers (leaf midribs) 10–15 in. long present; twigs green, drooping. **JERUSALEM-THORN PL. 19**
21. No green grasslike streamers present. **22**
    22. Only paired thorns present. **23**
    22. Single thorns present, alone or with paired thorns. **25**

E. ONLY PAIRED THORNS PRESENT:
23. Buds hidden beneath leaf scars, bundle scars 3, spur branches lacking. **LOCUSTS PL. 18**
23. Buds not hidden, bundle scar 1, spur branches common. **24**
    24. Twigs hairless, brownish; fruits dry pods.
    ACACIAS ETC. PL. 19
    24. Twigs hairy, usually green; fruits fleshy. **JUJUBE PL. 27**

E. SINGLE THORNS PRESENT, SOMETIMES WITH PAIRED THORNS:
25. Trees with both paired and single thorns. **26**
25. Trees with thorns only single, not paired. **27**

26. Stubby spur branches obvious. **MESQUITES PL. 19**
26. Spur branches lacking.
SOUTHWESTERN CORALBEAN, ETC. PL. 18
27. Twigs ending in sharp spines, no side thorns, desert trees.
ALLTHORN, ETC. PL. 26
27. Thorns present laterally along twigs or branchlets. **28**
    28. Thorns hooked. **29**
    28. Thorns straight or only slightly curved. **30**
29. Spur branches absent, bundle scars 3, fruits small, dark, fleshy. **PRICKLY-ASHES PL. 18**
29. Spur branches common, bundle scar 1, fruits dry pea pods.
CATCLAWS PL. 20
    30. Thorns slender, bare, without buds. **31**
    30. Thorns stubby, bearing buds. **34**
31. Trees of the arid Southwest. **GUAJILLO, PALOVERDES PL. 20**
31. Trees of more moist regions. **32**
    32. Thorns under 1 in. long, sap milky (in warm weather).
OSAGE-ORANGE PL. 28
    32. Thorns 1–10 in. long, sap not milky. **33**
33. Thorns about 1 in. long, not forked. **HAWTHORNS PL. 27**
33. Thorns 2–10 in., often forked. **HONEY LOCUST PL. 20**
    34. Trees of semi-humid areas. **CRABAPPLES, PLUMS, ETC. PL. 27**
    34. Trees of the arid Southwest. **35**
35. Thorny twigs dense, alternating at right angles.
CONDALIAS, ETC. PL. 28
35. Side twigs stiff, spiky, not alternating at right angles. **36**
    36. Trunk short, peeling. **ELEPHANT-TREE, ETC. PL. 23**
    36. Trunk otherwise. **DESERT APRICOT, ETC. PL. 27**

D. TREES NOT THORNY:
F. BUDS CLUSTERED AT OR NEAR TWIG ENDS:
37. Twigs with buds clustered at or near twig ends. **38**
37. Twigs without clustered end buds. **41**
    38. Spur branches absent. **39**
    38. Spur branches present. **40**
39. Buds scaly, species widespread. **OAKS PLS. 32–35**
39. Buds without scales, Pacific Northwest and n. Rockies.
CASCARA BUCKTHORN PL. 43
    40. Bundle scars 3, sap clear, n. U.S. **FIRE CHERRY PL. 42**
    40. Bundle scar 1, sap milky (*poisonous!*), s. Tex. and sw. Ariz.
    areas. **TALLOWTREE PL. 31, JUMPING-BEAN SAPIUM PL. 39**

F. END BUD NOT CLUSTERED:
G. BUDS ± ENCIRCLED BY O-, U-, OR V-SHAPED LEAF SCARS:

41. Buds encircled or nearly so by O-, U-, or V-shaped leaf scars.

42

41. Buds located above leaf scars. **44**

    42. Leaf scars with numerous bundle scars. **43**

    42. Leaf scars with 3 bundle scars (see also Honey Locust, thornless form, Pl. 20) **HOPTREES PLS. 22, 24; SOPHORAS PL. 24**

43. Buds often woolly with several obscure scales; bundle scars mostly in 3 groups. **SUMACS PLS. 22–24**

43. Buds not woolly, with only 1 caplike scale.

SYCAMORES PL. 29

G. BUDS LOCATED ABOVE LEAF SCARS:

H. LEAF SCARS DEEP, EITHER TRIANGULAR OR SHIELD-SHAPED:

    44. Leaf scars deep, either triangular or shield-shaped; twigs often stout, relatively inflexible; bundle scars 4 or more, sometimes in 3 groups (bundle scars 3 in Western Soapberry). **45**

    44. Leaf scars shallow, twigs mostly slender, bundle scars various.
       50

45. Pith chambered, buds woolly. **WALNUTS PL. 21**

45. Pith continuous, buds various. **46**

    46. Buds longer than wide, end bud larger. **HICKORIES PL. 21**

    46. Buds small, globular; end bud various. **47**

47. Leaf scars deeply triangular; bundle scars not grouped; fruits papery, winged, clustered. **TREE-OF-HEAVEN PL. 21**

47. Leaf scars 3-lobed, bundle scars in 3 groups, fruits neither papery nor winged. **48**

    48. Plants with several stems; fruits dry, pear-shaped capsules, 1½– 2 in. across. **MEXICAN-BUCKEYE PL. 22**

    48. Trees with a single trunk; fruits 1/2-in. smooth balls. **49**

49. Twigs greenish gray; buds 2-scaled, hairless, and often several at each leaf scar, above one another; fruits not always present.
WESTERN SOAPBERRY PL. 24

49. Twigs dark brown, buds single, hairy; fruits usually persistent.
   CHINABERRY PL. 25

H. LEAF SCARS SHALLOW, TWIGS MOSTLY SLENDER:

    50. Buds without scales. **BUCKTHORNS PL. 43**

    50. Buds with scales. **51**

51. Bud scale 1, mostly smooth, caplike. **WILLOWS PLS. 36–38**

51. Bud scales more than 1. **52**

    52. Pith chambered or at least partitioned at the leaf scars. **53**

    52. Pith solid, continuous. **56**

I. PITH CHAMBERED OR AT LEAST PARTITIONED:

53. Twigs encircled by narrow lines (stipule scars); buds 2-scaled, spicy when crushed.   **TULIPTREE PL. 29**

53. Twigs and buds otherwise (see also Walnuts Pl. 21). **54**

    54. Bundle scars 5, twigs rough-hairy, trunk not warty.   **PAPER-MULBERRY PL. 29**

    54. Bundle scars 3. **55**

55. Trunk warty; twigs hairy or not, twigs/buds brownish.   **HACKBERRIES PL. 30**

55. Trunk not warty; twigs hairless, purplish; buds green.   **INDIAN-PLUM PL. 40**

I. PITH SOLID, CONTINUOUS:

    56. Buds with a narrow base (stalked), blunt, reddish when mature, 2-scaled; small, woody, conelike catkins usually pres-ent.   **ALDERS PL. 40**

    56. Buds not stalked. **57**

57. Inner bark of small branches can be peeled in fibrous strips when cut. **58**

57. Cut inner bark weak, not especially fibrous. **60**

J. INNER BARK OF SMALL BRANCHES PEELS IN FIBROUS STRIPS WHEN CUT:

    58. Bundle scars 3; buds brown, scale edges often darker.   **ELMS PL. 41**

    58. Bundle scars more than 3. **59**

59. Bud scales 4–6, brownish; sap milky (in warm weather).   **MULBERRIES PL. 29**

59. Bud scales 2–3, red or green; sap clear.   **BASSWOODS PL. 30**

J. INNER BARK WEAK, NOT FIBROUS WHEN CUT:

    60. Twigs green, bundle scar 1 or indistinct. **61**

    60. Twigs not green, bundle scars various. **62**

61. Twigs 4-lined or 4-angled; trunk mottled. **CRAPEMYRTLE PL. 17**

61. Twigs smooth, trunk gray-green.   **CHINESE PARASOLTREE PL. 29**

    62. Spur branches present (See also Poplars 72). **63**

    62. Spur branches lacking. **70**

K. SPUR BRANCHES PRESENT:

63. Trunk marked with horizontal streaks (lenticels), bundle scars 3. **64**

63. Trunk bark without horizontal lines; bundle scars various. **65**

    64. Buds with 2–3 scales, broken twigs without an almond odor.   **BIRCHES PL. 41**

    64. Buds with 4–6 scales, broken twigs often with an almond odor.   **PEACH PL. 39; CHERRIES PL. 42**

65. Bud scales 2; fruits small, with feathery tails 1–4 in. long.
ALDERLEAF CERCOCARPUS PL. 43
65. Plants otherwise. **66**
    66. Trees of arid regions in Ariz. and Texas.
KIDNEYWOODS, ETC. PL. 23; LITTLELEAF LYSILOMA PL. 25
    66. Trees of more moist climates. **67**
67. Bundle scar 1, side twigs stiff, e. U.S. to cen. Texas.
POSSUMHAW HOLLY PL. 43
67. Bundle scars 3, side twigs flexible. **68**
    68. Buds long-pointed, reddish, scales often twisted and with
black notched tips; second bud scale usually less than half
length of bud.   JUNEBERRIES PL. 43
    68. Buds otherwise. **69**
69. Bud scales about 4; twigs not winged; fruits fleshy.
MOUNTAIN-ASHES PL.22;
DOMESTIC APPLE, DOMESTIC PEAR PL. 43
69. Bud scales about 6; twigs often corky-winged; fruits dry,
prickly balls.   SWEETGUM PL. 29

K. SPUR BRANCHES LACKING:
    70. Bundle scars 3 (sometimes more in California Hazelnut),
fruits various. **71**
    70. Bundle scar 1 or indistinct. **75**
71. Bud scales 2, buds small, wood yellow, cen. Texas.
AMERICAN SMOKETREE PL. 43
71. Bud scales many, buds elongate. **72**
    72. Buds with lowermost scale centered directly above the leaf
scar; bark often smooth and greenish on young trunks and
branches; end bud true.   POPLARS PL. 31
    72. Bud scales and trunk bark otherwise. **73**
73. Small (⅜–¾ in.) woody pine conelike catkins present; end bud
true.   ALDERS PL. 40
73. Woody conelike catkins lacking, end bud false. **74**
    74. Leaf scars raised, with 2 or 3 lines descending (on vigor-
ous twigs).   REDBUDS PL. 30
    74. Leaf scars not raised or at least with no descending lines.
HORNBEAMS, CALIFORNIA HAZELNUT PL. 41
75. Bundle scar lacking or indistinct, fruits dry capsules ⅜–½ in.
long, Mexican border region.   TREE TOBACCO PL. 43
75. Bundle scar 1. **76**
    76. Trunk smooth, dark gray outer bark peels to a silver gray
which in turn may peel to a whitish yellow; fruits fleshy
spheres.   TEXAS PERSIMMON PL. 46
    76. Trunk and buds otherwise; fruits thin, dry capsules 4–10
in. long; sw. U.S.   DESERT-WILLOW PL. 39

Appendix B
Plant Relationships

Field identification does not require a knowledge of major classification groups or even of family or scientific names. Yet it is often desirable to know general relationships within the plant kingdom. The following list indicates the family relationships of the genera of trees within our area. The listing of conifers (Division Pinophyta) is based on the work of Cronquist, Takhtajan, and Zimmermann (1966). That of the broad-leaved plants (Division Magnoliophyta) is the judgment of Cronquist (1981). Dr. Arthur Cronquist is late senior scientist at the New York Botanical Garden. All major and many minor botanical subdivisions are based on flower and fruit structures. Family names tend to be standardized by the ending *-aceae,* orders by *-ales,* subclasses by *-idae,* classes by *-opsida,* and divisions by *-ophyta.*

KINGDOM PLANTAE
SUBKINGDOM EMBRYOBIONTA
DIVISION PINOPHYTA
CLASS PINOPSIDA
SUBCLASS PINIDAE
Order Taxales
Family Taxaceae: *Taxus, Torreya*

Order Pinales
Family Pinaceae: *Abies, Cedrus, Larix, Picea, Pinus, Pseudotsuga, Tsuga*
Family Taxodiaceae: *Metasequoia, Sequoia, Sequoiadendron, Taxodium*
Family Cupressaceae: *Calocedrus, Chamaecyparis, Cupressus, Juniperus, Thuja*

DIVISION MAGNOLIOPHYTA
CLASS MAGNOLIOPSIDA
SUBCLASS MAGNOLIIDAE
Order Magnoliales
Family Magnoliaceae: *Liriodendron*

Order Laurales
Family Lauraceae: *Cinnamomum, Persea, Umbellularia*

SUBCLASS HAMAMELIDAE
Order Hamamelidales
Family Platanaceae: *Platanus*
Family Hamamelidaceae: *Liquidambar*

Order Urticales
Family Ulmaceae: *Celtis, Ulmus*
Family Moraceae: *Broussonetia, Maclura, Morus*

Order Juglandales
Family Juglandaceae: *Carya, Juglans*

Order Myricales
Family Myricaceae: *Myrica*

Order Fagales
Family Fagaceae: *Castanea, Chrysolepis, Fagus, Lithocarpus, Quercus*
Family Betulaceae: *Alnus, Betula, Corylus, Ostrya*

Order Casuarinales
Family Casuarinaceae: *Casuarina*

SUBCLASS CARYOPHYLLIDAE
Order Caryophyllales
Family Nyctaginaceae: *Pisonia*
Family Cactaceae: *Cereus, Opuntia*

SUBCLASS DILLENIIDAE
Order Malvales
Family Tiliaceae: *Tilia*
Family Sterculiaceae: *Firmiana, Fremontodendron*

Order Violales
Family Tamaricaceae: *Tamarix*

Order Salicales
Family Salicaceae: *Populus, Salix*

Order Capparales
Family Capparaceae: *Koeberlinia*

Order Ericales
Family Ericaceae: *Arbutus, Arctostaphylos, Rhododendron, Vaccinium*

Order Ebenales
Family Sapotaceae: *Bumelia*
Family Ebenaceae: *Diospyros*

SUBCLASS ROSIDAE
Order Rosales
Family Rosaceae: *Adenostoma, Amelanchier, Cercocarpus, Cowania, Crataegus, Heteromeles, Lyonothamnus, Malus, Oemleria, Prunus, Pyrus, Sorbus, Vauquelinia*

Order Fabales
Family Mimosaceae: *Acacia, Leucaena, Lysiloma, Pithecellobium, Prosopis*
Family Caesalpiniaceae: *Caesalpinia, Cercidium, Cercis, Gleditsia, Parkinsonia*
Family Fabaceae: *Dalea, Erythrina, Eysenhardtia, Olneya, Robinia, Sophora*

Order Proteales
Family Eleagnaceae: *Elaeagnus, Shepherdia*
Family Proteaceae: *Grevillea*

Order Myrtales
Family Lythraceae: *Lagerstroemia*
Family Myrtaceae: *Eucalyptus*

Order Cornales
Family Cornaceae: *Cornus, Garrya*

Order Celastrales
Family Celastraceae: *Canotia, Euonymus*
Family Aquifoliaceae: *Ilex*

Order Euphorbiales
Family Euphorbiaceae: *Sapium*

Order Rhamnales
Family Rhamnaceae: *Ceanothus, Condalia, Rhamnus, Ziziphus*

Order Sapindales
Family Staphyleaceae: *Staphylea*
Family Sapindaceae: *Sapindus, Ungnadia*
Family Hippocastanaceae: *Aesculus*
Family Aceraceae: *Acer*
Family Burseraceae: *Bursera*
Family Anacardiaceae: *Cotinus, Pistacia, Rhus, Schinus*
Family Simaroubaceae: *Ailanthus, Holacantha*
Family Meliaceae: *Melia*
Family Rutaceae: *Helietta, Ptelea, Zanthoxylum*
Family Zygophyllaceae: *Guaiacum*

SUBCLASS ASTERIDAE
Order Solanales
Family Solanaceae: *Nicotiana, Solanum*

Order Lamiales
Family Boraginaceae: *Cordia, Ehretia*

Order Scrophulariales
Family Oleaceae: *Forestiera, Fraxinus*
Family Bignoniaceae: *Catalpa, Chilopsis*

Order Rubiales
Family Rubiaceae: *Cephalanthus*

Order Dipsacales
Family Caprifoliaceae: *Sambucus, Viburnum*

Order Asterales
Family Asteraceae: *Artemisia*

CLASS LILIOPSIDA
SUBCLASS ARECIDAE
Order Arecales
Family Arecaceae: *Phoenix, Sabal, Washingtonia*

SUBCLASS LILIIDAE
Order Liliales
Family Agavaceae: *Nolina, Yucca*

GLOSSARY

See also Fig 1. Leaf and Twig Terminology, p. 3; Fig. 2. Leaf Shapes, p. 4; and Fig. 3. Twig and Bud Terminology, p. 6.

Alternate (leaves, buds). Not opposite but arranged singly at intervals along twigs.

Angled (twig, bud). Having evident ridges; not smoothly rounded.

Aromatic. Having a distinctive odor, at least when crushed.

Base (leaf). The lower portion, toward the leafstalk.

Berry (fruit). Strictly speaking, a fleshy fruit that contains small seeds (such as a grape). The mention of "berry" or berrylike fruits indicates fleshy fruits that are not true berries.

Blade (leaf). The broad, expanded portion.

Bloom (twig, leaf, fruit, etc.). A whitish powdery coating.

Bract. A somewhat leaflike, petallike, or woody structure occurring beneath a flower or fruit or their clusters.

Branchlet. Except for the twig, the youngest and smallest division of a branch. See **Twig.**

Bristle. A stiff hair, sometimes pricklelike.

Bundle scars. Tiny dots or lines within the leaf scar, caused by the breaking of bundles of ducts leading into the leafstalk. Sometimes elongate or curved.

Capsule. A dry fruit that splits partly open at maturity.

Catkin. A cluster of tiny flowers or fruits, usually fuzzy and caterpillar-shaped, often drooping. It occurs in oaks and in willows and their relatives. Where there are flowers of only one sex, male catkins usually are larger.

Chambered (pith). Pith divided crosswise by numerous plates or membranes. Term is here used broadly to include all types of segmented and transversely divided pith (diaphragmed, partitioned). When the twig is cut lengthwise, such a pith looks ladderlike. See **Partitioned.**

Coarse-toothed (leaf edge). With large teeth; dentate, serrate.

Compound (leaf). Divided into leaflets, each of which usually has the general appearance of a leaf. See **Major leaflet** and **Minor leaflet.**

Continuous (pith). Smoothly pithy, the twig center neither chambered nor hollow.

Crinkled (leaf edge). Irregularly curled, crisped, wavy (up and down). See **Wavy-edged.**

Deciduous (leaf, stipule, bud scale, etc.). Falls off seasonally, usually in autumn or dry season.

Dehiscent (seed pod). Splitting open.

Double-toothed (leaf edge). Each tooth bearing smaller teeth.

Egg-shaped (leaf). Broader near the base than at the tip, the base broadly rounded (but leaf tip sharper than apex of an egg); ovate.

Elliptic (leaf). Widest in the middle and tapering evenly to both ends like the cross section of an American football.

End bud (twig). True end bud or sometimes several, clustered, located at the precise end of the twig; terminal bud. False end bud occurs in some species when the end bud is shed and a nearby side bud acts as end bud. A scar marks the site of the shed bud and lies beside the false end bud. See Fig. 3, p. 6. See **Lateral.**

End bud scar (twig). Encircling lines, usually crowded, that mark the end of the branchlet and the base of the twig, the beginning point of twig groth. See **Ringed.**

Escape. A cultivated plant locally growing wild.

Established. An escaped plant freely growing wild and reproducing as a component of a natural plant community. See **Terminal, Naturalized.**

Evergreen (plant, leaf). Remaining green throughout the year. Leaves not dropping until new foliage is produced. See **Deciduous.**

Fan-compound (leaf). A compound leaf with leaflets radiating from a central area; palmate-compound.

Fan-lobed (leaf). Major lobes radiating from a central area; palmate-lobed.

Fan-veined (leaf). Main veins radiating from a central area; palmate-veined.

Feather-compound (leaf). Midribs of main leaflets branching from a central main midrib at several points in a featherlike pattern; pinnate-compound.

Feather-lobed (leaf). The main lobes more or less at right angles to the midrib, not radiating from a central point; pinnate-lobed.

Feather-veined (leaf). The main side veins branching more or less at right angles to the midrib; pinnate-veined.

Fine-toothed (leaf edge). With small teeth; denticulate or serrulate.

Form. Used here to include all populations of plants of the same species which vary slightly from the typical, whether such variation is limited geographically (see **Variety**) or not; forma.

Four-lined (twig). With 4 more or less equidistant lines running lengthwise along the twig.

Four-sided (twig, bud). Approximately square in cross section.

Fruit. The seed-bearing portion of a plant with its associated structures. The term does not imply that it is either fleshy or edible.

Genus. A group of species sufficiently closely related to be given the same generic name.

Gland. Strictly speaking, a surface or protuberance that secretes a substance, but generally any small knob or wart that is a normal part of the plant and has no other known function.

Glandular-toothed (leaf). Having teeth that bear glands. See **Tree-of-heaven, Pl. 21.**

Hairy. Covered with hairs.

Heart-shaped (leaf). The shape of the valentine heart; cordate.

Hollow (pith). Twig actually without pith but with the space present.

Hybrid. The offspring of a cross between 2 species or other categories.

Involucre. A circle or cluster of bracts beneath flowers or fruits.

Lateral (bud, flower/fruit cluster). To the side rather than at the end of twig or branchlet. See **Terminal.**

Leaf angle. The junction of leafstalk and twig.

Leaf scar. The mark left on the twig at the point of attachment of a leafstalk when the leaf falls or is removed.

Leaflet. A leaflike subdivision of a compound leaf. See **Major leaflet** and **Minor leaflet.**

Leafstalk. The stalk supporting a leaf; petiole.

Leathery (leaf). Of a smoothly tough texture; coriaceous.

Legume. A plant of the pea family or the one- to many-seeded podlike fruit of a pea-group plant.

Lenticel. A corky spot on the bark originating as a breathing pore and either circular or somewhat stripelike (see **Cherries, Pl. 42**).

Lobed (leaf, flower petal, sepal). Divided into rounded, incompletely separated sections.

Long-pointed (leaf). The tip gradually tapering to a point; acuminate.

Major leaflet. A primary subdivision of a compound leaf; pinna.

Midrib (leaf, leaflet). The central rib or main vein.

Minor leaflet. A subdivision of a major leaflet. See **Twice-compound.**

Naked (bud). Without bud scales.

Narrow (leaves). Shaped like the top view of a canoe; slender and pointed at each end. Often slightly wider near the base; lanceolate. Sometimes with more or less parallel sides.

Naturalized (species). Native to another area but fully established in a new range. See **Established.**

Net-veined (leaf). With a network of veins.

Node. The place, sometimes swollen, on a stem or twig where a leaf is attached or a leaf scar occurs.

Oblong (leaf). Longer than broad, with the longer sides somewhat parallel.

Once-compound (leaf). A compound leaf with a single set of undivided leaflets. See **Twice-compound.**

Opposite (leaves, leaf scars, buds). Two at a node; in opposing pairs.

Ovary. The ovule-bearing (egg-bearing) portion of the flower.

Ovule. See **Ovary.**

Palmate. See various *Fan-* prefixes.

Parasitic (plant). Growing on another plant and deriving food from it.

Partitioned (pith). The pith divided crosswise by woody plates, usually near the leaf scar. See **Chambered.**

Pendent. Hanging (usually from a stem or branchlet).

Persistent (scales, fruits, leaves). Remaining attached.

Petal (flower). One of a circle of modified leaves immediately outside the reproductive organs; usually brightly colored.

Petiole. See **Leafstalk.**

Pinna. Synonym for major leaflet (plural: pinnae).

Pinnate. See various *Feather-* prefixes.

Pith. The spongy or hollow center of twigs or some stems. See **Chambered** and **Continuous.**

Pod. The dryish fruit of some plants, especially legumes, containing one to many seeds and usually flattened, splitting down one or both sides; see **Legume.**

Prickle. A small, sharp outgrowth involving only the outer epidermal layer; generally more slender than a thorn. But in this book no stress is placed on the technical distinctions between prickles and thorns. See also **Bristle.**

Reclining (stem). The lower portion somewhat flattened along the ground but the terminal parts curving upward.

Resin-dot. Tiny circular or globular yellow spots, usually not obvious except under magnification.

Ridged (twig). Angular, with lengthwise lines.

Ringed (twig). With narrow encircling stipule scars at leaf scars. See **End bud scar.**

Rolled (leaf edge). Curled under; revolute.

Scale (bud, leaf, twig). (1) A thin, membranelike covering of the bud or, in some shrubs, the twig base, or (2) a fine, grainlike surface material.

Seed. That portion of the ripened fruit which contains the embryo and its closely associated essential coats.

Sepal (flower). One of the outermost circle of modified leaves surrounding the reproductive organs and lying outside the petals; usually green.

Sheath (conifer needle). Thin tissues present at needle bases and binding the needle bundles.

Short-pointed (leaf tip). Abruptly constricted and sharply pointed; not gradually tapering.

Short shoot (branchlet). See **Spur branch.**

Shreddy (bark). Dividing into fragile, thin, narrow sheets.

Shrub. A woody plant usually growing with several strong stems and less than about 1 3 feet maximum height.

Side buds. Buds in a lateral, not end, position.

Simple leaf. Composed of only a single blade, though frequently lobed.

Single-toothed (leaf edge). Bearing only a single set of teeth. See **Double-toothed.**

Sinus (leaf). The space between 2 leaf lobes.

Solid (pith). See **Continuous.**

Spathe. A large membranous bract or pair of bracts that encloses a flower cluster.

Species. For practical purposes: populations whose individuals freely breed with one another and vary only slightly from one another.

Spicy-scented. Aromatic, with a spicy odor.

Spike (flower, fruits). A cluster with a narrow, fingerlike shape, the individual flowers or fruits with short stalks or none.

Spine. See **Thorn.**

Spur branch. A stubby branchlet with densely crowded leaves and leaf scars. Often bearing flowers, fruits. See Fig. 3, p. 6. Synonymous with **Short shoot.**

Stalked (buds). Having a narrow necklike base.

Sterile (flower). Infertile, unproductive.

Stipule. A leafy growth at the base of the leafstalk, usually small and in pairs, leaving scars on the twig when it drops. See also **Ringed.**

Straggling. Semi-upright.

Terminal (bud, flower/fruit cluster). Growing at the end of the twig. See **End bud (twig).**

Thorn (twig, branchlet, branch, stem). A stout, sharp, woody outgrowth of the stem. Technically, prickles and spines are of different origin, but this book does not require a distinction to be made.

Thrice-compound (leaf). Divided into major leaflets that in turn are divided into minor leaflets, which are further subdivided into subleaflets; an uncommon type.

Tip (leaf). The apex.

Tree. A woody plant with a single main stem at least 3 inches in diameter at breast height (4½ feet) and growing more than 13 feet tall.

Trunk. The main stem of a tree.

Tubular (flower). With the basal portion hollow and tubelike.

Tundra. Vegetation type of very cold climates, especially in Far North, overlying permafrost and consisting of lichens, sedges, mosses, grasses, and low woody plants.

Twice-compound (leaf). With the major leaflets further divided into minor leaflets.

Twig. The end subdivision of a branch; the current year's growth.

Variety. That portion of a species which in a certain geographic area differs slightly from the remainder of the species elsewhere.

Wavy-edged (leaf edge). With flat, shallow, rounded undulations. See **Crinkled.**

Wavy-toothed (leaf edge). Wavy-edged but with more toothlike projections; crenate.

Wedge-shaped (leaves, leaf bases, leaf tips). With narrow, tapering bases or, less often, tips; cuneate, acute.

Whorled (leaves, leaf scars). Arranged in circles around the twigs.

Winged (leafstalk, twig). With projecting thin flat membranes or corky outgrowths.

Woody plant. With the stems and limbs containing lignin (wood).

References

Abrams, Leroy, and Roxana Stinchfield Ferris. 1960. *Illustrated Flora of the Pacific States,* 4 vols. Stanford, Calif.: Stanford Univ. Press.

Argus, George W. 1986. "Studies of the *Salix lucida* and *Salix reticulata* complexes in North America." *Can. J. Bot.* 64: 541–551.

Arno, Stephen F., and Ramona P. Hammerly. 1977. *Northwest Trees.* Seattle: The Mountaineers.

Baerg, Harry J. 1973. *The Western Tress,* 2nd ed. Dubuque: W. C. Brown Co.

Bailey, D. K. 1970. *Phytogeography and Taxonomy of Pinus Subsection Balfourianae.* Ann. Missouri Bot. Garden 57: 210–249.

Benson, Lyman, and Robert A. Darrow. 1954. *Trees and Shrubs of the Southwestern Deserts,* 2nd ed. Tucson: Univ. Arizona Press; Albuquerque: Univ. New Mexico Press.

Berry, James Berthold. 1966. *Western Forest Trees.* New York: Dover.

Bever, Dale N. 1981. *Northwest Conifers, A Photographic Key.* Portland, Ore.: Binford & Mort.

Correll, Donovan Stewart, and Marshall Conring Johnston. 1970. *Manual of the Vascular Plants of Texas.* Renner, Texas: Texas Research Found.

Cronquist, Arthur. 1981. *An Integrated System of Classification of Flowering Plants.* New York: Columbia Univ. Press.

Cronquist, Arthur, Arthur H. Holmgren, Noel H. Holmgren, and James L. Reveal. 1972. *Intermountain Flora,* Vol. 1. New York and London: New York Bot. Garden and Harper.

Cronquist, A., A. Takhtajan, and W. Zimmerman. 1966. On the Higher Taxa of Embryonbionta. *Taxon* 15: 129–124.

Davis, Ray J. 1952. *Flora of Idaho*. Dubuque: W. C. Brown Co.

Elias, Thomas S. 1980. *The Complete Trees of North America*. New York: Van Nostrand Reinhold.

Eliot, Willard Ayres. 1938. *Forest Trees of the Pacific Coast*. New York: G. P. Putnam's Sons.

Elmore, Francis H. 1976. *Shrubs and Trees of the Southwest Uplands,* Popular Ser. 19. Tucson: Southwest Parks & Monuments Assoc.

Fowells, H. A. 1965. *Silvics of Forest Trees of the United States.* Washington: U.S. Dept. Agri., Agri. Handbook 271.

Gerstenberg. R. H. 1983. *Common Trees and Shrubs of the Southern Sierra Nevada*. Reedley, Calif.: Kings River College.

Harrington, H. D. 1954. *Manual of the Plants of Colorado*. Chicago: Sage Books.

Hayes, Doris W., and George A. Garrison. 1960. *Keys to Important Woody Plants of Eastern Oregon and Washington*. Washington: U.S. Dept. Agri., Agri. Handbook 148.

Hickman, James C. 1993. *The Jepson Manual: Higher Plants of California*. Berkeley: Univ. Calif. Press.

Hicks, Ray R., Jr., and George K. Stephenson. 1978. *Woody Plants of the Western Gulf Region*. Dubuque: Kendall/Hunt Publ. Co.

Hitchcock, C. Leo, and Arthur Cronquist. 1973. *Flora of the Pacific Northwest*. Seattle: Univ. Washington Press.

Hitchcock, C. Leo, Arthur Cronquist, Marion Ownby, J. W. Thompson. 1972. *Vascular Plants of the Pacific Northwest,* 5 vols. Seattle and London: Univ. Washington Press.

Hoag, Donald C. 1965. *Trees and Shrubs for the Northern Plains*. Fargo: North Dakota Inst. Regional Studies.

Hosie, R. C. 1969. *Native Trees of Canada*. Ottawa, Ontario: Canadian Forestry Service.

Kearney, Thomas H., and Robert H. Peebles. 1969. *Arizona Flora*. Berkeley: Univ. Calif. Press.

Kelly, George W. 1970. *A Guide to the Woody Plants of Colorado*. Boulder, Colo.: Pruett Publ. Co.

Lamb, Samuel H. 1977. *Woody Plants of the Southwest*. Santa Fe, N.M.: Sunstone Press.

Lanner, Ronald M. 1984. *Trees of the Great Basin*. Reno, Nev.: Univ. Nevada Press.

Little, Elbert L., Jr. 1971. *Atlas of United States Trees, Vol. 1: Conifers and Important Hardwoods.* Washington: U.S. Dept. Agri. Misc. Publ. 1146.

———. 1976. *Atlas of United States Trees. Vol 3: Minor Western Hardwoods.* Washington: U.S. Dept. Agri. Misc. Publ. 1314.

———. 1977. *Atlas of United States Trees. Vol 4: Minor Eastern Hardwoods.* Washington: U.S. Dept. Agri. Misc. Publ. 1342.

———. 1979. *Checklist of United States Trees (Native and Naturalized).* Washington: Agri. Handbook 541, Forest Service, U.S. Dept. Agri.

———. 1980. *The Audubon Society Field Guide to North American Trees: Western Region.* New York: Alfred A. Knopf.

Lonard, Robert I., James H. Everitt, and Frank W. Judd. 1991. *Woody Plants of the Lower Rio Grande Valley, Texas.* Austin: Texas Memorial Museum, Univ. Texas, Misc. Publ. No. 7

Lyons, C. P. 1956. *Trees, Shrubs, and Flowers to Know in Washington.* Toronto: Dent & Sons.

Martin, William C., and Charles R. Hutchins. 1980. *A Flora of New Mexico,* 2 vols. Vaduz: J. Cramer.

McDougall, W. B., and Omer E. Sperry. 1951. *Plants of Big Bend National Park.* Washington: National Park Service.

McMinn, Howard E., and Evelyn Maino. 1980. *An Illustrated Manual of Pacific Coast Trees,* 2nd ed. Berkeley: Univ. Calif. Press.

Miller, Howard, and Samuel Lamb. 1985. *Oaks of North America.* Happy Camp, Calif.: Naturegraph Publ.

Mirov, N. T. 1967. *The Genus Pinus.* New York: Ronald Press.

Morin, Nancy R., ed. 1993, 1997. *Flora of North America.* Vols. 2, 3. New York: Oxford Univ. Press.

Muller, Cornelius H. 1951. *The Oaks of Texas.* Renner, Texas: Contrib. Texas Research Found. 1:21–23.

Munz, Philip A., and David D. Keck. 1968. *A California Flora.* Berkeley: Univ. Calif. Press.

Oosting, H. J. 1956. *The Study of Plant Communities.* San Francisco: Freeman.

Peterson, P. Victor, and P. Victor Peterson, Jr. 1975. *Native Trees of the Sierra Nevada.* Berkeley: Calif. Nat. Hist. Guides 36, Univ. Calif. Press.

Petrides, George A. 1972. *A Field Guide to Trees and Shrubs,* 2nd ed. Boston: Houghton Mifflin Co.

———. 1988. *A Field Guide to Eastern Trees.* Boston: Houghton Mifflin Co.

Preston, Richard J., Jr. 1940. *Rocky Mountain Trees.* Ames, Iowa: Iowa St. Univ. Press.

————. 1976. *North American Trees,* 3rd ed. Ames, Iowa: Iowa St. Univ. Press.

Reeves, R. G., and D. C. Bain. 1947. *Flora of South Central Texas.* College Station, Texas: Texas A. & M. Univ.

Ross, Charles R. 1985. *Trees to Know in Oregon.* Oregon State Univ. Exten. Bull. 697.

Sargent, Charles Sprague. 1965. *Manual of the Trees of North America,* 2 vols. New York: Dover (reprint of 1922 edition pub. by Houghton Mifflin Co.).

Stephens, H. A. 1973. *Woody Plants of the North Central Plains.* Lawrence, Kans.: Univ. Press of Kansas.

Sudworth, George B. 1967. *Forest Trees of the Pacific Slope,* 2nd ed. New York: Dover.

Trelease, William. 1967. *Winter Botany.* New York: Dover (reprint of 3rd edition, 1931).

Treshow, Michael, Stanley L. Welsh, and Glen Moore. 1964. *Guide to the Woody Plants of Utah.* Boulder, Colo.: Pruett Press, Inc.

Tucker, John M. 1952. "Taxonomic interrelationships in the Quercus dumosa complex." *Madroño* 11:234–252.

————. 1961. Studies in the Quercus undulata complex. I. A preliminary Statement. *Amer. J. Bot.* 48:202–208.

Van Dersal, William R. 1938. *Native Woody Plants of the United States: Their Erosion Control and Wildlife Values.* Washington: U.S. Dept. Agri. Misc. Publ. 303.

Viereck, Leslie A., and Elbert L. Little, Jr. 1972. *Alaska Trees and Shrubs.* Washington: Forest Service, U.S. Dept. Agri., Agri. Handbook 410.

Vines, Robert A. 1984. *Trees of Central Texas.* Austin: Univ. Texas Press.

Waterfall, U. T. 1962. *Keys to the Flora of Oklahoma,* 2nd ed. Stillwater, Okla.: Research Found., Okla. State Univ.

Wauer, Roland H. 1980. *Naturalists' Big Bend.* College Station, Texas: Texas A. & M. Univ. Press.

Welsh, Stanley L., N. Duane Atwood, Sherel Goodrich, and Larry C. Higgins. 1987. *A Utah Flora.* Great Basin Naturalist Memoirs 9. Provo, Utah: Brigham Young Univ.

Wiggins, Ira L. 1980. *Flora of Baja California.* Stanford, Calif.: Stanford Univ. Press.

Wooton, E. O., and Paul C. Standley. 1972. *Flora of New Mexico.* Reprints of U.S. Floras. New York: Wheldon & Wesley.

PHOTO CREDITS

DAVID CAVAGNARO: Jeffrey Pine, Gray Pine, Parry Pinyon, Mountain Hemlock (bark), Pacific Yew (bark), Western Juniper, Two-petal Ash, Red Elderberry, Tree-of-Heaven, Greenbark Ceanothus, California Sycamore, California Black Oak, Valley Oak, Silverleaf Oak, Pacific Willow, California-bay, Pacific Bayberry, Desert-willow, Western Juneberry, Parry Manzanita.

KATHY ADAMS CLARK: Rocky Mountain Juniper (bark), Pinchot Juniper, Rusty Blackhaw, Western Soapberry, Winged Elm.

MARY CLAY/PHOTO/NATS: Fremont Cottonwood (bark), Fremont Cottonwood, Narrowleaf Cottonwood.

DEREK FELL: Monterey Pine, White Spruce, Horsechestnut, Smooth Sumac, Coast Live Oak, Siberian Elm, American Holly, Bluegum Eucalyptus.

CHARLES MARDEN FITCH: Sugar Pine, Smokethorn.

LYNNE HARRISON: Lodgepole Pine.

ARTHUR LEE JACOBSON/PHOTOGARDEN: Grand Fir, California Buckeye, Oregon Ash, Mexican Elderberry, Western Mountain Maple, Oregon White Oak, Scouler Willow.

PETER MARGOSIAN/PHOTO/NATS: Mountain Hemlock, Pacific Yew.

JO-AN ORDANO/PHOTO/NATS: Bristlecone Pine.

JERRY PAVIA: Tamarack, Western Larch, White Fir, Rocky Mountain Juniper, Giant Sequoia, Ashleaf Maple, Mohave Yucca.

GEORGE A. PETRIDES: Subalpine Larch, Singleleaf Pinyon, Two-needle Pinyon, Ponderosa Pine, Western White Pine, Sitka Spruce, Engelmann Spruce, Subalpine Fir, Common Douglas-fir, Western Hemlock, Incense-cedar, Western Redcedar, Alaska-cedar, Arizona Cypress, Oneseed Juniper, Allligator Juniper, Texas Ebony, Velvet Mesquite, Elephant-tree, Common Hoptree, Crucifixion-thorn, Netleaf Hackberry, Quaking Aspen, Arizona Oak, Emory Oak, Weeping Willow, Red Alder, Paper Birch, Pacific Madrone, Anacua, California Washingtonia, Saguaro,

Organpipe Cactus, Jumping Cholla, Joshuatree Yucca, Schott Yucca, Torrey Yucca.

BEN PHILLIPS/PHOTO/NATS: Possumhaw Holly.

PHOTOSYNTHESIS: Common Juniper.

JENNIE PLUMLEY/PHOTO/NATS: Gregg Catclaw.

INDEX

Entries in **boldface** type refer to the plates that begin on page 21.

THE PETERSON SERIES®

PETERSON FIELD GUIDES®

BIRDS

FISH

INSECTS

MAMMALS

ECOLOGY

PETERSON FIELD GUIDE COLORING BOOKS

AUDIO AND VIDEO

EASTERN BIRDING BY EAR
cassettes 97523-9
CD 97524-7

WESTERN BIRDING BY EAR
cassettes 97526-3
CD 97525-5

EASTERN BIRD SONGS, Revised
cassettes 53150-0
CD 97522-0

WESTERN BIRD SONGS, Revised
cassettes 51746-x
CD 97519-0

BACKYARD BIRDSONG
cassettes 97527-1
CD 97528-x

EASTERN MORE BIRDING BY EAR
cassettes 97529-8
CD 97530-1

WATCHING BIRDS
Beta 34418-2
VHS 34417-4

PETERSON'S MULTIMEDIA GUIDES: NORTH AMERICAN BIRDS
(CD-ROM for Windows) 73056-2

PETERSON FLASHGUIDES™

ATLANTIC COASTAL BIRDS 79286-x
PACIFIC COASTAL BIRDS 79287-8
EASTERN TRAILSIDE BIRDS 79288-6
WESTERN TRAILSIDE BIRDS 79289-4
HAWKS 79291-6
BACKYARD BIRDS 79290-8
TREES 82998-4
MUSHROOMS 82999-2
ANIMAL TRACKS 82997-6
BUTTERFLIES 82996-8
ROADSIDE WILDFLOWERS 82995-x
BIRDS OF THE MIDWEST 86733-9
WATERFOWL 86734-7
FRESHWATER FISHES 86713-4

PETERSON FIELD GUIDES can be purchased at your local
bookstore or by calling our toll-free number, (800) 225-3362.

When referring to title by corresponding ISBN number,
preface with 0-395, unless title is listed with 0-618.